NORTHWARD

by

Anthony Hewitson

("Atticus")

Landy Publishing
2003

'Northward' was first published in 1900. This edition is a facsimile of that edition. A similar one was published by Landy Publishing in 1993 and another by S. R. Publishing in 1969.

© Landy Publishing; 'Acorns', 3 Staining Rise, Staining, Blackpool. FY3 0BU
Tel/Fax: 01253 895678
e-mail: bobdobson@amserve.com

Copyright in the cover design is held by Colin Billingham and in the foreword by Albert Clayton.

ISBN 1 872895 60 3

A catalogue record of this book is available from the British Library.

Layout by Mike Clarke. *Tel/Fax: 01254 395848*
Printed by Nayler the Printer Ltd., Accrington. *Tel: 01254 234247*

Landy Publishing have also published:

Cockersand Abbey by Brian Marshall
Preston in Focus by Stephen Sartin
Bygone Bentham by Joseph Carr
A Century of Bentham by David Johnson
A History of Pilling by Frank Sobee
Bolland Forest & the Hodder Valley by Greenwood and Bolton
Sketches of Grange & the Neighbourhood by Hudson

A full list is available from:

Landy Publishing
'Acorns' 3 Staining Rise, Staining, Blackpool, FY3 0BU
Tel/Fax: 01253 895678
Email: bobdobson@amserve.com

FOREWORD

by Albert Clayton of St. Michael's on Wyre

Anthony Hewitson begins **Northward** by describing the road between Preston and Lancaster as unquestionably one of the best made and most popularly used roads in the country. The first time I read this book was in the early 1960s at which time the M6 motorway had not been completed. The road he describes was, in the 1960s, the most congested and popularly-used road anywhere, and certainly one of the most dangerous, for motorists and pedestrians alike.

Anthony Hewitson was born in Blackburn on August 13th, 1836. His father, Anthony, was a stonemason, and at an early age, young Anthony was sent to Ingleton to live with his maternal grand-parents. He spent his formative years and received his education at Ingleton School. Hewitson later described his teacher (Mr Robert Danson) as *'an excellent teacher but a more accomplished thrasher'*. In 1850 he returned to live with his parents in Lancaster and served a seven year apprenticeship with the **Lancaster Gazette**. He later worked for several newspapers in the North and Midlands, perfecting his craft, and in 1868 he became proprietor of the **Preston Chronicle** newspaper which he retained until 1890, in which year it changed hands. He was a most humourous man and his writings reflect this in many ways. He often wrote under the pen-name of *'Atticus'* and died in 1912 aged 76.

Many of the villages, churches and country houses described by Hewitson remain much the same as they appeared at the turn of the century although many buildings have been demolished. But the way of life known to the author has changed forever. The traditional English village, with its ancient church, school, shop and pub, still remains and the annual garden party at the Parsonage often still takes place, but the old craftsmen of the village—the men who could plough a straight furrow with a team of horses, the village cobbler, blacksmith, wheelwright and tailor—are almost all gone and only memories of them remain. Farm workers in tied cottages have given way to young executives driving company cars, living on the new housing estates which are changing the face of the rural landscape—each estate looking very similar to the one in the next town—or county. But this is progress and whether we approve or not, we have to accept that change is inevitable, as it always has been. We do not live in museums. Since time began, changes have taken place.

We are fortunate that through the pages of this marvellous book we are privileged to take a look backwards in time and browse through historical facts, anecdotes and a wealth of information which will be invaluable to anyone remotely interested in local history—written in the distinctive style of one of the most accomplished journalists of his time, and written about the area where he spent so much of his life.

STONE BRIG
BROW

NORTHWARD

HISTORIC, TOPOGRAPHIC, RESIDENTIAL, AND SCENIC
GLEANINGS, &c.,

BETWEEN PRESTON AND LANCASTER.

BY

ANTHONY HEWITSON,

Author of a "History of Preston," "Churches and Chapels" (Preston and District), "Local Legislators,"
"Places and Faces," &c., and Joint-Editor of the "Tyldesley Diary."

WITH UPWARDS OF 100 ILLUSTRATIONS AND A ROAD AND REFERENCE MAP.

" By pretty roadside inns......, by old halls and parks, rustic hamlets clustered round ancient grey
churches, and through the charming, friendly, English landscape."

THACKERAY *(Vanity Fair).*

PRESTON :

GEORGE TOULMIN & SONS, THE GUARDIAN PRINTING WORKS.

1900.

PREFACE.

FACTS relating to history, topography, important individual actions and associations, buildings, scenery, &c., of a general character, are essential to both the culture and the material interests of the community. And equally necessary—if not in some respects more so—for the purposes of practical education and personal convenience are facts pertaining to local subjects of a like nature. But hitherto the main force of informative energy, tuitional and literary, has invariably been spent in the region of the widely comprehensive or the sphere of the distant and much diffused. There are plenty of people well stocked with generic or miscellaneous knowledge—persons even capable of dilating pretty freely on foreign questions—who are but indifferently acquainted with the history of their own immediate environment; there are many proficient in general knowledge who are surprisingly ignorant of local and district matters; and now-a-days there are any number of advanced "standard" scholars who can tell you about seats of government, the altitude of far distant mountains, and the length of rivers thousands of miles away, who know hardly anything about the buildings which surround them, and who are as completely in the dark regarding the height of the hills in their own locality as they are in respect to the source and course of the streams which pass their own homes. General knowledge ought always to be well regarded and diligently obtained; but that of the local kind should by no means be neglected—should be much more attended to than it is at present. The subject-schedule of every school ought to include history, topography, &c., of a local character. My principal object in writing the chapters which form this volume has been to promote the cause of Local Knowledge—to record, as the result of much research, personal inquiry, and friendly assistance, many curious particulars respecting roads and travelling methods, topography, personal and residential history, ecclesiastical and social matters, traditional and legendary affairs, &c., all pertaining to localities between Preston and Lancaster. The bulk of these particulars originally appeared in a series of articles which I wrote for *The Preston Guardian*, and which were published between March, 1899, and February, 1900; but, in revising them for republication, in book form, I have made numerous additions and emendations, thereby augmenting the details and contributing to the accuracy of the work—a work which will, I venture to hope, be found interesting to read and not without value for reference purposes. From some of the volumes of the Chetham, the Record, and the Lancashire and Cheshire Antiquarian Societies I have derived information as to certain names, dates, &c. In the course of my inquiries I have received help from many persons; and to the following I am specially indebted for information:—Major T. R. Jolly, Mr. W. Livesey, Mr. R. Veevers, Mr. H. Oakey, and Mr. J. Gregson, Fulwood; Mr. H. F. Wilson and Mr. J. Clarke, Broughton; Mr. J. Smith, Whittingham; Monsignor Gradwell and Mr. W. J. Fitzherbert-Brockholes, Claughton-on-Brock; the Rev. J. Wilson Pedder, Churchtown (Garstang); Mr. G. Singleton, Kirkland Hall; the Rev. G. Boys Stones, Garstang; Mr. W. Bashall, Nateby; Mr. Richard Hall, Forton; the Ven. Archdeacon Clarke, Cockerham; Mr. H. G. Smith, Ellel; the Rev. W. Poole, Dolphinholme; the Rev. D. Schofield, Wyresdale; Mr. W. G. Welch, Hampson; Mr. T. Carr, Galgate; the Rev. C. E. Golland and Mr. R. Nicholson, Glasson Dock; Mr. E. B. Dawson, Aldcliffe Hall; Mr. J. Diggens, Royal Albert Asylum, the Rev. W. Langley Appleford, Ripley Hospital, and Mr. L. Holden, Lancaster; Mr. W. Hewitson, Bury, &c. Nearly the whole of the illustrations are from sketches specially taken by a local artist.

A. HEWITSON.

PRESTON, *August 13th, 1900.*

NORTHWARD.

CHAPTER I.

Unquestionably, one of the best made, most popularly used, and variedly interesting roads—directly and collaterally—in the North of England is that which connects Preston and Lancaster. Numberless people, with vehicles of all kinds, regularly utilise it, in whole or in part; bicyclists innumerable, from near and remote places, pass briskly over its even surface in summer and autumn days; and by many who can't afford wheels of any sort it is much frequented all the year round. For the purposes of light and heavy traffic, for business and pleasure, for intermediate residential needs, for agricultural requirements, pedestrian movements, &c., it is most extensively patronised. It is also an old and very notable highway—has many attractive and singular associations, is flanked by much that is historically, structurally, and genealogically worth noticing, much that is replete with personal items and incidents of a striking and instructive character, and is altogether, when its lateral bearings are fully taken into account, one of the most interesting lengths of public road in the kingdom.

But, though such numbers of people as those alluded to use this particular section of the highroad northward, very few indeed are in any way acquainted with its history, and the same remark equally applies to the various objects of interest, past and present, on each side of it. No doubt, many of the persons who go along this road are somewhat curious, now and then, as to what they see—the suburban buildings and grounds, the mansions and parks, the woods, streams, turrets, towers, &c., on each side, the bridges they cross, the hamlets, villages, and "town" they go through, the hills and ravines, the placid vales and plateaus they observe in the distance; but, individually, they know very little about any of these things, and, as a rule, if any response to their curiosity be made, it is exceedingly meagre, or so vague as to be virtually worthless.

The distance between Preston and Lancaster is 21 miles. Generally speaking, the railway runs parallel with the highroad which connects these two old, historic towns, and is in no part more than about a mile, "as the crow flies," from it, whilst in several places, and in some for a considerable length, it is quite near to it. And much—the greater portion—of what comes within the view of those who travel on the highway can be seen by those who journey between the two towns on the railway. For full and satisfactory observation, however, I prefer the highroad, and, when time and weather permit, favour journeying along it, not on wheels of any description, but by means of my own feet entirely. I know, so to speak, every inch of the road. I have often walked the whole length of it —not straight on, at one go, but in sections, and at different times. And it is certainly a most pleasant, interesting way. The first reference to the highroad between Preston and Lancaster, which I have met with, is contained in a map of Great Britain, made about 1300; and in this map the length of the road is stated to be 20 miles. At such time, and for long afterwards, the track was narrow, tortuous in several parts, and, as compared with the present highway, a thoroughly bad, wretched road. But the measurement referred to must have been erroneous, else the miles were longer than those subsequently adopted, for after all the straightening which took place between 1817 and 1828, when the road was very greatly improved, in order to meet increased traffic, especially that of the coaches, the distance between Preston and Lancaster was put down at 21 miles, or one mile more than it was before the road was straightened at all! Obviously the old mode of calculating was defective, or different to that afterwards in vogue. In O'Gilby's "Britannia," published in 1675, the way from Preston to Lancaster, and thence northward to Carlisle, is named in the list of "direct roads"—the routes to or from London. The main road, north and south, through Lancashire, towards the end of the 17th century, in a very bad condition indeed. Celia Fiennes, a daughter of Col. Nathaniel Fiennes, of the Parliamentary army, says in her diary, entitled "Through England on a Side Saddle in the Reign of William and Mary," that it took her about four hours to travel from Wigan to Preston, and she afterwards observes that a longer time was required to go from Preston to Lancaster. "I can," she remarks, "confirm this by my experience, for I went to Gascoyne [Garstang], which is ten miles, and half-way to Lancaster, in two hours," and "thence to Lancaster town, ten miles more, which I easily reached in two hours and a half or three hours. I passed through abundance of villages, almost at the end of every mile, mostly of long lanes, being an enclosed country." And she notices, whilst going from Preston to Lancaster, as she had done in other parts of the county, that "at all cross-ways there are posts with hands pointing to each road, with the names of the great town or market town that it leads to, which does make up for the length of the miles, that strangers may not lose their road and have it to go back again." In Dr. Kuerden's MS. description of Preston, conjectured to have been written some time between 1681 and 1687, it is said, after a reference to the way out of the town, "allong the side of the river Ribble," towards Kirkham, &c., that "upon the right hand, northerly, lyes the great road towards Lancaster, by the way of Garstang." It is furthermore stated, in the same description, that "there is likewise, when you enter the town upon the south or eastern side, a way to pass by the body of the town over Preston More and Fulwood, by Broughton northward, by Garstang aforesaid, toward the burrough of Lancaster." The road "upon the right hand, northerly," was evidently a continuation, in somewhat better or broader form, of that which led out of the town by way of "Old Lancaster-lane"—a way which branched from the lower part of the road to Kirkham (supplanted by the present Fylde-road), went north as far as Savock Brook—now called Cadley Brook—then eastward, joining the south end of Cadley-road at a point near where Plungington Hotel now stands, and so over Cadley and into Broughton northward. The other road—"a way to pass by the body of the town," &c.—seems to have been one which took the line or followed not far from the course taken by the road which now passes Stephenson-terrace, Preston, and along the Barracks way, going left when over Preston and Fulwood Moors, and then joining the before-named road, by Sharoe Green-lane, in Broughton township. If the route of the second road were not thus west and northward, it could only have been along the existing way which traverses Fulwood, passes out of Watling-street, on the north side, between the Barracks and the Workhouse, proceeds round by Broughton Hall, and then, wheeling westward, along Durton-lane, enters the highway near Broughton Church. The more likely course for the road that passed "by the body of the town" would be across Preston and Fulwood Moors, and so on by Sharoe Green, as already explained, rather than round by Broughton Hall, &c. The northern way by Old Lancaster-lane was the more important of the two; but it was only of the pack horse kind when Dr. Kuerden wrote about it, and for some time afterwards. In those days, however, when the population of Preston was not more than about 6,000, and when the requirements of life and the operations of commerce, locally, were of a very primitive and limited character, such a road, in conjunction with that on the eastern side, which also, no doubt, came within the pack horse category, would be ample. It is singular

that neither of the two earliest extant maps of Preston.—"that drawn on the spott by P.M., Esq.," relating to the military positions here during the Rebellion of 1715, and evidently published soon afterwards, and the one made by George Lang, dated 1774—shows any actual connection, pack horse or otherwise, with the north road at the boundary of the town. The Rebellion map indicates three roads going towards, but not coupling up with, the northern highway outside the town, namely, a small way leading for about a quarter of a mile in that direction, crossing the Fylde-ward road not far from Tulketh Hall, and forming part of a narrow passage connected with a ford, opposite Castle Hill, in Penwortham; another in continuation of Friargate, and proceeding north to a point near the old Moor Brook; and the third on the eastern side, swerving from the south, and going north not quite so far as the second. Lang's map shows only a sort of lane, near the top end of Fylde-road, running northward less than a quarter of a mile, and the continuation of a road from the bottom of Friargate, up to the right—apparently on the line of the present Moor lane and down to a part near Moor Brook. But, notwithstanding this absence of full road continuation, northward, on the maps mentioned, there were in existence at the time three ways on that side, as already stated, capable of effecting the necessary junction, viz., Old Lancaster-lane, the road over the Moors, and that round by Broughton Hall. Shakeshaft's map of Preston, published in the early part of this century, shows a road going north from the town, on or in close proximity to the route of the present highway (Garstang-road) which runs straight to Fulwood, and right on northward. But it was a comparatively poor road. On reaching Watling-street it turned west, went down on that side as far as Cadley Brook, and then merged into Cadley-road, whose connection with the main northern way has already been explained. The road on Shakeshaft's map, from Preston to Cadley Brook (Savock Brook) would supersede to a very considerable extent the Old Lancaster-lane way, both to and from the town. A map published in connection with "Baines's Lancashire," in 1824, shows that then, or say a short time before, when the map was being prepared, there were two recognised roads out of Preston northward—one, evidently the principal outlet, being the Old Lancaster-lane way, and the other on the eastern side of the town, branching off in Ribbleton, then turning to the left, going over Fulwood Moor, merging into Sharoe Green-lane, and so onward, joining the main way opposite the Black Bull, in Broughton. In 1750 Parliamentary authority was obtained to take tolls for the repair and general improvement of the highway between Preston, Lancaster, and Burton-in-Kendal. According to the "Observations" of Adam Watkin, published in 1791, for "many ages," and up to the middle of the 18th century—the time when the Parliamentary authority just referred to was obtained—"a causeway of about two feet broad, paved with round pebbles, was all that a man or a horse could travel upon, particularly in the winter season, through both Lancashire and Cheshire." And we are further told, by the same writer, that "this causeway was guarded by posts at a proper distance to keep carts off it, and the open part of the road was generally impassable in winter from mire and deep ruts." For numberless years up to 1750 the cost of repairing the roads fell exclusively upon the people living in the districts through which they passed ; but, as the great majority of those upon whom this obligation devolved were of the rural order—persons located in very thinly populated parts—and the heaviest or main portion of the road traffic was that which came from towns, the injustice of the system, so far as the former were concerned, was obvious : the country people, consequently, kicked against it ; eventually, power to levy tolls, for road improvement and maintenance purposes, was obtained from Parliament ; and afterwards turnpikes—toll-gate roads—were gradually adopted throughout the country. From 1801 to 1826 inclusive at least 80 Turnpike Acts were passed for the county of Lancaster alone. The original Act of Parliament for turn-piking the road between Preston and Lancaster and Heiring Syke, near Burton-in-Kendal, was obtained in 1750 ; and the date of the expiry of the trust was—for the length between Preston and Garstang, February 1st, 1875, and for that running between Garstang and Heiring Syke, November 1st, 1882. I have not been able to meet with the exact date when operations for improving the highroad between Preston and Lancaster—beginning at Preston—were commenced ; but the length between the northern end of Moor-lane and the Withy Trees, Fulwood, was in course of construction in 1817 ; whilst that portion which extends from the Withy Trees to the Black Bull public-house, in Broughton, was made somewhat later. Up to the time of the completion of this second length, the Black Bull was located a short distance down Cadley-road—on the north-west side : when the new road was formed, the license of this inn was transferred to the present premises facing the highroad at the north corner of the old way referred to. About 1830 the whole of the road improvements deemed necessary, by those having charge of the turnpike trust, were finished. And by a particular kind of lateral evidence—mainly, in fact, by such evidence, which very few people, now-a-days, think about or have any idea of—are the position and extent of the respective alterations at present perceptible, or susceptible of identification. There are lengths of footpath, in different parts, some on one side and some on the other side, of the road, and wherever these are observable the main way parallel, and for a similar distance, is of the improved or altered kind. The old utilised parts, though somewhat levelled or straightened, or widened here and there, but not changed at all in their general course or line of direction, have not, as a rule, any adjoining footway.

The land immediately flanking the road on the northern side of Preston, between the summit of Moor-lane and the boundary of the borough at Fulwood, has since the original turnpike improvements were carried out here been very extensively utilised for building purposes. Prior to the making of the present Garstang-road—the length between Moor-lane and Fulwood—and, in fact, for numerous years after its construction, the contiguous land on each side consisted chiefly of rough sand-hillocks, meadows, pastures, and moory ground : at present much of the land—nearly the whole of that portion on the west side and almost half of that on the opposite side—is covered with houses, many being of a substantial, superior description. The only view of Preston from the north which I have ever seen is one which seems to have been taken at the part where the main road, as improved in the early part of this century, went through "Gallows Hill"—a rough, irregularly-shaped eminence, on which a number of the rebels of 1715 were executed, and which was removed entirely many years ago in order to provide sites for the Church of the English Martyrs (opened in 1867) and the buildings immediately adjoining. The view of Preston referred to is taken from a drawing, made about 1820, by William Westall, A.R.A. A reproduction, copied from Finden's engraving of the original drawing, is given on the next page.

Nobody would now be able to recognise this view as a picture of Preston from the north side, so great has been the change and so many the extensions in respect to new streets and buildings of all sorts during the interval. In the foreground of the view there is a wide, open-sided road, flanking which are some hillocks—the old sand heaps, &c., which used to be here. As to the town, which fills up the background, it has a peculiarly limited appearance : a couple of church towers, a factory, four windmills, and less than a dozen houses are the most striking objects depicted ! The major portion of the buildings which figure in the view are on the eastern side. The church towers are evidently those of St. John's (Parish) and Holy Trinity Churches. In respect to the four windmills, taking them in line, as they are ranged in the view, from east to west, the first seems to have been somewhere in the neighbourhood of Meadow-street—east end ; the second near North-road (a windmill tower now stands off North-road, between Sedgwick and Kirkham streets) ; the third tallies in position with that of the windmill tower still up near the west end of St. Thomas-street ; and the fourth is evidently intended to be on the summit of Moor-lane, where (eastern side) there is now the tower of one, and in the neighbourhood of which there is a public-house, the Windmill Inn, which no doubt got this name through its situation being adjacent to the mill. Formerly the way in which the name of this inn was spelled, on a sign in front, was a source of some attraction and amusement. It was spelled, in very big, striking letters, "Whindmill." The factory seen in the view standing off to the right, not very far from the fourth windmill, is evidently meant to represent that which Messrs. Watson and Collinson erected, not far from the summit of Moorlane, in 1777—the first cotton factory in Preston—and which was pulled down in 1860, to make room for

PRESTON FROM THE NORTH

WESTALL'S VIEW OF PRESTON FROM THE NORTH (ABOUT A.D. 1820).

certain extensions or alterations in connection with the Walker-street works of the Preston Gas Company. In the background of Westall's view there are indica-tions, by chimneys, of several factories; but, from his standpoint, that of Messrs. Watson and Collinson would be the only conspicuous mill.

CHAPTER II.

I will now "move on"—take the road northward, in a leisurely manner, noticing as I proceed many objects of interest, directly or indirectly, and numerous matters—the great bulk not hitherto popularised or made accessible to ordinary readers—of a curious and instructive character. The houses on the west side of the highroad, opposite Moor Park, Preston, were amongst the first villa residences built within the borough boundary. At the time of their erection there were no other houses near them: rearward there were fields and waste ground; southward there was about a quarter of a mile of open space, whilst the land between the "Ladies' Walk" and Moor Brook, extending to the south of "Gallows Hill"—land now covered with streets and a large population—was both bare and wild-looking. The late Alderman George Smith built and occupied a villa in the locality (opposite Moor Park) referred to, and there is a good story as to his definition of it. One day a local gentleman met Alderman Smith, and complimented him upon having got such a nice, substantial residence, whereupon the latter, who was a very loud-speaking, amusingly-illiterate individual, ejaculated: "A residence, sir? It's not a residence. It's an hall!" The Park named has an area of 100 acres—land which at one time formed part of "Preston Moor." Henry III., in 1253, granted to the burgesses of Preston this Moor, which at that time consisted of 324 acres, for building purposes; but the burgesses do not appear to have taken any practical advantage of this privilege. In the early part of 1642 Sir John Girlington, of Thurland Castle, near Kirkby Lonsdale—a strong Royalist and High Sheriff of Lancashire—read the King's Commission of Array at a meeting attended, it is said, by about 5,000 persons, on Preston Moor. During the proceedings dissension arose—one portion of the assembly was for the Royalist and another in favour of the Parliamentary side; and it is alleged that this meeting "was the signal for the commencement of hostilities in the county palatinate." Sir John Girlington was killed during a battle near Melton Mowbray. Between 1786 and 1833 horse races were held annually on Preston Moor, under the patronage of the Corporation of Preston, and in opposition to races, on Fulwood Moor, which were supported by Lord Derby and his party. When horse races in connection with Preston were originally established, or where first run, it is now impossible to say. In 1705 there were some races of this kind, got up by certain Prestonians, and the earliest of which I have met with any record, on Lea Marsh, a few miles westward. In 1834 the

Preston Corporation enclosed 100 acres of Preston Moor, dropped the old name, and called the separated or fenced-in part Moor Park. In 1867, after being "laid out"—a work involving much improvement, and costing £10,826—this Park was opened, in its present form, to the public.

Directly after passing the northern boundary of the Park just mentioned, the township of Fulwood is entered. Residentially, Fulwood is now what an American would term "quite a place," with a comparatively numerous and well-to-do population; the majority living between Watling Street-road and the brook which divides the township from Preston. Fulwood was at one time an "ancient and royal forest." King John gave the burgesses of Preston permission to take wood from this forest "towards building their town." The old Roman road between Manchester and Lancaster, via Wigan and Walton-le-Dale, passed through Fulwood on the eastern side. Watling Street-road is on the line of the Roman road which ran from Ribchester, via Kirkham, to Rossall Point, near Fleetwood. Up to the middle of the present century, Fulwood was an entirely rural region: it was mainly agricultural land, and the only buildings which could be seen in the township were, with the exception of the Barracks, a few scattered farmhouses and cottages. For many years that portion of the township, before referred to, which now contains the main portion of the population, was generally called "The Park" or "The Freehold"—a name due to the movement which originated or received a considerable impetus in the Midlands, and which spread to Preston about the time or soon after the triumph of the Anti-Corn Law agitation, in 1846, but which did not get into concrete form or bear any particular fruit here until a few years afterwards. Mr. James Taylor, of Birmingham, established what were called Freehold Land Societies, the object of which was to encourage thrift, self-reliance, home-improvement, &c., amongst the people, and especially to put them in the way of getting 40s. freehold properties, whereby they might be able, by the franchise thus secured, to vote for Parliamentary candidates, at election times, in favour of the Anti-Corn Law propaganda, and subsequently help on other reforms for the popular welfare. Mr. Taylor visited Preston, in the course of his labours, and whilst here fully expounded his views. Eventually a local Freehold Land Society was established. The president of the society was Mr. John Goodair, and the trustees were Messrs. Thomas Brewer, Richard Carr, Robert Charnley, Richard Fairclough, John

Hawkins, and Joseph Livesey. Directly after the formation of the Society a lookout was commenced for a suitable estate of land. Amongst others who took an active part in endeavouring to find such an estate was Mr. William Livesey; and, in the course of his many peregrinations, within a reasonable distance of Preston—for even then an idea to be out of the town, so as to keep clear of its rates, found favour—his eye fell upon what he considered the most eligible estate in the immediate neighbourhood. This was "Horrocks's Farm," in Fulwood, which was in the hands of the executors of Mr. S. Horrocks, and about 45 acres in extent—an estate bounded on the south by Eaves Brook which separates Fulwood from Preston; on the north by Watling Street-road; on the east by a footpath which leads from Moor Park, crosses the brook, and goes into Watling Street-road, opposite a part between Fulwood Hall and Sharoe Green-lanes; and on the west by Garstang-road.

Horrocks's Farm, Fulwood, had, shortly before being favourably viewed in the interests of the new Freehold Land Society, been offered for sale by Mr. Vallet, the predecessor of Mr. H. C. Walton, at his auction rooms, Fishergate, Preston; but, when thus "put up," the reserve was not reached, so the property was withdrawn. Mr. Vallet subsequently negotiated the sale of the estate, by private, on behalf of the trustees, for £4,995; Mr. William Livesey being the purchaser of it for the Freehold Land Society. At this particular time the law did not allow societies to hold estates of land; so the estate in question, after being sold as named, had to be conveyed to two private individuals; and the two selected were Mr. Michael Satterthwaite and Mr. William Livesey. The estate was surveyed and laid out, for the Freehold Land Society, by Messrs. Myres and Veevers, of Preston. This work was accomplished in 1850-51. A contract was afterwards entered into, with Messrs. Cooper and Tullis, of Preston, for the construction of sewers, the formation of roads, &c., on the estate; and in due time the work was done. The shares had previously been allotted; the drawing for them took place in the "Old Cockpit" (at that time utilised and known as "the Temperance Hall"), on the 29th of January, 1851. Altogether, there were 343 shares, the average price of each being £30; but of this number eight (relating to the land which forms the site of the present Park-terrace on the west side of Fulwood) were reserved to the vendors for sale, on yearly ground rents, in order to secure annually a sum of money sufficient to pay the tithe rent charge (due to the Vicar of Lancaster) on the whole estate, and thus free it from encumbrance in the future. For ecclesiastical purposes, Fulwood used to be in the parish of Lancaster; and, owing to this peculiar incorporation, Fulwood persons, when connubially inclined, had to go to the old county town—twenty miles distant—in order to get married! But, under Lord Blandford's Act, Fulwood was made into a separate parish, and the matrimonial inconvenience experienced through the old system was thus obviated. Fulwood, however,

though Blandfordised and virtually surrounded by the parish of Preston, is by no means entirely free from the old Lancastrian regime; the appointment of the Fulwood Church of England minister is still vested in the Vicar of Lancaster Parish Church, and that said Vicar draws tithe based on a £500 per annum estimate (at present it is about £90 a year below that sum) from the people of Fulwood. At the Freehold Land Society's allotment, in "the Temperance Hall," the written names of 183 persons, representing all the available shares (335), were handed in, on cards, which were put into a ballot box, and then the drawing was commenced. The first draw was in favour of Mr. James Drummond, "dispenser of knowledge to her Majesty's subjects," and the last was for Mr. Samuel Cragg, schoolmaster. The Society decided that there should be neither a public-house nor a beerhouse on the freehold property; and this restriction is still in force. But Fulwood must not, on this account, be set down as a place full of teetotallers or of persons enamoured of Maine Law principles. By importation it secures numerous fluids much more potent than water; some Fulwoodians convey, in an apparently serene good-humoured fashion, considerable quantities on the personally-internal plan, from Preston; and then "balm of Gilead" can be obtained from an inn on the western side and one or two on the eastern frontier of "the Park." In a fortnight after the Freehold Land Society's shares had been balloted for, several allotments changed hands at premiums ranging from £1 5s. to £5 each; and subsequent to that a local sharebroker offered for sale, more than once, plots "in the Park." The allottees, generally speaking, took formal possession on Tuesday, May 13th, 1851, on which day a farmhouse and some out-buildings on the estate, which had not been balloted for, were sold by auction. The house and certain of the outbuildings were demolished; but the barn was left standing. At a later period this barn was turned into a Methodist chapel; afterwards, for a time, it was used Episcopally as the predecessor of the present Church; and then it became—what it is now—a school. This is the double gabled building which stands in Victoria-road, near the Church. The part of it on the east side includes the old barn; the other portion is an addition. On the 1st of May, 1851, or twelve days before formal possession of the estate was taken by the allottees, the first foundation stones, intended for two houses on Fulwood Park—the Freehold Land Society's estate—were laid. The double ceremony was a very quiet one; only two persons (the layers of the two stones) being present; and it was performed on the day mentioned so as to synchronise with the opening day of the first great Exhibition, in Hyde Park, London! The two persons who laid these stones were Mr. William Livesey and Mr. Robert Charnley; and this dual lapidarious job involved a sort of race. Each wanted to have the honour of laying the first stone in the Park; both made a considerable rush to the places selected—they were on two separate, but immediately adjoining, plots; and Mr. Livesey managed to come in the "winner." Strange to say, however, the

ground in which he placed his foundation stone—
it is on the south side of Victoria-road, near the entrance to Lower Bank-road—has not been built upon
up to the present; and some years elapsed before a
building was raised above that which Mr. Charnley
laid. In respect to the general estate, for a number of
years building operations proceeded very slowly. The
first completed house on it was the present No. 18,
Victoria-road—north side, opposite the entrance to
Higher Bank-road. Mr. Henry Watson, brother of
Mr. Peter Watson, was, I believe, the builder of it.
The walls were made of rubble stones from Longridge.

FIRST NEW HOUSE ON FULWOOD FREEHOLD.

Since its original erection it has been considerably
altered, and the walls are now covered externally
with cement or stucco of some kind. One or two
houses, similar in wall construction and outside treatment, but of a later date, immediately adjoin it at the
rear.

On the northern side of Watling Street-road,
Fulwood, there is the Preston Union Workhouse,
which was built in 1865-68, and opened at the end of
the latter year, as the successor of an old Workhouse
in Preston, and certain establishments for Union purposes in Walton, Penwortham, and Woodplumpton.
In Fulwood, some distance east of the Workhouse,
there are the Military Barracks, erected in 1843-48, and
since then considerably enlarged. The Barracks
occupy a portion of the course, which went eastward,
on which were run the horse races patronised by Lord
Derby, as previously mentioned. For the general
management of Fulwood a Local Board of Health was
formed in 1863, Dr. Naylor being the chairman of
it for the first two years, and Mr. Richard Veevers for
25 years afterwards. The affairs of Fulwood
are now under the control of an Urban District Council. There used to be a toll bar
in Fulwood—across Garstang-road, close to the junction of Watling Street-road. It was put up here about
1842, in place of one at the south end of Broughton

village. The Fulwood tollbar was done away with
in or about 1875; and in 1877 there was erected, on
the site of the bar-keeper's's house, the building
now utilised as the Fulwood Urban District Council
Office.

CADLEY ROAD (SOUTH END.)

The old way through Cadley, into which the main
road north, out of Preston, formerly ran, is not far
from the building just alluded to—it is a short distance to the left, past the Withy Trees public-house.
Near the junction into this old way, and close to the
hollow down which runs Cadley Brook (the Savock),
there is the Home for the Blind. In 1874 a building
was erected in Glover-street, Preston, at a cost of
£4,000, for the purpose of accommodating local blind
persons whilst being taught various trades. In 1890
the Committee of Management felt that the establishment of a Home for blind children was an urgent
necessity. A bazaar for this object was held and the
sum of £5,000 was raised. To this was added £1,000
from the Gardner's Trust for the Blind, London. A
building committee was then formed and plans submitted to the Education Department. The plans
were on the Cottage Home system, and were adopted
by the Department—in fact, they were the first plans
of the kind sanctioned by the Department for the
object named. The Home (certified for 48 children)
was completed in 1895, and formally opened, by the
Countess of Derby, immediately afterwards. At
present there are 40 inmates, and in addition 12 blind
adults, who live off the premises, but are engaged
here, at day time, in skip, basket, and rug making,
as well as cane-seating. Rearward of the Home—
near the top of Cadley Brow, east side—Cadley old
school was located. It was founded in 1707, by the
Rev. S. Peploe, then Vicar of Preston, and afterwards Bishop of Chester. The building was discontinued as a school about 1863; it was afterwards pulled
down; and since about 1865 Cadley children have
received instruction in the school near Fulwood Church.

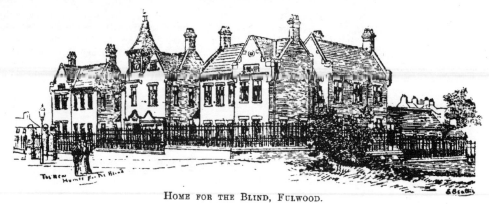

HOME FOR THE BLIND, FULWOOD.

At the top of the old way going through Cadley there branches a road, on the west side, which runs straight down to Cadley Bank, about three-quarters of a mile distant. This road—popularly called "Cadley Causey" (Causeway)—is on the line of the tury was partially occupied by a small cottage (there are now one or more old cottages at the rear of it). The cottage referred to was purchased by Mr. Platt, a woollen draper, who had a shop in Fishergate, Preston, after whom Platt's-yard, on the north side of the

CADLEY BANK.

Roman road which went westward as far as Rossall Point. The residence, now known as Cadley Bank, stands on ground which in the early part of this cen- same street, was named, and whose son, Mr. Walter Platt, has for years been a well-known official in connection with foot races, &c. The building at Cadley

CADLEY COTTAGE (WEST SIDE).

was much improved, if not actually reconstructed, on an enlarged scale, by Mr. Platt, who resided at it until his death. Afterwards Mr. J. C. Welch, tea and coffee merchant, Preston, became the owner of it. In 1872 Mr. J. J. Smith, hatter, &c., Preston, purchased Cadley Bank; he subsequently enlarged it; and, with the exception of a short time directly after becoming the owner, he has resided here ever since.

Near Cadley Bank there stands north-eastward, amid fields, Cadley Cottage. Formerly it was called Cadley House. There are two approaches to it—a road on the west and another on the south side. Trees, avenue-like, flank the latter way, which, though not much used now, was evidently, at one time, the main approach. Here there formerly resided—periodically, or in a summer-resort manner—one of the most notable men ever associated with Preston. This was Nicholas Grimshaw. He was, in 1781, elected the bailiff of Preston; he became a town councillor in 1790; in 1793 he was appointed Town Clerk of Preston; in 1797 he was the commander of the Preston Royal Volunteers; in 1801 he was made an alderman of the borough, and he was seven times Mayor of it—twice as Guild Mayor. In addition to the foregoing he was acting cursitor for the County of Lancaster for upwards of half-a-century, and clerk to the borough magistrates of Preston for about forty years. He died in 1838, at the age of 80, and was interred in the north-west corner of Preston Parish Churchyard, where a large, railed-in tomb covers his grave. In

Ncr. Grimshaw's Grave.

NICHOLAS GRIMSHAW'S TOMB.

this grave there had previously been interred two of his sons—20 and 17 years of age respectively—who, with two other local young gentlemen, were accidentally drowned in the Ribble, in 1822. Mr. Grimshaw's widow, Esther Mary, who died at Cadley Cottage, in 1853, in the 86th year of her age, was also buried in this same grave. On the death of Mrs. Grimshaw, Cadley Cottage was occupied by two old female servants—"pensioners"—of the Grimshaw family, and they remained at the place till their death, in the sixties, since which time the Cottage has been used as a farmhouse.

The road northward, after passing Fulwood Urban District Council office is, for about half a mile, very pleasantly flanked with houses and trees—nearly every one of the houses being of modern construction, and some of them quite new. About 300 yards up the road, beyond the Council office, a glimpse may be obtained, on each side, of a narrow, tortuously-channeled stream. It runs along a somewhat deep hollow, and passes under the road. The Ordnance map, issued in 1849, calls this "Savock Brook"; in old surveys and topographical works it is designated "Savig"; the Ordnance map based on the survey of 1890 designates it Savick Brook; and many people now term it "Savick." This brook has its source near Longridge, on the west side, and it debouches into the Ribble on the east side of Clifton Marsh. Dr. Charles Leigh, in his work, "The Natural History of Lancashire, Cheshire," &c., published in 1700, makes reference to this brook, with the view of proving a theory of ethnological combination or admixture in the case of the Brigantes—the people who, at the time of the Roman invasion, and for a number of years afterwards, inhabited Lancashire, Yorkshire, Westmorland, Cumberland, and Durham. Dr. Leigh says:— "The more clearly to illustrate that the Brigantes were a mixt people of Phœnicians and Britains, I shall produce but one instance more. . . . . The Instance is taken from a Rivulet, a branch of that River. . . . . stiled Ribbel. This Rivulet is at this day vulgarly stiled Savig. Now ig in the British Language being a Diminutive to shew the distinction betwixt a River and a Rivulet, which is therefore added to Avon, which in that Language signifies a River, Afonig and Savonig in the British Language signifying Rivulet, from thence may be easily accounted for the name of that Rivulet now stiled Savig. Since therefore in those parts we find a mixture of Phœnician, Armenian, and British Languages, we may thence make this reasonable Corollary, that those People lived together."

Highgate Park is on the east side of the main road in Fulwood; the principal entrance to it being a short distance north of the part which the Savock intersects. Here, on a gentle eminence, about 200 yards from the main road, is the residence of Mr. James Gregson, machine maker, Preston. Last century the land of this Park and that now attached to Oak House, in the immediate neighbourhood and on the same side of the main road, formed one estate. By will, dated 1780, Mr. Thomas Pedder devised this property to his son, Mr. Edward Pedder, of Darwen Bank, Walton-le-Dale, and certain other persons. In 1830, Mr. Pedder, of Darwen Bank, who was the uncle of Mr. Edward Pedder, banker, of Preston, sold the property to Mr. James Dandy, who, later, built Oak House. Alderman John Goodair, of Preston, subsequently purchased the Highgate portion of the estate and it was supposed that he intended building a residence for himself on the higher part of it. He made a road, on the south-eastern side, to

HIGHGATE PARK.

or not far from the top of the eminence on which Mr. Gregson's house now stands; but he refrained entirely from residential construction. Mr. Goodair died in 1873, and in May of the following year his Highgate property was offered for sale. It was bought by Mr. Gregson, who afterwards purchased Oak House and the land, &c., connected therewith. In 1876 Mr. Gregson built the residence which occupies the eminence before named, and here he has ever since lived. It is a substantial, excellent house, is well finished, has a spacious and beautifully decorated interior and adjoining it, at the rear, there is very good accommodation for horses, carriages, &c. Well laid out grounds are in front of the house, the Savock flows evenly through the land below it, trees surround and give a choice residential selectness to it, and on the north-western side there is an umbrageous, rustic-looking dingle, which adds to the picturesqueness of its environment. Mr. Gregson's estate comprises in its entirety an area of between 80 and 90 acres, and it has about half a mile of frontage to the main road on the west side. In a hollow, south-east of the residence, there is Highgate Park farm. The farm house here is the successor of one of a like kind which stood on the same site about 200 years ago. Oak House is a good, pleasantly-located residence, and at present it is tenanted by Mr. C. J. Pyke. The dwelling near it, which belongs to the estate, occupies the site of a farm house which was contemporaneous with the old one on the Highgate portion of the property.

CHAPTER III.

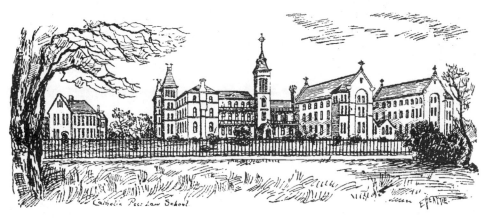

BOYS' "POOR LAW SCHOOL."

In Fulwood there is an institution for poor or destitute Roman Catholic boys. It is situated about half a mile north-east of that part of the highway under which Savock Brook passes. Structurally, it is made of red brick, is large, high, and turreted. This establishment was opened by the Roman Catholic Bishop of Liverpool, in whose diocese it is situated, in 1896. It will accommodate something like 300 boys, and at present about 120 are at the place, which is dedicated to St. Vincent de Paul, managed by Sisters connected with the Society bearing the name of that Saint, or some kindred charity, and spiritually looked after by Canon Pyke and the clergy of the Church of the English Martyrs, Preston. Amid the buildings nearer the road, on the same side, there is a "Home for the Aged," both male and female, attended to by Roman Catholic Sisters. There are at present about 120 old people in the Home, which receives considerable help by means of local gifts; the Sisters in charge having many warm supporters in Preston and the neighbourhood. The residence formerly known as "Springfield," and a contiguous building, are used for the purposes of the Home. Springfield was built and for some years occupied by the late Dr. Naylor, who was followed at it, successively, by Mr. Joseph and Mr. Henry Hawkins, after whom it passed, by purchase, into the hands of the Roman Catholic body. Directly opposite the Catholic Boys' Poor Law School, Fulwood, on the west side of and near to the highway, there is the Harris Orphanage. This Orphanage was erected and endowed by the trustees of the late Mr. E. R. Harris, of Whinfield, Ashton-on-Ribble. In 1880 the Committee of the Church Orphan Aid Society and the Orphan Home and School, Preston, approached the trustees, and pointed out the desirableness of establishing an institution for the care and welfare of the orphan children of Preston and the neighbourhood. As a result of this interview the sum of £100,000 was set aside by the trustees for the object named—£30,000 for building and furnishing purposes and £70,000 for endowment. In 1881 the Committee purchased 14 acres of land, pleasantly situated on the western side of the highway, in Fulwood, and exactly two miles from Preston Town Hall. Soon afterwards building operations were commenced, and the charming "village homes" now observable, and constituting the Harris Orphanage, were opened in 1888. Children are admitted whose parents have resided within eight miles of Preston Town Hall. The Orphanage has for some time past contained 120 children, and there are always cases waiting for admission. One "home" in connection with the Orphanage is empty, as, owing to the reduced interest from the invested capital, it has been found impossible to meet the extra expenditure which its occupation would involve. Early in 1900 Mrs. Jacson, of Lytham, widow of Mr. C. R. Jacson, sent to the Council the sum of £500, to be given, gradually, on behalf of certain objects which she specified for the improvement of the children in the Orphanage. Major T. R. Jolly is the Governor and Secretary of the Orphanage and Mrs. Jolly is the Matron of it.

HARRIS ORPHANAGE.

From the summit of the road, near the Black Bull, in Broughton, a striking view of Preston is commanded: the spires, towers, big chimneys, and main features of the town on its northern side, are not only very conspicuous, but constitute quite an imposing picture, which would be still more effective if the smoke nuisance were properly mitigated; whilst the hills north-east and south-east of Preston, as seen from here on a fine day—Longridge Fell, the rural heights of Mellor, the wooded eminence on which Hoghton Tower stands, the undulating moors of Brinscall, Anglezark, and Bromley, the dark brow of Belmont, and the cone-like form of Rivington Pike—make up a back-ground to the view of a finely-powerful and imposing character

About a mile north-east of the point from where the fine view which I have alluded to is observable there is a building called Broughton Tower; but it is not the original structure which went by that name. A lane opposite the Black Bull leads to it, by a branch to the left at Sharoe Green. Nothing of the original Tower is now standing; but the site of it can still be picked out—it is in the form of an ellipse, or oval, of moderate area, and is surrounded by a broad, partially filled-up ditch—the old moat. In the centre of the ground surrounded by the old moat there is a small cottage, and an idea prevails to the effect that this is a remnant—modified—of the original Tower, and that it formed part of its kitchen or cooking quarters. But an examination of this little building, which I recently made, did not reveal anything at all indicative of its structural connection with the Tower. Neither externally nor internally does it bear any marks, or any material of wood or stone, calculated to identify it as being any portion of the original residence here. The building which now goes by the name of Broughton Tower is a farm-house, situated about 100 yards north of the ground

on which the old Tower stood. From a very early time the de Singletons were owners of property in Broughton township. Baines conjectures that, as Gilbert de Singleton held a messuage in Broughton, in 1325-6, such messuage "was probably Broughton Tower." If so, then it is not unlikely that a member of the de Singleton family, who had property in or was connected with Broughton upwards of 100 years before that time, had an interest in the Tower. The tallage record of 3 Henry III. (1219) associates Alan de Singleton with the "Villat de Brocton" (Broughton). And the connection was continued for many generations. In a deed of enfeoffment, by "John Westbie, of Molebrecke" (Mowbreck, near Kirkham), bearing date January 16th, 1575-6, "Thomas Singletonn of Broughtonn Tower" is mentioned. The Harleian MS. (No. 2,042), in the British Museum, contains a list of Lancashire freeholders in the Amounderness Hundred, in 1600, and amongst them is "Thomas Singleton de Teower" (Broughton Tower, no doubt); but, as a member of the Langton family was, apparently, living here at or about the time named, the probability is that Thomas Singleton figures in the list as the owner, and not the occupier, of the Tower. With Broughton Tower the Langtons were long associated. There was a "Hu de Langton" Mayor of Preston in 1431; but I have not been able to glean any information showing that he had any actual connection with the Langtons of Broughton Tower. He may have been related—this is but conjecture—to Sir Thomas Langton, Knight, baron of Newton-in-Makerfield, who was an ancestor of the Broughton Langtons. The earliest Langton who resided at Broughton Tower, whose name I have met with, was Roger, who was baptised in 1559, and died in 1644; and the presumption is that this is the Roger Langton whose name appears four times in the Mayoral list of Preston,

BROUGHTON TOWER MOAT AND LANGTON ARMS.

viz., in 1605-16-32-39. William Langton, son of Roger Langton, was elected M.P. for Preston in 1645, and apparently continued as such till 1652. The letter which Oliver Cromwell wrote at Preston, on the 17th of August, 1648, describing his victory over the Royalist forces here, on that day, and which he despatched to "the Honourable Committee sitting at Manchester," was, according to the Commons' Journals, "enclosed in a letter from a Member of this House, from Manchester," on August 19th, and read to the House two days afterwards. The letter which accompanied Cromwell's description referred to certain "dispensations," "providences," &c., and was signed "W. L."; and Carlyle, in his "Oliver Cromwell's Letters and Speeches," says that the person whose initials are thus appended was "probably William Langton, the new Member for Preston." William Langton had a son, Richard, who lived in Preston, and there can be no doubt that this son is the "Rich. Langton" who appears in the Mayoral list as the chief magistrate here in 1692. John Langton, a brother of William Langton, was the founder of the Langton family of Kirkham. William's son, William, was living at Broughton Tower in 1714; and the latter's grandson, William, was the last of the Langtons who resided here; whilst a grand-daughter, Jane, was, in 1735, when 70 years of age, married to Lawrence Rawstorne, of Preston, ancestor of the Rawstornes of Penwortham, to whom she left Broughton Tower and other property bequeathed to her by her brother William. Broughton Tower, described as "a strong, heavy structure of stone," was pulled down about 1800. The property referred to passed from the Rawstorne family, by sale, in 1810—one portion of it going to the trustees of Kirkham

Grammar School, and the remainder to James Roth-well, of Hoole. In a small garden, immediately front-ing the farm house near the site of Broughton Tower, there are numerous carved stones which belonged to the old building. Two of them contain, on a shield, the Langton arms, or, rather, the "chevrons" thereof —strong bars joined at an angle; the "gules" (red, represented by perpendicular lines) accompanying the full bearings being apparently omitted. The chev-roned parts are clearer on one stone than those on the other; and a representation of that whereon the better definition appears is given on the left side of the Tower moat illustration. The arms and initials of the Langton family, along with those of certain other families, appear on a stone fixed in the eastern end of Broughton church. Against the wall, and above the font, in this church, there is part of a marble tablet, bearing an inscription, in Latin, relating to Robert Langton, of Broughton Tower. Beneath it there is a brass plate, containing the fol-lowing inscription:—"The memorial of Roger Lang-ton, of Broughton Tower in this parish, who died and was buried at Chester, September, 1714, was cast aside when the old church of St. Bridget, where the inter-ment took place, was pulled down. The Latin in-scription records the benefaction of Twenty Pounds, yearly, payable out of his landed estate, towards the stipend of the Incumbent of this Church. These fragments were discovered by accident, in October, 1888. They were removed to this spot by members of the family of the late William Langton, of Man-chester, a descendant of the first Roger Langton, of Broughton Tower, who served the office of Alderman and Mayor of Preston, and was buried there, April 3rd, 1644."

CHAPTER IV.

GREYFRIARS—UPLANDS HALL—PROSPECT HOUSE—PRIOR'S LEA—BRIDGE COTTAGE—
BROUGHTON CHURCH, HOUSE, PARK, AND VILLAGE.

GREYFRIARS.

From the high-road about 300 yards past the Black Bull, in Broughton, there may be seen, down to the west, clumps of trees. The trees to the left enshroud Greyfriars (originally called Broughton Bank), a very substantial residence, built in 1849, by Mr. Joseph Clayton, ironfounder, &c., Preston, occupied by him for 36 years—up to the time of his death, in 1885, and since then owned and occupied by Mr. Frank Hollins, of the firm of Messrs. Horrockses, Crewdson, and Co., cotton manufacturers, &c., of Preston and Bolton. Mr. Hollins has made some excellent additions to this residence. Originally, and up to the time of his purchase, the

and the general appearance of the building is most pleasing. The adjoining grounds have also been much improved, in respect to walks, floral and shrubbery arrangements, &c., by Mr. Hollins. At the chief entrance to the grounds, on the south side, there is one of the most substantial iron gates—with lateral supports, in the shape of clustered columns—in North Lancashire. The late Mr. Clayton had the gate and the supports made specially at his works (Soho Foundry) in Preston.

The thick, stately mass of trees to the north-west of Greyfriars encloses The Uplands (now called Uplands Hall), by which I am reminded of the Whitehead

UPLANDS HALL.

building had a bare, rigidly-isolated look; now, with varied flanking extensions, especially at the west end, the ornate is tastefully associated with the substantial,

family. There was a Ralph Whitehead living in Winmarleigh near the end of the 16th century. Richard Whitehead, his son, who was born in 1620 and died

14

in 1679, was, it is conjectured, the captain of a company of soldiers raised in Garstang, on the Parliamentary side, during the civil war. A grandson of this Captain Whitehead was the Rev. Thomas Whitehead, rector of Eccleston, near Chorley, for 42 years, and father of Thomas Whitehead who entered the army when young, became connected with the second European Regiment, was promoted to the colonelcy of it in 1824, subsequently distinguished himself in military matters in the East Indies, was made Knight, &c., in 1838, and Lieutenant-General in 1846. For some time Lieutenant-General Whitehead resided at Uplands Hall, Broughton, and here he died, in 1851, in the 74th year of his age. The Hall then was unoccupied for a while. In 1860 Mr. Paul Catterall, solicitor, of Preston, became the tenant, and he lived at the Hall for about eight years. One of the male members of the Whitehead family next occupied it for about two years, and during his stay made many alterations at the place. He was succeeded here by Mrs. Tempest (second daughter of Sir Thomas Joseph de Trafford, first baronet of Trafford Park), who was at the time widow of Henry, second son of Stephen Tempest, Esq., of Broughton, near Skipton, in Yorkshire, and she died at Uplands Hall, in 1883. The Hall was subsequently unoccupied until about 1886, when Colonel Oliver, late manager of the Preston branch of the Manchester and County Bank, purchased and went to reside at it, and he is living at the place now.

About half a mile past the Black Bull, in Broughton, on the east side of and near to the highway, there is Prospect House—a neat-looking little residence, whereat Alderman John Rawcliffe lived from 1852 to the time of his death in 1874. There does not

their present size, there could be seen from the upper windows, on a fine day, stretches of the south-western side of the Fylde, the estuary of the Ribble, and Southport, whilst occasionally, when the atmosphere was particularly clear, some of the Welsh mountains were visible. Since the death of Alderman Rawcliffe, Prospect House has been variously tenanted, and it is now, as it has been for some years, occupied by Mr. W. Dodgson.

PROSPECT HOUSE.

Spacious, elaborate, ruddy-hued, and standing back in its own grounds, nearly opposite Prospect House, is Prior's Lea. With its spirelets, high

PRIOR'S LEA.

now appear to be much of a prospect from this House in justification of the name it bears; but formerly, before the trees, &c., down on the west side, had got to

gables, &c., it has a very stylish and effective appearance. Prior's Lea was erected by Mr. Joseph Foster, machine maker, &c., Preston, and was occupied by him from 1892 till about the end of 1897, when it passed, by purchase, to Mr. Benjamin Sykes, C.E., of Preston, who has made considerable improvements at the place—including an electric light installation for the general establishment, an extension of the stables, the erection of a new entrance lodge, &c.—and has lived here since the early part of 1898. The gate adjoining the entrance lodge merits notice : it is a fine specimen of beaten iron work.

The little ivy-fronted house, down in the hollow, on the lower side of the road, facing Broughton Church, is called Bridge Cottage—a name derived from an immediately adjoining bridge, under which flows a brook which has its source among the high lands on the eastern side of Goosnargh. It is called Blundel Brook from its source to the highroad in Broughton, while from the latter point and for some miles westward it goes by the name of Woodplumpton Brook. Bridge Cottage was for a long time the residence of the late Mr. William Thornborrow, surveyor, &c. In or about

tains in its masonry, towards the top, a stone which bears the date 1533, and that is conjectured to have been the year in which it was erected. The body of the church was rebuilt in 1826. In the tower there is a sweet-toned peal of six bells—the gift, in 1884, of the late Alderman Daniel Arkwright, of Preston, and others (Alderman Arkwright's donation was £340). The Langton addition, in 1714, to the income of the minister at Broughton Church, was of the free or voluntary sort ; but in the previous century accretions for the same object were made in a different way. At a meeting of the "Committee for Plundered Ministers," held in 1646, it was decided that £20 per annum should be paid " out of the tythes of the towne of Broughton, sequestered from Sir Edward Wrightington, for and towards the maintenance of a minister in the chappell of Broughton annexed to the Church of Preston." In the same year the Committee ordered the sum of £50 to be paid out of the profits of the impropriate rectory of Poulton, sequestered from Sir Thomas Tildesley and John Greenhalgh, Esq., "delinquents," to increase the

BROUGHTON CHURCH AND BRIDGE COTTAGE.

1828, when the highway improvement work was being carried out in Broughton, Mr. Thornborrow (who was a native of a little place near Grange-over-Sands, and for some time worked in Wales, under Telford, the eminent civil engineer) appeared on the scene to superintend it ; he took lodgings at Bridge Cottage, with the intention of staying at it for a month or so ; but, through some cause, he got attached to the place, and, instead of staying here for a few weeks, he made the Cottage his home for 40 years—in fact, he bought the Cottage, never lived at any other place after first coming to it, and here he died.

Respecting Broughton Church, situated on the eastern side, it is dedicated to St. John the Baptist, and its original foundation goes back to a very early date. There was a church in existence here in 1112. The present church is the successor of one which stood on the same site, certainly, in 1527. The tower con-

maintenance of the minister of the "pochiall chappell of Broughton, within the pish of Preston. . . . the sd chappelrie consisting of 600 families, and the pnte maintenance belonging thereunto being but 4li p anu" (£4 per annum). In 1651 the Committee ordered that £50 a year should be paid out of the profits of the impropriate tithes of Leyland "sequestered from James Anderton, Esqr., papist and delinquent, for increase of the maintenance of James Knott, minister of Broughton and Barton, members of the parochiall chappell of Broughton. . . his present maintenance not exceeding twenty shillings a yeare." In a confirmatory or Committee order, made several months afterwards, "Ralph Banister and Wm. Osbolson, papists and delinquents," are associated with "Ja. Anderton" as contributories, out of the said impropriate tithe profits, in respect to the yearly payment of £50, and "all arreares thereof incurred" since the making of the original order. (For this, as well as for certain references, which will be found in subsequent parts, to grants made for the relief of "Plundered Ministers," I am indebted to the Minutes edited by W. A. Shaw, M.A., and published by the Record Society). The present Vicar of Broughton Church—appointed in 1886—is the Rev. S. E. Collinson. On the north side of the church is the school; the building above and at the rear of the latter is the schoolmaster's house; and the plain-looking structure which crowns the eminence on the same side is the Vicarage.

An excellent residence — Broughton House — is situated opposite the Vicarage, a short distance westward. The carriage way which branches from the highroad, on that side, near the summit of the

respected throughout the Fylde and Garstang districts. In 1823 Mr. France retired; and in the following year the late Mr. Richard Newsham, of Winckley-square, Preston, became a partner in the firm, which then took the designation of Messrs. Rawstorne, Wilson, and Newsham. In 1831 Mr. Newsham withdrew. The firm-name thereupon became Messrs. Rawstorne and Wilson, and continued so until 1847, when Mr. Rawstorne died. Mr. Wilson, after this, continued the business alone till the end of 1848, when his son, Mr. Edward Wilson, and Mr. Frederick Deacon became partners with him; the name of the firm then becoming Messrs. Wilson, Son, and Deacon. Mr. Wilson, senr., retired in

BROUGHTON HOUSE.

brow, leads to this residence. Owing to the many trees about, but very little of it can be seen from the highroad. Broughton House is a substantial, two-storey building. From the front of it there is a beautiful view of the vale-like land, on the south, between the highroad and the London and North-Western Railway. This House was built about 1833, by Mr. J. W. R. Wilson (father of Mr. Edward Wilson, senior partner in the present firm of Messrs. Wilson, Wright, and Wilsons, solicitors, Chapel-street, Preston); he lived here till 1856, when he went to reside at Silverdale, where he died, at a good old age, on the 10th of October, 1875. The firm alluded to is one of the oldest of its kind in the North. It owes its origin to Mr. Thomas Wilson, who in or about 1773, and when about 23 years of age, commenced business in the legal line with Mr. John Hankinson. In 1817, Mr. J. W. R. Wilson, son of Mr. Thomas Wilson, joined the firm, which at that time was composed of Messrs. Thomas Wilson and William Rawstorne—the latter being a member of the Rawstorne family of Penwortham. In the year last named Mr. Thomas Wilson retired, and his son then became partner with Mr. Rawstorne. At the same time there also joined the firm Mr. Thomas Robert Wilson France, known in after years as "the Squire of Rawcliffe," and much-

1859. For some time Mr. Edward Wilson and Mr. Deacon carried on the business, and then the former's two sons (Mr. Henry Francis and Mr. Edward Thomas Wilson) came in. At the end of 1883 Mr. Deacon retired. Subsequently Mr. Henry Lowndes Wright joined the firm, whose name then became what it still is—Messrs. Wilson, Wright, and Wilsons.

Broughton Park, on the eastern side of the highway, is approached by a carriage road a short distance beyond that leading to Broughton House. The residence of Mr. James Clarke, solicitor, Preston, is here. It was erected by him in 1891. A glimpse of the building can be got from the highroad: it is a spacious, selectly-located structure, with well laid-out grounds about it. The estate in connection with Broughton Park is about 140 acres in extent. On a part of it, at the north-east side, about 200 yards from the Goosnargh road, and fronted by an avenue of trees, now thin with age, there is a farm house, on the site of Broughton Old Hall. Many years ago this Hall was pulled down, and not a vestige of it can now be seen. Towards the end of last century General William Grinfield, commander-in-chief of some of the British forces in the West Indies, owned a portion of this estate. The Athertons (probably members of or connected with the Atherton family who owned or resided on the now much-built-upon

C

BROUGHTON PARK.

Greenbank estate, on the north side of Preston) afterwards held the property for numerous years. Later, the Haliburtons became possessed of Broughton Park estate. In 1841 Mr. Alexander Fowden Haliburton, of Wigan and Torquay (nephew of Mr. John Haliburton, who was a coal agent for Lord Balcarres, and at one time manager of or associated with the Canal Foundry, Preston), inherited it; and, when he died, he left the property to his widow—nee Augusta Louisa Neville Haliburton, daughter of Judge Haliburton, the author of "Sam Slick" and several other works. From this lady Mr. Clarke purchased the estate in 1889. Mrs. Haliburton died, at Torquay, on October 11th, 1891, and was interred in the Cemetery there.

A quarter of a mile north of Broughton Park there is "Broughton village"; it is made up of a few cottages, a shop or two, some joinering and blacksmithing places, a couple of public-houses, &c. The township of which it may be termed the "capital" contains five hamlets. In Doomsday Book Broughton is mentioned: it figures in the record as "Brocton"—a name suggestive of a fenced-in place at or near which badgers at one time existed; "Broc" being the Anglo-Saxon word for badger, and "ton" (i.e., "tun"), a word in the same language signifying an enclosure. In the Pipe Roll, 3 Henry III. (1219), the "Vill' de Brocton" (Broughton) is named for tallage (tax or toll) purposes. The Pipe Roll, 11 Henry III. (1226-7), mentions the "Villat' de Brocton" as one of the places which were at that time subjected to tallage, for the purpose of raising money to be used by the King, with the view of getting back his lost foreign inheritance. And amongst the Lancashire demesnes, talliated in 1261, was the "Vill' de Brocton." There is now, on the eastern side of Broughton village, a neat-looking, red-brick building for club purposes. It was erected in 1889, at the sole cost of Mr. Edward Wilson, of Broughton House, and was enlarged in 1897. Its cult is purely social—without limitation. In it

are reading and billiard rooms; the building also includes a caretaker's quarters; and contiguous to it there is a bowling green for the members of the club. The road which branches off to the east—at Broughton village—leads to Goosnargh, Inglewhite, &c.; that which strikes out westward goes to Woodplumpton. By the latter road Ambrose Hall, in Woodplumpton, can be reached; it is about a mile and a half from the village of Broughton. Some persons have conjectured that the Rev. Isaac Ambrose, a notable Puritan divine, was born at this Hall, whilst others have supposed that his parents lived at Ambrose Hall, in the township of Westby-with-Plumpton, and that in all likelihood his birthplace was there. But these surmises are, I believe, without any real foundation at all. In the 15th century there was an Ambrose family at Lowick, near Ulverston; early in the 16th century proprietary rights in Byreworth, near Garstang, were claimed by one Nicholas Ambrose, who has been taken to be the probable great-grandfather of Richard Ambrose, who sold the Ambrose Hall estate, Woodplumpton; and in the same century there was an Ambrose family at Ormskirk. There is no available proof that these Ambroses sprang from the same ancestors; but it is beyond doubt that the Rev. Isaac Ambrose came from the Ambrose family of Ormskirk, and that he was baptised at Ormskirk; so the fair presumption is that he was born in or near that town. In the early part of the present century the road between Broughton and Thornley, above Longridge, was one of the busiest country ways in England. Every day there were on it a large number of carts—not unfrequently seventy or eighty—laden with lime for Thornley, and intended for the tillage of farm lands below and on each side of Broughton. Corn-growing was greatly in vogue in those days. In fields on the north side of Broughton township, and in contiguous parts, water pits are remarkably numerous: evidently, they were made in the old marl-getting times.

CHAPTER V.

WHITTINGHAM HOUSE—BARTON HALL, BROOK, AND MILL—STONE BRIG BROW—NEWHOUSE CHAPEL—NEWSHAM HOUSE—HOLLOWFORTH.

Whittingham House, on the eastern side of Broughton village, is, on account of its age, family associations, &c., entitled to notice here. It is located about a mile and a half from Broughton, standing serenely in its own grounds, a short distance from, and on the south side of, the Goosnargh road. For upwards of 200 years Whittingham House was the residence of the Parkers, who, it is said—though I have not been able to meet with any genealogical warrant for this—"claimed to be a branch of the Parkers of Browsholme," near Clitheroe. Henry Parker (son of William Parker, of Bradkirk, near Kirkham) had a mansion in Whittingham—it was, no doubt, Whittingham House—in 1634. He died in 1642, and it is probable that his son John (bapt. 1610-11, died 1698) rebuilt the whole or a portion of Whittingham House in 1670. Tradition says that some of the wood work connected with Fernyhalgh old Catholic Chapel was utilised in the construction of Whittingham House. There used to be an old, strong, stud-faced door at the back of the place, and this, it was said, had come from the chapel named. The last direct male heir of the Parkers of Whittingham House was Mr. John Burch Parker. He was the only son of Mr. Henry Parker, was born at Whittingham House, died unmarried, in 1844, at the age of 22, and was interred at Goosnargh—the burial place of several of his ancestors. After his death Mr. Charles Fitzherbert-Brockholes,

youngest brother of "the old squire" of Claughton Hall, lived for some time at Whittingham House: he rented the whole of the Parker property here, was fond of the sports of a country gentleman, and kept greyhounds. Mr. William Paley, cotton manufacturer, of Preston, succeeded him as tenant of Whittingham House. And then there came to reside at it, after Mr. Paley, Captain James German, of Preston, previously married to Miss (Martha) Parker, who, on the death of her brother, Mr. John Burch Parker, inherited the family property in Whittingham. Captain (afterwards Major) German, who was Mayor of Preston in 1849-50, and an alderman of the borough from 1849 to 1853, did not stay at Whittingham House very long—he returned to Preston, where his wife died, in 1856, and afterwards (in the meantime marrying Miss Marion Cooke, daughter of Mr. Charles Cooke, of Ledbury, Herefordshire), he took up his residence at Sevenoaks, Kent, where he still lives. Mr. Paul Catterall, solicitor, of Preston, succeeded Captain German at Whittingham House, and occupied it for a few years. Two or three other gentlemen, including Mr. J. L. Harrison, now of Ladywell, Fernyhalgh, followed successively, as tenants, until about 1875, when Mr. Joseph Smith, cotton spinner and manufacturer, Preston, went to live at the place—in fact, he bought it—and he still resides here. After purchasing Whittingham House, Mr. Smith subjected

WHITTINGHAM HOUSE.

it to a very drastic process of improvement: he pulled down the whole of the old, plain, brick front, and in its place erected the present gabled, well-windowed, neatly-porched facade; he remodelled the building, internally, in several parts; and, altogether, the transformation he accomplished was of a striking and excellent character. At the front and the rear of the house there are—carved in stone—the armorial bearings of Mr. Smith's paternal and maternal families. His father was Mr. William Smith, of Clock House, Lea, whose ancestors belonged to a very old Bleasdale family: his mother was Jane, daughter and co-heiress of Mr. Robert Haydock, of Bartle, "the representative of the Haydocks of Cottam Hall." A small stone, which was in the old front of Whittingham House, is fixed in the porch wall on the right outer side. It contains some initials and a date; but, through being very far worn and quite tightly covered with ivy stems, I could only make out, when I last examined it, the letter "P" (obviously meaning Parker) and the figures "16." Mr. Smith informs me that, when he last definitely deciphered the date, it was 1670. If so, then the house must have been rebuilt, entirely or in part, by John Parker (a grandson of William Parker of Bradkirk), who was the owner of the place at that time. In the House there are now some very fine old pieces of furniture, in carved oak, including an arm-chair which, it is conjectured, belonged to the original 'Squire Parker here; a chest containing in front, in strongly carved letters, the name "Sarah Radclif"— a relative of the unfortunate Earl of Derwentwater (leader in the 1715 Rebellion); and a sideboard, bearing the Derby arms and the initials "I.S.," evidently referring to either James Stanley, 7th Earl of Derby, the great Royalist, who was beheaded at Bolton, in 1651, or to James, Lord Strange (son of Sir Edward Stanley, the 11th Earl)—1716-1771—who assumed the name of Smith, through his marriage with Lucy,

daughter of Mr. Hugh Smith, of Weald Hall, in Essex. There are also in one of the rooms a crucifix, a chalice, a mass book, and some embroidered vestments, from a domestic chapel which one of Mr. Smith's ancestors had in connection with his residence in Forton, not far from Forton Hall; likewise two paintings, on copper, from Stydd Lodge Catholic chapel, near Ribchester, and a triptych, &c., which once belonged to the old Haydock family.

On an eminence to the north, and about a mile from Broughton village, there nestles pleasantly amid trees Barton Hall. In 1834 the father of the late Mr. Charles Roger Jacson (Mr. George Jacson, who was a member of the first reconstituted Corporation of Preston elected in 1835 under the Municipal Reform Act, afterwards an alderman, then, in 1840, Mayor, and a cotton manufacturer in the town) purchased the whole of the property in the township of Barton, with the exception of about 25 acres, from Mr. James Shuttleworth, lord of the manor—a successor of Sir Richard Shuttleworth, of Gawthorpe, near Burnley, to whom the Barton property came through his marriage with Fleetwood, sole daughter and heiress of Mr. Richard Barton, of Barton, whose ancestors had been landowners here from some time prior to the middle of the 13th century. For nine years previous to purchasing the property, Mr. Jacson resided at what was then called Barton Hall. After making the purchase, he went to live at Barton Lodge (the building on the eminence before mentioned); subsequently the Lodge was called the Hall, and the old building—the original Hall—was turned into a farmhouse. In the spring of 1837 there died, at Barton Lodge, a Mrs. Birch, in the 100th year of her age. On the death of Alderman George Jacson, in 1846, his son, Mr. C. R. Jacson, succeeded to the Barton property, and took up his residence at the Hall, where he continued to live until the time

BARTON HALL.

of his death, in 1893. Mr. C. R. Jacson was an active, cultured gentleman. He completed his education at Rugby, under the celebrated Dr. Arnold. In 1836, when 19 years of age, he joined the manufacturing firm with which his father was connected at Preston. In 1846 he married Catherine, the only daughter of Mr. Henry Grenehalgh-Formby, second son of the Rev. Richard Formby, LL.B., of Formby Hall. His marriage was without issue. In 1863 Mr. Jacson became a Councillor, in 1865-66 he was Mayor, and in 1868 he was elected an Alderman of Preston. He was both a borough and a county magistrate, and for some time was chairman of the Preston Board of Guardians. He took a great interest in all the most important local movements and institutions, whilst in county affairs he was among the foremost workers—for years magisterially, and afterwards as an alderman of the Lancashire County Council. In 1894 Mrs. Jacson, his widow, a highly-accomplished lady, with a literary faculty, left Barton Hall. She now resides at Lytham. The whole of the Jacson property in Barton—the area of the land being upwards of 2,600 acres, and the buildings connected therewith consisting of the Hall, farm houses, corn mill, inns, cottages, &c.—was offered for sale, en bloc, in 1894. The highest bid was about £100,000—a sum deemed insufficient, and the property was withdrawn. On the 20th, 21st, and, 22nd of June, 1899, the property, divided into 72 lots, was sold by auction. Mr. W. Smith, of Newsham House, purchased the principal lot—Barton Hall and three farms, the area of the land being 395 acres—for £25,000. The sum realised for the whole of the 72 lots was £141,652. For many years the late Mr. John Logan was the steward of the Barton estate, and under his supervision various improvements, especially in drainage, were made. His son (Mr. J. H. Logan) became his successor in the stewardship, and held the position for a considerable time—until, in fact, the sale of the estate.

The stream which flows under the highway bridge (called Cardwell Bridge) in the hollow, facing Barton Hall, is Barton Brook, which takes its rise eastward, above Inglewhite. Verses have been written concerning Barton Brook, and some of the contiguous scenery, &c. A poem of nearly 200 lines, headed "Barton Brook and Barton Hall," and beginning with the words "Delightful, babbling Barton Brook," was written by the late Mr. E. Buller, of Preston. Something like a mile and a half above the bridge, close to the brook, there is Barton corn mill. About 1853 a serious flood overcharged the mill pond, and the weir gave way. A young fellow, named Henry Kirk—a native of Goosnargh, with an excellent poetic faculty—wrote some verses about this mishap. Where they were originally published—whether in one of the Preston papers or in some magazine—I do not know. Afterwards, I think, they appeared in an early edition of Harland and Wilkinson's "Lancashire Songs and Ballads" (several other verses of Kirk's composition may be found in the third and enlarged edition of that excellent collection). The following

were the verses he wrote respecting the mishap at Barton corn mill weir:—

THE OLD MILL WEIR.

The wild March winds came roaring
 O'er the snowy hills,
The turbid waters pouring
 Down a thousand rills;
In rocky chasms rumbling,
 Over cascades tumbling,
Flooding the valleys far and near,
 And downward bore,
 'Mid crash and roar,
  The old mill weir.

How often in my childhood
 Have I strayed from school,
Along the straggling wildwood,
 By the reedy pool,
To where the waters bounded,
 In a full curve rounded,
Like a mane of silver bright and clear,
 And broke into snow
 On the boulders below
  The old mill weir.

Fresh links are daily broken
 From that golden chain,
Whose links are each a token
 We would still retain
Of youth's resplendent morning,
 Our darker days adorning,
With those early memories fond and dear;
 And another went
 When fierce floods rent
  The old mill weir.

Not very long after writing these verses Henry Kirk enlisted as a soldier; he went through the Crimean war; and at a later period, after he had left the army and was residing in London, I became acquainted with him, and frequently received communications of a bright, sketchy character from his pen. The last time I saw him was at Preston, during the 1882 Guild celebration. He came down from London to witness some of the sights, then returned, and whether he be living or dead now I cannot say. The late Edward Kirk—at one time stationmaster at Worsley, then the editor of a newspaper at Eccles, and afterwards, up to the time of his death, in 1886, a frequent contributor of rural notes, &c., to the "Manchester Guardian"—was the brother of Henry Kirk. Barton Brook, after passing under the railway westward, runs into Hollowforth (traces of otters used to be met with at its sides in certain parts of this region), then wanders away into Sowerby, and eventually joins the Wyre between Myerscough and St. Michael's.

The steep part, just round the corner beyond Barton Brook bridge, is called Stone Brig Brow. The "Brig" refers to the bridge which spans the brook. At the end of the Rebellion of 1745, old Squire Butler, of Kirkland Hall, near Churchtown—a gentleman with strong Jacobite proclivities—was seized, at his residence, by some of the King's forces; and it was decided that he should go, as a prisoner, to Preston, his coachman being ordered to take steps for getting him there without delay. The coachman got two horses ready, one for the Squire and the other for himself; they speedily mounted the animals and set off, Prestonward, with the soldiers in proximity; but when they had got to Stone Brig Brow, the coachman quietly slipped off his horse, and ham-strung that on which the Squire was riding. The animal thus operated upon "gave way" speedily, the old gentleman fell off it, and, as he did not stir, the soldiers supposed that he had been either killed or very seriously hurt, so they left him, with the coachman standing or kneeling close by, and went on in the direction of Preston. When the soldiers had got well out of sight, the coachman helped the Squire (whose previous quietness had been due to "foxing," not injury) to his feet, assisted him in getting upon the other horse—the uninjured one—and then returned with him to Kirkland Hall. Stone Brig Brow used to be terribly steep, and very bad for horses to either ascend or descend, especially if they were heavily laden. In 1863 a very serious accident occurred here. A big boiler was being brought from Lancaster to Preston, on a waggon; while going down this brow the waggon, owing to the brake being either too weak or not properly applied, got beyond control—it over-ran the horses when not far from the bottom, near the bend, and then fell over, with the boiler, on the west side. One of the men in charge and three of the horses were killed. In 1869 this Brow was very considerably lowered; the cost of the alteration (about £800) being defrayed by the late Misses Cross, of Myerscough. Near the top of the Brow, on the east side, close to the fence, there is a polished granite tablet, which bears the following inscription:—"To relieve the sufferings of the animals labouring in our service the steep ascent of this hill was lowered at the expense of Mary and Margaret Cross, of Myerscough, A.D. 1869. This deed of mercy appeals to every passer-by that he, too, show mercy to the creatures God has put under his hand." The

tablet is bordered with freestone, and below, immediately in front, there is a plain seat for wayfarers, &c., to rest on.

The lane to the left of the main road, a short distance north-west of Stone Brig Brow, leads to Barton and Broughton railway station—(a most inconveniently located station, for the inhabitants of Broughton especially)—and also to Woodplumpton, Catforth, &c. From the summit of the bridge, at the station, a very extensive view—north, south, and west—is commanded on a fine day. Down the lane, to the left, past the railway station, there is Newhouse Roman Catholic Chapel. Newhouse is situated in Newsham; but the former appears to be an older place—anyhow, to have an older name—than the latter. In Doomsday Book Newhouse is mentioned; but there is no reference in that record to Newsham. A Roman Catholic mission was founded at Newhouse about 1730. During the No-Popery or Anti-Jacobite agitation, towards the end of last century, the chapel at Newhouse would in all probability have been destroyed, by an inflamed mob from Preston, had not a neighbouring Protestant given to them, as they were approaching, an excellent character of the resident priest, and then regaled them with meat and drink. In 1806 the present chapel supplanted the old one, on the same site. During the Parliamentary election campaign at Preston, in 1826, "Old Cobbett," who was the Radical candidate, frequently visited the Rev. J. B. Marsh, the then resident priest at Newhouse; they used to walk together, in conversation, up and down the lane which runs in front of the chapel; and for years afterwards the roadway here was called "Cobbett's lane." For some time the present Bishop of the Roman Catholic diocese of Salford (Dr. Bilsborrow) was priest in charge of Newhouse Chapel. The priest at

CROSS TABLET.

NEWHOUSE CHAPEL.

present in charge of Newhouse mission is the Rev. E. Kearney.

About a quarter of a mile south of Newhouse chapel there stands Newsham House—a very substantial stone structure built in 1851-2 by Mr. John Hawkins, cotton manufacturer, &c., Preston, and occupied by him up to the time of his death, in 1873. Directly afterwards Mr. Joseph Hawkins, his eldest son, went to Newsham House, and lived here for some years, up to the time of his death. Then Mr.

the structural specialities of this residence is the inclined plane of the external courses: the stonework is set at a slight angle of declination, outward, in order to keep out damp, from rain.

West of Barton and Broughton railway station—about a mile by ordinary road, but considerably less by footpath—there is a very good residence called Hollowforth. It has a strikingly ornate exterior, and amongst its immediate surroundings there are many curiosities in carved stone, &c. This

NEWSHAM HOUSE.

Thomas Coulthard bought the place, and lived at it for a while ; and now it is owned and occupied by Mr. William Smith, corn miller and merchant, who was M.P. for North Lonsdale from 1892 till 1895, and who has much improved the place— made various internal changes, put in the electric light, built new conservatories, rearranged and elaborated the front ground, &c. It is said that Newsham House was designed for Mr. Hawkins by Mr. John Stevenson, senr., who was for many years head of the firm of Messrs. Stevenson and Co., engineers, &c., Preston. One of

place derives its name from a ford which formerly existed a short distance southward—in a hollow part and across a deep-sided stream (a continuation of Barton Brook), over which there is now a bridge. Originally, the residence mentioned was a small farmhouse. In the 17th century one or more members of a family named Boadman lived at Hollowforth. The will of Maria Boadman, "of Hollowforth," was proved within the archdeaconry of Richmond in 1679. For many years the farm house at Hollowforth was occupied by Mr. Richard Threl-

fall, farmer and tanner; there was an orchard
in front of it, the farm land being continguous,
and the tannery just across the road on the east side.
When Mr. Threlfall died, his son Henry worked the
farm and the tannery; when the latter died he was
succeeded here by his brother, Mr. Richard Threlfall,
who was brought up at Hollowforth, and who, after
coming into possession, made many changes and improvements at the place. He extinguished the tannery
business, made extensive and elaborate additions to the
house, did away with the orchard in front, laid out
the ground very tastefully, and went in for much
curious stonework. The stones which formed the
obelisk in Preston old Market-place—a clustered
column obelisk, about 30 feet high, and taken down in
1853—were purchased by Mr. Threlfall, conveyed to
Hollowforth, and there utilised, the bulk in the front
gateway, and the remainder in a small structure at the
rear of the house. Several of the ornamental stones
connected with Preston Parish Church, but of no use

there, when the building was almost entirely pulled
down in 1853, for the purpose of being supplanted by
the present edifice, were bought by Mr. Threlfall, and
put in structural position at Hollowforth: numerous
finials, battlement stones, &c., figure on external portions of the house; and the two stones which formed
the circular casing for the church clock face do duty
here as door heads. Various ornamental stones—some
strikingly symbolic in character—from other places are
located in different parts of the grounds. Mr.
Richard Threlfall, while residing at Hollowforth, carried on business as a wine and spirit merchant in
Preston, of which borough he was once Mayor—
during the municipal year 1855-56. He died in 1870.
His widow continued to reside at Hollowforth until
her death in 1898. The house is at present empty.
On the whole, Hollowforth is a pretty place, though
perhaps rather overdone, here and there, with stony
embellishment.

OLD OBELISK STONES, &C., HOLLOWFORTH.

CHAPTER VI.

THE GRANGE—BOAR'S HEAD—BARTON CHURCH—GIP'S LANE INCIDENT—WHITE HORSE—
LONGEVITY—MYERSCOUGH COTTAGE, PLANKS, AND LODGE—THE TYLDESLEYS.

On the west side of the highway, and a little beyond the entrance to the lane leading to Barton and Broughton Station, &c., there is a farmhouse called The Grange. It is said that in the old days of religious intolerance, when the penal code bore very heavily upon Roman Catholics especially, this place belonged to a man of that order; that when he died it was found he had willed the property to either a Roman Catholic or for the benefit of a Roman Catholic mission; and that a Roman Catholic relative of the testator, knowing it could not be bequeathed to such a person or for such a purpose, turned Protestant, and so inherited the property himself. The main road, for about a mile north of the lane mentioned, is "as straight as an arrow" and perfectly level, whilst the high, numerously-wired telegraph poles on each side, fixed uniformly as far as the eye can see, give it an imposing, avenue-like appearance. William Black, in his novel, "The Strange Adventures of a Phaeton," makes reference to the strikingly level character of the road here and onward for some distance: he says

that "The western sands could not be much more level" than this road, and that it goes through a pleasant, rich, and well cultivated country. The small, yet neat and substantial-looking house, with a high, well-trimmed hedge in front of it, on the west side of the road, was occupied for many years by the Misses Cross before alluded to. They both died here —Miss Margaret, in 1888, in the 82nd year of her age, and Miss Mary, in 1893, at the age of 88. Their grandfather and the great-grandfather of the present Viscount Cross were brothers.

A little beyond the house which the Misses Cross occupied, and on the east side of the main road, there is the "Boar's Head" public-house. In Cary's directory of turnpike-roads, published in 1812, this house is mentioned. It was in existence before that work was issued, but for what length of time I have not been able to ascertain. A legend, or traditional story, runs to the effect that there was in this district, in the days of the Bartons, a wild boar which roamed about and did much mischief; that the principal of the Barton family pro-

BOAR'S HEAD AND BARTON CHURCH (OLD AND NEW).

mised to give his daughter in marriage to the man who would kill it; that a great hunt afterwards took place; and that on St. Lawrence's Day one of the Shuttleworths succeeded in killing the animal, near where the public-house now stands. A supplementary story says that the name of the inn originated from this old incident. For many years there has been in front of the building a sign bearing the representation of a huge boar's head. Contiguous, on the same side, and a little to the rearward, there is Barton new church. Viscount Cross laid the foundation stone of this church on the 22nd of April, 1895, and the building was consecrated for divine worship on the 29th of July, 1896. Miss Mary Cross gave a donation of £2,000 towards the new church, and Mr. C. R. Jacson left a legacy of £2,500 on behalf of it; the total cost, exclusive of many valuable presents for furnishing purposes, being £5,721. The new church—a neat, spire-adorned stone edifice—stands immediately behind the site of its predecessor, which was a very plain, externally-whitewashed little building, erected in 1845, and the successor of one with a pre-Reformation foundation. The school, near the lich-gate, was erected in 1840, to the memory of Mr. George Jacson, father of Mr. C. R. Jacson. The tree-surrounded, snug-looking brick house about a quarter of a mile north of the church, and on the same side of the road, is Barton Vicarage. It was built in 1842, through the efforts of the Rev. T. Duell, who was the minister at Barton Church for 38 years, and died at the Vicarage in 1870. Mr. Duell was a classical teacher, at Ripon Grammar School, in his early days, and whilst there taught numerous youths belonging to families of high position, five of the sons of Earl Grey being amongst the number. For many years, whilst minister of Barton Church, he acted as master of Bilsborrow School. With the exception of the first three years of his ministry at Barton, the Rev. T. Duell had with him, as clerk and sexton, Richard Curwen. For 21 years after Mr. Duell's death Curwen acted as clerk, &c., here. He died in 1891, at the age of 88 years. The Rev. J. D. Harrison was appointed vicar in succession to Mr. Duell, and he is still in ministerial charge here. The stipend now attached to the living of St. Lawrence's Church, Barton, may not be the analogue of an auriferous wonder; but it is quite a "gold-bearing reef" compared with the metallic situation here near the middle of the 17th century. The stipend then amounted to—nothing! And this, no doubt, accounted for another thing—the absence of a minister. In 1646, "by vertue of an order of both Houses of Parliament," it was directed that the yearly sum of £30 should be paid out of the impropriate tithes of Fulwood, sequestered from Sir Thos. Tildesley, Knt., "delinquent," and that £20 a year more should be taken out of the profits of the impropriate rectory of Poulton, sequestered from the aforesaid gentleman and John Greenhalgh, Esq., "delinquent," to and for "the maintenance of an able preachinge Minister, to be approved by the Committee of divines" assigned for Lancashire, "in the Chappell of St. Lawrence,

situate within the p'ish of Broughton. . . . .which Chappell hath noe Annuall mayntenance to the same belonging." Additional annual payments, equal to about £100—from the same sources and for the same purpose—were afterwards ordered. In 1650, a number of Commissioners, appointed by Parliament to inquire into ecclesiastical affairs, reported in regard to the chapel of St. Lawrence, Barton, that it had "neither Minister nor maintenance," and that the inhabitants desired that it might "bee made a Parochial Chappell to Broughton."

There are many places in England called Barton. The suffix "ton" means an enclosed part. "Bar" is an early form of bear, i.e., to yield or bring forth crops, &c.; and at one time it meant to surround with a fence or barrier. In several parts of England the word "barton" is applied to a rick-yard, meaning in this connection an enclosure for the bear or produce (corn, &c.) of the land. It is supposed that originally the various places called Barton must have been rick-yards, and they may have included the settlers' dwellings as well as their produce. It may further be remarked that in the 13th century—and, perhaps, earlier—the word "Bar" meant a wild boar; so that Barton might mean an enclosed place in a district which contained animals of this kind. There used to be wild boars in Barton, near Preston; but, then, such animals roamed about in other parts as well—in places with quite different names. The former hypothesis is the more probable.

The old, rustic-looking lane which branches eastward, at the corner of Barton vicarage grounds, runs up to Inglewhite; Barton Corn Mill, &c., being about three-quarters of a mile from the entrance of it. This is called Gips-lane. Some distance up it, on the right hand side, there is a water pit known as Melling's Gyll, which has various gruesome associations, and which receives a pretty wide berth at night time from certain of the natives superstitiously inclined. A horse was once mysteriously drowned in this pit, and one or two dead bodies of unknown infants have been found in or about it. As to the horse, tradition says that it belonged to an officer connected with the Rebellion of 1745. The story is, that during the north retreat of the rebels an officer in charge of some money—supposed to have been the paymaster—was seen coming down the lane, on horseback, by certain people living at a farm not far from Melling's Gyll, and that one of them, armed with a gun, went behind a fence at the side of the lane, and, as soon as the officer got opposite, "popped him off." It never transpired what amount of money the officer had with him, nor has anyone ever said outright that anybody robbed him; but the report which has come down, generation after generation, is that after the officer was shot the people at the farm "ne'er looked back no more"—that is to say, were in "easy circumstances" for the remainder of their days—and that his horse, which they declared they knew nothing whatever about, was found drowned in the neighbouring Gyll. Some years ago, when the thatch on the farmhouse alluded to was being removed, in order to be supplanted by slates, certain rusty old weapons, supposed to have belonged to the officer who came to grief, were found under it.

A little beyond Barton Vicarage, at the west side of the main road, there are several recently-erected villa-like residences, some of them with fine, fanciful names which must considerably stagger Bartonian and Myers-coughian minds; but they all seem nice dwellings, though perhaps a little too near the railway, which passes at the rear. The railway bridge, a short distance beyond, is called Whitehorse Bridge. It is a very wide one—probably wider, in its entirety, than any other country bridge crossing the line between Crewe and Carlisle—and it is, singular to say, the only bridge of the highway between Preston and Lancaster which goes over the railway. In May, 1840, when this bridge was being constructed, about 21 feet of the archway fell in; one man being killed and two severely injured by the accident. During the following July, in consequence of heavy rains, a portion of the bridge again gave way, but, fortunately, no one sustained any personal injury. There is a decidedly fine view from this bridge—a view which includes nearly the whole of the Fylde country, and various fells, mountains, vales, and pieces of woodland scenery eastward and northward. The hamlet immediately over the railway bridge is Whitehorse; and this name has evidently been derived from that of a public-house—the White Horse Inn—which is situated near one end of the place. The building at present used as the White Horse public-house is not an old one; but it appears to be the successor of an inn of the same name which stood upon the same site, or was in existence somewhere in the neighbourhood, about 240 years ago. Amongst the signatories (as Commissioners) of the return made for the Blackburn Hundred in respect to the sums raised by Act of Parliament (Car. II., 1660) "for the speedy provision of money for disbanding and paying off the forces of this Kingdome both by Land and Sea," were "Ric. Shuttleworthe" and "John Cunliffe"; and at the bottom of the return was the following statement:—"Delivered by the hands of John Taylor of St. Lawrence, Lancashire, at the sign called the White horse, 22 Dec." (1660). The "Ric. Shuttleworthe" here mentioned would be Mr. Richard Shuttleworth, who succeeded to the family property at Gawthorpe, near Burnley, and at Barton, near Preston, in 1607-8, was High Sheriff of Lancashire in 1618 and 1638, and twice M.P. for Preston—in 1640 and from 1654 to 1660. "John Cunliffe" would be a member of a very old North of England family, which for many years resided near Accrington, and no doubt an ancestor of the Cunliffes of Myers-cough House. (Near the end of the 15th or in the early part of the 16th century, Helen, daughter of Lawrence Shuttleworth of the Gawthorpe family, married a Cunliffe.) As to "John Taylor," he was evidently either the minister, or clerk, or an official of some kind at the chapel or in the district of St. Lawrence; this name (St. Lawrence) being formerly

applied, without any mention at all of Barton, as old maps, &c., show, to the place of worship just named and the locality in which it stood. Obviously, in the above quoted statement "St. Lawrence" meant this; the late old chapel near the roadside—a building used as a domestic chapel by the Shuttleworths, enlarged in 1845, and Blandfordised, &c., in 1850—being, as already stated, the predecessor of the new church in Barton. As to the "White Horse," that would have reference to a local inn, of which the present one with the same name, in the neighbourhood of the railway bridge, is, no doubt, the successor. There are old people in this region now; but not so many, I fancy, as formerly. It is reported that in May, 1821, there were living within a radius of one mile of Whitehorse 27 persons whose united ages amounted to 2,190 years, the average of which would be a little over 81 years for each individual. This beats what I have seen in a statement as to the longevity of sundry people who were living, a few miles farther north, about the same time; the statement being to the effect that, in the early part of this century, there were residing at Garstang 25 persons whose aggregate ages amounted to 2,000 years—average, 80 years each. How long these persons lived after the time when their ages were thus taken down I do not know; but none of them, I fancy, would reach the number of years attained by certain individuals who died in Garstang and the neighbourhood thereof during the latter part of last century, viz., Elizabeth Storey, Garstang, died 1762, aged 103 years; William Widnes, Garstang, died 1796, aged 110; James Swarbrick, Nateby, died 1790, aged 102; and William Dickinson, Scorton, died 1796, in his 110th year. In 1855 there died at Catterall a man named Ralph Green, who was 101 years old. A patriarchal person died in Barton, on the 30th of June, 1898: this was Edward Myers-cough, who was in his 93rd year. On the 3rd of January, 1899, there was interred, at Churchtown, Hannah Norris (a native of Bleasdale, which is a few miles north-east of Whitehorse), who died at Hambleton, aged 99. Her father died at 83, her brother at 93, and she had a sister who, like herself, was only a year off 100 when she died. A stone-throw from the hamlet of Whitehorse, northward, near the bend in the road, there is Myers-cough Cottage. It has a gloomy appearance at the end facing the road; but the front of it, looking north, is verandahed, and has a more pleasing aspect. Here, for several years—up to the time of his death, in 1890—the late Mr. T. Parkinson resided. He had in his possession the original MS. of the Tyldesley Diary—a very interesting personal record made during the years 1712-13-14, and printed, for the first time, with annotations, in volume form, at Preston, in 1873. It has for some years been in the "scarce" category of bibliophiles.

We are now in Myerscough. This township is supposed to be of the same area as the ancient Forest of Myerscough, which at one time contained herds of wild deer. Up to 1778 there were deer in Myerscough Forest. The long, level portion of the highway in front of Myerscough Cottage is now known as Myerscough Planks; it was in old days called Myerscough Plank. Under date December 23rd, 1713, Thomas Tyldesley, ot Myerscough Lodge, has this entry in his diary: "Went to dinr to Thurnham. In ye eivening Bror. Dalton [of Thurnham Hall] returned home, who tould us hee was apprehensive of beeing robed on Mirscough Planke by 3 well mounted." It is said that the road here was at one time in a very swampy, bad condition, and that it was improved or made passable by being covered with planks overlaid with earth, &c.—hence its name. It is furthermore stated that this part was formerly very lonely, and favourable for the operations of highway robbers. The "well mounted" trio referred to by "Bror. Dalton" were evidently either highwaymen or suspicious looking characters suggesting some connection with predatory work.

About a quarter of a mile beyond Myerscough Planks, northward, there is a lane which turns off to the left. The canal from Preston to Kendal, via Lancaster, goes close by here—within about a dozen yards of the highroad—and it is crossed by a very awkward, high-backed bridge. On the left side of the lane, just over the canal bridge, there is a barn, in the outer gable of which is a stone bearing the inscription—"Rev. T. D., 1834." This refers to the Rev. T. Duell, who either built the barn at his own expense, or had some allowance made for its construction, at the time named. The small house, situated near the barn, was occupied by him until the Vicarage in Barton was erected for his use. The lane alluded to leads to St. Michaels, Great Eccleston, &c. About a mile and a half down it, Myerscough Lodge is located; but it is not the old original Lodge of the Tyldesleys: that, with the farm buildings adjoining it, has been pulled down; this—a large, excellent farm house, with contiguous outbuildings—is its successor, and is situated about 40 yards eastward from the ground on which the old Lodge stood. In conse-

quence of their inconvenient structure and dilapidated state the Lodge, which had been used for a long time as a farm house, and the adjacent outbuildings were demolished in 1888. The old Lodge was a very interesting place, chiefly on account of its regal and family associations. For many years it was owned and periodically occupied by members of an old Royalist family, and it was twice Royally visited. In the first half of the fourteenth century (1320-46) the district of Myerscough formed part of a Royal forest. Leland, in his antiquarian researches, made in the reign of Henry VIII., alludes to "Merscow Park" as a possession of Lord Derby. In the reign of Edward VI., Thurstan de Tildesley, who was appointed Receiver-General of the Isle of Man, when Sir John De Stanley, "King and Lord of Man," was called to England, left to the children of his second marriage certain property in Myerscough. Edward Tyldesley, a grandson of Thurstan, resided at Myerscough Lodge: he was the father of Major-General Sir Thomas Tyldesley, a renowned fighter in the Civil Wars, who served under the Earl of Derby, in the Royalist cause, and was killed at the battle of Wigan Lane, in 1651. Edward Tyldesley, son of Sir Thomas, was a supporter of the Royalist party; during the time of the Restoration he built Fox Hall (now a public-house) at Blackpool (then an insignificant fishing village); and the presumption is that he alternately resided at Fox Hall and Myerscough Lodge. His son, Thomas Tyldesley, who was born in 1657, and died at the beginning of 1715, chiefly resided, during the latter portion of his life, at Myerscough Lodge, where he died. This Thomas (the last of the Tyldesleys who occupied the Lodge) was a supporter of the "Old Pretender's" cause: during the early unrest of the Jacobites which eventuated in the Rebellion he "got his sword and gun mended ready for use": and had he been living when the Rebels went south and passed, as they actually did, in November, 1715, within about a mile and a half of Myerscough Lodge, he would, in all probability, have joined them. His

MYERSCOUGH LODGE (OLD).

son Edward did join them, at Lancaster, and was afterwards taken prisoner, conveyed to London, tried there, and acquitted. A grandson (James Tyldesley) served in the army of Prince Charles in 1745. King James I., during his progress from Edinburgh to London, in 1617, stayed at Myerscough Lodge two or three days and nights. During his visit he had "a high old time" of it—hunted in the surrounding park, killing five bucks, feasted, revelled, made the Duke of Buckingham, who was in his suite, sing, and sang himself, all about hunting. His Majesty also indulged in speech-making. Nicholas Assheton, of Downham, in the parish of Whalley, who was with the company at the Lodge on this occasion, says, in his private dairy, that the King, in the course of his stay here, made a "speeche about libertie to pipeing and honest recreations." (Probably his Majesty had at this time some faint idea of the "Book of Sports," the preparation of which was, it has been conjectured, definitely "suggested to his mind on the banks of the Darwen," during his visit to Hoghton Tower, after leaving Myerscough Lodge. This "Book of Sports" was, in reality, a Royal proclamation, sanctioning certain sports or recreations on Sundays, after divine service. It was first issued in 1618. Charles I. reissued it in 1633; and it was burnt by the common hangman, by order of Parliament, in 1643). Charles II., while making his advance towards Worcester, in August, 1651, stayed one night at Myerscough Lodge. Dr. Charles Leigh, in his work, "The Natural History of Lancashire, Cheshire," &c., published in 1700, says that Edward Tyldesley, of Myerscough Lodge (father of Thomas, the diarist), presented to Charles II. a white crow, which was afterwards "kept as a curiosity in the Park at St. James's." At the eastern end of the Lodge there was a small, semi-hexagonally roofed apartment which was called "the King's room." This, according to tradition, was the room in which the two Royal visitors slept during their stay here. The stairway leading to this and the other rooms, on the same floor, was broad and of oak, with a low-set, massive balustrade. At one time there was, in a room at the north end downstairs, a lofty, elaborately-carved chimney-piece; but a few years before the Lodge was pulled down it was taken out and conveyed to some place in London. This chimney-piece was of dark oak, and contained eight surmounting panels, in two parallel rows—the upper lot relating, heraldically and otherwise, to the Tyldesley and Derby families, whilst those below had on them medallion heads, in strong relief (the second being coroneted and the third helmeted—possibly intended to represent James the seventh Earl of Derby and Sir Thomas Tyldesley, who were engaged in the battle of Wigan Lane). Two of the walls in the same room were panelled with oak. Over the doorway of a stable, immediately opposite the Lodge, there was an oblong stone, which contained, in large, clear letters, the inscription—"Old Dog Lad 1714." Thomas Tyldesley, the diarist, made certain structural improvements in or about the Lodge, in 1714, and it may fairly be presumed that he caused this inscribed stone to be fixed in the stable wall. The inscription has been construed to mean—taking the initial letter of each word—"Oswald Lord Derby, Demesne of Garstang, Lord Archer [of the] Duchy." But this is a very "far-fetched" guess. The probability is that the inscription related to a nickname adopted by Thomas Tyldesley, as deputy keeper of the Forest of Myerscough, in which capacity he would have to keep a strict eye upon dogs: indeed, there is an entry, bearing date March 28th, 1712, at almost the very beginning of his diary, in which he styles himself (as one of the guests of the High Sheriff) "ye Old: Dog: Lad." Above the door of a small outhouse, opposite the stable alluded to, there was a stone which contained a scroll bearing about a dozen letters; but some time before the stone was removed the letters had got very far worn—some being almost obliterated—and nobody appeared to be able to get at the meaning of them. On the southern side of the Lodge there was an old barn, the upper portion of which was at one time, according to tradition, used as a Roman Catholic Chapel. Thomas Tyldesley was a Roman Catholic. The chief approach to the Lodge was for years, and up to the time of its demolition, near the north-western corner of the building; formerly it was on the southern side, and there are still standing on that side two yew trees, between which, it is supposed, the road originally went. The inscribed stones before mentioned have been fixed in the centre of the western wall of the new outhouse enclosure. Whilst some drainage excavations, in connection with the new buildings, were being made—near the site of the old Lodge—several chiselled blocks of freestone were dug out of the ground. When afterwards put together, these stones took the shape of an octagonal pile, about a yard and a quarter high, the diameter being about one-third of the vertical measurement, whilst in the centre there was a circular aperture; and it is very probable they at some time formed one of the chimneys of the old Lodge. They

THE NEW LODGE, MYERSCOUGH.

are now, in built-up order, on a small piece of ground fronting the new Lodge, and assume the appearance of a rather antique-looking flower stand. The last descendant of Tyldesley, the diarist, died at Trenton Rectory, Ontario, Canada, on August 16th, 1889. This was the Rev. Canon Bleasdell, D.C.L., examining chaplain to the Bishop of Ontario, Canada. Canon Bleasdell, who was 72 years of age at the time of his death, was the eldest son of Mr. James Bleasdell, cotton spinner, &c., of Preston, and great grandson of Agatha, daughter of Thomas Tyldesley. He was born at Moor Hall, Preston—a building, on the northern side of the town, pulled down several years ago; was educated at Preston Grammar School; held for a time, on reaching manhood, the head mastership of Garstang Grammar School; then went to Manchester, and undertook private tuition there; next became a student at Trinity College, Dublin, taking his B.A. degree three years afterwards (in 1845), and his M.A. in the following year; was ordained by Bishop Sumner of Chester; was inducted to his first living at Collyhurst, Manchester; accepted a call from the diocese of Toronto, Canada, in 1848; did much excellent work therein; eventually became senior Canon of St. George's Cathedral, Kingston, and senior examining chaplain to the Bishop of Ontario; and, as already stated, died at Trenton Rectory in 1889. Reverting briefly to Myerscough, I may observe that land in it with an aggregate area of 1,500 acres belongs to the Duchy of Lancaster, and that of this quantity Myerscough Lodge farm absorbs about one-fifth. The land generally in Myerscough is flat; there is not a sufficient fall or outward drainal gradient for rain water, &c., so pumping has to be resorted to. About a mile north-west of the Lodge there is a steam pumping station which was completed in 1887. The engines are capable of raising 600,000 gallons of water per hour. They are brought into operation just as the accumulation of water renders pumping necessary, and the "out-put" is run into the river Wyre. Mr. T. Nevett, of Preston, is the agent for the Duchy property in Myerscough. The name Myerscough means marshy land.

CHAPTER VII.

MYERSCOUGH HALL—ROEBUCK—BILSBORROW AND ITS SCHOOL—DICKY TURNER—EARLY
RAILWAY ARRANGEMENTS AND INCIDENTS—BEACON FELL—CANON PARKINSON—
PARLICK PIKE, FAIRSNAPE, AND BLEASDALE.

About half a mile east of the Lodge, Myerscough Hall is situated; but, owing to a thick belt of trees, it can scarcely be discerned at all from the road which passes on the south side here. Adjoining the highway, and not far from the canal bridge previously mentioned, there is "Roebuck Village": it consists of a few small, rural-looking structures—cottages, &c.—and two public-houses, and is, in reality, a hamlet. One of the public-houses—that on the lower side of the road—is called the "Roebuck"; and somehow, this inn, though apparently much the younger of the two, has got its name implanted upon the village. The old name of the place was Myerscough—the name of the township in which nearly all the buildings in the village now stand. This name is generally pronounced "Maska" (final a short) by the natives; and this pronunciation somewhat tallies with the way in which I find the name spelled in certain old written and printed matter. Under date September 25th, 1725 (Sunday), the Rev. Peter Walkden, Nonconformist minister, and at that time living in the neighbourhood of Chipping, refers in his diary to a man "from Mascuh," who went to hear him; and Paterson, in the "corrected and improved" edition of his work on the direct and principal cross roads in England and Wales, issued in 1789, designates the small culvert, at the

south end of "Roebuck village," as "Maskay Bridge." The second public-house, a little to the north-west of the "Roebuck," is called the "White Bull." Tyldesley, the diarist, pretty frequently dropped in—occasionally stayed all night—here; but, whilst successful in obtaining fluids—anyhow, he does not complain of their scarcity—he was not always so fortunate in getting solids at the establishment. Under date "November primo," 1712, he says in his diary:— "Went a hunting with cos. Butler; meet a merry company; killed a brace off hares; went to ye White Bull with Sany Butler, Young Lord Gabrll Hesketh, and honest Tho. Lucas, where Sany B——r and Gabr H : devoured all the pyes in the house, but not one mouthful to us 3 poor pill garlicks." (Pill garlick means a slighted, ignored, or wretched person.) The land and the buildings proximately visible on the east side of the road are in the township of Bilsborrow. It is supposed that the "Bileuuarde" mentioned in Doomsday Book as consisting of two carucates (about 200 acres) of land under cultivation refers to Bilsborrow. Early in the 14th century Alan (son of Richard) and John de Billesburgh held from the King two bovates (probably about 30 acres) of land here; and a like quantity was possessed here, about the same time, by Alan de Singleton, from whom it passed, by marriage, to the Banastres. Edmund, Earl of Lancaster and brother

ROEBUCK VILLAGE (WHITE BULL ON THE RIGHT).

of Henry I., owned land in this part. Early in the
14th century the de Billesburghs had land in the township—a small quantity of it having been obtained
from the Abbot of Cockersand Abbey. About the
middle of the same century Elena, wife of Roger
Brockholes, possessed some land in Bilsborrow. In
the latter half of that century the de Balderstons held
the manor, by a small monetary service, from the
Prior of St. John of Jerusalem. One or more members of the Cottam and Barton families were property-
owners in Bilsborrow in the 16th century. The property in the township has since been, and is now,
variously owned. At the north end of the "village"
there is a good, substantial school, with master's
house adjoining. This school was erected, along with
the master's house, in 1873, at a cost of £1,500. It is
the successor of a school, &c., built here out of the
proceeds of property bequeathed to trustees, in 1718,
by Mr. John Cross, of Myerscough, only son of Mr.
Robert Cross, of Barton. The old school was intended
"for the education of the poor children of Myerscough and Bilsborough in reading, writing and the
principles of the Christian religion, according to the
doctrine of the Church of England", the new one is
open to children from any of the surrounding districts,
is under Government inspection, and has a curriculum which includes all the usual "standard" subjects of an ordinary public school. Life goes on very
quietly and primitively in the "village," and from
time immemorial it has, on the whole, been marked
by simplicity and serenity. I know an old Bilsborrow
man who used to keep a small grocery in the
"village"; he may do a little yet in the same line;
but his active business days are over. Several
years ago, he appeared to have come to the great
conclusion that the people about were made for his
shop, and not his shop for them. One day, at the time
alluded to, a servant girl was sent to the shop to make
a small purchase; just as the girl got to the shop door
she met the "tradesman," who was going out, and
who, as soon as he heard her mention some small,
ordinary article which she wanted, flew into a
very furious temper, blew her up in a tremen-
dously emphatic style, told her that she ought to have
had more sense than come to his shop at such a time
(it was about half-past two o'clock in the afternoon),
when he was going out for a walk, and altogether so
staggered the girl with his extraordinary indignation
that it took her some time to recover her normal
balance. Dicky Turner, who invented or first applied
the word "Teetotal" to temperance, was born in
Bilsborrow in 1790. It was whilst making a temperance speech in the Old Cock Pit, Preston, in 1833,
that Dicky used the word. He died in 1846, and was
interred in St. Peter's Churchyard, Preston. His
grave is in the south-west corner.

Near the Roebuck Inn, at the east end,
there is a road which goes up to Inglewhite,
&c. This is Bilsborrow-lane. About a quarter
of a mile up the lane there is a bridge which crosses
the Preston and Lancaster section of the London and
North-Western Railway. When this length of line

was opened, in 1840—and for some time afterwards—
there was a station close to the bridge mentioned: it
was the predecessor of the present one near the
Brock, and was called "Roebuck"—the name being
taken from that of the public-house at the bottom
of the lane. One day, a while back, I was
speaking to an old, retired locomotive engine
driver—one of the first drivers on the line
—about this old "station," when he said:
"Yes, I remember the station when it was
at Bilsborrow-lane bridge. How things have
changed since then! Nobody seemed to be so very
particular in those days. We were allowed upwards
of two hours for the run between Preston and Lancaster; and, on returning from the latter place, we
had generally to stay a while at this curious country
'station,' in consequence of there being then but a
single line between it and Whitehorse bridge, and in
order to let a passenger or goods train, from the south,
come on and pass us. Occasionally, when we reached
the little station at Bilsborrow-lane bridge, I and my
fireman would—when the season was on—get off the
engine, go into adjoining fields, and gather mush-
rooms. And now and then, when we reached this same
station, I would tell my mate, the fireman, that I felt
dryish, and he would say that he would like something to sup, and then, whilst we were talking, the
guard would come up to us, and, on learning what we
had in view, would say that he could do with a tooth-
ful; and so, leaving the train standing, we would get
into the lane, and walk right away down to the Roebuck public-house, there drink a pint apiece, and
then walk quietly back to the little station, the train
standing all the time, and the passengers sitting in the
carriages, patiently wondering when we were going
to start again on the journey! But nobody found
fault, and nobody thought of reporting us in those
days." Although another station, about half a mile
north, has long been regularly used for passengers, it
is only ten years since the last portion of the original
one was broken up, and then utilised for fire-kindling
purposes! How I came to know this was in consequence of a little conversation I had at the time
with the Brock station master—Swarbrick, since dead.
Whilst talking to him, he suddenly said: "I finished
the last of the old station—burnt it—this morning."
And when I asked what he meant, he rejoined: "Well,
you see, the old station, which used to be close to the
bridge, was a small, wooden concern, something like
an old watchman's sentry box, and, after the present
station was built, it was brought to the back of the
place, and when I came on here as station master I
found it, and made it do service as a hen cabin; but
in time it got too inconvenient, so I began breaking it
up, and setting the fire with pieces of it, and I used
up the last bit in making the fire this morning." There
is now in front of the present station-house, at Brock,
a small relic of the old signalling system. It is in the
form of an iron ring fixed in the wall. When in use,
in the early days of railway travelling, this ring held
a pole, to the head of which a flag was
hoisted when a passenger train was required to stop

at the station for persons wanting to travel by it. Upon the stationmaster devolved the duty of attending to this signal; but occasionally he was a little remiss. Once, certainly, owing to the contiguity of the Green Man inn, he forgot all about the signal, and a train dashed past the station at full speed (no colour being exposed to attract the engine driver's attention), and there were left on the platform a number of persons desirous of going by the train, but who were obliged to wait until another came up: and this involved the exercise of a lot of patience, for trains ran much less frequently then than now, whilst the majority of them did not take third-class passengers at all.

From the railway bridge referred to, in Bilsborrow-lane, an extensive view of the Fylde country can be obtained; whilst from different parts of the road, a little farther up, several of the distant north-western mountains—Blackcombe, Coniston Old Man, Langdale Pikes, &c.—can be seen on a clear day. Up the lane, on the north side, a few hundred yards from the bridge, there is an octagon-shaped, white-washed building, which has for many years been used as a Wesleyan Methodist chapel. It goes by the name of "Pothouse Chapel." Originally, it is said that pots—in all probability brown earthenware ones—were made in this building, and the clay for them would most likely be obtained when marl was being sought for in the locality. There are now visible some old, water-charged pits—large, deep holes, evidently due to excavations for marl—in the neighbourhood of the chapel; they are on the north-west side. In the early part of this century the application of marl to certain defective kinds of agricultural land was a common thing. About a quarter of a mile past the chapel, and on the same side of the lane, Bilsborrow Hall is situated. It is a plain, substantial, 17th century building, and is used as a farm house. The hills, east and north-east (Beacon Fell, Parlick Pike, Fairsnape, and Bleasdale Moors), form conspicuously-picturesque features of the landscape. They can be reached by going up Bilsborrow-lane, as far as the hamlet of Inglewhite, turning then leftward, and striking in above Whitechapel, for Beacon Fell, and, for the other hills named, keeping on the road from this point for about a mile and a half, then going up a lane on the right, passing higher Brock Mill and Admarsh Church. Another way to the latter goes beyond the entrance to the lane mentioned, descending by Snape Rake, and afterwards wheeling gradually to the right, past Bleasdale Tower and the North Lancashire Reformatory. The hills in this region are visible from the highroad between Preston and Lancaster for miles—nearly all the way from Preston to the southern end of the township of Cabus. A capital view of them can be obtained from the railway bridge in Bilsborrow-lane. Beacon Fell, the summit of which is 874 feet above the sea level, is the nearest. It is, "as the crow flies," about four miles from the bridge. In the generality of maps—the old Ordnance one included—this eminence is called Beaton Fell; but the title deeds of the farm here, which embraces 300 acres of the

land, term it Beacon Fell. And I feel convinced that this is the correct name. Beaton points to nothing, has no real meaning at all, that I can discover; but we all know what beacon means; and those who have been upon or seen the eminence in question will certainly be of opinion that it is a most likely, or would in old times be a very suitable, place for a beacon. Indeed, on a coloured map of Lancashire (now in the Record Office) which was forwarded to the Privy Council by the Lord Lieutenant of the County, along with a report as to the condition of Lancashire, in 1590, Beacon Fell is shown as one of the beacon hills of that period. A fire of the proper beacon kind, upon this hill, at night time, would be seen from a great distance. The white speck in front of Beacon Fell (a whitewashed farm house, with similarly-coloured adjoining outhouses) is visible many miles away—west, north, and south. Out on the Irish Sea, leagues off the Lancashire coast, it can even be descried. Formerly, it used to be said that the farm house on Beacon Fell was the highest regularly-inhabited building in Lancashire. The land constituting the farm here is entirely of the meadow and pasture character; and it is owned and "operated" by Mr. Joseph Smith, cotton spinner and manufacturer, Preston. The late Mr. James Teebay, of Ingol Cottage, Broughton, commenced the work of agricultural improvement on the front of Beacon Fell. All the land here was, virtually, in a state of wildness when he first tackled it. He reclaimed about forty acres. Mr. Joseph Smith purchased the general estate about 1868; and since then he has made many improvements. He has rebuilt the farm house and the contiguous out-buildings (this work was accomplished a few years after he became the owner of the estate); he has very considerably increased the area of reclaimed land; and he keeps here about ten times more stock than the late Mr. Teebay did. The land in this quarter is amongst the highest that is cultivated in the country generally; and, owing to the practical methods adopted by Mr. Smith, it is in excellent "heart." Some time after purchasing the property, and whilst making a new wall on the east side of it, Mr. Smith came across a section of the Roman road which originally ran from Ribchester to Galgate, where a similar road, on the south-western side, joined it, and at which place the two merged into one, proceeding thence northward, via Lancaster, &c. There is an excellent view, especially westward, from the top of Beacon Fell, and not unfrequently the Isle of Man is visible from it.

About two miles behind Beacon Fell summit there is Woodgates farm, on which, towards the western side, stands a good, plain house, which has in front of it a stone bearing the date 1768, and an inscription, in Latin, to the effect that nothing profane must enter the building. Canon Richard Parkinson, the author of that delightful story, "The Old Church Clock," and a poet of no mean order as well, was born here, in 1797. He got his elementary education at Brabbin's School, Chipping; to the well-known schools at Hawkshead and Sedbergh he subsequently went; and he "finished" at Cambridge. On leaving the University he was appointed master of the old school in Lea, near Preston; this post being obtained for him principally through the aid of Mr. William Smith (father of Mr. Joseph Smith, before named), who was then residing at the Clock House, Lea. For about twelve months, during his mastership at Lea school, young Parkinson edited the Preston "Sentinel" newspaper (the predecessor of the Preston "Pilot"); afterwards he was for several years curate at St. Michael's Church, and whilst there he was for a time the tutor of a son of the Rev. Hugh Hornby, the then vicar—the son in question being the late patriarchal Archdeacon Hornby, of St. Michael's; and eventually he became Principal of St. Bees College and Canon of Manchester. He died at St. Bees, in 1858, and was interred there.

North of and not far from Woodgates farm there rises Parlick Pike—a ravine-fronted, round-headed hill, 1,416 feet above the level of the sea. Yates's map of Lancashire, which was published in 1786, and gives "lines of sight" from different elevations, contains Parlick Pike, whose communications are specified as—Preston Church, Pendle, Billinge Hill the old mill at the east end of Kirkham, Treeall Mill, and Clougha above Lancaster. Some beautiful and comprehensive views are obtainable from the top of Parlick Pike—Chipping lying serenely below, to the left: eastward the curving vale of the Hodder, the pastoral knolls of Browsholme and Radholme, Whalley with its leaf-embowered abbey, Clitheroe with its gray, old castle, and Pendle with its commanding, skyward range; westward, the level Fylde country and the open sea beyond; and at the rear the wild, solitary knots of Bowland, &c. About a mile and a half north of Parlick Pike, in a sort of central position as observed from Bilsborrow-lane, and rising to a greater altitude 1,674 feet above the level of the sea), there is Fairsnape. Between the two hills there is a slight depression. The ascent of Fairsnape, from the Pike side, is easy. From the summit of Fairsnape, which is covered with soft peat beds, ling, millstone grit, &c., one of the finest, most varied, and wide-reaching views in the North of England can be obtained. I have been up here, on a clear, favourable day, and scenically—taking into account the proximity of the hill and the easiness of its ascent—know of nothing to equal it, certainly nothing to excel it, in the North. From the summit of Fairsnape, on a fine day, can be seen six watering places—Morecambe, Grange, Blackpool, St. Annes, Lytham, and Southport; five ports—Barrow, Glasson, Fleetwood, Preston, and Liverpool; ten inland towns—Clitheroe, Garstang, Lancaster, Carnforth, Ulverston, Millom, Kirkham, Poulton-le-Fylde, Chorley, and Ormskirk; and thirty villages—Heysham, Overton, Cockerham, Pilling, Singleton, Great Eccleston, Wray Green, Warton, Freckleton, Clifton, Longton, Hoole, Hesketh Bank, Tarleton, Meols, Croston, Leyland, Farington, Euxton, Bamber Bridge, Walton, Woodplumpton, Inskip, St. Michaels, Churchtown, Broughton, Mellor, Whalley, Longridge, and Chipping. And regarding hills and mountains, the scene is equally comprehensive. To the left there are visible the high hills, ranging eastward, above

Bolton, Bury, and Rochdale, as well as all the chief intermediate prominences up to Pendle; in front, far off, filling in the horizon, the mountains of North Wales; to the right, Clougha Pike and Warton Crag, and away beyond, northwest, the Furness fells, Blackcombe, Coniston Old Man, Langdale Pikes, &c.; whilst in the rear, about 20 miles distant—taking the "bee-line" course—there are visible Whernside, 2,414 feet above the sea level, being the highest hill in the West Riding of Yorkshire with one exception (Micklefell, 2,600 feet); wave-sided, level-topped Ingleborough, 2,368 feet high; and rugged, block-like Penyghent, with a summit altitude of 2,273 feet. Immediately northwest of Fairsnape are Bleasdale Moors—dusky, heavy-looking expanses of wild land, on the lower side of which are Hazelhurst, Brooks, and Oakenclough Fells.

Bleasdale, a view of which can be obtained from the bridge in Bilsborrow-lane, before mentioned, lies in basin-like, amphitheatrical serenity—in a diagonal line, about five miles from that bridge. It is hemmed in, with the exception of a portion on the front or south-western side—up which the view from the bridge is obtained—by Beacon Fell, Parlick, Fairsnape, and the moors and fells named. Formerly, Bleasdale was a forest, and down to the middle of the sixteenth century, if not somewhat later, there were herds of wild red deer in this region. On the northern slope of the dale, amid trees and well cultivated land, Bleasdale Tower is situated. This is a modern structure, and originally—anyhow, for some time—it was occupied by Mr. W. J. Garnett, who was one of the M.P.'s for Lancaster from 1857 to 1864. On the death of his father (Mr. William Garnett) in 1863, Mr. W. J. Garnett succeeded to the paternal property—a considerable quantity of it being in Bleasdale—and took up his residence in full at the mansion of the family, Quernmore Park, a few miles east of Lancaster. Here he continued to reside up to the time of his death, in 1873. His son (Mr. William Garnett) now lives at Quernmore Park. The North Lancashire Reformatory School is about half a mile east of Bleasdale Tower. This School was built by subscription in 1857; the cost of it being about £1,500. Mr. W. J. Garnett took a great interest in the movement for it; and the establishment was practically commenced under his auspices. The first governor of the Reformatory School was Mr. Grant King, and when he died he was succeeded in the governorship by his son (Mr. Alfred King), who still holds the position. There are now about 130 boys at the Reformatory, which, in its entirety, is an excellent institution. A little way beyond it, eastward, there is a solitary cottage or barn—all that remains now of the once active, flourishing hamlet of Hazelhurst! The river Brock has its rise up in the angle between Fairsnape and Bleasdale Moors. In 1899 Mr. S. Jackson, of Calder Vale, discovered in a circular mound on Bleasdale Moor, near Admarsh Church, two cinerary urns. They were in the centre of the mound, and at a depth of 22 inches; one was 8 inches and the other 7½ inches in height; both contained charcoal and calcined bones; and in the taller there was a small urn or vase, with contents of a similar character.

CHAPTER VIII.

MYERSCOUGH HALL—BROOKHOUSE—SIGN-PAINTING INCIDENT—GREEN MAN INN—BROCK—
STANZACRE—MYERSCOUGH HOUSE.

I have already made reference to Bilsborrow school at one end of "Roebuck village." About 50 yards past the school (north), on the left side of the high road, there is a semi-circular gateway. This is the entrance to a lane which leads down to Myerscough Hall, about a mile distant. The Hall, with its park-like grounds in front, comes pleasingly into view soon after the canal bridge, over which the lane goes, has been passed. It is but a short distance from Myerscough Lodge. Tyldesley says in his diary, under date September 1st, 1714—"Alday att Lodge till eivening; then went to see my nigbr [neighbour] Greenhough [Greenhalgh]. Stayed with him 2 howers." Possibly this "Greenhough" lived at Myerscough Hall. Mr. William Greenhalgh, who was High Sheriff of Lancashire in 1729, resided at Myerscough Hall, and by him it was rebuilt. He died in 1741,

"of Myerscough Hall," in 1810. For some time during the first half of the present century Mr. James Greenhalgh, a descendant of his, lived here. A subsequent tenant for a while was the late Major Cunliffe. Then the Hall was occupied by Mrs. Salisbury, who died here, and whose daughter, Miss Salisbury, is now the tenant of the place. The present owner of the property is Mr. Algernon Joy, of London (a descendant of Mr. Hall Joy, of Hartham Park, Wilts, who married Mary Charlotte, daughter of Mr. James Greenhalgh, of Myerscough Hall, in 1831).

The white, tree-fronted dwelling, nearly opposite the gateway of the lane which leads to Myerscough Hall, is Brookhouse. It is said that John Wesley, when on his journey north, in April, 1765, either preached or stayed a night at Brookhouse. When this house was built I cannot definitely

MYERSCOUGH HALL.

and was succeeded at Myerscough Hall by Mr. Edward Styth, of Great Eccleston, who—as a condition of the inheritance of this property—took the surname of Greenhalgh. In 1769 he died and was succeeded in the ownership of the Myerscough Hall property by his only son James, of Lancaster, who took the additional surname of Greenhalgh. Edward, son of the last-named, is mentioned, by an indenture, as being

say; probably it was erected about the middle of last century. At the end of a barn belonging to Brookhouse farm, which adjoins, there is a stone on which is the date 1742. An elderly gentleman, named Greenhalgh—a member of the Greenhalgh family of Myerscough Hall, no doubt—once lived at Brookhouse. He was of the substantial, straightforward order—had a good deal of "John

35

Bull" in his composition. One day a fine-talking, smartly-dressed young gentleman called upon Mr. Greenhalgh, at Brookhouse, in respect to certain personal accommodation, and met with a reception so peculiar that it would not in a hurry be forgotten by him. The young gentleman stated that he was on his way to join a hunting or shooting party in the neighbourhood—at Squire Brockholes's, Claughton Hall—but, having found out that he was a few days too early for the gathering, he had taken the liberty of calling at the nearest substantial-looking residence he could find (this being Brookhouse), thinking that the master

BROOKHOUSE.

of it would have no objection to his staying there until the time arrived for going up to the Hall. Mr. Greenhalgh, who had never seen the young gentleman before, and knew nothing whatever about him, felt very angry at this intrusion, and, looking straight at the stranger, he said, "When you get an invitation from me to come and stay here, we shall be glad to see you; but not till then. Be good enough to leave the house, sir." The young gentleman, very much taken aback by this rebuff, thereupon withdrew—the front door being instantly closed when he got on the step—and he blushingly wended his way to the Green Man public-house, a short distance northward, and there arranged for the needful lodgings. But he could not forget the repulsion experienced at Brookhouse, and he sighed for some means whereby he might be enabled to give old Mr. Greenhalgh a "Roland" for his "Oliver." Next morning, whilst talking with the landlord, he made reference to the sign in front of the inn—a large, wooden concern, bearing the painted figure of a "Green Man" (a gamekeeper, dressed in green)—intimated that it had faded very considerably, and offered to repaint it, gratuitously, if he could be provided with certain oil colours, which he specified, and a brush or two. The landlord jumped at the offer, got the requisite colours, &c., had the sign taken down, and as quickly as possible gave the young gentleman an opportunity of commencing operations. In due time the job was finished; the "artist" went away; the sign was refixed; and the new Green Man

picture quickly became the conversational topic of the district. The unknown young gentleman who painted the sign had not only depicted on it a good-sized, effectively-attired "Green Man," but had actually given him, by way of revenge for the rebuff received at Brookhouse, the features of old Mr. Greenhalgh! The likeness was a very striking one indeed. Before long, Mr. Greenhalgh got wind of what had been done; soon afterwards he either went personally to look at the sign, or sent someone from Brookhouse to examine it; there was no question at all as to whose features those of the new Green Man were meant for; and Mr. Greenhalgh—greatly exasperated at this liberty taken with his face by, as somebody informed him, a stranger who had been staying at the place for a few days, and who, from the description given of him, was identified as the young gentleman who had called at Brookhouse—forthwith made an intimation to the effect that, if the face of the Green Man on the sign were not quickly changed, he (Mr. Greenhalgh) would, at the earliest opportunity, endeavour to get a change made in the tenancy of the inn. The facial resemblance was soon obliterated; and Mr. Greenhalgh, who had been in a high state of dudgeon about the exposition of his "phiz," in front of the Green Man public-house, quickly regained his wonted equilibrium. Amongst those who followed Mr. Greenhalgh, as tenants of Brookhouse, were Mrs. Salisbury, Mr. Humber, Mr. Rodgett, and Mr. R. Cunliffe. For some years—form about 1875 to 1885—Brookhouse was utilised for educational purposes by a person named Hilton. Afterwards—for about six years—I resided at the place. Mr. Isaac Simpson, gold-thread manufacturer, Preston, is the present tenant of Brookhouse.

The main road crosses, by a fairly good stone bridge, the river Brock, a little to the north of Brookhouse. It is probable that in old times there were badgers in or about certain parts traversed by this river. "Broc," as previously mentioned, is the Anglo-Saxon word for badger. Otters, or traces of them, are occasionally found nowadays in the Brock; but no badgers are met with. In the oldest road books I have seen Brock bridge is mentioned; but the present structure, though pretty gray with age, is not, I suspect, the original one—if very old, it would have been considerably narrower than it is. Brock railway station is nearly opposite and not far from the bridge. The chimney which rises amid trees, about half a mile from the station, eastward, is connected with Matshead Paper Mill—an old, steady-going mill which has for many years been owned and worked by the Bateson family. It is close to the river Brock, from the water of which a portion of its motor power is derived. Some distance up the course of the river there is an umbrageous, picturesque part called "Brock Bottoms"—a charming spot in summer time, considerably patronised by sketchers, botanisers, &c., and much frequented by rural ramblers and persons of the holiday, picnic order. In this sequestered region, on the Claughton side of the Brock, there used to be a cotton mill. For some time, up to 1829, it was worked, jointly, by Mr. Richard Kenyon and Mr. Kilshaw; from 1829 to about 1854 Mr. Kenyon, who lived in Claughton, had the mill entirely in his own hands, using it first for cotton spinning and afterwards for weaving, but, not being able to make the concern pay, he had to relinquish it. Messrs. Burton and Whitehead succeeded Mr. Kenyon; and they were followed by a co-operative society, during whose occupation the mill was burnt down. This disaster occurred about 1860. Subsequently, Messrs. W. R. and J. Bond fitted up the building and used it for roller making; Mr. Thomas Crossley next occupied it in the same line; and now file making is carried on here by Messrs. T. Parker and Son.

The Green Man inn, already named, stands on the side of the highway—in one part very near it—about 220 yards past Brock bridge. It is a quaint-looking structure—seems like two or three buildings, strongly made and variously sized, in combination—and in front of it there is a sign on which appears the painted figure of a gamekeeper or forester, of the old-time sort, dressed in green, with a bow and arrow in his hands, and a buglehorn by his side. The Green Man is an old-established, well-known halting place for refreshment and baiting purposes. Drivers of

cough, figures in the list of Lancashire Royalists, whose estates were sequestered in 1652. The same list contains the names of three other Myerscough persons, viz., Thomas Pearson, Andrew Thistleton, and Francis Westby. The highroad crosses the canal a short distance north of the Green Man inn. Just over the canal bridge, and on the left-hand side of the road, there is a barn (connected with a small adjoining farmhouse) which contains in the front gable wall a stone bearing the initials and date, "T.B.C., 1844." These refer to Mr. Thomas Butler Cole, of Kirkland Hall, who died, after an odd career, in 1864. The farmstead here formed part of his general estate. In a subsequent part additional reference is made to "T.B.C."

The main road goes over the canal twice between Preston and Lancaster; the points of traversion being near the Green Man, Myerscough, and on the south side of the village of Bonds, near Garstang. (At the top of Penny-street, Lancaster, the main road again crosses the canal; but this occurs at a part within the boundary of the borough.) This canal, which on the north-west side of the Green Man has a very straight and somewhat attractive course, was opened between Preston and Tewit

GREEN MAN INN, MYERSCOUGH.

carts, waggons, and miscellaneous vehicles seldom attempt to hurry past it. Lots of people out for a drive make a point of pulling up here; and, in summer time, anglers, of the working class sort mainly, from various parts of Lancashire—particularly from Bolton and the neighbourhood—make the Green Man their headquarters; they sometimes turn up in numbers suggesting the influx of a small crowd, and the bulk of their fishing is done in the canal, which takes a wide curve a short distance from the house, on the rearward side. For a considerable number of years William Butler was the landlord, and a relative of his has now charge of the place. The name of Butler is a pretty old one in Myerscough. A William Butler, of Myers-

Field, near Burton-in-Westmorland, in 1797; and in 1819 the length from Tewit Field to Kendal was opened. On its route between Preston and Tewit Field there are 114 road and occupation bridges and two road aqueducts. Between Preston and Lancaster the canal runs entirely on the west side of the railway; between Lancaster and Kendal it goes mainly on the opposite side. The canal route from Preston to Lancaster is 30 miles, and from Lancaster to Kendal 27 miles, or altogether—from Preston to Kendal—about 15 miles more than that of the railway and the highroad. In 1863 the canal was leased to the London and North-Western Railway Company for a fixed annual rent or dividend in perpetuity.

The avenue on the west side of the highroad, and something like a quarter of a mile past the canal bridge near the Green Man inn, Myerscough, goes in the direction of Myerscough House. At the top end of the avenue, which is very straight, finely flanked with large trees, and about 600 yards long, there is Stanzacre Hall—now a farmhouse, or utilised for something of the kind. This is an old place—older, I

STANZACRE HALL.

believe, by very many years than Myerscough House. Very little, if indeed any, of the original building is now in existence: if there be any part left, it is at least about 350 years old. "Stannesacre, Myrescoghe Park," is referred to in the records of the Duchy Court of Lancaster as far back as 6 Edward VI. At one time Thurstan Tyldesley lived at "Stanacre" (Stanzacre). It was his grandson Edward who entertained King James I., at Myerscough Lodge, in 1617. Stanzacre Hall forms part of the property included in the Myerscough House estate. By whom Myerscough House, which stands about three-quarters of a mile west of Stanzacre Hall, was originally built I have not been able to discover. In 1696 Mr. William Butler (probably a descendant or relative of the Butler whose name appears in the sequestration list of 1652)

of Mr. Robert Gibson, Recorder of Lancaster about that time. Subsequently, Mr. Charles Gibson, a grandson of the Recorder, lived at Myerscough House (he had also a simultaneous proprietary or residential connection with Quernmore Park, near Lancaster). In 1810 Mr. Henry Fielding, calico printer, lived at Myerscough House—in all probability simply as tenant, and not by virtue of any ownership rights here. Mr. Charles Gibson died in 1823. Afterwards Mr. John Cunliffe purchased Myerscough House and its estate. In Reynold Clarke's "Gazetteer," published in 1830, Myerscough House is mentioned as the seat of Mr. Cunliffe. But in 1825, if not for some time earlier, Mr. Cunliffe was residing at Myerscough House. He was a county magistrate—a member of the Garstang bench—and was much respected. On the 15th of October, 1829, the "freedom of the borough of Garstang" was conferred upon him. For many years Mr. Cunliffe resided at Myerscough House, and he died here in 1871. In 1874 Mr. W. J. Parkinson bought the property forming the estate, and went to reside at Myerscough House. He not only greatly improved the estate, but by purchase added considerably to its general area. In 1000 the whole of the estate, including the House, was sold by auction to Mr. Leeming, of Lancaster, for £48,000. Directly afterwards he sold the property: it was bought by or on behalf of Mr. Joseph Eccles, cotton spinner and manufacturer, Preston, who in a short time went to reside at Myerscough House, where he is still living, and at which he has made many improvements. It has an antique, serenely-pleasant appearance, and from a pretty. octo-gabled structure, with central tower, which surmounts the general building, a very good view of the surrounding country can be obtained. Myerscough House has for some years been fitted up with the electric light; it was one of the earliest

MYERSCOUGH HOUSE.

sold Myerscough House and the estate at that time connected with it to Mr. Richard Cross, of Barton (supposed to have been an ancestor of the Cross family of Red Scar, near Preston), whose representatives sold the same, about 1731, to Mr. Charles Gibson, brother

country residences in North Lancashire—if not actually the very first—supplied with this luminant. In a field adjoining Myerscough House, on the east side, there is one of the largest boulder stones in the country.

CHAPTER IX.

About 300 yards past the entrance to the avenue on the Myerscough House property a road branches, on the east, from the highway; this leads into Claughton, Barnacre, &c. Claughton Hall is about a mile and a half distant, north-east. From certain parts of the diverging road—on the northern part—it can be seen. The Hall stands on the east side of a spacious, wooded park: a long, winding sheet of water, centred by an ornate bridge, fronts it, and laterally as also at the rear there are fine, ancestral-looking trees. For many generations the name of Brockholes has been associated with the district of Claughton. The original home of the Brockholes was, however, at Brockholes, on the Ribble, near Preston, the earliest record being of a Roger de Brochol, who married Mabil, sister of Huctred de Bradsac, in 1254. In 1286, his second son, Adam, who lived at Byreworth, near Garstang, was one of the viridars in a forest assize, at Lancaster; but it does not appear that a Brockholes possessed any property in Claughton previous to a purchase of land from the heirs of William de Tatham, a priest, by Roger de Brockoles (great-grandson of Adam) and Ellena, his wife, about the middle of the 14th century. His grandson John married Catherine, heiress of William de Heton, and afterwards the family lived sometimes at Heton (Heaton in Lonsdale) and sometimes at Claughton until 1600, or perhaps later. A subsequent Roger de Brockholes, whose inquisition was taken in 1499, founded a chantry in the parish church of Garstang (Churchtown), for the perpetual singing of divine service. A younger scion of the Claughton Brockholes (Anthony Brockholes), who went to America in 1674, as second in command to Major Edmund Andros, the first Governor of New York, became the second Governor of that city in 1677. In 1715 John Brockholes, eldest son of the then squire of Claughton, and William, his youngest brother, joined the army of the Chevalier; and there is reason to believe that John was wounded during some fighting in or near Preston, and removed in a hopeless condition to his father's residence, in Claughton, where he died in September, 1717. William Hesketh of Mains Hall, near Poulton-le-Fylde, married Mary, daughter of John Brockholes, of Claughton, and had issue a son Thomas, who succeeded his uncle, William Brockholes, and took the name and arms of Brockholes. Dying unmarried, Thomas Hesketh Brockholes was succeeded by his brother Joseph, who married, in 1768, Constantia, daughter of Basil Fitzherbert, of Swinnerton, in Staffordshire, and,

dying without issue, his estates passed to his brother, James Hesketh, who devised them to William Fitzherbert (second son of Basil Fitzherbert), who took the name and arms of Brockholes. William Fitzherbert-Brockholes was very fond of the then fashionable sports and pastimes. In 1810 he was one of the stewards of Lancaster races; and during the races there for five years in succession—1813 to 1817 inclusive—he fought mains of cocks with one Mr. Rawlins Satterthwaite. Cockfighting was at that time quite a high, fashionable sport. Three times out of the five fighting meetings at Lancaster his "birds" were beaten; but he was successful with those he brought into the pit when the principal main of the series was fought during the races in 1814, the stakes then being 10 guineas per battle and 200 guineas for the entire main. He was also evidently a very ardent sportsman with his gun. Once he was fined £5 5s. 0d. for absenting himself from the Grand Jury, at Lancaster, to which he had been summoned, and tradition says that he had heard of a flight of woodcocks, the previous evening, and went after them instead of obeying his summons to Lancaster. In the latter part of 1817 he died, leaving as his heir his son Thomas, who, being only 17 years old at the time, did not enter into possession of the property till 1821, when he attained his majority. Thomas Fitzherbert Brockholes (the son just referred to) was a great sportsman, and was an excellent shot as well as a good fisherman. It is said that he shot 99 woodcocks to his own gun in one year, and spent days trying to find a straggler left behind to make up the 100. He only seems to have fought a main once at Lancaster races, viz., in 1821; but there are records of his having, along with the Lord Derby of that time, fought many mains at Preston, and they were evidently two of the principal cockfighters of the day. He was also very fond of hunting, and he kept a pack of foxhounds for many years. For the first few years, he rode to them; but, meeting with an accident that prevented him from riding, he followed them on foot, and he continued to do so till he was over 60 years of age, and there were few who could keep up with him when hounds were running. It is well-known that the fox possesses an excellent "head for country." Referring to this subject in an interesting article in the "Zoologist," Mr. Harting says a fox has been known to return seventy miles to its "earth," and this not once, but three times. A fox was once caught in Yorkshire, and sent into Lancashire to be hunted by the hounds of "the old Squire, of Claughton, and the identity of it was established by its having been marked in the ear by the fox-catcher. This story Mr. Harting had from his friend Captain F. H. Salvin, who was living in Yorkshire at the time, and was well acquainted with Mr. Brockholes, who gave him all the details." "The old Squire" resided at Claughton Hall for upwards of 50 years. In 1842 he was High Sheriff of Lancashire. He was never married, and died in 1873. Whenever referred to, by those now living who knew him, he is called "the old Squire." He was an excellent specimen of the English country gentleman. "The old Squire" was succeeded by his nephew, James Fitzherbert, who took the additional surname of Brockholes. This gentleman died in 1875, and was succeeded by his cousin, William Joseph Fitzherbert (son of Francis Fitzherbert, of Swinnerton), who assumed the name, &c., of Brockholes, and is still living—a genial squire, an active county magistrate and county council alderman, and much respected by all who know him. There is a tradition to the effect that one of the members of the old original family (John de Brockholes) was a member of Parliament for Preston in the 19th of Edward III. (1346); but this is incorrect, as no members of Parliament were returned for Preston during the reign of the monarch named; indeed, owing to the indifference or straitened pecuniary circumstances of the inhabitants of Preston, who had to pay their members so much per day during each session, the town was not represented in Parliament from 1326 till 1547. Claughton Hall is built of light-coloured free-stone, is three storeys high, and has a serene, stately

older portion, now the back and the offices, must have been built 100 years previously—probably even more remotely. There is no record of the Claughton Brockholes having ever lived at any house in Claughton other than the original one on the site of the present Hall; but some of the earlier generations resided at Byreworth, near Garstang, which formed part of the family property from a very early date until a comparatively recent time. On the south side of Claughton Hall there are some large, excellent gardens: they are adjacent to the mansion. On the 5th of July, 1836, there was a tremendous hailstorm, and much damage was done here—principally at the conservatories. The floors were strewn with bunches of grapes, riven from the vines by the hailstones, and altogether about 8,000 squares of glass were broken! In the summer of 1863 there was, I remember, quite a rush of amateur florists, gardeners, &c., to Claughton Hall gardens, in one part of which an American aloe (Agave Americana Variegata) was flowering. An idea prevails that the American aloe does not flower at all until it is 100 years old; but the fact is, the flowering time of this plant "depends almost wholly on the rapidity of its growth. In hot countries it will flower in a few years; but in colder climates, the growth being slower, it is necessarily longer in arriving at maturity." This aloe flowers but once, whatever may be its age at the time of efflorescence, and then it begins to gradually decay until life eventually leaves it. The aloe in Claughton Hall gardens was about 70 years old when it flowered. Many of its leaves at that time were about 15 feet in length, from 12 to 14 inches wide, and quite a number of them, if not the bulk, weighed about 12lb. each. The central stem, when about a third of the flowers were out, was 19 feet high, and

CLAUGHTON HALL.

appearance. The main portion of the Hall—the front and residential block—was erected by William Fitzherbert-Brockholes (father of "the old Squire"), and was barely finished by him when he died, in 1817. The

when they were in complete bloom its altitude was about 22ft. On a fine day this stem would grow two and sometimes two and a half inches. There used to be a heronry in Claughton Hall grounds—not very far from the Hall—and once (in 1870) "the old Squire," upon whom I had had occasion to call about something or other, went with me to it, and appeared to take much pleasure in pointing out the nests and referring to the habits of the herons. Some of these big birds were at the time sitting on large, rough-looking nests at the tops of trees; others were flying about in a heavily-flapping style. About a dozen years ago, whilst walking along a road on the north-east side of Myerscough I noticed a heron on the wing; it appeared to have come from some part of Claughton. In his latter years "the old Squire" took a particular interest in feeding and fattening Highland cattle—rough-looking, thick-haired Scots—and the carcases of some of them (very fine ones) used to figure in Preston butchers' shops during the "show" at Christmas. The railway between Preston and Lancaster runs some distance through the lower portion of Claughton Hall estate, and for a length on each side of the "New Lane Bridge" the telegraph wires pass underground. When the property required for railway purposes here was purchased, one of the conditions insisted upon by "the old Squire" was that the railway company should build an ornamental bridge to carry the road over the railway, and that there should be no disfiguring telegraph wires or posts for a certain distance on each side of the bridge. Not only is this bridge a handsome, well-built structure, with the crest of the Brockholes' family (a badger) conspicuously introduced into the stonework, but the railway is made to interfere as little as possible with the picturesqueness of the park by means of so-called "invisible slopes" and iron park fencing. In fact, it is said that "the old Squire" insisted on the railway company complying with very special conditions before he allowed them to pass through his estate at all. For a while, after the railway was opened, "the old Squire" looked very dubiously upon the engines, or rather upon the sparks which flew out of their funnels, as they were passing his property. He thought that the sparks might, in dry weather, set on fire some of his trees near the railway, or damage certain of his fences, or ignite patches of his park grass. Not unfrequently, in summer time, he was recognised in his characteristic attire—white trousers, &c.—standing in an adjacent field, watching a passing train, and particularly eyeing the funnel of the engine; but the fiery outbreaks he apprehended did not occur, and in time quite a friendly feeling supplanted his suspicions, and he used to wave his hand at a train when it went by him, and if very near the line when one passed would indulge in a genial ejaculation—shout out "Good day," or something of the kind, to the driver or guard. The old fish-ponds of Claughton Hall are on the western side of the estate, between the railway and the canal. In the "Archæological Journal" for March, 1849, there appeared an interesting account of the finding of an urn of baked clay in a small tumulus in Claughton Hall park, near the group of cottages called "the Street," and close to the line of the Roman road leading from Walton-le-Dale to Lan-

caster, &c. The urn contained burned bones, along with some weapons and ornaments. From the character of the weapons and ornaments, it is thought that the tumulus covered the remains of a Danish viking, killed perhaps in some raid.

A short distance from the Hall, on the east side, Claughton Roman Catholic Church is situated. The mission here is a very ancient one, and Roman Catholic services have been regularly held in this locality since the time of the Reformation. The present chapel was built in 1792. Externally, it has a plain appearance; internally, it is strikingly beautiful. Members of the Gradwell family have been priests at this mission for upwards of 90 years. The Rev. Robert Gradwell was here assistant to Father Barrow from 1809 to 1811, and then priest in charge from the latter date till 1817, when he left for Rome, subsequently becoming coadjutor bishop to Bishop Bramstone, of London; his brother, the Rev. Henry Gradwell followed him, at Claughton, being in charge here from 1817 to 1860; and he was succeeded by his nephew, the Rev. (now Monsignor) Robert Gradwell, who is still at the head of the mission, and who this year has been raised by his Holiness Leo XIII. to the dignity of Domestic Prelate. Monsignor Gradwell's father (Mr. George Gradwell) was elected an Alderman of the first "reformed" Corporation of Preston, on the 31st of December, 1835, and continued an Alderman till his death, in 1849. A very neat-looking priests' house adjoins Claughton Catholic Church.

About half a mile from Claughton Hall is Claughton House, built in the reign of Henry VIII. This is an old residence of the Whitehead family, who at one time owned a good deal of land in Claughton and the neighbourhood. In the time of the Civil Wars, a Whitehead of Claughton House and a Whitehead of Matshead—possibly brothers or cousins—took opposite sides. Early in this century the Claughton House property was purchased and incorporated with the Brockholes estate.

On the east side of the main road, and about two-thirds of a mile past the avenue which runs up to Stanzacre Hall, in Myerscough, there stands, near a timber yard, one of the finest chestnut trees in North Lancashire. It is lofty, its branches spread over three-fourths of the road opposite, and when in flower it looks splendid. The few adjacent cottages on the opposite side form what is called "Pump-street." One day, as I was passing along here, I said to a rotund, middle-aged woman, who was gossiping with a couple of females at the higher end of the cottages, "Why is this called Pump-street?" She promptly rejoined—"Because there's a pump in it." But, there being no pump of any sort visible, I interrogated—"Where is it?" when she replied to the effect that it was up a passage, covered in, amongst the cottages, and that the people here had to rely upon it solely for drinking water. And then she began to find fault with the name of the place—said she didn't like the name "Pump-street" at all; and when I interposed—"A finer name—Victoria-

terrace, would that do?"—she answered, "Yes, or
Fern Villas—something like that, you know;" and
then she smiled humorously, and I moved away.
A few hundred yards beyond Pump-street, close to
the highway, there is the Brockholes Arms Inn—a
very good-looking, substantial stone building, with
the Brockholes' armorial shield, fully charged and surmounted by the family crest, in front.

The diverging road to the west, at Pump-street,
leads to Kirkland, St. Michael's, &c. At the
north-east corner of it there is the stone base of an
old cross. In the township of Kirkland, which on
its south-eastern side is about a mile and a half from
the Preston and Lancaster high road, the village of
Churchtown, including the old parish church of Garstang, is situated. Kirkland Hall is about half a mile
north of Churchtown. It stands on a gentle, wood-en-
vironed slope, and the main approach to it is by a gateway, adorned with the Butler crest, &c., on the eastern
side of the village. William de Lancastre, third
baron of Kendal, held Kirkland in the 13th century:
the Butlers, a branch of the Butler family of Rawcliffe, became owners of Kirkland in the 16th century,
and for generations afterwards members of the same
family, in a direct line, held property here.
A daughter of Mr. Edmund Cole, of Beaumont Cote,
near Lancaster, who was high sheriff of Lancashire in
1707, married Mr. Thomas Butler, of Kirkland. Pre-
deceased by his father by but a little more than a
year, this Thomas Butler died in 1748; his heir being
his eldest son Alexander Butler, who, according to a
monumental inscription, in Churchtown church,
"served his country in the important office of high
sheriff, constable of Lancaster Castle, deputy-lieu-
tenant, and magistrate," "chose an elegant retirement
as most congenial with his literary and philosophical
pursuits," and died on the 6th of May, 1811, aged 79

brother Thomas, rector of Bentham), who was at the
time only 16 years old. This great nephew, in 1816,
when he "came of age," entered into possession of
the property, and the rejoicings at Kirkland, in commemoration of the event, were kept up for three days.
With permission granted by the Prince Regent,
Thomas Butler took the additional surname of Cole,
on the 16th of December, 1817. At the Lancaster
March Assizes, in 1818, Mr. Butler-Cole figured as
defendant in a breach of promise case. The plaintiff,
Miss M. A. Orford, was the daughter of a Warrington surgeon, and after his death, in 1810, she resided
in Liverpool. The Assize proceedings resulted in a
verdict for her of £7,000 damages. Defendant's
counsel (Mr. Scarlett) "moved for a new trial, on the
ground of excessive damages;" but the application
was refused. Mr. Butler-Cole married Louisa,
daughter of a very prominent Preston gentleman—
Mr. John Grimshaw (brother of Mr. Nicholas Grimshaw, previously referred to), who was five times Mayor
of the borough. After living with Mr. Butler-Cole
for a good many years she separated from him (the
marriage being without issue), and afterwards resided,
up to the time of her death, in Preston. She made
Dr. T. Dixon, of Preston, her legatee—indeed, willed
to him everything she possessed; but he gave the bequest to her niece, the daughter of Mr. Bland Walker,
of Preston. Mr. Butler-Cole was a very curious
person, and I have, at time and time, heard various
stories illustrative of his eccentricity. Here is one,
giving a fair sample of his latter-day oddness, which
was told to me by the late Mr. Alexander Tullis (of
the firm of Messrs. Cooper and Tullis, contractors),
Preston. Mr. Butler-Cole (he was more frequently
designated "Cole-Butler," and not unfrequently
"Old Cole") had the building or renovating of something in or about the Hall in contemplation, so he

KIRKLAND HALL.

years. Through some cause, he had got imbued with a
dislike of his brothers' sons, and left his estates to his
great-nephew, Thomas Butler—(a grandson of his

sent word about it to the firm named, and Mr. A. Tullis
went over to see him. As near as I can remember,
the following was Mr. Tullis's version of his encounter

with this very curious gentleman:—"After being admitted into the main lobby or passage of the Hall, I expressed a wish to see Mr. Butler-Cole, and a servant directed me to the door of a room which he was occupying at the time. I knocked at the door; it was promptly opened, and there stood before me, looking somewhat serious, old Cole. I told him my name and the object of my visit, when he requested me to come into the room, but said that I must not enter it with my boots on—that I must first pull them off, and leave them outside near the door mat. Cole was awfully afraid of catching cold—he persistently nursed a delusion on that point—and he fancied that as I had walked along the road from Brock station the soles of my boots would be somewhat damp, and that, if I entered the room with my boots on, the atmosphere of it would get chilled, and that he would thus run a risk of catching cold! Well, I pulled off my boots, walked into the room, and Cole explained what he wanted. But he was a fearful while about it. I tried to get away—anyhow, wanted many a time to go out; but he persisted in discussing matters, and he actually kept me standing in my stocking feet in the room for three hours! I was glad to get out of the room, and didn't want any more encounters of this kind with old Cole." This was a sample of the style in which the old gentleman operated for the purpose of avoiding colds. But, notwithstanding his whim-whams and fatuities, Mr. Butler-Cole was very kind to the poor of Kirkland; in winter-time, for several years, he distributed food, clothing, &c., amongst them; and occasionally his benevolence overflowed into one or more of the adjoining townships. And on a certain occasion he evinced quite a strong religious spirit. This was during the choleraic outbreak in 1849. Government had not appointed a "day of humiliation and prayer" to stay the ravages of the malady, so Mr. Butler-Cole selected the 28th of September in the year named as a day to be kept by his tenantry for this purpose; and it is reported that "At his request they and their wives and families met at Kirkland Hall, when prayer was offered up, and Mr. Cole preached an excellent and appropriate sermon," and that "in the afternoon he again offered up prayer and preached another sermon." Owing to a misunderstanding or quarrel with the Vicar of Churchtown, Mr. Butler-Cole opened some sort of a place of worship of his own, in or near Kirkland Hall, and for a while regularly conducted religious service in it. Mr. Butler-Cole died in 1864, aged 68 years, and was buried in Churchtown Churchyard. He left the Kirkland and Beaumont Cote property to Major Thornton, for life, with remainder for life to Captain Clarke—a relative on his (Butler-Cole's) mother's side—the subsequent remainder for life going to Captain Clarke's second son, "with succession to his son, and, failing issue, then to the heirs of the Butlers." The present owner is the Rev. Henry Clarke, who for some time, up to about 1805, was vicar of Wray, Windermere, and now resides at the Cote, Torquay. He came into possession, following Major Thornton, deceased, about 1887, and restored Kirk-

land Hall, &c., which had been empty some years—receiving £1,000 from the executors of Major Thornton for dilapidations. The estate has been in Chancery since the death of Mr. Butler-Cole. As to the occupation of the Hall, for a short time after the death of Mr. Butler-Cole, a person named Butler lived at it; subsequently the late Mr. H. C. Owtram, cotton manufacturer in Preston, resided at the Hall for some years—till 1878; it was next occupied for a time—chiefly in summer—by Mr. Woolright, of Liverpool; then it was in the hands of a caretaker for five years; and in 1890 the present tenant (Mr. George Singleton) entered on, renting in addition to the Hall three cottages at the rear for labourers, &c., and a contiguous farm connected with the estate. Externally, the hall, though plain in design and built of brick, has a substantial and somewhat commanding appearance. It is a combination building, and includes structural work done at four different times—if not more. The oldest part appears to be in the rear, at the north-west corner, where there is a stone bearing the initials and date, "B.T.E., 1668." The initials refer to Thomas Butler and Elizabeth his wife. This Thomas, who was the son and heir of John Butler, a captain in one of the Royalist regiments, who was slain in 1644, on Marston Moor, died about 1717. His wife Elizabeth was the daughter of Mr. Edmund Fleetwood, of Rossall. The next oldest part is near to and south-west of that just mentioned; it bears on a gable stone the same initials (referring, no doubt, to the said Thomas and his wife), and the date 1679. On the opposite side—north-east corner, rear—there is a substantial, choicely-carved door-way; and the door is of a very superior, an-

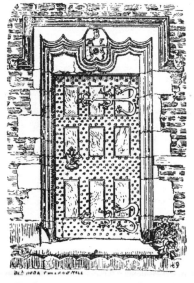

OLD DOOR AND DOORWAY, KIRKLAND HALL.

tiquely-ornate character. The surmounting portion of the door-way contains, centrally, the initials "B.A.E." (Butler—Alexander and Elizabeth), and the date 1695. The letters and figures are very clear. This Alexander (a son of Thomas Butler, who was a captain of foot, under Charles eighth Earl of Derby) was born in 1673, married Elizabeth, daughter of Thomas Parker, of Browsholme, and resided at Kirkland Hall. The issue of the marriage was seven children—two sons and five daughters. His wife died in 1726, and he died in 1747. Surmounting the south or front of the hall, in a pediment, there are the arms of the Butler family, and below, over the front door, are the initials and date "A.B., 1760," which refer to Alexander Butler (grandson of the above Alexander), heir to the Kirkland estate, and a very influential county gentleman, as already mentioned. Internally, the Hall is large and contains many rooms; and, as to furniture, apart from that of the tenant, there are numerous articles belonging to the estate—massive chairs and tables, elaborate chests of drawers, rare engravings, paintings (including a large portrait of eccentric Butler-Cole), a splendidly carved old oak bedstead (the armorial bearings of the Derby and Butler families being prominent on it, as well as initials, a central exhortation in rhyme, &c.), and a considerable number of strongly-bound antique-looking books—all of which have come down as Butler heirlooms. Some of the wall paper in the library is curiously pictorial: I presume it was put on when "old Cole" lived at the Hall: it depicts runaway marriage scenes chiefly. In a lumber room at the top of the building there are two or three huge steel or iron traps—locally called "man traps." They are so constructed that no ordinary man, if caught in one, could possibly get out of it without assistance. Traps of this sort formed part of the paraphernalia once in vogue for the special benefit of poachers. Fifty years ago, when walking through a certain country district in North Lancashire, I used to pass the corner of a wood where there was fixed up a notice board which said— "Beware of spring guns and steel traps." But the use of such things is now—has, in fact, long been— illegal.

Churchtown is a neat, clean-looking little village. On the south side of a fine avenue of trees, at the entrance to Churchtown, there is the village school. Taking into account its foundation, it is the oldest school in the parish: it was founded for free education about 1602. The present school, which stands on the site of one built in 1812 as the successor of the original school, was erected in 1876, at the sole expense of Mr. Edward Moon, of Aigburth, near Liverpool, who got his early education here, and was a relative—uncle, I believe—of the late Sir Richard Moon, who for many years was chairman of the London and North-Western Railway Company. In one part of Churchtown there is "The Cross"—a round stone column, fixed upon a strong, heavy, stone basement. In the early part of this century large pot fairs were held annually at Churchtown. The Parish Church, on the south side of the village, is a very old and interesting building. The exact date of its original foundation is not known; but there was

CHURCHTOWN VILLAGE AND CROSS.

certainly a church here in the 12th century. There are some old, genealogically-striking mural tablets, &c., in the church; whilst in the churchyard, chiefly in the eastern portion of it, there are several curious and ancient stones. In the ground, near the principal entrance to the church north west corner there is the stone on which in old times the clerk used to stand and read out notices, &c., on Sunday, after the morning service, for each of which he got a fee of sixpence. Prior to 1863 the church here was in a very dilapidated condition—the body of it was filled with box pews of various shapes and sizes, the floor was sunk in many places where bodies had been buried, a long, low, gallery filled the west end, and a large stone vault blocked a portion of the east end, the roof was ceiled in lath and plaster, and the walls and arches were covered with lime-wash, which had become dingy to a degree. A restoration committee, consisting of the vicar and the churchwardens, was formed in 1864; Mr. Albert Simpson, of Elmhurst, Bowgrave, acted as honorary treasurer; and subscriptions were gradually obtained to restore the church, under the directions of Mr. Paley, architect, Lancaster. The whole church was reseated (in oak) and refloored, the stone-work was cleaned and pointed, and the gallery and plaster ceiling removed. It took about five years to complete the work, and the total cost of it was £1,371 13s. 1d. During the restoration, how to deal with the big vault in the east transept—a vault so large that it blocked the transept from floor to ceiling—was a difficult problem to solve. The vault contained two coffins—one having in it the remains of an ancient lord of the manor, who in his day had been a sort of king in the district. Eventually a faculty was obtained—after due public notice had been given—for the removal of the vault: the two coffins were placed in the ground below the stone shelf on which they had rested, and the material of the vault was, as far as possible, utilised in the restoration of the church. Since the restoration scheme was carried out, the church has undergone certain alterations—improvements—in the chancel. Taking the building in its entirety, it is now one of the best specimens of an old English parish church to be met with. In 1750, Mr. Richard Pedder, of Preston, purchased the advowson of this church for his son James, who was instituted vicar here during the autumn of the same year. Mr. Richard Pedder was twice Mayor of Preston, viz., in 1748 and 1756, and he died in or about 1763. His grandfather, Mr. Thomas Pedder, was a "gentleman soldier" under Captain William Lynley, Newington Butts, Surrey, in the latter half of the 17th century. He married, in 1650, Elizabeth ffeilden, of Preston, and died in 1679. It has always been understood that the Pedder family had been at Preston some time before the first-named date, but that owing to either civil or religious troubles had migrated to Ireland, whence the aforesaid Mr. Thomas Pedder subsequently returned to Preston. The Churchtown advowson has been owned by the Pedder family ever since its purchase in the year named; and, with the exception of a period of 22 years in the latter half of last century, the vicars of the church, from 1750 till now, have been members of the same Pedder family— the present vicar (the Rev. J. Wilson Pedder) being the great-great-grandson of Mr. Richard Pedder, of Preston, who purchased the advowson.

St. Michael-le-Wyre—usually called St. Michael's, and by some simply Michael's—is about two miles south-west of Churchtown. It is a small, but very ancient place, and is mentioned in Doomsday Book as Michelscherche. The Wyre runs through the village. The original church at St. Michael's was one of the three (those of Preston and Kirkham being the others) built in the Hundred of Amounderness "soon after the introduction of Christianity into the north of England." Nothing whatever of it now remains. The present church, which is near the river, on the south

ST. MICHAEL'S CHURCH.

side, is a re-erection of the time of Henry VIII. Since 1789 the vicarial position here has been held by members of the Hornby family. In the year mentioned the Rev. Hugh Hornby became the vicar; in 1847 he was succeeded by his son William (afterwards Archdeacon), who, in 1885, was succeeded by the present vicar, his son (the Rev. Phipps John Hornby).

Archdeacon Hornby died in 1899, at the patriarchal age of 89. The stipend in connection with St. Michael's Church, though, perhaps not as substantial now as it was some years ago, is still a good one, and it is, certainly, most excellent when contrasted with that attached to the place at one time. In 1646 a Committee appointed or sanctioned by Parliament ordered that the yearly sum of £50 should be paid out of the profits of the impropriate rectories of Poulton and Bispham "seqd from Sir Tho. Tilsey, delinqt," for the "increase of ye maintennce of Henry Jenny, ministr of Michaels, in ye county of Lancr, the vicarage whereof is not worth above 50li (£50) a yeare." Some time after this, Jenny complained to the Committee that he could "reape noe benefit of ye augmentacon by reason the proffitts of ye sd rectory are granted to other ministers by way of augmentacon." So the Committee discharged the order previously made, and decided that £50 a year should be paid to Jenny out of the profits of the impropriate tithes "arising within ye rectory of Holland & Dalton, seqd. from ye late Earle of Derby, delinquent, and out of ye impropriate tythes of Ellen (Ellel), Thirnham, & Cockerham, seqd. from Mr. Bradshaw & Mr. Calvert, recusants; together with all arrears thereof incurred" from the time the grant was originally made by the Committee. The sum of £50 per year to augment the same living was also ordered to be paid by the Committee out of the surplus of the profits of impropriate rectories in several parts of North Lancashire; but, being afterwards informed that there would not be enough to secure the sum named, with arrears, from such source, the Committee ordered that the money should be provided out of the profits of the impropriate rectories of Mawdesley, Bispham, Dalton, and Holland, sequestered from James, seventh Earl of Derby. The vicarial stipend in con-

INTERIOR OF ST. MICHAEL'S CHURCH.

nection with St. Michael's is now derived, by tithe rent, from Upper Rawcliffe-with-Tarnacre (in which township the church is situated), Out Rawcliffe,

Great Eccleston, Elswick, Inskip-with-Sowerby, and Woodplumpton. The interior of the church has an unassuming, ancient appearance; the roof, which is open, being supported by strong beams and rafters of a particularly plain character. On the northern side there is the chantry or chapel of the Butlers of Out Rawcliffe—ancestors of the Butlers of Kirkland. On the door of it there are the arms of the Butler, France, and Wilson families. In the neighbourhood of the church there are good schools. A Sunday school was established at St. Michael's, in 1807, by the Rev. Hugh Hornby and Mr. William Harrison; this was amongst the earliest of its kind opened in England. St. Michael's village is a neat, serene, little place, and is environed by rich agricultural lands. The bridge which crosses the Wyre here is a strong and shapely one. The age of it is not exactly known. A number of the Royalist forces, under Colonel Goring, went over this bridge, or one in the same part, in 1644; Colonel Ashton's troops having crossed it in the immediately preceding year. It is said that the soldiers under Goring's command were very strong in numbers—so strong that before the last of the companies had passed over the bridge at St. Michael's the first was supposed to be at Kirkham. They must, indeed, have been either remarkably numerous or very straggling, to have extended over a distance so considerable as that.

ST. MICHAEL'S BRIDGE.

CHAPTER X.

CATTERALL AND ITS WORKS—BAYLTON'S CHARITY—CATTERALL COTTAGE—STURZAKER HOUSE —BONDS MEETING HOUSE—DIMPLES—BOWGRAVE—ELMHURST—ROMAN ROAD—BYRE- WORTH—GARSTANG WORKHOUSE—STONE-BREAKING PERFORMANCE.

The "village" of Catterall, which is about a mile and a half, by road, from Churchtown—east side, and quite close to the northern highway—consists of a very few houses, with the inevitable "public" amongst them. The township of Catterall is an old one. In the reign of King John there was a mill—no doubt one for grinding corn—in Catterall. A family named Catterall soon afterwards owned Catterall. In the reign of Henry VIII. the whole or major portion of the property in the township passed into the hands of the Sherburns; afterwards it belonged, successively, to the Banastres of Bank, the Winckleys, and the Shelleys, and now it is mainly owned by the successors to the property of the late Lord Winmarleigh, by Mr. J. Jackson, the Fylde Waterworks Company, &c. North-west of the "village," about a quarter of a mile, "Catterall Works" used to be located. They were of very ancient date, and many kinds of indus- tries were, at time and time, carried on in them. Calico printing, bleaching, cotton spinning, and paper making had all their day here, and all of them ended disastrously for the promoters. The works from first to last must, it has been calculated, have lost between £100,000 and £200,000. The Fieldings, the Berhens, the Catteralls, a Paper Company, and two or three firms in addition, all tried their hands at the place, and failed to make their operations remunerative. Finally, the property—a large mill-like building, two long rows of adjoining cottages, &c., with the land forming the sites thereof—was acquired, in 1885, by Mr. A. Simpson, of Elmhurst, on behalf of himself and the other directors of the Fylde Waterworks Company, who foresaw that, sooner or later, the river Calder, on which the property was situated, would be required by the Company. An amusing scene took place before the Committee of the House of Lords when the Company applied for their new Act, in 1891. The opposing counsel, on hearing that the directors of the Company had bought Catterall works, &c., on their own account, about six years before, felt sure they were going to make some "plunder" out of the property, and pressed Mr. Simpson, in cross- examination, with the view of ascertaining if this were their "little game." Mr. Simpson, having had con- siderable experience before Committees, led the learned counsel on until that gentleman thought he was on the verge of a discovery, and then he quietly told him that the directors had sold the property to the Com- pany on the same terms as those on which they had themselves acquired it. The Company afterwards gradually demolished the buildings, and now there are only two or three cottages left on the ground. In con- nection with the works there used to be a small calico- printing establishment, eastward, between the canal and the railway; but the building wherein operations were carried on was gutted about 1878, and the place has now a very deserted, ruinated appearance. The population of the township of Catterall has fluctuated very remarkably during this century. It was at its maximum point towards the middle of the century; the cause of this, no doubt, being the large influx into the locality of working people, single and married —the latter, probably having considerable families— through the fuller employment afforded at the "works." In 1801 the population of the township was 560; in 1841 it was 1,102; when the census was taken in 1891 it had gone down to 336; and the presumption is that now it is somewhat lower.

A person who conducted a grocery business contiguous to Catterall works once had an extraordinary news- paper controversy with the trustees of a local eleemosy- nary foundation called Baylton's Charity: the tussle lasted for months—it was, I should say, the longest contention which ever took place about anything in this locality. Baylton's Charity was left by a Mr. Wm. Baylton, whose will is dated 1679. By his will he left certain parcels of land for the benefit of the poor of the townships of Catterall, Barnacre, and Garstang —one half of the rents of such land to go to the poor of Barnacre, and one quarter each to the poor of Catterall and Garstang, provided that the total rents did not exceed £10 a year; the surplus, if any, to go to the trustees for their trouble in the matter. The property of this Charity consists of three parcels of land—one in Barnacre, one in Catterall, and one in Forton; the total area being 26 acres and 8 perches. The yearly rents now amount, in the aggregate, to something like £36. As the value of the property increased, the surplus over and above the £10 became larger, and was devoted partly to increasing the amount doled to the poor in the three townships named and partly to providing a yearly dinner—a spread to which the trustees invited the chief householders. In 1874 the trustees (who were all advanced in years) felt that the doles were much abused—were being received by many who had no claim to them; so they asked Mr. Simpson, of Elmhurst, to become a trustee, and to take the active management of the property. Mr. Simpson consented, and it was agreed to at once give notice that a change would be made in the administra- tion of the trust. Letters were sent to prominent resi- dents, of every sect and political party, asking them for suggestions as to the best way in which to apply the income from the property of the Charity. From the replies received a scheme was formulated which is still being adhered to, and is as follows:—£10 annually doled to the poor as named in the will; £6 divided between Preston Infirmary and the Idiot Asylum at Lancaster; £16 divided amongst the four schools of the three townships; and £4 for repairs to the property as required. When this new plan of administration came into force, the £10 was apportioned amongst the really deserving poor—widows having a first claim, and then working men with large families of non-workers. Of course, numerous persons who had received doles for many years, and others who enjoyed a good dinner gratis, were much dissatisfied with the new arrangement; and subsequently an agitation was got up by the then Chairman of the Garstang Board of Guardians, and a public meeting was called to pass a vote of censure upon Mr. Simpson in particular. The meeting was held, and amidst considerable opposition, &c., the Chairman was about to declare the vote carried when he was requested to read a letter which had been received by Mr. Simpson from the Charity Commissioners that morning, in which they expressed their approval of the new scheme which had been formulated. The meeting thereupon broke up in disorder, and the scheme has ever since been carried out. But the administration of the charity does not in some respects appear to have given full satisfaction. On the 11th of October, 1898, Mr. A. Cardew, Assistant-Commissioner, held an inquiry, at Garstang, into, amongst other charities, this one. During the proceedings it was alleged that the money which accrued from Baylton's Charity was not sufficiently distributed amongst poor people; that the control of the Charity was, personally, in too circumscribed a form; that some of the property from which the income was derived was very much out of repair; and that the accounts had not been submitted to a meeting of the parishioners. The Assistant-Commissioner intimated that, if the administration of the Charity were in hands deemed to be not sufficiently representative, the Garstang Parish Council should communicate with the Charity Commissioners with the view of securing an alteration, and that so far as the accounts were concerned the law rendered it necessary that they should be submitted to a parish meeting. Mr. Simpson, the acting trustee, was from home at the time, but on his return he convinced Mr. Cardew as to the absolute incorrectness of the complaints which had been made. On the 2nd of January, 1900, the Charity Commissioners issued an order by which the Charity is to be managed in future by three co-optative trustees and four representative trustees, these latter to be chosen, two by the Parish Council of Barnacre, one by the Parish Council of Garstang, and one by the Parish Council of Catterall; the first co-optative trustees to be Albert Simpson (the only surviving trustee), Bernard Simpson, his son, and the Rev. G. Boys Stones, vicar of Garstang.

On the east side of the main road, between Catterall village and the old water cut which was con-

nected with Catterall works, there is a very neat residence which few persons see, owing to a somewhat high wall in front of it. This is Catterall Cottage. The original portion of it was, apparently, built in the latter half of last century. An addition was made to the front, giving the facade its present appearance, numerous years ago. Catterall Cottage, formerly known as "The Pickerings," was owned in 1795 by Richard Curwen, yeoman, of Poulton, and by him in that year it was sold to William Myers, of Manchester, and Henry Fielding, of Catterall, merchants, then carrying on the business of calico printers at Catterall. This firm was known by the name of Watson, Myers, Fielding, and Co. In 1797 William Myers sold his half share to Henry Fielding. On October 9th, 1816, Henry Fielding died intestate, leaving an only son, Henry B. Fielding. On November 18th, 1851, this son died, leaving his property to his wife, Mary Maria Fielding, by whom "The Pickerings," with other property, was sold in February, 1852, to Mr. Jonathan Jackson. In February, 1853, Mr. Jackson sold "The Pickerings," then known as Catterall Cottage, and about thirty acres of land to Mr. William Boys, on whose death, in March, 1881, it became under his will the property of his sister, Miss Margaret Boys. On her death, in January, 1895, she left this property to her nephew, the Rev. G. Boys Stones, Vicar of St. Thomas's, Garstang, to whom it now belongs. Very little can be traced as to the occupants of this house. It was in the occupation of the Rev. James Pedder for some years, while he was incumbent of St. Thomas's, Garstang, and up to the time when, on the death of his father, in 1835, he became Vicar of Garstang. For some time afterwards (previous to 1847) it was occupied by a family of the name of Holmes. In the year named (1847) Mrs. Boys, formerly of Ingolhead, near Preston, went to reside at Catterall Cottage, and members of her family lived here afterwards, until the death of her daughter, Mrs. Boys Stones, in 1897, when it became the residence of Mr. James Butler, corn merchant, of Preston, who still lives here. Some fine old trees, intermingled with a number of the ornamental kind, surround the house, and in front of it there is one of the prettiest lawns in North Lancashire. From the rear there is visible—north-east—choice moor and mountain scenery.

On the river Calder, below where the Catterall works used to be located, there is a tannery, which has been worked by the Holden family for many years. And a little lower, situated at the junction of the Calder and the Wyre, there is what is known as the old Bobbin Mill—a place which belongs to Mr. Crossley, and at which he carries on the business of roller making and machine repairing. Above where Catterall works stood, about 200 yards from the entrance to the grounds, the highway crosses, by a small bridge, the Calder. Sturzaker House is situated about half a mile east of the bridge. In the Bursar's rent roll of Cockersand Abbey, for the year 1451, the name "Laur Sterysacr," of "Sterysacre," appears. Tyldesley the diarist, of Myerscough Lodge, occasionally called at this House. North of the bridge a few hundred yards, and not far from the corner of a road which passes on the right side from the highway, there is a small building, with a few trees in front and a thick set plantation behind: this is Bonds Friends' meeting house. It was built about 1828, by Mr. Richard Jackson, assisted to some extent by Mr. John and Mr. Jonathan Jackson, his brothers, all natives of Wyresdale, who began business—John as papermaker, at Oakenclough, and Richard and Jonathan in the cotton trade at Caldervale—about 1820. In front of and a short distance from the little place of worship named there is Calder House.

About half a mile beyond—north-east, near the side of the road branching from that which passes Calder House—there is a place which used to be called Dimples Hall: it is now named Dimples. In a deed made during the latter part of the 14th century the transfer of some land in the Garstang district from Richard de Dimples—a name derived from Dimples—to Richard de Plesington is mentioned. It is conjectured that a branch of the Plesington family of Plesington (now spelt Pleasington), near Blackburn, resided at Dimples in the second half of the 14th century. Certainly, there was a Robert Plesington at Dimples in 1520. Members of the same family apparently lived at Dimples and owned the estate thereof for upwards of 130 years afterwards, and at a later time for nearly half a century. During a portion of the Civil War, in the 17th century, Mr. Robert Plesington, of Dimples, was governor of Greenhalgh Castle (about three-quarters of a mile due north of Dimples) for the King. Some of the Plesingtons of Dimples were unfortunate on account of their religion and dynastic allegiance. In the list of Royalists whose estates were sequestrated in 1652 there appears "Robert Plesington, Dimples, gent." This was, no doubt, the Plesington before named who had been governor of Greenhalgh Castle. John Plesington (son of Robert Plesington, who attained his majority at Dimples in 1619) was educated for and became a Roman Catholic priest; he lived mainly in Cheshire; and in 1679, after being convicted of having said mass, delivered the sacrament, &c., he was executed at Chester. When the Stuart dynasty was restored, the Plesingtons got back again the Dimples property. Tyldesley the diarist, of Myerscough Lodge, who was a Roman Catholic, occasionally called at Dimples, evidently to participate in religious service. There was a domestic chapel at Dimples, and when Tyldesley went to it mass was said by a priest conjectured to have been the Rev. James Gant. In 1716 Mr. John Plesington, then of Dimples, was attainted of high treason—probably he had either openly supported or sympathised with the Rebellion in the latter part of the previous year, and his estates were forfeited. His sister Alice's husband (Mr. Roger Muncaster, attorney, and Town Clerk of Garstang) was, on the 28th of January, 1716,

executed on Gallows Hill, Preston, for high treason. After the forfeiture of his property it is not known where Mr. John Plesington went to, or what his ultimate fate was. Two of his sons were buried at Churchtown—one sixteen years before and the other a year after the property was forfeited; and it is supposed that his widow was interred there in 1754. Dimples estate, since its forfeiture, has successively been the property of the Greenhalghs of Myerscough Hall, the Fieldings of Myerscough House, Mr. Jonathan Jackson, and Mr. James Jackson—the last-named gentleman being also the present occupier of the place. To the outside observer Dimples looks like two fairly-sized dwellings joined together—one immediately before the other. In front it has a placidly-

DIMPLES.

substantial, though somewhat retiring, appearance. This is not the original Dimples house; but it stands upon the site of the first residence here. The front portion is of more recent date than the rear part; but the latter, in its entirety, does not appear to be at all ancient. In parts of the back wall there are some bricks evidently from a very much older building: they are small, bear marks as if, when in the soft clay state, they had been laid upon grass-covered ground, and they were evidently sun-dried. In the land contiguous to Dimples there are gentle depressions—dimples: the site of the house is also, when contrasted with the land on the south-west side, in a hollow; and it may fairly be assumed that the name of the place was originally derived from the concavities observable. Frequently in modern times—since the addition in front was made—this residence has been called Parrdimples. Par (equivalent in etymological value to Parr) means equal, and the word pair comes from the same or a cognate root. The added front part at Dimples is of the same size and shape as the rear structure; they are equal or resemble a pair of buildings quite closely joined; and the probability is that the equality and conjunction observable account for the name Parrdimples. In old times, as already stated, there was a Roman Catholic domestic chapel at Dimples; and there is a tradition that a priest was buried under one of the hearth-stones in the house.

The hill up which the highway goes, north-west of the Friends' meeting house, in Bonds, is called Bowgrave. I have seen it designated Baugrave and Bow-greave; but it is now, according to ordinary spelling and the definition of the Ordnance Map, known as Bowgrave. As to the meaning of the name, only the latter portion of it admits of actual or reliable explanation. "Grave," as a final syllable, and "greave" (both derived from the Anglo-Saxon "graf") mean the same thing, i.e., a grove. Respecting the first portion of the word, if "Bau," it might pertain to some ancient chief of that name (Baugrave being thus the grove of Bau); or if "Bow," as now spelt—and this is not at all improbable—then it would refer to a bending down, or frontal, or projecting grove. All around Bowgrave the land is characterised by a considerable angle of declivity—it slopes a good deal, and, viewed from the north and the south especially, the western side has a strikingly frontal or projecting appearance. Bowgrave is in Bonds, which, for township purposes, is attached to Barnacre. The summit of Bowgrave is 123 feet above the level of the sea, and commands a very extensive and excellent view—the whole of the Fylde country, the ravines and purple hills east of Scorton, the northern slopes of Wyresdale, several of the mountains of Westmorland and Cumberland, &c. In the eastern side of the highway, and not far from the top of Bowgrave, there is Elmhurst—a very pretty

station, at the north-west corner, near the top, was the first building erected on Bowgrave: it was put up in 1855-6, the total cost—land, &c., included—being £1,300; and the site was chosen in order that the station might amongst other things be a protection for the road, which at this point was very lonely, and on which—not far distant—a murder had been committed. Shortly before Bowgrave police station was erected, the general county constabulary system, rendered compulsory by Act of Parliament, had been adopted. For years this system had been a desideratum in rural districts. Only the old parish constable plan had previously been in vogue, and so lethargic and peculiar were its operations that the thing was to a great extent a farce—a mere formal fatuity. On the northern road, as elsewhere, a considerable amount of lawlessnes prevailed through its slowness and indifference. Singular to remark, the first report of the Constabulary Force Commissioners, issued in 1839, regarding the "Practices of Migratory Depredators," contains an extract showing the state of affairs at Garstang (the town of Garstang is about two-thirds of a mile from the summit of Bowgrave) and the necessity for constabulary improvement which existed at that time. The extract in question is from an entry dated January 14th, 1838, found in the

ELMHURST.

place. This is the residence of Mr. Albert Simpson. It is almost entirely shrouded from view, by trees, on the western and northern sides; but from the south and the east it is picturesquely conspicuous for a considerable distance. The grounds in which Elmhurst stands are beautifully laid out; they are terraced to the south, contain many ornamental trees, fine conservatories, &c.; and altogether the place has a charming appearance. Mr. Simpson built Elmhurst, in 1867, and he has resided at it ever since. Bowgrave, on the summit and at the north and west sides, is now "quite a place," residentially. It is getting covered with dwelling-houses. The county police

Itinerary of a thief. This thief, who was accompanied by a man of the predatory class, after referring to certain pocket-picking performances at Chorley and Preston (at the latter place it is mentioned that "a decent sum" was realised), says:—"Thence to Garstang—market day; just as we got in met a drunken man, we knocked him down, robbed him, did not hurt him much, got £12, and went on without stopping, got to Lancaster at night by coach which overtook us soon after we left Garstang."

The Roman road between Walton-le-Dale and Lancaster crossed Bowgrave. Mr. W. Thompson Watkin, in his "Roman Lancashire," says that this road "appears to have passed through Broughton, by Barton Lodge and Brook, between Myerscough and Bilsborrow Halls, through Claughton, where a portion of it is in old maps called 'Fleet-street'" (now known as "The Street"—two or three cottages, &c., being immediately contiguous—about half a mile north-west of Claughton Hall, and a short distance from the railway); and so northward. But Mr. Watkin's details are very meagre as to the localities or parts traversed between Claughton and Lancaster, and his statement as to this particular road passing east of Garstang is very doubtful: indeed, it seems to be erroneous. An antiquarian friend of mine some time ago made a close inquiry into the route of the road, and I have a copy of his observations in regard to it. After intimating that in or about 1884 a portion of the Roman road was discovered on Bowgrave, he says that its route from Claughton northward was across the Calder, at a point near Sturzaker House, then over Bowgrave, across the Wyre between the highway bridge and the canal aqueduct—"very close to the aqueduct"—and that from traces of the road "found on the north-west side of Garstang there is an angle [of it] near where Moss-lane crosses the canal, and the course is changed from a north-westerly direction—going north—to one of north-north-west. This shows that the line of road lies just south of Garstang, and near to the canal basin. From the angle near Moss-lane bridge the road crosses Green-lane, about midway, and at a point where a lane leading from Garstang enters it. It crosses the turnpike road a little north of Manor House, and, although the investigations have not been fully made northward, the course has been ascertained to lie, from an angle here, almost due north, passing Ratcliffe Wharfe and Clifton Hill on the west side. It passes Windy Arbour a little to the east, and after skirting Hay Carr on the same side it runs almost straight into Galgate. The section of the road which was laid bare on Bowgrave shows the road to have been about 21 feet in width and laid—not regularly paved—with small boulders such as are used in ordinary light pavement, the stones having evidently been taken out of the neighbouring streams." The route of the road on leaving Galgate was through Burrow and so on, straight, to Lancaster. In the 18th century, says Mr. Watkin, the Roman road between Lancaster and Preston [passing on the east side of Preston] was still used as a means of communication; but "it was so much destroyed that in places vehicles and pack-horses had to divert from its straight line, making a sort of curved track." It is supposed that, northward, the road went from Lancaster to Kendal, and also that a branch of it either ran east of Lancaster into Yorkshire or secured some communication with the Roman stations in that county.

Nearly opposite Elmhurst, on the west side, there is a narrow, winding, green lane, which leads to Byreworth, about half a mile distant. This is a farmstead—a very old one. The earliest proprietary name in connection with Byreworth which I have

met with is that of Brockholes. In 1289-90 Adam de Brockholes, an ancestor of the Brockholes of Claughton Hall, possessed Byreworth; and about the middle of the next century Roger de Brockholes and his wife Elena had land here. Early in the 16th century Thomas Butler owned Byreworth. Towards the end of the same century it was the possession of Thomas Brockholes, and from him the estate descended to his son John, who conveyed it, in 1621, to Ralph Wilson and Richard Bancke, of Borwick, near Lancaster. The former and Sir Robert Bindloss, of Borwick Hall, were next the joint owners of Byreworth, which they sold, in 1652, to John Wilson, of Over Kellett, and John Bailman, of Overton. Later the property was possessed by the Leighs, of Lyme, in Cheshire, from whom it went by purchase to the Brockholes family, of Claughton Hall. In 1784 Byreworth was conveyed by William Fitzherbert-Brockholes to Richard, Joseph, and William Jackson—members of the Jackson family, of Spout House, Nether Wyresdale. Richard Jackson, of Spout House, left Byreworth to his son Joseph, who bequeathed it to his brother William, from whom it descended to Jonathan Jackson, and it is now owned by James Jackson, of Dimples. Byreworth House is

BYREWORTH.

situated in a very quiet, secluded part of Bonds; it has a plain, mildly-rustic appearance, and is, probably, a somewhat enlarged or reconstructed building on the site of the original house. There are neither name initials nor dates visible on any part of it. The oldest portion of the building is apparently at the north-east side, where the walls are low, and in which there are some indications of re-arranged masonry.

Near a bend in the high road—east side—below Bowgrave police station, &c., there is Garstang Union Workhouse. Formerly the Workhouse of this Union was in Claughton, up a lane about a quarter of a mile east of Brockholes Arms, and consisted of a range of low buildings now turned into cottages. It got into a most dilapidated condition, and for years the Local Government Board endeavoured to impress upon the Guardians of the Garstang Union the necessity of building a new Workhouse. At last the suggestions or recommendations of the Local Government Board were succeeded by commands, and then the Guardians, having secured about six and a half acres of land on

Bowgrave—in the quarter already referred to—advertised for suitable plans. Only two architects competed, and on a given day all the ex-officio and elected Guardians of the Union were invited to inspect and to vote upon the rival designs. Mr. Simpson, of Elmhurst, was the only ex-officio Guardian who attended the meeting, and he, on being asked his opinion, inquired whether the Guardians had quite decided to expend only £3,000 on the erection of the new Workhouse. Being assured that they had so decided, he told them that they would have to accept the plainer design, as the other would cost far more than £3,000. The Guardians replied by calling attention to the written description of the design, which read as follows:—"The estimated cost of the whole is £3,400 (exclusive of heating apparatus, w.c.'s, baths, and fittings), which can be abated as already described to the extent of £400." On putting the question to the vote, every one except Mr. Simpson went in for the more elaborate and costly plan. Mr. Simpson thereupon left the meeting, saying "they would find out their mistake, and he would be ready to help them when that time came." The plan was then sent to the authorities in London, and accepted and sealed by them, the date being March 11th, 1872. When the tenders came in, the lowest was found to be about £8,000, exclusive of the bricks; and the Guardians were so astonished—so wroth—at this that they decided not to build a Workhouse at all! Before long the Local Government Board began to inquire as to the progress of the new undertaking, when a reply was sent to the effect that the project had been abandoned. The Local Government Board informed the Guardians that this could not be allowed, and, after some correspondence, threatened to dissolve the Garstang Union. The Guardians did not believe in the threat; but they were disillusioned one day, when it was made known to them that an order for dissolving the Union had been received. It was then deemed prudent to consult Mr. Simpson, and he, along with Mr. Henry Garnett, of Wyreside, arranged an interview with the Local Government Board, on the introduction of Lord Winmarleigh; and, as a result of that interview, the Local Government Board rescinded the sealed plan, which was a proceeding without precedent, and allowed the substitution of the less pretentious, or less costly, design, in accordance with which the House was built. The work was completed about 1874, and the total cost of it, exclusive of land, bricks, and architect's fees, was £3,345, as against the £8,000 before named. Up to the present the Workhouse has never been more than half filled with inmates.

In the summer of 1878 Mr. Simpson, of Elmhurst, feeling some doubt as to the propriety of having sent to prison certain vagrants or tramps, brought before him as a magistrate connected with the Garstang bench, on the charge of having refused to complete their task of stone-breaking in the vagrant cells, at the Garstang Union Workhouse, decided to test the matter himself, in order to ascertain what the stipulated stone-breaking task really amounted to. So he one day walked to the Workhouse, and somewhat astonished the officials there by stating that he was going to personally break a quantity of stones. He then entered the stone-breaking department, pulled off his coat, rolled up his shirt sleeves, and commenced hammering at a heap of stones—a heap exactly similar to the lot which every male tramp or vagrant lodging for a night in the Workhouse had to break before leaving the place next day, or else render himself liable to be sent to Preston House of Correction for not finishing the task. Well, after labouring vigorously at the heap for about five hours—much of the time being taken up in breaking a few big, very hard stones, but neither bigger nor harder than those which figured in every heap—after wearying his muscles, blistering his hands, and wetting not only his shirt, but his waistcoat right through with sweat, Mr. Simpson managed to accomplish the task. After this experience on the part of Mr. Simpson, the impropriety of giving such a stone-breaking task to casual male vagrants—especially men unused to this sort of work, and in considerably poorer physical condition than himself—became quite clear; so he wrote to the Garstang Board of Guardians on the subject, and in the course of his observations very properly stated that to the "casual" vagrant this stone-breaking system not only amounted to positive punishment, but also more or less incapacitated him from work; and he suggested certain changes with the view of mitigating the severity of the task in the case of men of the class named. Subsequently a committee was appointed to inquire into the subject, and, as the result of a report which it submitted, the Guardians adopted a plan calculated to obviate the severity complained of. An account of Mr. Simpson's stone-breaking experiment, together with certain comments approving of his desire for a change in the system, appeared in several English newspapers, daily and weekly; "Punch" devoted a column to it; and it even formed a subject for editorial observations in one or more Canadian journals.

CHAPTER XI.

BONDS ROMAN CATHOLIC CHURCH—SION HILL—GREENHALGH CASTLE—TURNER'S FARM—
SULLAM—CALDERVALE—OAKENCLOUGH—FYLDE WATERWORKS.

The village of Bonds is just beyond the bridge which crosses the canal at the northern base of Bowgrave. The church near the side of the road is of the Roman Catholic order; the Rev. J. R. Hennessey being the present priest in charge. It was built in 1858, as the successor of a place of worship which was erected in Garstang, for the Roman Catholics, in 1784, and which, after the church in Bonds village had been opened, was transformed into the Garstang Institute. The large house at the north end of Bonds village—west

Mr. John Taylor Wilson, a Lancaster solicitor of some eminence as a conveyancer, who resigned the coronership), and he held the post until he died in 1852, at the age of 83. His successor in the coronership was Mr. John Cunliffe, solicitor, of Preston (son of Mr. John Cunliffe, of Myerscough House), who retained the post until his death in 1855. Mr. Lawrence Holden, solicitor, of Lancaster, next succeeded to the coronership—a position he still occupies. The great predecessor of the whole of the foregoing—the earliest

BONDS VILLAGE.

corner, near the Wyre bridge—is called Sion Hill. Tyldesley says in his diary, under date May 11th, 1714, that, after going with some foxhounds from Thurnham to Nateby, he called at Bowers House, and "thence to Sion's Hill [Sion Hill, Bonds, no doubt], to Charles Sollom's, all night." For many years Sion Hill was the residence of the Gardners, who were connected with the legal profession. On the 7th of March, 1834, when Mr. John Gardner, solicitor, was residing at this house, it was broken into, and property said to be of the value of £500 stolen from it. At Lancaster Assizes, in August of the same year, two men (James Lunt and William Maddox) were each sentenced to seven years' transportation for committing this robbery. Mr. John Gardner was the coroner for the Lonsdale Hundred—the south portion of it, at any rate, if not some of the northern part—for nearly half a century. He was appointed to the office in 1803 (his immediate predecessor being

"Crowner" for their district whose name I have met with—was Mr. Thomas Covell, whose "brass" is in Lancaster Parish Church. On the metallic memorial in question there is a portrait, and the following inscription:—" Brass of Thomas Covell, 6 times Mayor of Lancaster, 48 years Keeper of the Castle, and 46 years one of the Coroners of the County of Lancaster. Died 1639. Ætat 78 years." Since the demise, about 1875, of the last of the Gardners who resided at Sion Hill (Mr. Henry Gardner, barrister-at-law), the house has been mainly occupied, in succession, by medical gentlemen—Drs. Irvine, Gorham, and Roberts. The last-named now lives at it.

Greenhalgh Castle—or rather a very ruinated remnant of it—stands on a moderate but picturesque eminence, in a field in Darnacre, about half a mile from Bonds village, eastward. A lane, the entrance to which is near the Wyre bridge, opposite Sion Hill, runs close by it. Greenhalgh Castle was built in 1490, by Thomas Stanley, the first Earl of Derby of that family, who obtained a license for its construction, and for its occupation by a garrison, principally for protection against certain of the nobility of the country, whose estates had been given to him by Henry VII., for services rendered at the battle of Bosworth Field, in 1485, and whose vengeance or hostility he strongly apprehended. The castle seems to have been "a rectangular building, with a tower placed diagonally at each corner about fifteen yards asunder." A moat ran round it; and portions of oblong depressions apparently on the line of the moat —in all probability remnants of the original work— are still visible. It is said that on the old bridge (the predecessor of the present one) which crossed the Wyre, at Garstang, there was a small watch tower, put up for the purpose of signalling with the garrison at Greenhalgh Castle. In 1640 the Castle was

saw it in 1772 when on his journey to Scotland, refers to a single tower as being "the poor remains of Greenhaugh Castle." In the same year Prebendary Gilpin, vicar of Boldre, passed through this district, and in his "Observations," which he published in 1786, he says, after making some rather deprecatory remarks as to the scenery of the locality (he was on the hunt for the grand and the beautiful, "particularly the mountains and lakes" farther north)—"As we approached Garstang, the castle [Greenhalgh] tho' ruined into a mere block, and without beauty, becomes an object, where there is no other." In 1780 Roger Dewhurst, of Halliwell, made a sketch of the tower as it then existed. This sketch was engraved and it appeared in the first edition of Baines's History of Lancashire; in the edition of 1868-70, edited by Harland and Herford, it was reproduced; but it did not secure a place in the edition published in

GREENHALGH CASTLE (1900).

garrisoned for the King by James Earl of Derby; the governor of it being Christopher Anderton, son of Sir Christopher Anderton, of Lostock, near Bolton. It was subjected to a "close siege" during the winter of 1644-45; but the soldiers within it stoutly held their own. Greenhalgh Castle was one of the eight garrisons north of the Trent which held out for the King. It was also one of the two places in Lancashire (Lathom House being the other) which for a time effectively resisted the Parliamentary forces. The garrison, it is said, held out until the death of the governor, when a capitulation took place, and in or about 1650 the castle was dismantled. Since then, time and weather have done much, and certain local tenantry, &c., desirous of securing stones for wall-building, more to reduce the proportions of Greenhalgh Castle. Thomas Pennant, the traveller and naturalist, who

1888-93, and edited by Croston. Mr. J. Britton, in his work on Lancashire, published in 1818, says that Greenhalgh Castle, "seems to have consisted originally of seven or eight towers of great height and strength." Mr. John Briggs, an able northern editor in the early part of this century, observes, in the first of his published letters, that he and some relatives, whilst on their way from Preston to the Lake district, in 1820, visited "Greenalph [Greenhalgh] Castle," and that one of them, evidently attracted by a portion of the old moat bed, exclaimed—"Where, in the name of antiquity, did they get water to fill this trench?" May-be, a good many persons since then have, on looking at the altitude and dryness of the surrounding ground, indulged in a kindred interrogation. In old times, however, a considerable portion of the adjoining ground was swampy, and lagoons or deep holes might be made for concentrating the water, which could then be carried by garrison hands to the moat. In the ratio of existing portions of the tower, the altitude of the highest part of it, as sketched by Dewhurst, would be about 54 feet. This highest part of the tower was at the south-west side. In 1871, during a visit I paid to the castle ruins, I noticed a rough pinnacle at the side mentioned— evidently that which appears in Dewhurst's sketch— and it had been patched up with mortar as if to preserve it from further disintegration. Towards the end of 1898 I revisited the old castle ruins, and found that nearly the whole of the south-eastern side of the tower and about two-thirds of the wall on the south-western side had disappeared. Numerous stones were lying in a deep hollow on the south side of the tower and a few on the ground eastward, but these would by no means be equal to those which formed the walls that had disappeared since my previous visit. More recently I again visited Greenhalgh Castle. The main portions of the ruins, as now visible, are parts of the walls on the north-east and north-west sides of the tower. Externally, they are about 18 feet wide. The interior of the tower, at the base, is about 15 feet square. On the north-west side there were originally three embrasures in the lower part of the wall—the form of them being now quite distinct, internally; but externally the bordering masonry of each is very much broken— in fact, gone entirely. Two tall, deep, indentions —one above the other—appear in the wall (inside) on the north-east side. They are not connected with any embrasure apertures. The higher one is in line, centrally, with what seems to have been an outlook, about a foot deep and half a foot wide; the lower indention is backed entirely by stones. On the north-west side of the interior, about 12 feet from the ground, there are a few evenly-formed holes in the wall, as if they had been used for joist ends—the joists being for the support of a floor. Several feet above these holes—on the same side, and in the centre of the wall—there is a large, broken-sided, open-topped aperture, but whether this was originally a look-out or embrasure it is now quite impossible to tell. The present external height of the wall on the north-east side is about 30 feet, whilst the altitude of that on the north-west side and of the strip of joining wall at the south-west angle will be about 27 feet. The ground floor is now a mere chaos of stones. Originally, there was apparently, at the south-east corner, a narrow door-way or passage. Adjoining the north-east side there is a broken, irregularly-projecting wall, about 18ft. high and 9ft. long at the most extended part. The existing walls of the tower are about five feet thick, are formed of rough freestone—pieces of all sizes and shapes—centred with grouted rubble; the mortar in several parts being now almost as hard as the stones which adjoin. The roughness of the masonry is accounted for by the fact that the castle was built for defensive and not residential purposes. An old writer says that the castle had but one door, and that the building "was thot impregnable with any ordenance whatsoever." Concerning the name of this castle, Whitaker, in his "Richmondshire," says that the more proper form of it would be Greenhow, "for 'halgh' always signifies a meadow or spongy place, and 'how' a hill, which last agrees with the situation of this fortress on a green and beautiful knoll." In the "Palatine Note-book" (Volume 4) "E.K." (Mr. Edward Kirk) observes that the elevated ground on which this castle stands was at one time "nearly surrounded by a low, marshy swamp [would not "halgh" as before defined apply here?], the only natural connection with the hard land in the past having been on the north-east side," that "most of the old swamp is now [in 1884 when E.K. wrote this] drained and cultivated;" that "there are traditions still of a lake having existed here;" that about 1850 there was found in an adjoining field, whilst it was being ploughed, one or more cannon balls; and that in 1881 a leaden ball 2½ inches in diameter was picked up within the precincts of the castle. The father of the present Lord Derby sold Greenhalgh Castle and some adjoining land to Lord Kenlis (afterwards Lord Bective, who died in 1893), and it now forms part of the Barnacre property belonging to the latter's daughter, Lady Henry Cavendish Bentinck. Though not very high, the site of the castle is a most commanding one, owing to the openness and flatness of a great deal of the surrounding country. From the ground at the base of the castle, outside, a view extending many miles can be obtained; and in old times, when all the castle walls were up, and the place was in its original completeness, the external scene, from the higher parts, must have been not only very picturesque, but of a most wide-reaching, comprehensive character. Taking into account the object of this castle—it was solely for military or defensive purposes—the site would be excellent: it would command the ford or bridge-way across the Wyre, at Garstang; and, as all foot and horse soldiers going north or south on this side of the country would be obliged to pass there, the advantages involved in such a site would, unquestionably, be very great. The castle ruins can be very distinctly seen from the Wyre Bridge, at Garstang; and, though the eminence on which they stand is considerably shrouded by trees on the eastern edge, travellers on the London and North-Western Railway, which is about half a mile off, on that side, can get a glimpse of them as they ride past. Before it gets too late, an effort should be made to preserve the remaining portion of this old, historic castle. Near the ruins, on the south-east side, there is an ash tree which very markedly manifests the virtues of self-help and self-reliance. All the earth originally under the trunk has fallen away, and below the overhanging base of the tree there is a root, which has developed vertically, down to the nearest ground. This root is about half a foot in diameter, and it forms a direct prop for the tree—is such a thorough support that if it were removed the tree would fall.

In Barnacre, about half a mile east of Greenhalgh Castle, there is a farm called "Turner's," which up to a few years back had, according to common tradition, been occupied successively by members of a family named Turner for upwards of 300 years. A relative of the family, who at present resides in Preston, informs me that the Turner occupation of the farm extended back over a period of about 500 years! The last member of the Turner family who lived here (her husband being the tenant) was Elizabeth, daughter of the late Lawrence Turner. With respect to Lawrence Turner, he occupied the farm from February, 1829, to the time of his death, in January, 1879, being then 88 years of age. He was one of a family of 18, and his own children numbered 12. A stone relic of the family may now be seen in Bonds Catholic Church; it has been converted into a receptacle for holy water, and bears the following inscription: "T.—R.T." "I.T.—1639." An oak bedstead, still in the possession of a relative of the family, and bearing family initials and a date, is said to have stood in a room at Turner's Farm—in one particular part of the room—for over 200 years. R. Turner lived at the farm in 1636 : the initia's R.T. and the date 1636 are carved behind the stable door. In front of the stable, over the door, there is a stone bearing the initials T.I.E. and the date 1696. The original burial ground of the Turner family was at Garstang (Churchtown) Parish Church. On a tombstone in the churchyard there may be seen an inscription relating to Martin Turner, who died in 1765, aged 55 years. In the same graveyard there is another stone, referring to one or more members of the Turner family, but the general inscription is not decipherable: nothing can be made out except the date 1584. The family pew of the Turners, who were always Roman Catholics, is or was in a range known as the "Barnacre Row." There is a traditional story respecting a very plucky, but personally unfortunate, adventure which a member of the Turner family once had in connection with a horse robbery. The story is to the effect that during the rebellion of 1715 some of the Pretender's soldiers stole a white horse from Turner's Farm and took it to Preston; that Turner, the owner, unwilling to be deprived of the animal in such a way, followed the soldiers, and on the way was roughly handled by them—was thrown down an embankment, and had his spine badly injured; that notwithstanding this maltreatment he got up, walked on to Preston, ascertained where the officer in charge was quartered, interviewed him, and asked for the restoration of the horse, but was advised to return home, without making any bother, if he did not wish to be further hurt; that he then left the officer, but was determined, notwithstanding the warning he had got, to recover, if possible, the horse; that he found out where it was stabled, waited about till night, then quietly crept into the place, brought out the animal, got on to its back, and hurried home with it as quickly as he could. To commemorate this restoration of the horse, the family for some time kept up its breed, and to each foal gave the name "Pepper's Breed," the stolen and restored horse

being called "Pepper"; but Turner, the hero of the affair, never recovered from the spinal injuries he sustained, and ultimately they proved fatal to him. The dwelling-house connected with Turner's Farm is a plain, simple-looking building. A considerable

TURNER'S FARM HOUSE.

part of it (west end) is ancient; the remainder, which is flush with such part on one side, but wider and higher on the other, being of much later construction. The latter portion evidently covers ground which was occupied by what was originally the eastern half of the old building; a doorway, now walled up, being in the centre, south side. On the same side of the present old part, which is thatched, there were formerly four small windows; but two of them are now blocked up. In a garden, on the south side, and opposite the centre of the general building, there is a dial column of carved stone; but the dial plate has either decayed away or been removed. There is no date on the column; but near the top of it are the initials "I.M." Martin Turner, at the time of his death, in 1765, left a son, an only child, named John Turner. During legal infancy this son had for his guardian an uncle named John Miller, and the initials on the dial column are those of this guardian-relative. It is said that many stones used in the construction of the existing house and outbuildings were taken from the ruins of Greenhalgh Castle. The Castle was not dismantled until about 1650, and the bulk of the present structural work on Turner's Farm appears to be of a subsequent date. If members of the Turner family lived here so long ago as tradition alleges, then the oldest portions of the present house, &c., may be but parts of the successor of a still older structure. Before Barnacre passed into the possession of the Duke of Hamilton it was in a wild state, covered with bush and woods. The Turner family and others settling in the neighbourhood were given one half of their holdings for bringing the land into a state of cultivation. These farmers were afterwards known as "Barnacre lords"; their farms were called after their surnames, and each of these "lords" had a pew in Garstang (Churchtown) Parish Church. This was in pre-Reformation times. After the Duke of Hamilton got a proprietary footing in Barnacre, he disputed the title of the "lords," and a trial took place at Lancaster. The proof in their favour was indisputable; they had their title deeds with them, and they won. But the triumph of the "lords" was very transient. Being greatly elated on account of their victory, they called, on returning home, at a public-house in Galgate, and, taking much more refreshment than was good for them, they either lost their deeds or somebody stole them. Another trial was afterwards forced upon the unfortunate "lords," and at the conclusion of it the former verdict was reversed, so the land passed to the Duke of Hamilton. Father Edward Bamber, who was the last to suffer martyrdom, on account of his faith, at Lancaster, on the 7th of August, 1646, was related to the Turner family. A direct descendant (Lawrence Turner) is now living, with his family, at Barrow-in-Furness.

The round-headed hill on the south-east side—about a mile and a half from Turner's Farm, Barnacre, and rising by an easy gradient at the rear of Garstang and Catterall Railway Station—is Sullam. The summit of this hill is 548 feet above the level of the sea. Though this is not much of an altitude, there is obtainable from the top of Sullam, owing to the open, level land in front, a very extensive and delightful view. The whole of the Fylde, with its fringe of watering-places; the spires, towers, &c., of Preston; the castle, church, and various other buildings at Lancaster; Morecambe Bay, clear and placid, and the serrated range of mountains away north-west from Blackcombe to Helvellyn; also Great Ormes Head, Snowden, and at times the Isle of Man, are visible from Sullam. About the middle of the fourteenth century, "certain wastes

"Went early to Sollom ffox-hunting, to meet Bros. Dalton and ffrost; found two ffoxes but could get nether off them into ye earth." June 18th, 1713, "On Calder [south-east of Sullam] unkennelled a ffox, ran him a howr, but the severity of ye day being so hotte made us loos him." April 12th, 1714, "Went on ye morning a ffox-hunting to Sullam, where a great company met, but I left the ground by 7 to meet Mr. B—dsworth, who was gon." May primo, 1714, "Went to Sullam a ffox hunting. Had a ffine chace; but Mr. Smith of Wedacr [Woodacre] spoy'd our sport with his grey hound, wch made us loos the ffox by running him." May 3rd, 1714, "Went a hunting to Sullum and ffound ditto ffox in ye same kenell or within 2 yards. Had a noble chace, but he proved to stout and bette us quit outt, thoh some in our company belives the doges killed him." May 12th, 1714, "Went to Solom a fox hunting with severall young Dimples, &c. Found a bitch fox and ffor an howr ye doges running here briskly; but as soon as ye sun appeared they could hunt no ffurther." There used to be wild deer on Sullam; and in the early part of the present century a fair for the sale of toys, gingerbread, &c., was annually held in summer time on its summit!

Caldervale village is about a mile north-east of Sullam. About 1848 a cotton mill and a shed were built in Caldervale, by Mr. Jonathan Jackson, who first appeared in the locality—connected in some way with the cotton trade—about 1820. For a number of years the mill and shed were worked by Mr. Jackson, and afterwards by his sons, who were unsuccessful. Eventually the property was bought by the Fylde Waterworks Company. The mill is now in ruins. The

CALDERVALE.

called Salome" were held by Thomas de Twenge. In or about 1431 Sir John de Lumley died, seized of, amongst other property, "a messuage and 50 acres called Sulan" (Sullam). Sport for fox-hunters, &c., appears to have been very plentiful on and about Sullam, and Thomas Tyldesley, of Myerscough Lodge, figured amongst the "Tally-ho" men here. In his diary I find these entries:—May 6th, 1712,

shed is worked by Messrs. Liver and Co., who purchased it from the Waterworks Company. Oakenclough paper mill is about a mile and a quarter north of Caldervale village. It is situated on the river Calder, is one of the oldest paper mills in the country, and was acquired by Mr. John Jackson, grandfather of the present proprietor (Mr. Harold Jackson) about 1820. It has been kept going very regularly, and is a great boon to the locality. At a picturesquely-conspicuous point between Caldervale and Oaken-c'ough, east side, Caldervale Church is situated. This church was built by public subscription, on a site given by Mr. W. J. Garnett, of Quernmore Park, near Lancaster; it was endowed by him and the Rev Wi'son Pedder, of Churchtown, who became alternate patrons; and in 1863 it was consecrated. The present vicar here is the Rev. G. H. Wilson.

About two miles north of Sullam there appears to be—as viewed from its summit—a flat-topped hill; but in reality it is the embankment of a large reservoir connected with the Fylde Waterworks. From the western part of this embankment I one summer evening saw the Isle of Man. On the northern side—down in a deep ravine, through which Grizda'e Brook used to flow—there is another reservoir, connected with the same system of waterworks. Through leakage or weakness in the dam of this reservoir, when originally constructed, very considerable delay was occasioned and a good deal of additional expense incurred. The excess water or by-wash from the lower reservoir flows into the remaining portion of the old brook channel, and debouches therefrom into the

river Wyre, about half a mile south of Woodacre Hall. From these reservoirs water is supplied to Garstang, Kirkham, Lytham, St. Annes, Blackpool, Fleetwood, and intermediate country places in the Fylde. The water is said to be of the purest quality. The Fylde Waterworks Company was formed in 1860, and for many years had but poor success. During late years, however, it has advanced rapidly, and is now a prosperous concern. In 1891, an Act was obtained to divert the river Calder into the Company's reservoirs. By means of this diversion the supply of water has been increased three or four-fold. The mains have been nearly doubled, and before long the Fylde country will be adequately covered with service pipes from them. In 1898 an Act was obtained by the authorities of B'ackpool, Fleetwood, Lytham, and St. Annes, to buy up the property and works of the Fylde Waterworks Company. Mr. Simpson was the chairman of the Company at this time, and, after protracted negotiations, the purchase was effected without litigation. On its conc'usion the shareholders presented Mr. Simpson with an elaborate illuminated address, together with a cheque for £5,000.

CHAPTER XII.

To the Wyre and the only inland town—quaint, little Garstang—which it closely passes, I must now draw attention; by-and-by, when somewhat north of the " finished " place, I shall have occasion to revert to Barnacre—shall have something to say about Woodacre Hall and its wood, Barnacre Lodge, the Hamilton bathing well, &c.

The river Wyre runs between the townships of Barnacre-with-Bonds and Garstang: it takes its rise in the lonely, wide-spreading hills at the head of Wyresdale; and from its source, in the wild, high region named, to its debouchure, at Fleetwood, into Lune Deep, the course of it is of a very crooked, wandering character. Michael Drayton, in his " Polyolbion " (published 1612-22), gives a graphic, compactly-picturesque description of the Wyre. He refers to it as

Arising but a Rill at first from Wyersdales lap,
Yet still receiving her strength from her full Mothers pap
As downe to Seaward she, her serious course doth ply,
Takes Caldor coming in, to beare her company,
From Woolscrags [Wolf Crag's] cliffy foot, a Hill to her at hand,
By that fayre Forrest known, within her Verge to stand.
So Bowland from her breast sends Brock her to attend
As she a Forrest is, so likewise doth shee send
Her child, on Wyresdales Flood, the dainty Wyre to wayt,
With her assisting Rills, when Wyre is once repleat;
Shee in her crooked course to Seaward softly slides,
Where Pillins [Pilling's] mighty Mosse, and Mertons [Marton's], on her sides
Their boggy breast out lay, and Skipton [Skippool] downe doth crawle
To entertaine this Wyer, attained to her fall.

In the Lancashire section (published 1720) of " Magna Britannia " reference is made to the Wyre as a river that " affords pearl fishing, which are frequently found in a sort of large Muscles called by the Inhabitants Hambleton Hookings, a name taken from the manner of catching them, they plucking them out of their Beds by Hooks." There is no allusion whatever in the work to salmon, trout, or any kind of fish except " Muscles." In 1871 I received from a person living in the neighbourhood of Hambleton a small bagful of " Hookings "—large, rough-shelled mussels with an excellent flavour. Since then I have neither seen nor heard of any, and I believe that now the " Hookings " have, with very rare exceptions, disappeared from the Wyre. It is conjectured that the original bridge over the Wyre between Bonds and Garstang was built near the end of the fifteenth century, by the Earl of Derby, for the purpose of securing communication with Greenhalgh Castle. Owing to its inconvenient formation—it was high and very

narrow—this bridge was pulled down, and the present one erected in its place about the year 1750. A stone at the termination of the parapet of the bridge (north-east end) bears the inscription, " J. Threlfall, B.M., 1829." On both sides of the bridge, at the Garstang end, there appears to have been an addition of several yards made to the parapet of the original structure. The record at present in the County Bridgemaster's office, at Preston, respecting this bridge, does not go as far back as 1829; but the presumption is that the parapet was extended in that year, when a person named J. Threlfall was the bridgemaster. Just below the bridge there is the weir of Bonds corn mill, and this by its back-watering influence causes the Wyre here to be broad and somewhat deep. On the north side of the river, immediately below the bridge, there is a fish-ladder, which was put in several years ago by the Wyre Board of Conservators, and it has materially facilitated both the production and protection in the Wyre of the finer kinds of fish. In October, 1898, the Wyre was restocked with 5,000 yearling brown trout, out of money voted for this purpose by the Lancaster Corporation to the Fishery Board in charge of the river.

As soon as Wyre bridge is crossed, northward, the town of Garstang is entered. Antiquarians and persons fond of philological matters have been sorely puzzled as to the exact meaning of the name Garstang. I can give no positive or reliable explanation of it; in fact, I can do no more than supply data—fuller, perhaps, than any the reader has hitherto met with—for theorising on the subject. In the Doomsday Book Garstang is designated " Cherestanc;" the land area of it, or connected with it, being " six carucates." In other records, &c., not so old, the name appears variously as Geirstanke, Gairestang, Gairstang, Gayrestang, Gairstange, Garstrenge, Garstrang, Garsting, and Garstang. In old times—indeed, up to nearly the end of the 18th century—there was no fixed rule for the spelling of names or words of any kind: very much of the spelling was done on the phonetic plan—as a word or name sounded, when pronounced, so it was spelt. For instance, an old road book to which I have already referred mentions " Maskay " (Myerscough), also " Gaugut " (Galgate), &c. This book was printed 100 years ago, and, singular to observe, the way in which the names just mentioned are spelt in it, tallies exactly with the style in which the bulk of the local people pronounce them at present. In the same book reference is made to the seat of " Mr. Brocas " (Mr. Brockholes, of Claughton Hall), and " Brocas " exactly corresponds with the

59

pronunciation of the name by many people now liv-inig in and about Claughton. Taking the earliest spelling of Garstang met with—"Cherestane" in the Doomsday survey—the first syllable of it (Chere) may have involved the idea of something valuable, worth looking after, or being careful of. In certain old English books the word "Chere" (now obsolete) was used. As applied to persons, it meant dear; when associated with things, it indicated being precious, valuable, goodly, &c., and, in a secondary sense, fond, loving, careful (over)—to cover or be above, which is also expressed by the word "Ker." According to the Oxford English Dictionary—the most exhaustive modern philological authority I have met with—the letter G, which now both commences and terminates the place-name in question, was originally a differen-tiated form of C, whilst in very old times—times pre-ceding the Norman Conquest—the letter C, which begins and ends the said name in the Doomsday Book, had the function of both G and K. So that the present way of spelling the name—Garstang—harmonises in letter value with much of that met with in the Norman record, and the form it presents in that record is based upon or derived from a very old mode of letter con-struction. As to the meaning of "Chere," it may have implied or had some affinity to the Anglo-Saxon word "Chare," meaning care, attention, separate, or turn. The second syllable "stane" may be taken as the equi-valent of "stang"—an Anglo-Saxon word pertaining to a land measure; so that the full name might originally relate to some valuable, much-to-be-prized and cared-for boundary or particular length or portion of land. If, however, the first syllable were pronounced hard, in the initial part (Ch being uttered like K), then it would sound somewhat similar to Ker—a contraction equivalent to the old English word cover, which, tak-ing the terminal portion (stang) in the sense above referred to, would make the name mean something equal to a comprehension or covering, or protecting by prescription, or possession of a certain quantity of land. The first syllable of the name as now spelt (Gar) is Anglo-Saxon for long or narrow, with pointed head. The second syllable (stang) may be a mis-spelling, or contraction, of the Anglo-Saxon word "stan," meaning a stone. If it be an error in spelling or an abbreviation, and if "stan" be the real terminal, then the name would mean a long, narrow stone, with a pointed head—perhaps something of the nature of, or analogous to, a boundary or distance-recording or measuring stone. As having some possible bearing upon the meaning of the first portion of the name (Gar), I may state that there are the following old, obsolete words:— Gear, to dress or make ready—also business matters, concerns, and affairs; gair, an aquatic fowl; gare, gaure, to look or stare at, or take keen notice of; gair, gare, stripe or streak; gar, a dart, or spear or lance—something long and sharp-pointed. Similarly spelled to Garstang, in the first part, is Gargrave—a place in the West Riding of Yorkshire; and, strange to say, two of the old first-half variations in the spel-ling of the latter name correspond with two in that

of the former, viz., Gair-grave and Gayr-grave. Ac-cording to Dr. Whitaker, in his "History of Craven," Gar, in Gargrave, refers to a personal name—Geri or Garri; and Gar in Garstang might be deemed equally applicable. By many country people the name Gar-stang is pronounced "Gahsting," which reminds me of some humorous verses relating to the Garstang and Knot End Railway, published in a Preston paper, in 1873. The first verse contained the name spelt as now pronounced by numerous persons in and about the Garstang district, and ran thus:—

I was in Gahsting years ago, and two years since, I know,
I had some business in the town—a town uncommon slow.
I asked the way to Fleetwood, where I had a night to spend,
And folks all told me of a line—the Gahsting and Not-End.

(In a humorous note explanatory of the latter part of the name of this peculiar little railway, the author of the verses says: "Not-End. The line is so called because it does not end; it only stops in a field at Pyllynghe.")

There is nothing at all of a definite character on re-cord concerning Garstang before the reference to it in Doomsday Book—a book compiled in the latter part of the eleventh century. No information of any sort is available as to the condition or character of the place during the twelfth century. But after this period facts become fixed and tangible, in documentary and other ways. Early in the thirteenth century the manor of Garstang belonged to the Lancastres, barons of Kendal and Wyresdale. Agnes, widow of William de Lancastre, the third baron, held the manor as her dower about the middle of the same century. Two nephews (Peter de Brus and Walter de Lindsey) after-wards became possessed of it. Subsequently the manor was owned by the Lindseys. Sir John Haver-ington, of Farleton, near Kirkby Lonsdale, was, during the latter part of the fourteenth century, the owner of the manor or of certain property in it, through marriage. Proprietary rights in Garstang were then successively exercised by Henry Duke of Lancaster, and a descendant, the Multons descendants of the de Lancastre family, one or more of the Twenge family, Sir William de Mollineux, the de Couoy de Gynes, the Rigmadens, &c. In 1535-36 the manor became the property of the Crown. Afterwards, with certain reservations on behalf of the tenants, it went to the Savoy Hospital, in London. The manor next passed, by lease, successively, to Henry Saville, his servant William Saville, William Holden, the Rigmadens, and the Gerards. In 1738 the manor reverted to the Crown. In 1742 it was granted to Mr. William Hall, of the Middle Temple, London, for a term of 30 years. Later, in the same year, the Hon. Edward Walpole obtained the manor for the remainder of the term, and, soon afterwards, the King, by Act of Parliament, conveyed to him—with the view of giv-ing encouragement to the trade of Garstang and pro-viding security for improvements made therein—the manor in fee; and a descendant of his, by marriage (Mr. Bertram William Arnold-Keppel, who resides near Swaffham, in Norfolk), is now lord of the manor, and owns the major portion of the property in Garstang. The town of Garstang was incorporated by a charter, granted in the reign of Edward II. (1314). This charter was surrendered to Charles II., and renewed by him on August 5th, 1680. By this renewed charter the town was made a "free burrough"; its governing body consisting of a Bailiff and seven Burgesses, and locally designated in after years "the Mayor and Corporation of Garstang." Owing to a fire which occurred about 1750 nearly the whole of the "Corporate" documents or records were destroyed. A banquet in connection with the "Corporation" used to be held annually in the Town Hall. In 1883 the old system of government by the "Mayor and Corporation" was done away with, and in 1889 the town's property was put into the hands of a board of trustees, designated the Garstang Town Trust, appointed by the Charity Commissioners, and consisting of two ex-officio, five representative, and four co-optative members. The present Town Hall, which is the successor of one pulled down about 1755, is now used for District Council purposes, miscellaneous meetings, entertainments, &c. For many years Garstang Petty Sessions were held in the Town Hall; but since the middle of May, 1893, the sessional business has been transacted in the Garstang Institute. Adjoining the Town Hall there is the Market House, which was built in 1843, at the expense of the Lord of the Manor. An antique piece of mechanism —Garstang fire engine—has had its headquarters in the Market House for a considerable number of years. It is an engine of the manual sort, was purchased about the middle of last century, and is said to be the oldest of its kind in Lancashire—anyhow, the iron portions of it, for the whole or main of the original wood work was some years ago supplanted by fresh material. Originally the engine was kept in an outhouse behind the premises of Mr. Hartley, ironmonger, on the west side of the Market-place. At first it was placed on heavy wooden block wheels, and dragged by a chain when required for extinguishing purposes, and when needed at a fire in any outside district it had to be carried on a cart! At the north end of the town there is a school, which stands upon a piece of land granted to the "Mayor and Corporation" of Garstang, in 1756, by the Right Hon. Sir Edward Walpole, for a term of 200 years at the nominal annual rent of 2s. 6d. Mr. John Morland, of Winmarleigh, gave £150 for the endowment of the school. When the building was put up and ready for use, the £150 was handed over to the "Mayor and Corporation," who cleared a debt on the Town Hall with the money and allowed annually out of their funds £6 15s., which sum was handed over to the Schoolmaster, and for which he had to give free tuition to four scholars selected or nominated by the town's Bailiff. The School is now conducted on modern lines, and periodically subjected to Government inspection, same as all ordinary public schools in the country. Richard Brathwaite ("Drunken Barnaby"—a northern gentleman, with a passion for rambling up and down the country and a strong penchant for versification) passed twice through

Garstang, and in his "Itinerarium," originally published in 1638, there are allusions to what he saw and experienced in the old town. In Part 2 of the "Itinerarium," after describing his "progress" through Lancaster and Ashton, he says:—

> Thence to Garstang pray you hark it,
> Ent'ring there a great beast market;
> As I jogged on the street
> 'Twas my fortune for to meet
> A young heifer, who before her
> Took me up, and threw me o'er her.

In part 4 of the same work, under the heading "Tramontane Fairs," Barnaby, after referring to certain places (beginning with Appleby and going south), observes:—

> Thence to Garstang, where are feeding
> Herds with large fronts, freely breeding.

The November cattle fair at Garstang used to be a very large one. For instance, at the fair in 1805 there were, from the North alone, nearly 3,000 cattle; at that in 1814 there were 2,300; and at the fair in 1821, in addition to a large number of English cattle there were between 2,000 and 3,000 head of Scots. Formerly there was a fair or market for cheese at Garstang. William Stout, a Lancaster Quaker and tradesman, says in his diary that in 1691-2 he "went to Preston fair, principally to buy cheese; the market for cheese then being mostly at Garstang and Preston." Fairs are now held, yearly, at Garstang —on November 22nd for cattle, and on November 23rd for horses and the hiring of farm servants. The "country about Garstang" at one time produced a "peculiar breed of cattle," smaller than the ordinary Lancashire kind, but "of elegant shape, beautifully curled hair, with wide horns and straight backs." Pennant, the traveller, &c., before referred to, passed through Garstang in 1772, and thus describes the place:—" A small town, remarkable for the fine cattle produced in its neighbourhood: a gentleman has refused 30 guineas for a three-year-old cow, has sold a calf of a month's age for 10 guineas, and bulls for 100, and has killed an ox weighing 21 score per quarter, exclusive of hide," &c.; so that, as Pennant says, Drunken Barnaby might well refer to the cattle in this locality. The same writer also observes:— "Abundance of potatoes are raised about the place and sent to London, Ireland, and Scotland." Potato-growing, to the point of "abundance," is still a characteristic of the district, especially on the westward side. In respect to cattle, Garstang is not so noted now-a-days as it formerly was; the fairs do not draw so many to the place as in old times; but on farms in the district there are still many good animals; and occasionally, I dare say, a wonderfully fine calf turns up for the dealer or the butcher. That mentioned by Pennant, which fetched 10 guineas when it was a month old, must have had its speciality in its breed. For weight, I fancy that the calf which Mr. John Knowles, butcher, of Lancaster, bought from Mr. Robert Ray, of Garstang, in 1848, was not often equalled in the old, palmy days, and has since been seldom excelled. This particular

calf was eleven weeks old when Mr. Knowles slaugh-
tered it, and it weighed 60lb. per quarter, or, in its
entirety, just over 17st.! According to Dr. (Bishop)
Pococke, iron-smelting was formerly carried on in
the neighbourhood of Garstang. In his "Travels
Through England," he says that on the 10th of July,
1750, whilst going northward, he passed through "a
very poor town called Garstang," and that he "saw
to the east the smoak of some iron smelting houses
which were erected there on account of the great
plenty there is of wood." Directly east of and contiguous to Garstang there is a portion of the country
which may be called the centre of Barnacre; but,
apart from Dr. Pococke's statement, I have never
met with any evidence showing that there was ever
"great plenty" of wood in that part. For generations
there has been a good deal on the Woodacre side of
Barnacre, and also on the opposite or Claughton side;
and the "smoak" noticed had, perhaps, drifted from
either one or the other of those parts. As to the "iron
smelting houses," this is the first time I have seen
any reference to such places in the Garstang district.
Perhaps the "smoak" came from one or more ordinary forges, or was due to charcoal burning. In the
old coaching days Garstang came in for a large

the ink on Annie's pelisse. Misfortunes seldom come
single. ''Tis not alone the inky cloak, good daughter,' but I forgot at Garstang my two breastpins—
one with Walter and Jane's hair, another a harp of
pure Irish gold, the gift of the ladies of Llangollen"
(Lady Eleanor Butler and the Hon. Miss Ponsonby).
It was whilst temporarily halting at Garstang, in 1829,
that Brougham and Macaulay (at that time barristers
on the Northern Circuit) met, and where the former
informed the latter of the result of a division in the
House of Commons on the Roman Catholic Relief or
"Emancipation" Bill. In a letter to his father,
written at Lancaster, on March 14th, 1829, Macaulay
says:—"All minds seem to be perfectly made up as
to the certainty of Catholic Emancipation having
come at last. The feeling of approbation among the
barristers is all but unanimous. The quiet towns-
people here, as far as I can see, are very well con-
tented. As soon as I arrived I was asked by my land-
lady how things had gone. I told her the division,
which I had learned from Brougham at Garstang."
William Black, the novelist, made a halt at
Garstang in 1871, and some of the incidents in
one of his best stories have their venue at the
Royal Oak, in the old town, and along the

GARSTANG (1900) FROM GREENHALGH CASTLE.

measure of patronage, and was a particularly well
known place. Being on the great north-west highway between London and Edinburgh, all the coaches
which ran on this road were pulled up for passenger
refreshments, horse-changing, &c., at Garstang. Not
unfrequently, also, some of the passengers who had
travelled a long distance broke their journey on
reaching Garstang—stayed all night, taking advantage
of such hotel accommodation as the old place provided for persons of their order. During his journey south, per coach, in 1828, Sir Walter Scott stayed
a night at Garstang; but the "Wizard's" experience
here was not of a particularly felicitous character.
The entry in his "Journal," for April 4th, 1828, includes the following:—"Slept at Garstang; an indifferent house. As a petty grievance, my ink holder
broke loose in the case, and spilt some of

banks of the Wyre, &c., in the neighbourhood.
At one time there appeared to be such a dislike of,
or unwillingness to adopt, "modern improvements"
in Garstang, and the place was evidently so completely locked up in the hands of one family—nobody being able to buy either a piece of land or a
building—that it was called "the finished town."
About 1836, when the survey was being made for the
Preston and Lancaster railway, much indifference, if
not even a strong aversion, to the project was shown
in Garstang by either the inhabitants or the family
owning the town; and it is said that in consequence
of this the present route of the railway, on the eastern
side—a mile distant, as the crow flies, and nearly two
miles off by the ordinary road, from Garstang—was
adopted. The "Market Place" of Garstang is a
sort of triangular space in front of the Royal Oak

Hotel, and in the centre of this space is the old Market Cross—a far-worn stone pillar, on a stone base. A small metal plate, fixed on one side of the pedestal, bears an inscription to the effect that the Cross was repaired by public subscription, in 1897, in commemoration of the Queen's Jubilee (the Diamond Jubilee which occurred in the year named). Originally, the column would, no doubt, be surmounted by a cross—hence the name Market Cross. For several years, up to the time when the reparation work was done, a lamp stood on the top of the column. It is now surmounted by a ball. Once upon a

GARSTANG MARKET PLACE.

time Garstang evinced a species of dread or hatred of gas light—virtually tabooed a small company formed for the purpose of supplying gas, indeed cold-shouldered it almost as signally as it did the original railway project, and persisted in illuming, or making dismal, its streets with a few ancient oil lamps. But now it has not only a considerable regard for railway facilities—would prefer to have them much fuller and nearer than they at present exist—but goes in freely for gaslight, for even "incandescent" auxiliaries, and hugs to its bosom two big gas lamps in the Market Place! Reminders of old Garstonians are occasionally met with in strange and unexpected places. For instance, in John Le Neve's "Monumenta Anglicana," published in 1717, it is stated that there was at that time, in the Charter House Chapel, London, a tablet or monumental slab, bearing an inscription which ran as follows:—"Here lyeth the Body of Mr. James Sidgrave, born at Garstang, in Lanc. He was 21 years housekeeper of this Hospital, to which he gave by will £50, to the poor of Clerkenwell £50, to 20 poor familys £100. He dyed the 26th day of April, A.D. 1707, aged 57 years." In 1879 attention was drawn to this in a Lancashire and Cheshire antiquarian publication ("Local Gleanings"), and the question was asked, "Is anything known of Mr. Sidgrave's parentage or descendants?" A reply, of a theoretical character, shortly afterwards appeared in the same publication, to the effect

that the name Sidgrave should, probably, be Sidgreaves, and that, if so, the keeper of the Charterhouse hospital referred to was, perhaps, a member of the Sidgreaves family of Inglewhite Lodge, near Goosnargh—a son of James Sidgreaves, who died in 1671. But the members of this Sidgreaves family were all staunch Roman Catholics, as are those of their descendants now living in Preston; and as "James Sidgrave" was for many years connected with and left some of his money to a Protestant place (Charterhouse Hospital) it may fairly be presumed that he was not of the Roman Catholic faith, and consequently not a member of the Sidgreaves family of Inglewhite Lodge. Furthermore, his natal associations were not at that place: he was "born at Garstang." In 1604-5 there was a James Sydgreaves living in Bonds, close to Garstang; at Garstang or in the neighbourhood there resided, about the same time, one Nicholas Sidgreaves; and amongst those persons in the parish of Garstang who, in 1641-2, signed a declaration "to maintain the true Protestant religion of the Church of England against all Popery and Popish innovation" was John Sidgreaves, who is described as being "within Garstang quarter." In all probability, James Sidgrave was lineally descended from or was laterally connected with one of these. The monumental slab is still in the Charterhouse Chapel. The present Master of Charterhouse (Dr. Haig Brown), in a letter I have received from him, has supplied me with a copy of the inscription which it bears. Le Neve's copy is correct, with the exception of two or three very trifling deviations in spelling, &c., which I have rectified in that given. The Master of Charterhouse says, in his letter, "The inscription which I have copied, is on a black leger slab at the west end of the north aisle of our chapel." About eighty years ago there were actually 13 public houses in Garstang! Their names were—the King's Arms, Royal Oak, Eagle and Child, Golden Ball, Wheat Sheaf, Pack Horse, the Horns, Brown Cow, Blue Anchor, Red Lion, Holy Lamb, Swan, and Shovel and Broom. Some of these inns have been done away with; the names of one or two have been changed; and the number at present open is 10, namely, the Royal Oak, Golden Ball, King's Arms, Eagle and Child, the Horns, Pack Horse, Crown, Brown Cow, Wheat Sheaf, and Farmers' Arms. Over the front door of the Brown Cow there is the date 1685. There are several very old shops in Garstang—some renovated—also various new shops and other buildings. The shop (opposite the Royal Oak—east side) in which "Old Tommy Clarke" —as he was commonly called—carried on business as printer, stationer, newspaper seller, &c., is still used for like purposes; whilst extensions of the premises are utilised for the Garstang postal and telegraph business. He was a native of Garstang—his father being Mr. Robert Clarke, attorney, Garstang, who died in 1797, and whose father, Mr. Joseph Clarke, was also a lawyer in the old town. In the list of Bailiffs of Garstang there are the following:—1761, Mr. Jno. Clarke;

1770, Mr. Thos. Clarke; 1777, Mr. Thos. Clarke; 1783, Mr. Jos. Clarke, junr.; 1788, Mr. Jos. Clarke, junr.; 1792, Mr. Robt. Clarke; 1796, Mr. Thos. Clarke. "Old Tommy" was a man of many parts, and quite a character; he was not only a printer, stationer, and newsagent, but ran a lending library, and took an active part in local affairs; being also, it is said, "Mayor several times." He used to figure conspicuously as a speaker at the "Corporate" banquets held in the Town Hall, and took a special pleasure in eulogising Garstang and glorifying its inhabitants. Whilst carrying on business in the fore-named lines, he for a while simultaneously acted as editor of the "Preston Pilot" (now defunct), which at that time was owned by his brother, Mr. Lawrence Clarke. Previously he had done reporting work for the same paper. "Old Tommy" for a considerable time went regularly from Garstang to the newspaper office in Preston, every Tuesday, and returned on a Saturday morning to Garstang, by the highway—trudging on foot the entire distance, and carrying with him a bundle of newspapers, some of which he personally delivered, or gave to a nephew of his, who accompanied him, to leave at certain houses on the way. In his editing and bundle-carrying days newspapers were, comparatively speaking, very dear; they were in the order of scarce articles; and ability to read them was by no means a common or plentiful thing. And before he had any connection with newspapers they were still scarcer and dearer, whilst the number of those persons who could properly read them was correspondingly smaller. Every week end, about 90 years ago, a number of Garstang working men subscribed for a paper, in their individual turn or in certain sections—it was the old "Lancaster Gazette," now in the non-existent category, which was purchased—and at a convenient hour they met at "the Cross" (opposite the Royal Oak), where a man named William Carter read the news to them, and afterwards had the paper given to him for his trouble. Carter was a very distinct, good reader; and during the latter part of his life, when he lived in Forton, he was a most assiduous newspaper peruser. He used to say that, when he got a newspaper, he read it all through—"advertisements and everything." He died in Forton. "Old Tommy" had in his family a son and a daughter who were very smart, mentally. The son (it is supposed he was befriended by Lord Stanley some time after the latter was summoned to the House of Lords, in 1834) got a post in connection with the Customs, at Liverpool, and eventually became Superintendent of the North-West coast. He died at Leamington, in 1896, aged 72 years. The daughter alluded to had a remarkable memory—so remarkable, it is said, that she could, after coming from church, repeat every word of the sermon! "Old Tommy," whose full name was Thomas Walker Clarke, and who died in 1863, in the 70th year of his age, was succeeded in his business at Garstang by Mr. John Wrightson

(brother of the late Mr. George Wrightson, auctioneer, of Preston), whose widow carried it on for many years after his death, and whose sons, Herbert and John, have now charge of it along with the postal and telegraph work of the town and district. A daughter (Miss Mary M. Clarke) of the old gentleman alluded to now resides at Ivy Bank House, Bolton-le-Sands, near Carnforth.

St. Thomas's Church, Garstang, is the successor of a chapel-of-ease, originally licensed for divine service in 1437. The Plundered Ministers' Committee ordered, in 1646, an annual payment of £50 out of the tithe profits of the impropriate rectory of Goosnargh, sequestered from Sir Thomas Tildesley, "delinquent," for the "maintenance of a minister at the chappell of the Market Towne of Garstange"; and subsequently the same Committee ordered the sum of £50 to be allowed and paid out of impropriate tithes arising within the parish of Kirkham, sequestered from Thomas Clifton Esq., "papist and delinquent," "to and for the maintenance of such minister as shall be approved of by the classis" of the county of Lancaster, to officiate in the said "chappell." This place of worship was rebuilt in 1666, and again in 1796, whilst in 1876 it was restored and enlarged. It has been a parish church, in accordance with the provisions of the Blandford Act, since 1880, in which year a separate district, taken out of the civil parish of Garstang, was assigned to it. The Rev. G. Boys-Stones is the present vicar of St. Thomas's Church. At the north end of Garstang there is a small Congregational chapel: it was built about 1777. On the south-western side of the town there is a Wesleyan Methodist chapel—built in 1879, at a cost of something like £2,000, and the successor of a chapel, connected with the same denomination, erected in 1814, at a cost of £670. Prior to 1814 the Methodists here had a place of worship of some kind: they had, certainly, a school four years before that date, and the local Independents were evidently very kindly disposed towards them; for a notice I have seen states that on the 21st January, 1810, "a charity sermon was preached in the Independent Chapel, Garstang, for the Methodist Sunday School in that place." The Liberal Club building, at the southern end of the town, was opened on February 18th, 1889. The present Institute adjoins the old one, and was built in 1896; the cost of it being about £800. The population of the township of Garstang is very little if any more now than it was 50 years ago.

From the Garstang and Catterall station—the station of the Preston and Lancaster (now L. and N.-W.) Railway—there is a junction line to Garstang, and thence westward to Pilling. This line, called the Garstang and Knot End Railway, was opened for traffic on the 5th of December, 1870. Originally, it was intended to form a section of quite a big affair: its western terminus had to be at Knot End, opposite Fleetwood; there had to be docks at Knot End to secure coasting business, particularly in connection with Ireland, and for certain American trade, &c.; the line had to go eastward as far as Hull, or run into some railway having a direct route to that seaport; and at the first open meeting in support of the project—a meeting held at the Royal Oak Inn, Garstang —a wonderfully fine picture of prospective traffic and dividend-earning was drawn.   Up to now the line has got no farther eastward than the Garstang and Catterall station, whilst westward it stops at Pilling; but communication between Pilling (from the old terminus point there) and Knot End will, by-and-bye, be secured by means of a light railway. The first sod in connection with the work of extension was cut by Sir Matthew White Ridley, M.P. for the Blackpool Division, on the 25th of January, 1899. At the end of May, 1900, owing to some pecuniary trouble or misunderstanding, a large quantity of materials connected with the new undertaking was sold by auction. The distance from the Garstang and Catterall station to Pilling is seven miles, and from the latter place to Knot End about four and a half miles.   From 1872 to 1875, the line was entirely closed, through difficulties of a pecuniary or kindred character.   Near the Garstang and Catterall station (north end) there is a district creamery: it was opened in 1897, and it is, productively, very well spoken of.

CHAPTER XIII.

On the side of the highway, three-quarters of a mile north of Garstang, there is a stone with the name Cabus cut in at its base. This refers to the township of Cabus, which is here entered. There does not appear to be any great antiquity about Cabus. Its name is not met with "earlier than 8 Hen. VIII. (1516)," when Margaret Rigmaden, the widow of Nicholas Rigmaden, died, "seized of certain lands here." The Lady Chapel or chantry in Garstang Parish Church (Churchtown) was founded by this Margaret Rigmaden, during her widowhood, and some time after her death it passed, through marriage, to the Butler family, of Kirkland Hall. Cabus is a purely rural region, and during the present century the number of its inhabitants has very considerably decreased. In 1830, the population numbered 277; when the census was taken, in 1891, it was only 179; and the probability is that since then there has been a further decrease. The northern end of Nateby township immediately adjoins Cabus; and about half a mile west of the wayside stone referred to, in a direct line, there is Nateby House. So far as documentary evidence goes, Nateby appears to be first mentioned as the property of the Travers family, of Tulketh, near Preston, in the time of Henry I. Subsequently, members of the Northman, the de Lancastre, de Nateby, de Plesington, and Travers families had proprietary rights in Nateby. The chief, or amongst the best known buildings in the township of Nateby are Nateby Hall, Bowerswood, and Bowers House. There is a tradition that a subterranean passage used to run between Bowers House and Nateby Hall. No trace of this has, however, been met with in modern times. In a wall of one of the outbuildings of Bowers House there is a stone bearing the date 1627, and the initials RG GG. To members of a Green family, of Nateby or Garstang, it is conjectured these initials refer. Bowers House, which is about a mile and a half west of Garstang, is now a farm house belonging to the same estate as that on which Bowerswood stands, and about 50 yards north of the latter. Bowerswood is owned and occupied by Mr. William Bashall, grandson of the late Mr. William Bashall, of Farington. It was built as a shooting box by Mrs. John Bashall, aunt of the present owner, for her son, the late Mr. Warwick Bashall, about 1890, and was considerably enlarged in 1899. The late Mr. William Bashall, of Farington, purchased the land from the Duke of Hamilton in 1853. There will be, roughly, some 2,000 acres of it in Nateby. And then there is the Bonds property in addition. On the death of Mr. Bashall the estate

was split into two halves, his eldest son, William, taking the larger portion of the Nateby property, and his second surviving son, John, the Bowerswood property and that in Bonds. When William (the son) died, the property passed to his daughter, who married Norris Bretherton, of Leyland, and who still owns it. On the death of John Bashall, the Bowerswood property was held in trust by his wife until Boardman Bashall came of age. He had it but a short time, and on his death it passed to his brother Warwick, and held it until his death in 1899, when it passed to the present owner (Mr. W. Bashall), considerably encumbered and in a poor state of repair.

A short distance from the boundary stone named, a road, apparently not much used, runs down to Nateby. At the entrance to this road there are two very strong, round gate posts. They belonged to the toll bar, which formerly existed about a quarter of a mile north; the big gate was fixed to these posts; and when the bar was done away with the late Mr. Peter Ormrod, of Wyresdale Park, Scorton, bought them, and caused them to be fixed at the opening of Nateby lane. In the old coaching days there was a range of buildings, including a number of stables—the whole going by the name of Rochdale—at the head of this lane, near the highway. The stables were for the accommodation of the coach horses, which were, as "coach time" got near, taken to the front of the Royal Oak, Garstang, and there yoked up and driven on in place of the animals which had run the regulation distance. In the vicinity of the stables, &c.—long since pulled down—there is now a dwelling called "Rochdale House."

From the highroad, near the boundary stone, a fairly good view can be obtained of Woodacre Hall—a white-fronted, high-roofed, strong-chimneyed building, about three-quarters of a mile to the north-east, in a straight line, and about a mile and a half distant by the ordinary road. Woodacre, or Wodeacre, now in the township of Barnacre, was once the name of a manor. It was originally in the Forest of Wyresdale, and gave its name to a family that owned or tenanted it for a considerable time in the early part of the 13th century. The Rigmadens afterwards became possessors of the manor. The property remained chiefly, if not entirely, in the possession of the Rigmaden family till about 1600. After the Rigmadens had gone off the scene, there came the Fyfes, who resided at Woodacre Hall—the old Hall, which stood a short distance from the present building. Dr. Fyfe died here in 1671. Mr. William Spencer next lived at Woodacre Hall (at the new building, I believe), and, through a descendant of his, the place went to

James, fourth Duke of Hamilton, who met with his death in a duel, with Lord Mohun, in 1712. The Duchess of Hamilton, his widow, resided at Woodacre Hall for some time after this fatal encounter. She died in 1744. The Woodacre property was sold by the 11th Duke of Hamilton in 1853. It was purchased by the late Alderman Thompson, of Underley Hall, near Kirkby Lonsdale. Woodacre Hall has, for many years, been used as a farm house. The old Hall, it is said, stood in a small field a little to the east and on the higher side of the railway which runs through Barnacre, near the present Hall, and about the same distance from the supposed site of the old place. It is not accurately known when the old Hall was pulled down, but the presumption is that it was demolished in the latter part of the 17th century. Neither names nor dates of any kind can be found on the masonry of the present Hall, and the chief characteristics of it are its simplicity or plainness and strength. An outhouse on the south-

WOODACRE HALL.

eastern side has had walled into it several curiously chiselled stones, evidently from the old Hall; but they give no definite clue at all to the history of the place. An excavated part of the railway, called Barnacre Cutting, is not far off. Here, on the 31st of August, 1848, there was a very considerable block to the passing of trains. The line was covered with water, to the depth of three feet, for about a mile—an inundation due to the bursting of a water-spout on one of the contiguous hills. About seven years before this there was a somewhat similar flood, in the same part, through a like cause. There is a broad, dark mass of trees (Woodacre Great Wood) on the northern side of the Hall; and with this wood the Rev. Isaac Ambrose, a Puritan divine, was periodically, for some years, religiously associated. Ambrose was born in or near Ormskirk, in 1604. He became vicar of Preston about 1640, being preferred to the position by the Hon. Lady Margaret Hoghton. Whilst vicar of Preston he was on very friendly terms with the Hoghton family, and he used to spend much of his time in the woods (near Hoghton Tower) on the edge of the Darwen, which was then a clean, beautiful stream. In 1655 he became vicar of Garstang (Churchtown) Parish Church. On the 4th of January, 1657, he preached in Preston Parish Church the sermon at the funeral of the Hon. Lady Margaret Hoghton. He was ejected from the

vicarage of Garstang, through the Act of Uniformity, in 1662, and two years afterwards he died, at a house in St. John-street (then called Church Weind), Preston. There is a tradition that, while the Rev. Isaac Ambrose was vicar of Garstang Parish Church, he "went into retreat," or withdrew, for a month every year, to a hut in Woodacre Great Wood, and that during his retirement there he wrote a book. It is very probable that he either thought out or composed the latter portion of his chief or most effective work, entitled "Looking unto Jesus," in Woodacre Great Wood. This work was first

WOODACRE GREAT WOOD.

published in London in 1658, consisting of about 1,200 pages, and it has been several times reprinted. The Rev. John Wesley edited two of Ambrose's works—one being that just alluded to, and the other entitled "Ministration of, and Communion with, Angels"—and contributed thereto a sketch of the life of Ambrose, which Lieut.-Colonel Fishwick, in his "History of Garstang," describes as being "Brief and full of errors." The late Rev. C. H. Spurgeon, in the course of the first of two sermons or addresses he delivered in the old area of Preston Corn Exchange, on the 26th of February, 1861, made reference to Ambrose's periodical withdrawals to the wood named, and spoke highly of the religious works which the old divine wrote. During his brief stay in Preston, Mr. Spurgeon was the guest of Mr. John Gudgeon, who, I believe, induced him to call upon Mr. John Hogg--a well-known local tradesman at that time, whose shop was at the top of Cannon-street (north-east corner). Anyhow, the notable preacher visited Mr. Hogg's place, and there had shown to him one of the works of the Puritan divine whose merits he had emphasised in the Corn Exchange. This was Ambrose's "Prima, Media, et Ultima—the First, Middle, and Last Things" (sixth edition, printed at Glasgow College, in 1738)—a work originally dedicated "to the Worshipful the Mayor, Aldermen, and other Inhabitants of the Town of Preston, in Amounderness." The book belonged to Mr. Hogg. After looking at the volume, Mr. Spurgeon got a pen and ink, and wrote on a blank leaf, at the beginning of it, in his characteristically clear, strong style of caligraphy, the following verse:—"Is the Lord's hand waxed short? thou shalt see now whether my word shall come to pass unto them or not"; and beneath the verse he wrote his own name—C. H. Spurgeon.

One of the London comic papers made reference to Mr. Spurgeon's visit to Preston—said it was singular that, whilst Mr. Spurgeon was in the town, he went to a Hogg and stayed with a Gudgeon. Reverting to the Rev. Isaac Ambrose, I may remark that there used to be an ardent admirer of him at Scorton: this was Thomas Smith, the Duke of Hamilton's gamekeeper. In or shortly before 1836, Smith made a "tour of inspection" in Woodacre Great Wood, with the view of discovering, if possible, the site of Ambrose's hut. Eventually he hit upon what, in his opinion, seemed to be the actual or the most likely spot; there he built a hut; and on Saturday, July 16th, 1836, he entertained to tea, in it, at his own expense, about 50 children as well as a number of ladies and gentlemen. The Preston and Lancaster section of the London and North-Western Railway runs through this wood, and it is conjectured that the hut to which the Rev. Isaac Ambrose periodically resorted was on the higher side; anyhow, it was in a part of the wood, on that side, where Smith put up the "memorial" structure—a primitive sort of hut, which remained up until shortly after the railway was opened, in 1840, when it fell into decay. This hut was made of wood, stones, and sods; it stood just a third of a mile north of Woodacre Hall—was in the wood on the east side of the deepest part of Barnacre Cutting, and about half a dozen yards from the present railway fence. A small mound and a few scattered gray stones, intermingled with brackens, thistles, creeping plants, &c., and overhung with tree branches densely frondent, now occupy the site of the hut. Of course, the trees which at present constitute the wood are not those that formed it when Ambrose paid his

SITE OF THE AMBROSE HUT.

annual visits: the timber has been cut down several times since then, but replanting has always followed. Smith, the Duke of Hamilton's gamekeeper, must, on account of his position, have had a particularly good knowledge of this wood, and he may have found some remnant of structural material, or noticed some peculiarity in the surface of the ground, pointing to or indicating the locale of the original hut; he was, at any rate, so convinced of the genuineness of the site he selected, or of the soundness of the evidence he possessed in its favour, that he had no hesitation in building on it his Ambrose "memorial." The Ordnance Map issued in 1849 shows a small oblong mark at the very spot now covered by the mound; but it does not give any explanation of the mark.

About a mile and a half S.E. of Woodacre Hall there is Barnacre Lodge. It is located in a well-wooded district, abounding in game. The approach to it is up an umbrageous, picturesque gill or small glen. The building is serenely embosomed in trees; its roofs and gables of deep ruddy hue are very conspicuous from numerous parts away down south-west; but in the immediate neighbourhood, near the head of the carriage drive, a high, tree-studded bank in front cuts them off from view, and not until one gets to the summit of this bank by a winding, curiously rustic pathway, which goes up the breast of it, or by the drive which passes round the higher end of it, can the general body of the building be seen. The site of the Lodge is 300 feet above the level of the sea. From the west side there is a very fine view of the Fylde country, Morecambe Bay, &c., whilst from the higher windows of the Lodge, and especially from the surmounting "lantern," there is a most extensive and charming outlook in almost every direction. The original drawing of this building was on view at the Royal Academy in 1877. The design was noted with interest by architects, particularly on account of its involving a revival of the half-timbered style which was so much in vogue during the Elizabethan period. The external panels of the building are of bordered cement, ornamented with incised floral work. The hall roof is very choicely panelled and ornamented. The stairway is in the Elizabethan style, and on the nowels are grotesque figures for lamp-supporting purposes. Generally, the building is fitted up with the most improved and suitable requisites. Excellent stables, harness rooms, and a coachhouse are in proximity. Mr. T. H. Myres, of Preston, designed the Lodge, &c., and superintended the building thereof. The total cost of the work was about £10,000. Barnacre Lodge was built by the late Earl of Bective as a shooting-box. It was commenced in 1875, and completed in 1878. The late Earl was the eldest son of the third Marquess of Headfort, by the marriage of that nobleman with Amelia, the only child of Alderman Thompson, of Underley Hall, near Kirkby Lonsdale. In 1853, when the North Lancashire property of the Duke of Hamilton was sold, Alderman Thompson purchased the Barnacre portion of it. In 1867, the Earl of Bective (then Lord Kenlis) married Lady Alice Maria, only daughter of the fourth Marquess of Downshire. His princi-

BARNACRE LODGE.

pal residence was Underley Hall. He took very considerable interest in agricultural affairs, was a noted owner and breeder of Shorthorns, earned the respect and goodwill of his tenantry by the kindly regard he showed for their general welfare, was a promoter of the allotment system—in fact was one of the first landowners in the country who personally supported it—and appropriated part of an estate, which he owned, near Kendal, for allotment purposes. In his younger days he associated himself with the Volunteer movement, and became an officer of the Westmorland Rifle Volunteers. He was also connected with the Yeomanry Cavalry of the county. In 1868 he was High Sheriff of Westmorland. When his father, who was M.P. for Westmorland from 1854 to 1870, was raised to the peerage, he succeeded him in the representation of that county: he was member for it till 1885, in which year, through a reconstitution of electoral areas, he was returned to Parliament for the Kendal Division, which he continued to represent till 1892, when failing health necessitated his resignation of the seat. In 1893 he died, at Underley Hall. The surviving issue of his marriage is a daughter (Olivia Caroline Amelia): so that from the foregoing it will be noticed—and this is, indeed, singular—that the late Lord Bective was the son of an only daughter, the husband of an only daughter, and the father of an only surviving daughter. In 1892 his daughter married Lord Henry Cavendish Bentinck. For seven years after the Earl's death, the Countess of Bective, his widow, principally resided at Barnacre Lodge. She is a lady of broad and generous sympathies. Whilst living at Underley Hall she took part in numerous movements for the progress and welfare of the people of Westmorland. But her activities for good were not limited

to that county. In the eighties, she very ably and energetically helped forward a plan for securing a fuller use of English-made materials for ladies' wear, which was to a large extent for the benefit of certain depressed places in Yorkshire—Bradford especially. Subsequently she evinced a warm regard for many local and district movements, notably in North Lancashire, of a practical and beneficent character. To the extent of her opportunities and ability she continues to pay attention to matters of this kind, whilst in the wider and more general spheres of philanthropy and social reform she takes a very commendable part. In the summer of 1899, Barnacre estate, along with Barnacre Lodge, was sold to Mr. Thomas Rushton, of Bolton, and he has since mainly resided at the Lodge. About the same time as the Barnacre property was disposed of, the Countess of Bective purchased Lunefield, near Underley Hall, and this is now her country residence. For many years the agency of the Barnacre property has been in the hands of Messrs. J. W. Fair and Rea, of Preston, and they still hold it.

Half a mile south-west of Barnacre Lodge, in a quiet hollow, there is "The Spa Well." This well (most copiously supplied with very clear water, which springs from the base of an adjoining hill, and is believed to possess medicinal properties) is square in form, and is enclosed by a plain, strong wall, with inward steps, at one corner, going down to the water. Originally, the front wall appears to have been surmounted by a rail, for a screen—there is a rail socket at each end of the wall. Tradition says that members of the Hamilton family, when residing at Woodacre Hall, used to bathe in this well, the inner walls of which have now in some parts fallen into the water. A short distance from and opposite the well there is a cottage which has in front of it a stone bearing the

SPA WELL, BARNACRE.

initials and date " I. H., 1753." The cottage stands on land which for many years, up to 1853, belonged to the Hamiltons; the date given relates, of course, to the year in which it was erected; and the initials no doubt refer to the then existing head of the Hamilton family—James, the 6th Duke—who succeeded to the dukedom in 1742. Ten years later his Grace indulged in a curious marriage ceremony. At half-past 12 o'clock at night, on February 14th, 1752, he married, at Mayfair Chapel, a famous beauty—Miss Elizabeth Gunning—with, according to Horace Walpole, " a ring of the bed curtain." There were children by the marriage, and one of them (a daughter named Elizabeth) married Edward, the 12th Earl of Derby —great grandfather of the present Lord Derby. The Duke of Hamilton referred to died in 1758.

Just past a bend in the highway, a few hundred yards north of the Cabus boundary stone, there is a house with a very broad, low gable facing the road. There was formerly a toll bar here—the bar previously named—and the gatekeeper lived at this house. Extending on the western side, for about a mile and a half, chiefly parallel to the highway, there are many fields, the bulk laid out in a very systematic manner, and in a good state of cultivation. Some of the fields are square, others are oblong, and all have excellent thorn fences. On the opposite side of the highway, and in line with it for a somewhat similar distance, though not, in their entirety, so effectively cultivated, there are fields shaped and fenced in the same style. The whole of the fields at one time belonged to the Duke of Hamilton; and the work of planning, superintending, and executing the work essential to their improvement, in respect to size, drainage, fencing, &c., was done by men chiefly brought from Scotland by his Grace. The fine, full, thorn fences here show that the land which forms the fields directly adjoining is of superior quality, and that there has been proper husbandry in connection with it. Good fences are not found in connection with poor soil and bad farming: defective agricultural methods and inferior land do not encourage their growth. I am acquainted with a North Lancashire gentleman who not long ago bought an estate in the Midlands: the land constituting it is good, and one thing which particularly tended to convince him of its excellence was the appearance of the thorn fences—they were full and strong. Something like a quarter of a mile past the old toll-gate house, in Cabus, Gubberford-lane branches off the highroad. This lane, which goes to Scorton, &c., crosses the river Wyre, by a very good stone bridge, at a point where there used to be a ford—it was called Gubberford. The bridge, which takes this name, was completed in 1848; the cost of it being defrayed by the Duke of Hamilton and Mr. J. Keppel, the latter being at that time the lord of the manor of Garstang. A branch from the lane, just over the bridge, on the south-east side, leads to Woodacre Hall.

At a point on the highway, a short distance beyond Gubberford-lane, there are visible, on the west side, the spired tower, gables, and chimneys of Winmarleigh House: they rise above a dark mass of trees, and give a picturesque relief to the landscape. The House is about a mile and a quarter—in a straight line—from the main road. Winmarleigh is a very old township. It is supposed that a portion of it was granted, in the 13th century, to Cockersand Abbey. The Gentyll or Gentill family appear to have had property in Winmarleigh during the first half of the 14th century. Some time afterwards, Roger de Wynmerlegh owned half of the manor; and by marriage the property next passed to the Rowalls and the Radcliffes. For a considerable number of years the old Manor House, in Winmarleigh, was the residence of the Radcliffes. In 1561, on the death of William Radcliffe, who had no children, the manor went to his sister Ann, wife of Sir Gilbert Gerard who was successively Attorney-General and Master of the Rolls. The Winmarleigh property was held by male members of the Gerard family until the latter half of the 17th century, when it passed to the Hon. Elizabeth Gerard (daughter of Dutton Lord Gerard), who married William, son of the second Baron Spencer, who about this time was residing at Ashton Hall. near Lancaster. Elizabeth, granddaughter of the Hon. William and Elizabeth Spencer, married Robert Hesketh, of Rufford, whose sole daughter and heiress was, in 1714, married to Sir Edward Stanley, afterwards the 11th Earl of Derby. In 1743, the Spencer property in Winmarleigh was sold, in order to "pay off Lady Derby's portion"; the purchaser being Thomas Patten, whose descendant, John Wilson Patten (ultimately Lord Winmarleigh), became its owner, and held it—in fact the township of Winmarleigh generally—up to the time of his death. After the decease of William Radcliffe, in 1561, the manorial residence in Winmarleigh was occupied as a farm house, and it continued to be so occupied until the latter part of the 18th century, when it was pulled down. This Manor House stood in the neighbourhood of the present mansion—adjoining the entrance to the grounds, at the side of the road which passes there. On the site of the Manor

WINMARLEIGH HOUSE.

House another building was erected, and it is used in connection with the "home farm." Formerly, Lord Winmarleigh (when he was Colonel Wilson Patten, M.P. for North Lancashire) was in the habit of going every year to Winmarleigh, and spending a few months there in shooting, &c.; but at that time the thought of building a residence for himself in Winmarleigh had never been seriously entertained by him, if, indeed, it had ever struck him at all. Eventually, when Bank Hall, Warrington, his regular residence, became less select, or more closely surrounded by miscellaneous buildings (it is now utilised as the Town Hall of Warrington) he decided to erect the present Winmarleigh House, which was built in 1871. It is a large, substantial structure, formed of red brick and freestone; the style of its architecture being Elizabethan domestic. A church, neat and pleasing in appearance, stands a short distance from the House: it was consecrated in 1876, and its cost (£2,000) was wholly defrayed by Lord Winmarleigh. In 1887, a north aisle was added, and the cost of this, too, was defrayed by Lord Winmarleigh: his Lordship built this aisle as a memorial of the Queen's Jubilee. Winmarleigh School and teacher's house were completed in 1870; the money required for the same being provided by Lord Winmarleigh. The Rev. T. B. Armitstead is the present Vicar of Winmarleigh. From August 5th, 1830, to April 23rd, 1831, Lord Winmarleigh (then Mr. John Wilson Patten) along with Lord Stanley (afterwards Lord Derby—father of the present Earl) represented in Parliament the whole County of Lancaster. From 1832 to 1874 he was one of the members for North Lancashire; and on the 16th of March in the latter year he was created a peer. His son and heir, Eustace John Wilson Patten, died in 1873; and John Alfred, son of Eustace John, and the only grandson and heir of his lordship, died

in 1889, and was interred at Winmarleigh Church. Lord Winmarleigh died at Winmarleigh Hall on July 11th, 1892, in the 91st year of his age, was interred in the Patten vault, in Warrington Parish Churchyard, and left as his only successors two daughters and two granddaughters. On Winmarleigh Moss, about a mile and a half west of the House, there is a place to which seagulls resort in remarkable numbers during the breeding season. They gather here in thousands, lay eggs amid the grass in all directions, and when the hatching has taken place the ground swarms with young gulls, whilst the air immediately overhead suddenly becomes thick with flapping and screaming old ones, when visiting parties appear on the scene. The eggs and subsequently the young gulls—indeed, the whole of the birds, young and old— are protected by one or more keepers connected with the Winmarleigh estate. The best time to see the gullery is towards the end of May. Up to about 1844 a great number of sea-gulls used to assemble annually on Walney Island, near Barrow; but through some cause they were disturbed, whereupon they crossed Morecambe Bay, eventually assembling in an enclosure about a mile and a half south-west of Pilling village; and, yearly, gulls congregated in that enclosure till about 1877, when, through either disturbance or preference, they migrated to Winmarleigh Moss, where every year since then has been a great gathering of them in the breeding season. At "The Island," in Winmarleigh, about three-quarters of a mile south-east of the gull moss, there is and has been for years one of the most extensive entire horse establishments in the country. For a long time coursing meetings have been held in Winmarleigh; but the first gathering of this kind, between Preston and Lancaster, to which I have met with any reference, did not take place at Winmarleigh. There was a coursing meeting at Cockerham on the 4th of November, 1832; a like meeting took place in Barnacre on the 19th of December in the same year; and there was one at the Old Holly, in Cabus, in January, 1833. The first Winmarleigh coursing meeting of which I have found any record was held on November 19th, 1835; and with few exceptions there has been a meeting here, yearly, ever since—occasionally, but not very recently, two within twelve months. Mr. Patten (afterwards Lord Winmarleigh) and Mr. Hinde not infrequently figure in the reports as runners of dogs, &c., at the Winmarleigh meetings; but those whose names are oftenest met with in the early records are Mr. William Lamb, then of Hay Carr, Ellel, and Mr. E. G. Hornby, of Ellel Hall. In Winmarleigh there are a good many hares; they are fine ones; and for a great number of years such animals have found quarters in this district. Tyldesley, the diarist, says, under date October 2nd, 1712:—"Meet Bro: ffrost att Winmarley: killed 2 hares."

Soon after the point has been passed whence a partial view of Winmarleigh House is obtained, the main road winds over a slight eminence called Fowler's Hill. At the west side of the road on this hill, and near the junction of a lane which runs down into Winmarleigh, there is a small, white-washed cottage. At one corner of it, and fixed pretty high in the wall, there is a small triangular iron frame; and to the great majority of persons the cottage and the frame amount to a sort of mystery. Some probably think that the little building must originally have been a shop; others that it was, perhaps, at one time a beerhouse; and so forth. The fact is, it was used as a toll-bar house before the one previously named—that nearer Garstang—was erected, and the iron frame at the corner contained a lamp, which when lighted at night time showed persons in charge of vehicles the gate and enabled the keeper of it to do his work expeditiously. The bar at Fowler's Hill was done away with about 1840.

excellent stone front, containing in one part a large representation, in carved stone, of the arms and crest of the Hamilton family. The earliest reference to this public-house which I have seen is in the diary of Thomas Tyldesley, of Myerscough Lodge. Under date June 15th, 1713, Tyldesley makes mention of a hunt, which lasted two hours, after a "martran" (marten) found in Scorton Park, and says that after it had been killed "12 of us went to ye Old Hollings," and there "spent 3d. each." On the 1st of October, in the same year, he records the fact that he "spent at Old Hollins 6d." And on the 28th of April, in the following year, he states that he called at "the Hollins," where "Mr. Walker, Mr. Rigby, and the tenants were keeping a courtt." For generations—from "time immemorial"—a Court Leet for Nether Wyresdale has been held in Cabus, and doubtless the "courtt" referred to by Tyldesley was this Leet one. An agricultural show—one of the best in the North of England—used to be annually held on some land connected with and adjoining the Old Holly Inn. It was under the auspices of the "Ashton (near Lancaster) Agricultural Society." A great quantity of the property—chiefly farms—between the Lune and the Calder was at this time owned by the Duke of Hamilton, who had a residence in Ashton (Ashton Hall): the agricultural society was established by the Duke (through his agent, Mr. William Lamb, of Hay Carr, Ellel), for the benefit of his tenants; and the Old Holly was a good centre for them—hence the annual shows in this quarter. The first of these shows was held on the 17th of October, 1838 (in which year an important ploughing club was established here, under similar auspices, and for the same tenantry, and it flourished for a considerable time). The agricultural shows were continued yearly until the sale of the Hamilton property, in Lancashire, in 1853. After each show there was a dinner, at the Old Holly, in the large room at the north end —a room exceptionally spacious for a country inn,

OLD HOLLY INN.

A little over a mile north of Fowler's Hill there is a well-known inn at the side of the highroad. This is the Hamilton Arms, commonly called the Old Holly or Old Hollins; and it is a very large inn—the largest, in fact, between Preston and Lancaster. It has an

and no doubt specially made to accommodate the large number of persons who met for dining and post-prandial purposes on such occasions. Usually one of the principal gentlemen in North Lancashire occupied the chair at the dinner. In a list which I have

seen, the following appear amongst the chairmen:—
John Cunliffe, Myerscough House; R. W. France,
Rawcliffe Hall; W. J. Garnett, Bleasdale Tower; G.
Jacson, Barton Lodge; T. Greene, M.P. for Lancaster; J. Wilson Patten, M.P. for North Lancashire;
Pudsey Dawson, Hornby Castle; J. Talbot Clifton,
Lytham Hall; C. R. Jacson, Barton, &c. At the
dinner, and during the after proceedings, wine used
to flow freely; and especially by the reporters—a very
thirsty tribe in those old clay-moistening days—was
it patronised. From a veteran press-man, who
occasionally attended this Old Holly agricultural
symposium, I learn that the majority of the reporters
not only took a full note of the proceedings, but got
full personally; that they considered nothing less
than a couple of bottles of wine their fair individual
share; that some of them evinced a capacity for even
more; and that on one occasion a reporter, after
leaving the Old Holly, had rambled up and down, or
tumbled about so vigorously and peculiarly, that he
ultimately lost his note book, which was found,
several days afterwards, in the canal, at Glasson
Dock! Owing to its position and the accommodation it afforded, magisterial and other meetings in
connection with North Lancashire matters were occasionally held at the Old Holly. The stone-cut
Hamilton arms and crest in front of the building are
of the full relief kind, and are very beautifully finished.
Particularly well carved and equally conspicuous are
the armorial "supporters"—two antelopes, which, in
the lingo of heraldry, are "arg., armed, ducally
gorged, chained, and hoofed." The horns now on the
heads of the supporting antelopes are not those which
they had in the first instance. In 1858 a tall, finely-
built young man (Mr. James Hardcastle), son of Mr.
J. Hardcastle, banker, of Bolton, became through
some cause mentally deranged, and for the sake of
improving his health he was removed to Cabus;
rooms for his accommodation being taken at the Old
Holly. Whilst here, and during a very serious fit of
aberration he got out of one of the upper front windows, jumped on to the porch, and then began to at-
tack the armorial carved work, apparently with the
object of demolishing it. But, as soon as he had
broken or torn off the antelopes' horns, someone happened to spy him, and he was promptly secured, and
taken inside the inn. Afterwards he was removed to
Bowers House, Nateby, and before long a very sad
affair occurred. He one night, in the early part of
August, 1858, eluded the men in charge of him. Next
morning a search for him was commenced, and eventually his dead body was found in a water pit, on the
low road side near Nateby House. And, strange to
say, a wheelbarrow was found at the same time, by
the side of the same pit. The young gentleman who
came to this sad end was only in the 20th year of his
age. The Hamilton Arms Inn (Old Holly) is now a
favourite baiting place, and in summer-time numerous
pic-nic parties halt at it for tea or the stronger sort
of " refreshments." The main road, up to the time
when it was improved, about 1824, used to pass on
the west side of, and quite close to, the Old Holly;
the present back of the inn being then the front. Immediately north and south of the inn the old way took
the course of the existing road.

CHAPTER XIV.

Past the Old Holly, a very short distance northward, and on the right hand side, there is a lane which leads to the village of Scorton—about a mile distant. Scorton is in Nether Wyresdale—at the very base of that township. Its name signifies an enclosure (A.S. ton) at or near a score (A.S. scor), or mark, or long incision. Scar, in respect to incisional marking, is a sort of equivalent of Scor; but it refers more to rocks or cliffs than to moorland, like that adjoining Scorton; and the presumption is that the Scor which here forms part of the name has been derived from the long, slanting rores or certain marks in the hills, at the rear of the village. Though it bears an Anglo-Saxon name, Scorton is not a particularly old place. It is not mentioned in the Doomsday survey, and the earliest reference to it which I have seen does not go further back than 1587. The village of Scorton is a neat, picturesque-looking little place, the generality of the buildings in it being cottages—serene, whitewashed, and with bright little patches of flowers in front of them. Scorton has been designated a "model village": it is without either a resident lawyer, or doctor, or policeman, and it does not contain any drinking place—has neither a public-house nor a beershop within its boundaries. About 1830 a beershop was opened in the village, but it was given up—closed—in about two years afterwards. Either the Duke of Hamilton (when he owned Scorton) or his agent determined that there should be no place in the village whereat intoxicating drink could be obtained; and this prohibition has prevailed here ever since. But the restriction does not preclude the importation of bottles, or hampers, or cases from Preston, Garstang, Lancaster, or anywhere else; there are also three public-houses—the "Holly" trio—not such a great way off, and it is conjectured that the majority of adult Scortonians are not absolutely aquatic in their liquid procedure, and would not send for a policeman to take you up were you to show them, in a neat, quiet way, a bottle of "special Scotch"—unless, perhaps, you put it into your pocket again with the cork undrawn. In 1793 a school was built, by subscription, at the east side of the village, on a site given by the Duke of Hamilton. The building is still standing, and there may now be seen in front of it a stone tablet, bearing an inscription, which records the two facts just named, and in addition declares that "the appointment of a master is invested in his lordship and his lordship's heirs for ever."

But another school has supplanted this, which has been turned into a private house, and the power of appointing a master now rests with persons quite unconnected with Hamiltonian heirs. The North Lancashire possessions of the Duke of Hamilton embraced the great bulk of the property in Nether Wyresdale (the village of Scorton included), and very much, if not the whole, of that in three or four adjoining townships; and when it was sold, through some embarrassment in the financial circumstances of his Grace, in 1853, Mr. Peter Ormrod, then of Halliwell Hall, near Bolton, was a very extensive purchaser. I may here observe, parenthetically, that Mr. Ormrod was a descendant of the Ormrods of "The Hill Farm," Harwood. In his younger days he was connected with the cotton works of his father, in Bolton; afterwards for many years he was the head of the banking firm of Hardcastle, Cross, and Company, of Bolton; and, though deemed by not a few to be a somewhat unsympathetic, mundanely-minded gentleman, he was at bottom kind-hearted and generous: he was considerate towards the sick and the poor, and he built Bolton Parish Church at a cost of many thousands of pounds. Estimates I have seen as to the church in question specify the sum he spent upon it very variedly—from £30,000 to £60,000. At the sale of the Hamilton property Mr. Ormrod bought 4,027 acres in Nether Wyresdale for £110,500, 693 acres in Cleveley for £39,100, 1,359 acres in Cabus for £54,100, and, had it not been for some strong competition on the part of Alderman Thompson, of Underley Hall, near Kirkby Lonsdale, the Barnacre estate, which formed part of the Hamilton property, would likewise have been purchased by Mr. Ormrod for £84,000. It is said that, after purchasing the property mentioned, Mr. Ormrod spent about £50,000 in improving the Nether Wyresdale portion of it—especially on the south-eastern side. The wood-surrounded residence, on an eminence north-east of Scorton village—a very substantial, stately-looking structure, surmounted by a tower, and bearing the name of Wyresdale Park—was built by Mr. Ormrod. It was commenced in 1856; afterwards the design of it underwent, in one or more parts, some change involving an enlargement of the structure; and the place was not completed until 1865. All the adjoining shrubs and trees were planted by Mr. Ormrod. The land connected with the mansion and the home

74

SCORTON.

farm is about 300 acres in area. At the north end of Scorton there used to be a cotton mill. It was erected at the beginning of or very early in the present century for the purpose of spinning and weaving cotton by water power, and was, it is said, the first cotton mill of the compound sort, with a motor obviating hand and foot operations of the old kind, built in Lancashire. Scorton mill was not a financial success to the gentleman who built it, and through this the property passed to Mr. Webster Fishwick, of Burnley, whose son George eventually became the owner of it—this would, I believe, be about 1824—and lived at Scorton for many years up to the time of his death, in 1854. When Mr. Ormrod became the owner of the mill, he carried on certain work associated with the production of yarns, and mainly for the purpose of finding employment for a number of persons living in the village. The machinery required was supplied from mills which Mr. Ormrod was connected with at Bolton, and doublers were sent by him, from that town, to Scorton, in order to give the villagers the necessary instructions for efficiently working it. Mr. Ormrod alternately resided at Halliwell Hall and Wyresdale Park. When he purchased the Hamilton property named, there were two places of worship in Scorton village—a small Roman Catholic Chapel, the successor of an old, thatched, primitive-looking building, and a Wesleyan Methodist Chapel, at the south end, built in 1842—the site of the latter being given by the Duke of Hamilton, whilst the cost of the building was defrayed solely by Mr. Geo. Fishwick, when he was the master of the factory. (Shireshead Church, in Cleveley, was the place of worship attended by the " Establishment " people of the locality in those days.) In 1861 a new Roman Catholic Chapel was built at Scorton ; the small building which it superseded being afterwards utilised for educational purposes, and it is still so used, essential improvements having in the meantime been adopted to keep up its tuitional effectiveness. In 1878-79 the neat, picturesquely-situated church, of the Episcopal order, at the south end of the village, was erected,

the cost of it—about £13,000—being defrayed by Mr. James Ormrod, of Halliwell Lodge, near Bolton, brother of Mr. Peter Ormrod. The vicar of Scorton Church is the Rev. A. T. Davidson. Near the Church there is a pleasant vicarage, and contiguous is a good, modernly-built school. Scorton Hall is at the north end of the village : it is a plain, ordinary-looking structure, and is supposed to have been erected early in the 17th century. Mr. Peter Ormrod died at Wyresdale Park on the 17th of May, 1875, in the 80th year of his age, and was interred in the graveyard attached to Garstang (Churchtown) Parish Church. The remains of Mr. Ormrod were removed —with the sanction of the Home Secretary, of course —from Churchtown, and interred in the yard connected with Scorton Church, soon after its consecration, in 1879. Mrs. Ormrod, his widow, was a daughter of Mr. Thomas Hardcastle, a well-known bleacher, and one of the founders of the banking firm of Hardcastle, Cross, and Co., of Bolton, whose establishment was afterwards incorporated with and became the Bolton branch of the Manchester and Salford Bank : she resided at Wyresdale Park after Mr. Ormrod's decease and up to the time of her own death, which took place when she was 84 years of age, on the 1st of June, 1890. Her remains were interred in Scorton Churchyard. Colonel Cross Ormrod (nephew of Mr. Peter Ormrod) succeeded to the property in Wyresdale, &c., and took up his residence at Wyresdale Park. The greater portion of Scorton cotton factory, which as a working concern received its quietus soon after Mr. Peter Ormrod died, was pulled down by Colonel Cross Ormrod : there now remains only the bottom storey (originally the factory was three storeys high), and it is used as a joiner's shop. Colonel Cross Ormrod resided at Wyresdale Park up to the time of his death, which took place on June 12th, 1895. His son (Captain Peter Ormrod) afterwards inherited the property, and he resides at Wyresdale Park. In fish hatching Captain Ormrod takes great interest. In 1894 he purchased the hatchery which was for some time in operation at Halton, near Lancaster, and transferred it to a specially prepared place in Nether Wyresdale;

its location being on a good stream near the base of Hayshaw and Harrisend Fells, not far from the Wyresdale road, and about two and a half miles north-east of Scorton village. Since the transfer, numerous extensions and improvements have been made; the hatchery is now about the largest and best in the country; and from it are sent fishes of various kinds—salmon, trout, &c.—to many parts of the United Kingdom, whilst some are despatched to places on the Continent. The hatchery, after being run for a while by Captain Ormrod solely, became limited company property, the shareholders being the Captain and certain of his relatives. There is a large and excellent extension or branch of the Wyresdale hatchery in Cleveley, contiguous to what was a corn mill, and the water here used runs direct from the Wyre. The old corn mill is now, after much alteration, utilised for business purposes in connection with the hatchery. In 1900 the Company placed 7,000 yearling rainbow trout in the tributaries of the River Wyre. Captain Ormrod has also turned his attention to deer-keeping. In May, 1899, the large herd of fallow deer which belonged to the late Sir Frederick Milbank, of Barningham Park, near Barnard Castle, was purchased by Captain Ormrod, brought to Scorton, and turned out upon some land connected with Wyresdale Park. It is said that this herd is one of the finest in the North of England. Captain Ormrod has likewise an excellent pack of staghounds. The opening day of the hunt was Wednesday, November 8th, 1899. Harriers, for hare-hunting, are, in addition, kept by Captain Ormrod.

In the locality of the fish-hatchery before mentioned—indeed, close to it, at the junction of the road which comes over the high moorland southeastward and slants down Harrisend Fell to the base—there is a small building known as Cross Hill School. About 200 yards past the school, north-east, the Wyresdale road goes over a small hill, on the summit of which there is the stone base of an old cross. This base stands on one side of the road. The elevated ground here would, no doubt, at one time—when the cross was up—be known as Cross Hill; this is its present name; and proximity to the Hill clearly accounts for the name of the old school The original foundation of Cross Hill School dates back as far as 1487. Early last century—in 1717—Robert Browne willed £20 for teaching and catechising "at Cross Hill School"; and four years later Richard Browne devised the interest of £30 on behalf of the same objects. Owing to the dilapidated state which the school had got into, it was rebuilt, by subscription, about 1816; and a little while afterwards the master was here provided with house accommodation and a garden. Some years ago school teaching at this place was given up. The road which crosses the neighbouring hill, south-eastward, is a portion of the old way from Clitheroe to Cockersand Abbey.

A little to the west of Scorton Church, and between the ordinary road and the railway, there is an old May pole. It stands in a field which fronts a substantial house called Springfield. About five and forty years ago, whilst passing Scorton by train, I first noticed this pole. At that time there was a circular shaped frame, almost like a large, wide-barred cage, at the top of it—this, which would revolve, was for the attachment of light ropes or ribbons, reaching almost to the ground, for dancers to take hold of; and, altogether, the pole seemed to be then in good order. But, with the lapse of years, the surmounting frame has gone, and the pole now appears to be in a poor, decaying condition. Springfield was, I believe, built by—it certainly was the residence of—Mr. George Fishwick. Since his death it has been successively occupied by Mr. Hopwood, who came from East Lancashire, and worked Scorton mill for a time; by Colonel Archer, son-in-law of Mr. James Ormrod; Mr. Tyrrell; Mr. (now Alderman) James Burrow, of Preston, from 1875 to 1880; Mr. George Dickson, solicitor, Preston, from 1880 to 1885; and Mr. John Noble, clerk to the Garstang Union, &c., from 1885 to the time of his death, on the 20th of February, 1899. Mr Noble's family at present occupy the place.

The attractive, antiquely-designed red-brick building on the side of the hill, about a quarter of a mile south-east of Scorton Church, is Ghyllwood Lodge. This residence was erected about 1890, by the late Colonel Cross-Ormrod, for his estate agent, Mr. Bailey, who lived at it up to the time of the Colonel's death, in 1895. Towards the end of 1896, Mr. Titus Thorpe, of Preston, became the tenant of this Lodge, and he still resides here. From the front of it a beautiful view is commanded of the western waters—sea and bay, and several of the Lake mountains, &c.

The small, tower-like elevation, on the summit of the hill at the rear or east side of Scorton village, is a pile of stones, put up in 1887, in commemoration of the Queen's Jubilee. There was a large bonfire here on the Jubilee night, and it was visible for many miles. Though the altitude of the hill, at the point where the stones are piled up, is not very great—615 feet above the sea level—a very extensive and delightful view can be obtained from the summit on a clear day: the range of the view, north to south, extends from the Lake mountains to Rivington Pike, near Horwich; in front, the entire of the Fylde country and the lower region of South Lonsdale Hundred spread out fully, level and many-coloured, like an immense mosaic, with Morecambe Bay and the Lune on one side, and the estuaries of the Ribble and the Mersey on the other; whilst away, beyond, there are the waters of the Irish Sea, and occasionally there is visible—when the atmosphere is very clear—the lonely outlines of the Isle of Man. "Nicky Nook" is immediately behind the hill on the east side of Scorton. To this region many pleasure parties resort in summer time. Towards the north-east end of the hill there is a small gull moss.

Near the side of the highway, about a third of a mile north of the "Old Holly," in Cabus, there is another, though considerably smaller, public-house called the "Middle Holly." A triangular piece of land fronts it, and here there is a good specimen of

MIDDLE HOLLY.

the road-altering system which was carried out in the early portion of the present century, and of the improvement effected by it. On the west side there is an old road; on the opposite side there runs the highway which superseded it—broad and smooth, with a gentle ascent for some distance, then dropping a little, but perfectly straight as well as uniform in width for nearly a mile, and with a parallel footway on the eastern edge. The old road looks like a country lane: it passes close to the "Middle Holly," is steep and tortuous, winds up and round to the north-east, crossing the newer way—the broad, straight length mentioned—then going into or forming what is known as Hollins-lane, and afterwards proceeding northward. Opposite, and a few hundred yards west of the part where the old road crosses the highway, there stands at the head of an oblong, tree-flanked field, a residence, known as Forton Lodge—a pretty large, substantial building, with a somewhat peculiar roof centred by a massive chimney block. Mr. Wiliam Brade, a Liverpool gentleman, built Forton Lodge, probably soon after 1801. He purchased the land for its site, as well as that for the garden, &c., at the rear, in 1801, from Mr. Thomas Feckener (spelt Faulkner some time afterwards, and associated, no doubt, with the present Faulkner's Fold and Faulkner's-lane, which are a little to the west of Forton Lodge); whilst the oblong, tree-flanked field in front he subsequently bought from Mr. Edward Crossfield. In the last decade of the 18th century, when the canal—the length between Preston and Tewit Field, near Burton-in-Kendal—was being made, there resided in Faulkner's Fold, a labouring man named Thomas Hall. And if he had been called a pedestrian as well as a labourer, the definition would have been quite accurate. During the construction of the canal aqueduct which crosses the Lune, above Lancaster, this Hall, while continuing his tenancy in Faulkner's Fold, was employed at the bridge as a

labourer; and each working day, from the commencement of the aqueduct till its completion, in 1797, he walked there and back, and did a full day's work as well: in other words, he walked about 18 miles and laboured ten hours every working day for about four years! And his wage would, perhaps, be 15s. per week—probably less! What Hall did in his con-

nection with other jobs I have not ascertained; but the performance just named would, I should say, form a "record" of its kind which has not since been broken in any part of the country. William Brade, who built Forton Lodge, was, I believe, a successful merchant or man of business, in Liverpool; and it has been conjectured that he built Forton Lodge as a summer residence. He may have had such a

FORTON LODGE.

residence in his mind when he erected this Lodge; but the presumption is that old family associations with the district very considerably influenced him in selecting a site in Forton. The name of Brade or Braide was in old times a by no means uncommon one in this locality, and in contiguous parts too; it was to be met with in Forton, Holleth, Cockerham (especially), and Pilling. The Bursar's rent roll of Cockersand Abbey, for the year 1501, includes, in the Forton section, the name "Ric. Brade." Amongst the Lancashire wills proved within the archdeaconry of Richmond in 1665, and now at Somerset House, there is one of William Brade, of Forton; and amongst those from Lancashire, proved within the same archdeaconry, in 1763, and at present in the Probate Office, Lancaster, is the will of William Brade, ycoman, Forton. In all probability these persons were ancestors of William Brade, who built Forton Lodge. By will dated February 20th, 1818, William Brade devised the Lodge to his daughter Isabella, of Liverpool. After her death, James Brade, of London, a descendant, held Forton Lodge. In 1852 he sold it to Mr. Preston Kelsall, of Lancaster, from whom it was purchased by the trustees of Mr. Robert Rawcliffe, and it is still in their hands. Mr. Thomas Paget occupied Forton Lodge from about 1825 to 1843, if not a little longer. He died here, leaving a widow and three daughters. On the death of the widow, Miss Paget became the tenant. In September, 1857, her sister, Miss Letitia Paget, whilst accompanying home a lady friend, who had been on a visit to the Lodge, was killed in a railway collision, in the South of England. She was 42 years years of age. Her remains were brought back to Forton, and interred in the south-east corner of old Shireshead Churchyard. Miss Paget, her sister, lived at Forton Lodge for some time after this sad event, and then went to Greenfield, Lancaster, where she resided till her death, in 1893. She was 90 years old at the time of her decease, and was interred in Shireshead Churchyard—in the grave containing the remains of her sister Letitia. When Miss Paget left Forton, Mr. Roger Bowling went to live at the Lodge for a time; Mr. Winder followed him as tenant, and resided here for about 20 years; the late Colonel Cross Ormrod occupied this place from about 1885 till the death of his aunt (Mrs. Ormrod, of Wyresdale Park), in 1890; then, after being empty for a while, the Lodge was taken by Mr. W. G. Welch, sharebroker, Lancaster, and occupied by him till the spring of 1899. The present tenant is Mr. Lloyd Evans, who is connected with the Agricultural Department of the Lancashire County Council. From the upper windows of this residence—especially those facing the west—some delightful views are commanded.

The first house on the right side of the highway, after passing the part crossed by the old road, in front of Forton Lodge, is an inn—the third of the "Holly" kind: it is called the "New Holly." The propinquity of this trio of "publics" is remarkable.

NEW HOLLY.

As country way-side inns, distinctly detached from any village or hamlet, they are probably in closer proximity than any other three houses of the like kind in the North of England—the distance which covers the lot is well within three-quarters of a mile; and it may be taken for granted that in nearness and close similarity of name they are unique. As an inn, the Middle Holly is—by name, certainly—the youngest of the trio.

Hollins-lane runs behind the New Holly Inn. Of course, Hollins is the plural of Hollin, i.e., holly. The Anglo-Saxon equivalent of holly is "holen," so that the parentage of hollin is obvious. There can be little if any doubt at all that the prevalence of the holly in Cabus and Forton prompted the names which the three inns bear. There are still visible, especially in Forton—in the fences of lanes, fields, &c.—numerous holly trees and bushes. The bark of the holly is a febrifuge: the berries are of an extremely purgative and emetic character. In old times holly branches were occasionally used in connection with religious processional displays.

CHAPTER XV.

FORTON—OLD OWNERS AND TENANTS—FORTON HALL—CURIOUS PRESENTMENT—NEW HOLLY ITEMS—HOLLINS LANE—WEAVING AND DRINKING—SHIRESHEAD CHURCH, OLD AND NEW—FORTON BANK—INDEPENDENT CHAPEL—BOARD SCHOOL.

Forton, whose name means a fore enclosure, or fenced-in place to the front, is a very ancient township. In Doomsday Book it is mentioned as Fortune, with a land area equal to about 100 acres. In the early part of the 12th century the whole of Forton belonged to Warin de Lancastre, who granted or rented half of it, for 111s. per annum, to Aldred, the son of Hugo. Afterwards Warin's son (Henry de Lancastre) and several other persons conveyed property in Forton to the Abbot of Cockersand Abbey; and towards the end of the 15th century nearly the entire of Forton belonged to the Abbot thereof. In the reign of Henry VIII., when the monasteries, &c., were broken up, Thomas Holt, who was knighted in Scotland, near the middle of the century in which the dissolution occurred, had the manor of Forton granted to him, and for many years—probably until about 1642—his descendants owned it. In 1643-44 Richard Newsham, John Fox, and James Clifton, of Forton, and John Corles, of Ellel, purchased the manor, and they afterwards sold to their tenants, in Forton, the particular portion of property which such tenants had respectively paid rent for. In Forton the property is now, so far as ownership goes, split up amongst numerous persons. Forton Hall, about three-quarters of a mile west of Forton Lodge, is a small, neat place.

FORTON HALL.

In the course of last century it went into the possession of Elizabeth Whitehead, of Claughton, who conveyed it to her younger son Thomas, and a descendent of his (Mr. Alexander Whitehead) now owns and occupies it. Forton is in two parishes—Cockerham and Garstang. In 1785 eighty acres of "Forton commons" land were enclosed under Act of Parliament authority. The whole of the land in the township is now enclosed, and the bulk of it is of the meadow and pasture kind.

A presentment made at Lancaster Assizes, in 1307, respecting a man charged with committing a murder in Forton, three years previously, shows the peculiar state of the law and of procedure at that time as to the criminal responsibility of drunkards. The presentment, which is contained in an Assize Roll, and was quoted some time ago by the "Law Journal," is as follows:—"Amundernesse. The jurors present that Thomas Le Porter, of Forton, killed Robert Le Porter at Forton, near Lancaster, in the 32nd year of the King that now is [Edward I.], and the said Thomas comes, and being asked how he wishes to acquit himself of the death aforesaid, defends the death and all felony, &c., and pleads that he is not guilty of the said death, and puts himself for good and ill on the county. The jurors upon their oath say that the aforesaid Thomas, in the year aforesaid, and long before, was at intervals lunatic and mad, and was a near neighbour in the said vill of Forton of the said Robert, of whose death he is charged; and it so happened that the said Thomas, on a certain night in the year aforesaid, at the invitation of the said Robert supped with the said R. in his house; and when they had suppered both one and the other became drunken with wine; and when they had sat and drunk long after supper, at length the said Thomas, so drunk as aforesaid, went away and went to his own house, and the said Robert pursued him, and caught him up to lead the said Thomas to his own house; and the said Thomas, being wholly drunk and in madness immediately running at him, became lunatic and furious, and in his madness (morbus lunaticus), arising alike from insanity and drunkenness, drew out his knife and pierced the said Robert, who was neither speaking nor talking with him, through the middle of the body, whereby he forthwith died. Wherefore the jurors say that the said Thomas slew the said Robert without malice or felony aforethought, but that lunacy, madness, and drunkenness led him to do this. Therefore he is remitted to gaol awaiting the King's pleasure."

Before the great road-improving movement set in, coaches and other vehicles going north or south ran through Hollins-lane, Forton. On one side of Hollins Hill, which is an open, slightly elevated part, towards the south end of this lane, there were stables for coach horses. The coaches used to be drawn up here whilst the horses were changed; and there was a public-house close by—it was called the "New Holly"—for the refreshment of passengers, &c. The building is still standing, but has been transformed into two cottages. Over one of the doorways there is a stone on which are the initials and date—"R.A.A. 1714." But, if this date refers to the time when the building was erected—and I suppose it does—then this structure was not the original "New Holly," and there must have been another inn, bearing the same name, here or somewhere not far off, prior to 1714. Under date, May 30th, 1712, Thomas Tyldesley, of Myerscough Lodge, has an entry in his diary which states that after dining with "Doctr Farington" (of Preston), at the house of "Bro Frost" (Walter Frost, of Cockerham Hall), he "went with him and Mr. Ion to ye New Hollings," and there "stayd

NEW HOLLY BUILDING, HOLLINS HILL.

an hour." In the same diary other references are made to the same public house, viz.: September 25th, 1712, "Spent att New Hollins, 2d." September 29th, 1712, "Stayd at New Hollings one hour and halfe; pd. pro mee and servant, 1s. 6d." Oct. 1st, 1713, "Spent at New Hollins, 1s." Oct. 14th, 1713, "To ye New Hollins; spent 2d on Ned Malley and selfe in nance" (brandy imported from Nantes, in France). August 8th, 1714, "Spent 1d. of Robert Walker, att New Hollins." The Rev. Peter Walkden, Nonconformist minister, who lived near Chipping, states in his diary that after conducting service at Forton Chapel, on Sunday, January 10th, 1725, he "called at the New Hollins, and being in a cold, and the day cold, I resolved to get a gill of hot ale; so told Brother Miller. He and John Gardner went in with me, and we got one pint among us, and paid pence apiece and came away."

About 1790 there was a linen-weaving place in Hollins-lane, the master of it being Mr. Matthew Hall, grandfather of Mr. Robert and Mr. Richard Hall, who now reside in Forton. The linen was produced by handlooms, and the weavers—men mainly, if not exclusively--could earn very good wages, and had a powerful regard for drink as well as a great idea of their own personal consequence. Every Monday and Tuesday, from morning to night, they were, as a rule, engaged in drinking at the New Holly, and yet their weaving was so remunerative that they could, in the other four working days of the week, earn about £4 each! They considered themselves quite a superior set, and would not drink in the company of local farmers, whom they looked down upon as a common class of persons.

The present high road west of Hollins-lane was made in 1822-24, and when opened it, of course, got the great bulk of the wheeled and pedestrian traffic—coaches, miscellaneous vehicles, people of all sorts on foot, &c., left the narrow, rough, and crooked old

way for the broad, smooth, and straight course; and in 1825, owing to this abandonment of Hollins-lane, the license of the New Holly on the Hill was transferred to the present building with the same name at the side of the highroad, and previously referred to—a building specially erected for the purposes of an inn. About midway in Hollins-lane there is a small Wesleyan chapel, which was built in 1822; the whole or principal portion of the cost of its erection being defrayed by Mr. George Fishwick, of Scorton.

Something like half a mile east of Hollins-lane there is Shireshead Church. It is usually designated, by the local people, "Shireshead old Church," or "old Shireshead," and it is situated in the township of Cleveley. Shireshead means the head of a division of land—ground rising to a point with lateral depressions—or the apex of a gradually separated eminence. "Shireshead old Church" stands on high gently rising ground, flanked with depressions, especially on the south-eastern side, where the Wyre runs; and the form and altitude of the land in this quarter quite justifies the name which it bears. "Shireshead chapel"—a place of worship which has, probably, had a more curious or fluctuating career than any other building of the kind in the North—is named as being in existence in 1520: when it was originally established is not known. The Rev. William Harrison, topographer, historian, &c. (1534-1593), mentions, in one of his descriptive notes, "Shireshead chapel"; the date pertaining to it, in his allusion, being apparently 1577. In 1646 the "Committee for the Relief of Plundered Ministers" ordered the payment of £40 yearly "out of the impropriate tithes arrisinge wthin the townes ffields & peinots of fforton and Clevely wthin the Chappelry of Shireshead & pishe of Cockerham. . . sequestred from John Bradshawe, papist & delinquent, to & for the maintenance of such minister as (vpon approbacon of the Divines appointed by ordynance of Parliamt for examinacon of ministers. .) shall officiate in the Chappell of Shiershead aforesaid, being above 2 miles distant from the pish Church of Cockerham aforsaid & wch consisteth of above 300 soules." In the Lancashire Parochial Church Survey, made in 1650, the Commissioners observe that the "Chappell of Shierside hath no certain Maintenance to their knowledge, the minister there for ye Tyme being Mr. John ffisher." The "Committee for the Relief of Plundered Ministers" ordered, in 1652, that the sum of £50 a year should be "allowed and paid out of the impropriate rectory of Cockerham. . . . seqd from Mr. John Calvert & Mr. John Bradshaw, papist and delinqts, to and for increase of the maintenance [of] Wm. Ingham, minister of ye chappell of Shyershead." Some Nonconformists had possession of this place of worship, for a time, after the Restoration: later it was deserted or fell into disuse; about the beginning of the 18th century it was, apparently, occupied "on suffrance," by a body of Nonconformists, whose tenure (according to tradition) was cut short, one Sunday while they were worshipping, by the Duchess of Hamilton, who horsewhipped them out of the building; then it reverted to the Episcopal party; afterwards the structure got into a ruinous state; and in 1805 it was rebuilt. A small stone at

positional crisis. It was originally placed here to the memory of a little boy, who was killed by getting entangled amongst some machinery at a place in Ellel. After the tablet had been up for a while, the little boy's father, owing to some extra pressure

SHIRESHEAD OLD CHURCH.

the west-end (outside) bears the inscription, "This Chapel of Shireshead rebuilt A.D. 1805." After being reconstructed, the building was used regularly, on Episcopal lines, until 1889, when it was superseded by a small new church, about three-quarters of a mile westward, near the vicarage. The two bells used up to the time the old place was closed still hang in the little double-arched belfry above the west-end gable. Externally, the building seems to be in a fairly good condition; but internally it is otherwise. One day I had a look into this old place, and found it in a very forlorn, dingy state—a sort of ecclesiastical derelict. The pews on the ground floor were all there as in by-gone times; the pulpit and the reading-desk remained undisturbed; the large gallery on the south side and at the west end was still up; but the whole interior had a strangely abandoned, pathetically forsaken appearance, whilst the processes of decay were actively going on, and very visible in the place generally. There are several large, old-fashioned pews in the gallery, and name-plates, &c., relating to the owners, are on some of them. When there was no available Episcopal accommodation at Dolphinholme, the late Mr. and Mrs. Henry Garnett, of Wyreside, with their family, regularly attended for years "Old Shireshead Church." Some time ago whilst conversing with a middle-aged person, in the neighbourhood of Cleveley, I chanced to make reference to the numerical character of the Garnett family, when a rejoinder, in an ejaculatory tone, came thuswise, "A—my—yes; I remember them; when they used to go to Shireshead old Church, Mr. and Mrs. Garnett and their twelve children, and all got into one pew, in the gallery, they did look a lot." The "children" in question consisted of nine sons and three daughters. When I looked into the old church I noticed, fixed against the northern wall, a little marble tablet, which once went through a sort of trans-

of temper or misunderstanding between himself and the minister, had it taken down and carted off to his own private residence. But in a very short time the minister, having ascertained what had been done, communicated with the gentleman, to the effect that, if the tablet were not forthwith replaced in the church, legal proceedings would be taken against him. The tablet was immediately refixed in its original position, and it has remained in it, undisturbed, ever since. A graveyard, in which many interments have taken place, and which is still used for burial purposes, directly adjoins the church, which now merely provides mortuary accommodation.

A little distance south-west of the graveyard there is a building which was erected in 1832, as a day and Sunday school, used as such for years, then abandoned, and in 1898 transformed, with additions, into a gamekeeper's house. Between 1836 and 1850 it was, as a country Sunday school, one of the best in the North of England, its regular attendance for some time consisting of ninety boys and seventy girls. A boy whose colour attracted a great deal of notice amongst the country children attended this Sunday school for a time. He was a "blacky," and had been brought from some foreign part, as a servant, by Mr. W. Talbot Rothwell, of Foxholes, near Bay Horse Station. This lad was much mystified when he first went to the school, and used to move about, quickly and anxiously, from one part to another, asking to be instructed—saying to this teacher and that, "Teach me; will you teach me?" None of the ordinary teachers seemed to be able or willing to tackle him tuitionally, so at length there came to the rescue the incumbent (the Rev. Robert Brickel), who took the lad well in hand, and gave him such instruction, each Sunday, as he appeared to need. Mr. Brickel, who was a native of Furness, received his first clerical appointment in 1836, as curate of Cockerham; in 1838 he was appointed incumbent of Shireshead, and he occupied that position till 1848, when he became rector of Hoole, near Preston, and as such he continued until his death, at the age of 68, in 1881. There was formerly in this township (Cleveley) a day schoolmaster with a somewhat comprehensive tuitional programme as well as a very original conception of syntax and the rules of punctuation. I refer to Thomas Blezard, at one time a soldier, for a short time (in or a little prior to 1848) master of Shireshead day school, and whose brother James kept a school before that time in a cottage in Hollins-lane. Early in May, 1848, Thomas figured off, by advertisement, in one of the Lancaster newspapers, in the following style:— "Notice, Is, Hereby Given, To the Clergy, Gentry and Inhabitants, of Lancaster and its Vicinity; also, to the Community, throughout Great Britain. That, Mr. Thomas Blezard, School-master, of Cleveley; in, the Parish of Cockerham; in the County of Lancaster. Most humbly begs leave to Publish his Scholastic qualifications; as a Preceptor. Namely, Reading, Writing, Arithmetic, Mensuration, and English, Grammar Classic; also, Ancient Latin Grammar Classic. Who, being desirous of ameliorating his Situation. He is, therefore willing to accept, the first Vacancy; as a Schoolmaster, or, any Other Suitable Situation: in England. I hope, that, I shall receive the Approbation; of the Commonwealth, of the Community. Notum, benum. Application, may be Made, Personally, or Correspondingly. To the aforesaid Place, of Abode. I am, gentm., Yours Respectfully, THOMAS BLEZARD. Dated, April 29th: 1848." Instructive skill and peculiarity of faculty for announcement-making of this kind remind me of a northern individual who, in the range of his curriculum, could beat even Thomas Blezard. I refer to a parish clerk of that remarkable clergyman whom Canon Parkinson, whose career I have already particularised, makes allusion to so frequently and interestingly in "The Old Church Clock." This parish clerk was a schoolmaster and a "surgeon" as well, and in the course of a notice he thus specified some of his abilities, &c.: "Blisters on the lowest terms, and fysicks at a penny. Sells Godfather's cordial, cuts corns, and undertakes to keep anybody's nails by the year or so on. Young ladies and gentelmen tort their grammar language in the neatest possible manner; and also grate care taken of their morals and spellin; also sarme singing and teaching the Ho, boy, cow Tillions and other dances tort at home and abroad. Perfumery in all its branches. Sells all sorts of stationery wares. . . He also performs fleebottomy in a curious manner, old rags bought and sold here, not any ware helse, and new-laid eggs every day. . . P.S. I teeches joggrefy and all them outlandish things. N.B. A bawl on Wednesday." This beats Blezard of Cleveley, and even out-distances the Great Eccleston genius, who some years ago made an announcement to the effect that he knew and desired

public patronage in respect to eleven different avocations, including umbrella mending, saw sharpening, watch cleaning, and pig killing. But it did not equal —indeed, did not come up to—the programme of a man who was living at Much Hoole, near Preston, in 1840, and who, according to report, knew thirty-four different trades; and yet was not happy; for in the year mentioned he made it known that he wanted a wife.

Three-quarters of a mile N.E.E. of Shireshead old church there is Nan's Nook—a rustic little place, consisting of a few dwellings, &c. The first mention of this place which I have met with occurs in a record of wills proved within the archdeaconry of Richmond: in it reference is made to the will of Richard Holden, yeoman, of "Nanns Nook," which was proved in 1762. A road runs past Nan's Nook to the river Wyre, which is about 300 yards distant, south-east; but there is no bridge over the water, and those who go across have to do so by ordinary wading or stilting. At one time, a man named Richard Sergeant lived at Nan's Nook. He had in his house hand looms: here also he had a family, and no mistake. His family consisted of 18 children—17 sons and one daughter! If any person chanced to ask him how many children he had, he would promptly and definitely reply that he had 17 sons, that all of them, barring one, were Sergeants, the exception being a corporal, and that they had each a sister. Occasionally he would endeavour to puzzle a company by imparting the same information, without being interrogated on the subject at all. In his younger days, this Sergeant was at Ashton Hall, near Lancaster, in the service of the Duke of Hamilton; and his son Matthew, with others of the same family, were also for some time at that Hall—remained there until 1860, when he (Matthew) died, at the age of 74. A brother (Gilbert), who lived for a while in Nether Wyresdale, was clever in the taxidermy line—could stuff birds, &c., in excellent style.

The Roman road from Ribchester to Lancaster, &c., passed on the north-eastern side of Shireshead—something like a mile and a quarter beyond where the old church stands. From the lane, at the bend, about 150 yards past the church, eastward, there is a fine view of Wyresdale, with its long, sloping sides, and its fell-formed, dark-purple head. Wyreside, a handsome residence on a pleasant, tree-embordered eminence; the woods which enwrap Dolphinholme; Newland Hall, high and serene; umbrageous Undercroft; the lofty, lonely environments of Abbeystead, &c., also come well into view here; but later on I shall have something to say about these, so at present refrain from further observations concerning them.

The round-headed eminence in a field about half a mile south-west of Shireshead old church is Corless Hill. It is not very high—only 175 feet above the sea level—but it commands a particularly fine, wide-reaching view: from it can be clearly seen the towers of Lancaster Castle, Parish Church, &c., on one side, and the spires and tall chimneys of Preston on the other, with all the varied intermediate scenery down to the sea. A building which is now utilised in connection with Captain Ormrod's fish-hatching establishment, but which for many years, up to about 1897, was known as Cleveley corn-mill, is in the neighbourhood of Corless Hill—on the east side, in a hollow. Three hundred yards east of this building there is an old ford which crosses the Wyre and connects the ancient road from Clitheroe to Cockersand Abbey, via Bleasdale, previously referred to.

Shireshead or Forton Vicarage is situated close to the road which runs between the north end of Hollins-lane and the highway. The little church near it, on the west side, was built to supplant the old place of worship already mentioned, and it was opened in 1889. The cost of it was about £1,700, and something like two-thirds of this amount was paid by the late Rev. John Bickerdike, vicar here, out of his own private means. The reason why he did this—had, apparently, to do this—was because, whilst he was strongly in favour of the new church, a considerable number of the parishioners thought it was not required. Having many of their associations with the old church through marriages, christenings, and bygone attendance at services therein, or on account of the burial of relatives and friends in the adjoining graveyard, and taking into consideration the fact that, structurally, the building was not in such a bad condition, they were of opinion that restoration, or the carrying out of certain improvements here and there, would amply meet the case. But the Vicar thought otherwise—contended that the situation of the building was inconvenient for the majority of the people in the district, as it was for himself, he being old and infirm at the time; so he selected a site at the west end of the vicarage garden, and the present church, which is a very neat one, was the result. I believe he spent upon this church, out of his own pocket, about £1,100, including the purchase of a new organ. The Rev. J. Bickerdike took the living of Shireshead as an "exchange," on account of his advancing age, &c., in 1879, having previously been Vicar of St. Mary's, Leeds, for 32 years. He died in 1892, and was buried in the graveyard attached to Shireshead old church. He was succeeded, at the new church, by the Rev.

NEW CHURCH, FORTON.

U. S. Brocket Spooner, who is still the vicar here. From the top of a small hill in a field on the west side of the highroad, opposite the end of the

lane near which the church stands, a remarkably good view—picturesque and extensive—can be obtained. The lane just referred to was formerly a continuous one to the Cockerham road: from the point which is now its west end it took the line of the present highway for about 150 yards southward; the lane on the lower side being its continuation to the road named.

Near the north-east corner of the lower lane just mentioned there used to be a malt-kiln: it was pulled down about 40 years since. To this corner old Mr. Corless, of Wallace-lane, Forton, was in the habit of sending his dog, every Saturday, for a Lancaster newspaper! The Poulton-le-Fylde carrier, who went to Lancaster every Friday, to be ready for the market there, on the following day, brought the paper back with him, and the dog had been trained to wait at the corner of the lane for him. On passing, the carrier would throw out of his cart the paper, and the dog would then pick it up and trot off home with it in its mouth. A farmhouse with outbuildings stands near the site of the old malt-kiln.

The residence on the west side of the main road, nearly opposite Forton Church Lane-end, is Forton Bank. It was built by Mr. John Allen, rail-

FORTON BANK.

way contractor, who originally came into this district when the Lancaster and Preston line was commenced, and was at that time in very poor circumstances. He was a peg carrier, &c., when the railway was staked out; but gradually, by steadiness and attention to his duties, he gained the confidence of his employers, made headway, afterwards went with some of the civil engineers who had been engaged on the line into Scotland, there began contracting on his own account, returned before long to England, and then kept in order, under contract, from 1841 to 1848, the permanent way of the Lancaster and Preston railway. This line was opened on June 25th, 1840. In the forenoon of that day the directors and a number of friends proceeded from Lancaster to Preston in a train of 11 carriages: there were several stoppages on the way, and the time taken up in the journey was one hour and 40 minutes. After halting for a while at Preston, the train returned to Lancaster, with an additional number of passengers; the back run being accomplished in one hour and ten minutes. There was afterwards a banquet in the "carriage repository" at Lancaster; Mr. G. Burrow, a highly influential local gentleman, and chairman of the directors, presiding. The Preston party were taken back, by train, in 55 minutes. The line between Preston and Lancaster is almost unequalled for the soundness of its construction and the excellence of its grading: it is one of the best and most substantial pieces of railway work in the United Kingdom. At the Bay Horse Inn, Ellel, in July, 1848, Mr. Allen, railway contractor, was presented with a beautiful silver stand with silver topped decanters, along with an elegantly chased cup, by tradesmen, workpeople, and friends, "as a token of their respect and esteem for his upright character, kind consideration, and courteous manner to all Ellel." Mr. Allen built Forton Bank house in 1848, died at it, in 1851, when only 46 years of age—worth, it has been estimated, about £40,000—and was interred in Cockerham churchyard. The house was subsequently occupied, successively, by his son and grandson; and by the latter (Major Allen, now of Lancaster, the owner of the place) it was considerably enlarged. Mr. W. Saul, solicitor, Lancaster, is the present tenant.

The residence on the eminence, about a quarter of a mile south-east of Forton Bank, is Hill House. It was built by Mr. John Gardner, cotton manufacturer, Preston, about 1881. Mr. Gardner, who was a native of Forton, resided at Hill House from the time of its completion until his death in 1891. Mr. John Isherwood, son of the late Alderman Isherwood, of Preston, now resides here.

A quarter of a mile from the highway, down the lane which leads into the Cockerham road, there is Forton Independent Chapel. It stands opposite the south end of a narrow, crooked, old by-way called Wallace-lane. Tradition says that Wallace, the Scotch warrior and hero, during one of his southern raids, near the end of the 13th century, passed with his forces through this lane—hence its name. But there is nothing to verify this tradition; and it is quite possible that the derivation of the name had nothing whatever to do with the northern warrior, &c. If Wallace and his soldiers ever moved north or south, through this district, the presumption is that they would avoid a tortuous by-lane like the one in question and proceed along the old and more direct road—once the highway—which for some distance goes east of and parallel with the present main road. Through a portion of Forton there runs, north and south, a by-passage designated Winder-lane; and, as this name was, in all probability, derived from one or more persons called Winder (several generations ago there were Winders in and about Forton), so likewise Wallace-lane, which is adjacent, may have been thus designated through some person or family named Wallace either living in or possessing property close to it. The will of James Wallace, yeoman, of Forton, was proved in the archdeaconry of Richmond, in 1764; and probably he had both predecessors and successors in Forton. The Independent Chapel is a gray, high-roofed, particularly plain-looking building, exter-

nally viewed; but internally it has a commendable appearance, whilst historically it is of considerable interest. It was built in 1706-7, under the Five Mile Act, and after the displacement from Shireshead Church of a number of Nonconformists who, through the Episcopal desertion of that place, had for a time worshipped there. The Act in question, which was passed in 1665, stated that all Dissenting teachers who refused to take the oath of canonical obedience, or to express in writing their willingness to conform to the rules of the Established Church, and pay obedience to the King and the bishops unconditionally, would be debarred from approaching, for the purpose of teaching their religious doctrines, within five miles of any Corporate town or any place where they had previously preached. Independents and Presbyterians declined to take the oath—would not comply, &c.—and, as a consequence, places for teaching and preaching their doctrines beyond the prescribed boundary were built in different parts of the country; the chapel in Forton being one of them—for Independents. On the accession of William III., the disabilities and penalties of the Five Mile Act were done away with by the Toleration Act; and by the repeal of the Corporation and Tests Act, in 1828, the civil disabilities placed upon Dissenters were also removed. The original Independent chapel in Forton was supplanted, in 1760, by the present building (on the same site), which was altered a good deal in 1870, and considerably renovated and internally decorated in 1898. The decorative work included the introduction of coloured glass windows. At the time the chapel was thus improved there was placed within it, on the south side, a massive carved oak tablet, bearing this inscription:—"In memory of Isabel Dawson, of Aldcliffe Hall, Lancaster, who, from the time of the Presbyterian Church in Lancaster becoming Unitarian, used to worship in this place till the erection of High-street Chapel. These windows were restored by her great grandchildren in the year 1898." Mrs. Isabel Dawson went to Forton Independent Chapel for about 10 years (1765-1775), from the 50th to the 60th year of her age, and it is said that she walked every Sunday from Aldcliffe Hall to the Chapel and back again—a total distance of about 13 miles! She was accompanied by a favourite dog, and there is a tradition that after her death, which occurred in 1781, this dog went for several Sundays, by itself, to Forton Chapel. The Dissenting or Independent element originally got into or was very considerably strengthened in Forton through a number of people who were brought from Scotland by the Duke of Hamilton to improve his Grace's property in some of the contiguous townships. In 1717-1729 the congregation at Forton Chapel was, comparatively, very large—one of the largest of its kind in the North of England. The Rev. Eleazar Aray, who for some time officiated in Shireshead old Church—at the time, evidently, when it was deserted by the Episcopal party—was the first minister at Forton Chapel; and he continued his labours here till his death, in 1729. The graves of four of the old ministers are in the burial ground, which surrounds the chapel; one of them being that of a very patriarchal pastor—the Rev. James Grimshaw, who died in 1838, in the 97th year of his age. The Rev. Peter Webster is the present minister.

Forton Board School is near the chapel, on the north-west side. The School Board here was established in 1877. The school building, with the master's house adjoining, cost about £1,600. Upon a portion of the ground now occupied by the school there was formerly a black felt hat-making place. The maker of the hats was William Gornall, a native of Tarnbrook, in Over Wyresdale. William was a very "lish" (agile) fellow, and when learning to dance, with certain young Fortonians, he was so enamoured of the job, or so bent upon accomplishing it, that they used to say he could not keep his feet down on the floor at all—seemed to be in a state of abnormal buoyancy, as if floating or flying up and down and round the room all the time. The hat-making place was done away with about 60 years ago.

FORTON INDEPENDENT CHAPEL.

CHAPTER XVI

Clifton Hill—The Gillows, &c.—Richard Tongue and his Cottage—Burglarious Activity.

Between half and three-quarters of a mile west of For on Board School there is Clifton Hill. This is the name of a beautiful residence, which stands on the crown of a gentle eminence, and commands a very pleasant southern view. Clifton Hill was built in 1817, by Mr. Robert Gillow, of the firm of Gillow and Co., noted cabinet makers, of Lancaster—a firm which was established by two brothers in the reign of Queen Anne. Pennant, the traveller, in his account of the journey to the north which he made, in 1772, after alluding to "some ingenious cabinet makers," in Lancaster, "who make most excellent and neat goods at remarkably cheap rates, which they export to London and the plantations," observes that "Mr. Gillow's warehouses of these manufactures merit a visit." The whole structure of Clifton Hill is of stone, and architecturally it combines elegance with strength.

when the place became empty. After remaining in this state for a time, Clifton Hill was, along with the adjoining land, &c., forming its estate, sold by Miss Gillow to Mr. W. Margerison, of Hareden, near Whitewell. Miss Gillow died in Paris, in 1871. For about a dozen years Mr. Margerison lived at Clifton Hill. In 1877 Mrs. Fitzherbert-Brockholes (widow of Mr. James Fitzherbert-Brockholes, of Claughton Hall, who died in 1875) purchased Clifton Hill and the general estate, and she has resided at the mansion here ever since. Mrs. Fitzherbert-Brockholes has a strong liking for rural life and agricultural matters. Amongst other things she has a beautiful herd of Channel Island cattle, which, when I last saw them, were grazing in a field directly fronting the mansion, and formed a very pleasing picture. There is a small, neat Roman Catholic Chapel connected with Clifton

CLIFTON HILL.
FORTON

CLIFTON HILL.

The facade is broad and elaborate—has a choice centre with ornate wings. The ordinary people of the district used to say, with a smile, that in form the structure was a copy of some fine wardrobe or other piece of ornamental furniture which had caught the eye of Mr. Gillow or been made by his firm. Mr. Gillow was "one of the old sort," and was much respected. He was in the habit of riding about on a white pony, and though very wealthy he was equally genial and homely. At one time he owned nearly the whole of Forton. Mr. Gillow resided at Clifton Hill 21 years—up to the time of his death, in 1838—and was succeeded at the mansion by his daughter, Miss Sarah Ann Gillow, who lived at it for a while, and then went away,

Hill—at the west end; the Rev. Father R. Barton being at present the resident priest. The lower Roman road from Ribchester to Galgate passed, it is understood, immediately west of Clifton Hill. There used to be an old poor-house in this locality.

I now return to the north-eastern side of Forton township, and get near to the highway again. About 500 yards past Forton Bank, northward, and close to the high road, there is a one-storey, primitive looking building called "Tongue's Cottage." Two beautiful Irish yew trees adjoin it; and at the rear there is a semi-circular, open space, looking as if it had been made by scooping out a portion of the side of the adjoining field, and, when I last saw it, mainly a refuge for stunted bushes, briars, &c. In a field, north-west of the Cottage, there are fruit and ornamental trees ; over the highway fence, in a field on the north-east side, there are several fruit trees, and one or two fine, red-flowering thorns. These are all that remain of what was once a very beautiful floral and horticultural estate, laid out and owned by Mr. Richard Tongue, who also regularly looked after it himself without any assistance. He not only planted a great number of fruit and ornamental trees, but studded the semi-circular space alluded to, as well as the ground at the base of it, and some at the sides of the highway, opposite the Cottage, with beautiful flowering plants. So very attractive, florally, was the place, that swift-going coaches were not unfrequently pulled up for a few moments, when they got opposite

TONGUE'S COTTAGE.

the Cottage, in order that a view of the flowers might be more fully obtained by the passengers, who were greatly charmed by the display ; some of them even declaring that this was the prettiest sight met with on the road between London and Edinburgh. Mr. Tongue resided at Forton Cottage, about 250 yards north-west of his floral domain. Before taking up his abode in Forton, he was the proprietor and editor of the "Preston Sentinel," the predecessor of the

now defunct "Preston Pilot"; and it has been said of him that he was "a poet, a traveller, and a man of talent." When he sold flowers, or won cash prizes by his exhibits at floral shows, he gave the money thus realised for the benefit of Shireshead old Sunday school. Mr. Tongue died in or about 1853. On one occasion the house in which he resided, in Forton, was "patronised" by thieves. This was in 1842, during a portion of which year housebreakers were, evidently, exceptionally busy in about half-a-dozen country districts, including Forton, south and south-east of Lancaster. On the 12th of March, 1842, the house of the Rev. R. Watson, Over Wyresdale, was entered by burglars in disguise, who seriously maltreated him, and then made off with a watch and a £5 note. On the 27th of April the Fleece Inn, between Bay Horse and Dolphinholme, was broken into, and about £15 stolen from the box of an Oddfellows' lodge, which was in one of the rooms. On the 4th of June some armed men got into the house of Mr. Tongue, in Forton, and stole from it money amounting to about £16. On the 25th of the same month a burglarious gang effected an entrance into the house of Mr. Richard Parkinson, Scotforth, and, after binding him hand and foot, took away about £12 in money and some domestic articles. On the 10th of July, a set of burglars got into a house on Scotforth Moor, occupied by Mr. William Parr, who was abused very considerably and actually tied in bed ; but in this case the depredators did not get much money—only about 8s. Twelve days afterwards the house of Mr. John Gardner, situated between Galgate and Quernmore, was broken into by several men who, unable to obtain money after demanding it, fell foul on Mr. Gardner and his brother—nearly killed them—then ransacked the place, and disappeared with their booty, which was but very trifling. Three years afterwards a predatory gang evinced considerable activity, though neither so cruelly nor successfully, a few miles further south. In five weeks, near the end of 1845, six burglaries were committed in and about Garstang.

CHAPTER XVII.

Not quite half a mile from "Tongue's Cottage," in Forton, northward, the highway is crossed by the Cockerham-road. Cockerham village is about two miles westward from this point. There is a pretty deep, wide hole in a field, near the entrance to the road—on the north-west side of it. This hole was caused by quarrying operations. The stone required, in 1839, for the erection of Bay Horse railway station (about a third of a mile to the north-east) was obtained here. The eminence near which the Cockerham-road goes, just past the old quarry hole, is Cross Hill, and no doubt it originally got this name through being the site of a wayside cross. A dwelling on the northern side of the road, at the summit of the eminence, bears the name of Cross Hill House; another dwelling on the same side, about 100 yards southward, is named Cross Hill Cottage, and a short distance south-east there is Cross Hill Farm. The way to Cockerham, from the main road, is in certain parts of a decidedly up and down character. The highest part of it—about three-quarters of a mile from the Preston and Lancaster highway—is called Windy Arbour. On one side of the road, at the summit of the elevation named, there is a cottage, south of which, and adjacent, is a large, new red-brick residence of the bungalow kind, built in 1896-7 by Mrs. Brockholes, of Clifton Hill. Originally, Mrs. Brockholes intended to erect here, for a couple of lady friends, a two-storey residence; but, soon after operations had been commenced, one of them was unexpectedly called away, and, as a two-storey house would have been too large for the other, the design was changed to one of the bungalow kind; hence the present structure. In respect to Windy Arbour, owing to its altitude and comparative bleakness, an ordinary observer would have no difficulty in seeing the appropriateness of the first part of the name; but what about the second portion of it? An ordinary observer would, certainly, fail to see the force of Arbour. Well, from all I can learn, Windy Arbour is a name which indicates bygone proximity to a Roman road. The Roman road between Walton-le-Dale and Lancaster went either directly over the elevated ground here, or a little to the east of it. Arbour seems to be analogous to or synonymous with harbour. Mr. Watkin, in his "Roman Lancashire," says that the name Windy Harbour is "a sure sign of a Roman road;" in other words, that, wherever a place with such a name is found, a Roman road

has crossed or gone not far from it. There are numerous Cold Harbours as well as Windy Harbours in England; and the presumption is that both names have one and the same meaning. The Rev. Isaac Taylor, in his "Words and Places," intimates that Roman villas originally stood at those parts which now bear the names mentioned, and that the deserted rooms or ruins of such villas afforded shelter—refuge—for travellers; hence their designation as Cold or Windy Harbours. An old antiquarian friend of mine—the late Mr. E. Kirk, of Pendleton—was of opinion that Harbours of this character could not have referred to exposed places, "for," says he, "in the Chipping Valley, nearly opposite where the Roman road crosses the crest of Longridge Fell, at Jeffrey Hill, there is a place called 'The Harbour' without qualification," and if the canal bridge, which is called "Arbour Bridge," over which the Cockerham-road passes, "nearly indicates the site of Windy Arbour," then, he argues, such Arbour "must have been in a sheltered spot." The elevated ground now named Windy Harbour, across which Cockerham-road passes, may not have been the actual site of a Roman villa; but, if not, a villa of that sort was, in all probability, near it—on the west side; and the name would be derived from this proximity.

About 300 yards beyond the canal bridge, Cockerhamward, and on the north or Holleth side of the road, there is the base of an old cross. The township of Holleth is the smallest in respect to area and population, as well as the most northern, in the Garstang Union: indeed, as to size, I believe it is the least, and, so far as population goes, the most sparsely inhabited township in Lancashire. It has an area of only 358 acres; and there are not more than about half-a-dozen houses in it. The population of Holleth has fluctuated curiously. In 1831 it was 50; in 1861 it was 30; in 1881 it got up again to 50; in 1891 it was but 25; and at present it will be but little more than, if as much as, it was in the last-named year.

There runs most crookedly and quietly, down in a hollow to the west, a few minutes' walk from the base of the wayside cross I have alluded to, the river Cocker. It has here more the appearance of an extremely dull little beck or softly-going syke than a river; but nearer its source it is more rapid and ripply, whilst towards the point of its debouchure it is broader and deeper. A good stone bridge—called Cocker House Bridge—carries the Cockerham road over the "river." On the north inner side of this bridge, fixed against the centre of the parapet, there is a County Hundred boundary stone: it indicates the dividing point between the Amounderness and

COCKER HOUSE BRIDGE.

South Lonsdale Hundreds. Old Harrison, in his topographical work, says that the Cocker "from its shortnesse deserueth no descriptio." Drayton, in the second part of his "Polyolbion," originally published in 1622, thus refers to it:—

—— Coker a coy Nymph, that cleerely seemes to shun
All popular applause, who from her Christall head,
In Wyresdale, neere where Wyre is by her fountaine fed,
That by their naturall birth they seeme (in deed) to twin,
Yet for her sisters pride she careth not a pin,
Of none, and being help'd, she likewise helpeth none,
But to the Irish Sea goes gently downe alone
Of any vndisturbd, till comming to her Sound,
Endangered by the Sands, with many a loftie bound,
Shee leaps against the Tydes, and cries to Christall Lon,
The Flood that names the Towne, from whence the Shire begun,
Her title first to take, and loudly tells the Flood,
That if a little while she thus but trifling stood,
These pettie Brooks would bee before her still preferd.

As to the head of the Cocker, Drayton is wrong: it is not in Wyreside, but in Ellel, near Crag End, on the N.E.E. side of the township. The "river," on leaving its source, runs southward to the Hole of Ellel, near Bay Horse Station, then winds away on the south-west of Hay Carr and Ellel Grange, next goes nearly due south for about two miles, afterwards takes a north-west course, about a mile from Cockerham village, and, ultimately, after crossing Cockerham Sands, flows into the estuary of the Lune nearly opposite Cockersand Abbey. A topographical work, published in 1719, says that near the mouth of the Cocker "there are deceitful and voracious sands (commonly called Quick sands), very dangerous for travellers, who, when the tide is out, are so venturesome as to cross them (because much the nearest way) into Furness." Improved main roads and good railway facilities resulted in the abandonment of the old plan of "crossing the sands" into Furness; but, when such plan

was in vogue, there could be no direct way across the estuary of the Lune and Morecambe Bay from any point near the mouth of the Cocker. The only possible way at low water contiguous to the outer channel of the river would be across the sands, north-east. Having got over these sands, persons for Furness would next have to go through Thurnham, Ashton, &c., via Lancaster, to Hest Bank, and thence across the sands to Kent's Bank, about a mile and a half south of Grange. Guides used to take parties across the sands between Hest Bank and Kent's Bank; the distance traversed—at low water, of course—being something like eight miles. In 1857, when the Furness railway was opened, the services of these guides were no longer required. Leland, who was authorised by Henry VIII. to make an antiquarian expedition throughout England, and who apparently accomplished it between 1533 and 1539, refers to the Cocker, to its dangerous sands, and to a curious salt-gathering plan in vogue on the coast which the river traverses in its way to the Lune estuary. He says:—
"The Coker river maketh no great course on he come to the sands of Cokerham village . . . upon the which sands I past over Coker river once again, not without some feer of quicksands. At the end of the sands I saw divers salt cootes where were divers heaps of sandis taken of salt strondys, out of the which by often weting with water they pike out the saltness, and so the water is drived into a body and after scdde." Camden, in his "Britannia," a work first published in 1586, says:—"In many places on this coast one sees heaps of sand, on which they pour water till they contract a saltness, which they afterwards boil over turf fires to white salt."

The village of Cockerham—a small, quiet-looking place, consisting of a few little, plain houses, &c., flanking part of a level, winding lane—is about half a mile north-west of Cocker House Bridge. The name Cockerham means a home or place of abode adjoining or not far from the Cocker. Cockerham is a very old place: it is mentioned in Doomsday Book as Cocrcham, and as belonging to Roger de Poictou. The Lancastres, barons of Kendal, were the owners of Cockerham shortly after the Norman Conquest. The manor and church of Cockerham were given by William de Lancastre to the canons of Leicester, in the latter half of the 12th century. The Abbot of St. Mary, Leicester, had "free warren" granted in the manor at the beginning of the 14th century. During the same century the manor was given to the Abbot of Cockerham. In the course of the 15th century (some reversion of interest or reclaim of proprietary right having taken place) a release of claim in the manor was made in favour of the then Abbot. In 1597 the customs of the manor were farmed by John Calvert, gentleman, of Cockerham, who died, in 1620, seized of the manor and rectory. A daughter of his became the grandmother of a man whose skull figures curiously in the legendary lore of Lancashire. She married Roger Downes, who settled at Wardley Hall, about seven miles west of Manchester, at the beginning of the Civil War in the 17th century, and who was vice-Chamberlain of Chester to William, Earl of Derby, &c. Their grandson (Roger Downes)—a courtier in the time of Charles II.—had his head cut off, during a brawl, on London Bridge; the head (so says tradition) being sent to his sisters, at Wardley Hall, where it was preserved, and where it became the subject of the strange legend of the Wardley Hall skull—a skull which, as per the legend, would, if removed, or thrown into a neighbouring pond, or actually buried, return to the Hall again, and which "never failed to punish the individual severely who should dare to lay hands upon it with any such purpose" as that of disturbing, taking away, or destroying it. This skull—anyhow, a skull—is now, I believe, preserved in a locked aperture at Wardley Hall. Reverting to Cockerham manor, it was, some time after the death of John Calvert, owned by the Charteris family. In or about 1798 it was sold, by Lord Wemyss, to four conjoint lords of the manor, whose present successors, manorially, are Colonel C. H. Bird, Crookhey Hall, Cockerham, who holds two lordship rights; Lieutenant Greene, Whittington Hall, near Kirkby Lonsdale; and Mr. J. Clarke, of Summerhill, Newton-in-Cartmel. By the inhabitants of the district these gentlemen are designated "the Lords of Cockerham."

Down amid fields, about a quarter of a mile S.W.W. of the village, Cockerham Parish Church is situated. It is conjectured that the church here was

parish, sequestered from Richard Calvert and John Bradshaw, recusants; but afterwards, for some reason, the Commissioners for Sequestrations in the county refused to pay the appointed minister (Gerrard Browne) the money, whereupon he lodged a complaint, and they were enjoined to pay him what was due, and to continue the payment yearly of the £50 "according to ye Act of Parliamt." The condition of ecclesiastical affairs in Cockerham parish, in 1650, is described as follows in the report of the Commissioners or Jurors appointed at the beginning of the Commonwealth to inquire into the state of the different parishes in the country:—"And ye said jurors doe further say vpon their Oathes, that ye Parish Church of Cockerham, within ye said Hundred of Loinsdale and County of Lance., is a Vicaradge Presentative, John Calvert, Esqr., a Papist Delinquent, Patron; That ye Tythes of Corne and graine within ye whole parish are Impropriate to ye said Mr. Calvert and to Mr. Bradshaw, another Delinquent papist, worth one hundred and sixteene pounds p ann, vizt Eighty pounds p ann in Ellell, sixteene pounds p ann in Cockerham, and Twenty pounds p ann in fforton; And That there is another Tyth of Corn in pt of Thornham, within ye said pish, impropriate to ye said Mr. Bradshaw, worth Ten pounds p ann; And ye said pish of Cockerham doth containe within it ye

COCKERHAM CHURCH.

originally founded about 1160. Towards the end of the 13th century the vicarage of Cockerham came under the control of de Newark, Archdeacon of Richmond. In the first half of the 17th century a new church was built. Near the middle of the same century the "Committee for the Relief of Plundered Ministers" ordered £50 a year to be paid towards the maintenance of a minister at Cockerham out of impropriate tithes in connection with property in the

severall Townshipps, hamletts or Villages of ye severall distances from ye said Parish Church heretofore following, vizt, Cockerham, where ye Church is seated; Ellell, distant as aforesaid Three miles; fforton, one mile; pt of Cleveley Three myles; pt of Thurnham Three myles; one howse in Lower Wyersdale, vizt, Robert Websters, of ye Holmes; And that there is belonging to ye said Church a Vicarage house and Six acres and a halfe of Glebe land, and also Tyth of Salt and Wooll, lambe and pigge, Goose, hay, hempe, flax, and small Tyths, in most of ye places within ye said Vicaradge; That there is some Composicon Rent from Thurnham Hall, about Six shillings p ann: That ye pffitts thereof were anciently reputed to bee about Sixty pounds p ann, but by reason of ye decay of Sheepe ye said Vicaradge hath beene ffarmed ye last yeare for Thirty five pounds And ye said Jurors likewise say That ye said Parish of Cockerham doth containe within it ye severall Chappelles distant from their said pish Church as followeth, vizt, Ellell Three myles, Shierside Three miles; And that ye Incumbent officiating att ye said Parish Church for ye Tyme being is one Mr. Thomas Smith during ye Sequestracon of Mr. William Calvert, ye Vicar, for delinquency. And ye said Jurors further say that ye said severall Chappells belonging to ye said pish Church of Cockerham are pvided for as followeth; vizt, ffifty pounds p ann allowed by Order from ye Comittees of plundered Ministers to ye said Chappell of Ellell; ye Minister there Mr. Peter Atkinson; And that ye said Chappell of Shierside hath no certain Maintenance to their knowledge, the Minister there for ye Tyme being Mr. John ffisher." The 17th century church, at Cockerham, was superseded (with the exception of the tower, which is still standing) by the present church, which was built in 1814. It is a very plain, solitary, strong-looking structure. In the tower there is a very good peal of bells, which, according to tradition, came from Cockersand Abbey. But this tradition is not correct. There may have been in the tower, for a time after the break-up of Cockersand Abbey, one or more bells which originally came from that place; but the present peal—six bells, the tenor being 11cwt. —was cast, in 1748, by Mr. A. Rudhall, of Gloucester. The bells were rehung by Taylor, of Loughborough, in 1888, and they are now in capital order. They bear the following legends:—Treble "Peace and good neighbourhood. A.R. 1748." 2, "Prosperity to the parish. A.R. 1748." 3, "We were all cast at Gloucester, by Abel Rudhall, 1748." 4, "Robert Gardner, Edward France, Robert Fell, Stephen Bond, churchwardens. A.R. 1748." 5, "The Rev. Mr. Thomas Winder, Vicar. A.R. 1748. Tenor, "I to the Church the living call, and to the grave do summon all. 1748." The general body of the Church internally is large—apparently very spacious for a country place—but it has a somewhat dull, heavy look: the chancel, however, is spacious, ornately-effective, pleasantly-bright. There was once a very singular dispute about a Rood (a crucifix, or image of our Saviour) ordered and made, but not approved of, for Cockerham Church; and, strange to say, the particulars of this dispute I have obtained not from any record or tradition at Cockerham, but by means of a communication made by a Furness gentleman, and published many years ago in a Westmorland periodical! The writer states that in the early part of this century there were two curious old books chained in the wardens' seat, in

Cartmel Church—they may be somewhere in the place still—and that one of them contained the following:—"A Story of a Roode Set up in Lankashire. In this visitation of Bishop Boner [a bad 16th century English prelate] . . . you see how the Bishop tooke on for not setting up the roode, and ringing the bells at Hadham. Yce heard also of the precept, which commanded in euery parish a Roode to be erected both well fauroured, and of an able Stature. By the occasion thereof, it cometh in minde (and not out of place) to story likewise what happened in a certain Towne in Lankashire neere to Lancaster called Cockram, where the Parishioners & Churchwardens having the same time a like charge for the erecting of a roode in their parish church, had made their bargain & were at a price with one that could cunniglie karue and paint such idols, for the framing of their Roode: who according to his promise, made them one, & set it up in their Church. This done, he demanded his money. But they misliking his workmanship refused to pay him, whereupon he arrested them, and the matter was brought before the Maior of Lancaster, who was a very meete man for such a purpose, and an old fauourer of the Gospell, which is rare in that countrie. Then the caruer began to declare how they couenanted with him for the making of a Roode, with the appurtenances ready carued and set vp in their church, uhich he according to his promise had done, and now demanding his money, they refused to pay him. Is this true, quoth the Maior to the Wardens? Yea, Sir, said they. And why doe you not pay the poore man his due, quoth he? And it please you Maister Maior (quoth they) because the Roode we had before was a well fauoured man, and he promised to make us such another: but this that he hath set vs up now is the worst fauoured thing that euer you set your eies on, gaping and grinning in such sort, that none of our children dare once looke him in the face, or come neere him. The Maior thinking that it was good enough for that purpose if it had been worse, My Masters (quoth he) howsoeuer the roode like you, the poore mans labour hath been neuer the less, and it is a pittie that he should have any hindrance or loss thereby. Therefore I will tell you what you shall doe: Pay him the money ye promised him, and go your wais home and looke on it, and if it will not serve for a God, make no more adoe, but clap a pair of horns on his head, and so will he make an excellent Deuill. This the Parishioners tooke well in worth, the poore man had his money, and diuers laughed well thereat: bt so did not the babylonish Priests." In old times, notices which we should nowadays deem very peculiar and out of place were put up on the door of Cockerham Church. And some of them, in respect to bad spelling, exceeded even that wonderful production—before quoted—of the clerk to the notable minister specialised by Canon Parkinson in "The Old Church Clock." For instance, at the beginning of 1824 a notice, of which the following is a copy, was fixed to the door of Cockerham Church, for the information of those who attended the services there:—"To be sould By ockso at they house of —— in Pilling Stake pool 6 February 1824 they sale to begin at twelve o'clock at noon all the stock of Katel con sisting of 2 good work hors his and 1 yong mare rising 3 years old and 1 foile 2 spr ing calvers cows and 2 draps and 2 wite face sheeps and hall sorts of husberny gears such as carts and weles plu and hares and house sold furturner.—Thomas —— Pilling Ockinhearer." The present Vicarage, which stands on a pleasant eminence at the north end of Cockerham village, was built in 1843, when the Rev. John Dodson was the vicar. It is situated 70 or 80 yards west of the site of the old vicarage house, which it superseded—a house the materials of which were, by order of Mr. Dodson, carted away to Tong Moor, in Littledale, where he utilised them in the construction of a residence. Not far from the old vicarage, on the north-west side, there was a windmill, which occupied a prominent position, and could be seen for miles. Indeed, its position was so prominent and exposed that occasionally the concern got more wind than was good for it. In January, 1802, a gale made the sails whirl round so rapidly that the friction which ensued set on fire the mill, which was gutted. In 1849 another mill, built on or near the same site, was burnt down from a supposed similar cause. A third mill was then built, but it was pulled down many years ago. When Mr. Dodson was appointed the vicar, in 1835, Cockerham was a "lively" place. Horse races were periodically run; bowling was freely indulged in on some enclosed ground opposite the old Manor Inn; cock-fighting was in vogue; and every fortnight there was coursing. Mr. Dodson, who was a very earnest, serious man, set his face against these things, deeming even the most innocent of them (bowling) a source of gambling or inebriety; and eventually he succeeded in putting an end to the whole lot. In 1850 he resigned his vicarial position at Cockerham, without assigning any reason to the parishioners for such step, and went to live at Tong Moor, Littledale—at the residence previously mentioned, which was a very good one; and in this lonely, upland region he built a Dissenting chapel, apparently of the Independent order, and regularly conducted service in it himself. After leading this sort of out-of-the-way ministerial life for some years, he went to the South of England, and there he died. The present vicar of Cockerham is the Ven. Archdeacon A. F. Clarke.

At the south end of the village of Cockerham there is a good school, which was built in 1829, and to which additions have since been made. In the front wall of the master's house, directly adjoining the school, there is a stone which bears the date 1681. This stone was brought from the old school (the predecessor of the present one), and the date on it has been generally understood to refer to the time when such school, which stood in the north-east corner of the churchyard, was built. But that school

was erected some time earlier. At an inquiry into the charities of the parish of Cockerham, held on the 11th of May, 1899, it was stated by Assistant-Commissioner Cardew that the earliest document relating to Cockerham School Charity was under the episcopal seal of the Bishop of Chester, that it was dated 1679, and that it cited that there had been a school house built, and also a school in the north-east corner of the churchyard. A legend says that the Devil once alighted in Cockerham Churchyard, afterwards wrought considerable havoc in the district, then had a peculiarly severe encounter with the master of the old school, and was at last completely foiled by that individual. Sundry doggrel verses, said to have been the production of "some local rhymster," describe with considerable detail the whole affair. After referring to the arrival of his sable majesty, to the fear produced and mischief wrought by him, the rhymster says that the people at length met, and appointed the schoolmaster to try his skill, and see if he could not "the devil bind faster." With pride the master accepted the appointment, and (so says the rhymster)—

One day in the school, in the corner of the churchyard,
The windows all fastened, the doors all barred,
With the gypsies' blarney, and the witches' cant,
He drew him forth with his horrible rant.

Terror seized the master as soon as he had done this, and he was informed that, if he did not by his "lore"—by three questions—entangle the sable one thus met with, the latter would diabolically transform, mangle, and fly away with him. The schoolmaster thereupon set to work in the interrogatory line. He first asked the devil how many dewdrops there were on some adjoining hedges. The number was given. Then a question was put as to how many stalks there were in a particular wheatfield. "His Majesty" operated upon the field with a scythe, and told the number of the stalks. The Cockerham dominie had now got into a very tight corner, and this is what the rhymster says—

Now the poor fellow's was a pitiful case,
As plain might be seen from his long length of face.
"Now, make me, dear sir, a rope of your sand,
Which will bear washing in Cocker, and not lose a strand."
The devil and mate then went down to the strand,
In a jiffy they twisted a fine rope of sand,
And dragged it along with them over the land;
But when they brought the rope to be washed,
To atoms it went—the rope was all smashed.
The devil was foiled, wroth, and gave him a shaking;
Up he flew to the steeple—his frame all a-quaking,
With one horrid frig—his mind very unwilling,
He strode to the brig o'er Broadfleet at Pilling.

And so the Cockerham people got shut of Dabol; but cynics hint that he still occasionally drops in, and bothers folk there, notwithstanding the legendary exorcism. A legend somewhat similar to the foregoing is associated with other country districts. It transpired during the inquiry in 1899, previously mentioned, that the late Mr. John Mason, of Cockerham, left a charity of £10 per annum for the education of bastard children in the parish; that the charity, consisting of certain land at Skerton, near Lancaster, realised but £7 10s. a year, less commission; that an arrangement had been made whereby, when there were but few illegitimate children in the parish (there were only two in it at the time of the inquiry), the master of Cockerham School could pay half of the school fees with the money; and that the managers of the school did not deal with, in fact kept aloof from, this charity "because of its character."

Cockerham Hall is about 300 yards west of the Vicarage. It is now a farmhouse. Originally this Hall was a private residence. In 1712 Mr. Walter Frost lived at it. Under date October 21st, in the year named, Thomas Tyldesley says in his diary:— "Meet Mrs. and two girlles at Cock-ham Hall, to see Sisr. Frost, very ill." There used to be two public-houses in Cockerham—one in the middle and the other at the north end of the village. The former (Manor Inn) was done away with as a public-house, and set apart for private use, a few years ago; but periodically —when the important and well-known Cockerham horse sales take place—its old functions are revived for the refreshment of equinely-interested visitors, &c. The present inn at the north end was formerly called the Plough; but it has now taken the name and is kept by the person who was the landlord of the extinguished public-house. Cockerham village is located near the summit of a ridge of moderate altitude, from which there is a good view of the south-western parts of the parish, the whole of the Pilling district, Fleetwood, &c., as well as the waters of the

About three-quarters of a mile from Cockerham village, southward, there is Crookhey Hall, the residence of Colonel C. H. Bird. It has a handsome, commanding appearance. Crookhey House is not far from the Hall.

CROOKHEY HOUSE.

Colonel Bird's father was Mr. William Smith Bird, a native of Needham, near Boston, Mass., U.S.A.; his mother (who was married to Mr. Bird after he had settled in this country) being Elizabeth, only daughter of Mr. William Gardner, of Crookhey House, near Cockerham. In their married life they resided at Ivyhurst, Aigburth, near Liverpool; but they occasionally came to Crookhey House, which, with neighbouring property, had been a family possession of the Gardners for generations; and, on the

CROOKHEY HALL.

sea stretching away to the west. The parish includes the township of Cockerham and parts of Holleth, Forton, Cleveley, Ellel, and Pilling; the total area of it being 14,750 acres. During the present century its population has been almost stationary; in 1801 it was 714; in 1871 it was 803; when the census was taken in 1891 it stood at 705; and it will not be much different now.

death of her father, Mrs. Bird inherited the place. One Edward Barben lived at "Crookey in Cockerham," in or shortly before 1636—probably at a much smaller house standing on the site of the present one. The will of William Gardner, "of Crookey," was proved within the archdeaconry of Richmond in 1661, and that of Bridget Gardner of the same place in 1662. Crookhey House is about a mile south of Cockerham village, near the river Cocker, and contiguous to the Forton and Garstang road. It has no architectural embellishment, yet its size, its substantial, well-pointed walls, its numerous windows, and its enclosed, tree-centred front ground give it a definite air of re spectability clearly pointing to ownership of the better order and to superior original associations. Periodically, for some years, Colonel Bird, whilst having his home at Ivyhurst, Aigburth, came over to Crookhey House, which he used as a shooting-box. His father, who was very kind to poor families in Cockerham, during the winter season, died in 1858, and was interred in Cockerham Churchyard. Afterwards Mrs. Bird, his mother, occasionally visited Crookhey House. She died at Ivyhurst, in 1870, and was buried in the churchyard at Cockerham. Crookhey House is now, and has for some years been, a farmhouse. In 1874 Colonel Bird began the erection of Crookhey Hall, on a site above and a short distance north of Crookhey House, and it was completed in 1878. Crookhey Hall is a fine, large building, in the Elizabethan style of architecture. Fronting it there are beautifully laid-out grounds, about five acres in extent; north-east, at a convenient distance, there are capital stables, &c.; contiguous to the mansion, excellent gardens and conservatories are located; whilst, on the south side, park lands, with an area of about 50 acres, give a picturesque completeness to the place. The mansion occupies the crown of a gentle eminence, and it commands excellent views of the north-eastern hills, the Fylde region, and the sea off Fleetwood. Colonel Bird and his wife (nee Isobel Eveleigh Wyndham, of Clearwell Court, Gloucestershire) take a steady interest in all that concerns the welfare of the district in which they reside.

CHAPTER XVIII.

The road which crosses the highway at the north end of Forton, going in one direction to Cockerham, runs up on the north-east side into the township of Ellel, &c. A few yards from the point where it branches off, on the latter side, there is a small bridge under which runs a stream that divides the townships of Forton and Ellel. This stream is called Potters Brook, and the same name is applied to some buildings a short distance northward. I one day asked an old Fortonian why this stream was called Potters Brook, and the reply I received was—"Because there used to be a nest of potters near the side of it." Afterwards, on questioning another local person on the subject, I was told that formerly potters camped or hung about the banks of the brook, not far from where it runs under the main road. If the name of the brook were originally derived from the presence of potters, so far as I can learn they must have been very old or early patrons of its borders. In 1617 the will of John Harrison of "Potterbrooke," Forton, was proved within the archdeaconry of Richmond. The small bridge previously referred to is called, on the Ordnance Map, Tanners Bridge. At one time there was a tannery near it, on the east side. This tannery was done away with about 1856, and was succeeded by a fellmonger's place, which was kept going for some years. A dwelling-house, known as Lower Abbey, is situated near where it stood. About 150 yards up the road, on the west side, there is a house called "Upper Abbey." But there appears to be nothing at all ancient about either "Abbey," and so far as I can learn neither of them has ever been associated with any religious order or foundation.

Ellel is a rurally-pleasant region, and it is of high antiquity. It has also, like not a few other localities, been subjected, so far as the spelling of its name goes, to a good deal of variation. In Doomsday Book it is called Ellhale: in other records, &c., which I have seen, it is designated Ellal, Ellall, Ellhall, Ellale, Ellill, Elhill, Ellyll, Ellell, and Ellel. The last-mentioned form of the name—i.e., Ellel—is that which has been chiefly in vogue during the present century. The meaning of the name is now a matter of pure theory or speculation. It will be observed that the variations in the spelling of the name occur almost exclusively in the second syllable. With one exception, there is exact uniformity in the spelling of the first part of the name—Ell. To a measure of 45 inches in England, but of varying lengths in some other countries, the word ell applies. The ell measure is now used chiefly in respect to cloth; but

formerly, in some parts, it was adopted for determining land quantities. If the name of the township into which we have now got be spelled correctly in Doomsday Book, viz., Ellhale, then it might mean a place where an ell measure of a hale (old word for full or whole) kind, and differing, probably, from that of certain neighbouring districts, was employed. Or it might mean a loneliness—an isolatedness—of a full or complete sort, if Ell be viewed as having come from a root-prefix cognate to that of the old South of England word "ell-inge," or the Teutonic "el-end," i.e., lonely, separated, out-of-the-way, &c. Taking some of the other forms of spelling, the name might refer to the originally projecting hill now called Ellel Crag, on the higher side of and the most prominent object in the township; Ell, coming from the Teutonic Elle, meaning very high, or from the English word Ell, which involves a jutting point as well as a measure—elbow being derived from the same root. Ell is also derived from or a modification of the Gaelic word All, meaning white. The breast of Ellel Crag has a somewhat light appearance now: in early times, when there was more stone on it, the lightness, or tendency to whiteness, might be still greater—hence the appropriateness of Ell, or, for the purpose of emphasis, a sort of duplication thereof in the form of Ell-ell. But, of course, this is mere hypothesis; and all I can with accuracy say about the name is that it is a very curious one. There is a story to the effect that once, when an Ellel man was being examined in an assize court, he was asked by the Judge where he came from; that the reply was given in a rather hurried, indistinct manner—only the first part of the name being really audible; that the question was, in consequence, repeated, when the man coolly and plainly answered—Ellel, whereupon the Judge, previously somewhat confused or irate, smilingly rejoined, "Oh, Ellel; I thought you mentioned another place." Near the end of the 11th century, when the Doomsday Survey was made, Ellhale (Ellel) was owned by Roger de Poictou, one of William the Conqueror's great barons. Some time afterwards Ellel was connected with the manor of Warton, north of Lancaster. There was an ancient "forest of Ellal," and from it Herbert de Ellal gave 30 loads of wood to Furness Abbey. Early in the 13th century Sir Grimbald de Ellal was one of the principal persons, if not the chief landed proprietor, connected with Ellel. The Thweng and Molyneux families possessed the manor in the 14th century. Towards the end of the 14th or the beginning of the

15th century the Plesingtons, of Pleasington, near Blackburn, had some property in Ellel. Early in the 16th century Sir James Lawrence was an owner of property here. The Molyneux and Lawrence interests in Ellel were at a later time disposed of, and the land in the township eventually got into various hands. In 1756 authority was given, by Act of Parliament, for the enclosure of "Ellel commons"; and it is said by a writer in 1794 that Ellel was the "only instance"—in Lancashire, I presume—where efforts made up to that time for the improvement of waste lands had been unsuccessful. In the course of the efforts made, lime was applied, and Ellel land was dealt with in the manner generally observed elsewhere; but we are told that, when a few crops had been got, the land showed signs of reverting to its original waste condition. Since then a decided change for the better has taken place, and the land is now, on the whole, of a good, productive character. Mr. J. Fenton Cawthorne, who was for three separate periods member of Parliament for Lancaster, and who died in 1831, was for some time the reputed lord of the manor of Ellel. The old manor house was situated above Bay Horse railway station, near the road which crosses the ridge of the "moor"; but many years ago it got into a state of decay, and about 1850 the ruins were removed. Ellel Crag is about a mile and three-quarters north-east of Bay Horse Station, and has long been known for its freestone quarry. This Crag is 418ft. above the level of the sea. John Housman, of Corby, near Carlisle, alludes in his topographical work, first published in 1800, to the freestone in certain parts of North Lancashire as being of the best quality, particularly that on a common between Lancaster and Garstang. He must here be referring to the Ellel Crag quarry. About half a mile east of Ellel Crag there is a plain dwelling called Crag House. In an inquisition of Jacobus Laurence, made on the 20th of August, 1490, Crag House, Ellel, is mentioned. Probably the present Crag House stands on or near its site. Up in this high region there were coal pits, or shafts sunk for the purpose of getting coal, in the early part of last century. Tyldesley, of Myerscough Lodge, says in his diary, under date May 22nd, 1714:—"After dinr went to Ellall col-pitts, and mett Mr. B—dsworth there." On the 27th of the same month he was at Aldcliffe Hall, and "from thence to Ellall colle pitts." Two days afterwards he went "to ye More col-pitts, thence to ye Crage [Crag] colepitts." And in an entry of his for the 4th of the following month, he remarks:—"Pd 5d. pro tobaco pro Ellal Crag colliors, whither I went ffrom Cockerham." In another country district, a few miles north of the Crag, coal-getting operations were simultaneously going on. In 1714 there were coal pits in Quernmore; but I fancy they would be somewhat like those in Ellel—not up to very much. And in the early part of the present century numerous attempts to get coal were made within about half a dozen miles of Ellel Crag, and two much nearer, but

not one was really successful. They were made on Grassyard Hall estate, near Caton, in 1804; on Scotforth Moor, in 1821; at Bazil Point, Overton, opposite Glasson Dock, in 1825; on Halton Moor, in 1826; and on Wham House estate, Ellel, in 1836.

In his autobiography, William Stout, a Quaker tradesman at Lancaster (born 1665, died 1752), makes reference to a native of Ellel, named John Hodgson —a very singular person, whose career was characterised by enterprise, ambition, prosperity, extravagance, and impecuniosity, followed by death in or about 1703. According to Stout, this John Hodgson, whom he describes (evidently taking him at the zenith-point of his prosperity) as "the greatest and most respectable merchant in my time," was born in Ellel (when or in which part of the township is not stated); and after serving his apprenticeship with John Greenwood, grocer and apothecary, Lancaster, he commenced business on his own account, and did well. His first wife was a Wilson, of the Dallam Tower (Westmorland) family: his second wife was Isabel Hodgson, a native of Lancaster. He got connected with the Virginia trade; was part owner of the first ship that ever sailed into the port of Lancaster from Virginia; was also part owner of several ships engaged in bringing wine and brandy from Bordeaux; paid little duty in respect to what he received, through being, for some reason, in favour with the Customs officers; made himself a great name, indulged in high living, and was for many years very successful in the French and Virginia trade; got to be a justice of the peace for the county; set up a sugar-refining house, but, not understanding the business, was supposed to suffer loss by it; secured, from Bristol, an excellent spinner of tobacco; built a residence which cost nearly £1,000; took gentlemen's sons as apprentices, who with other persons— servants—made too free with his wine cellars and warehouses; spent £500 a year in entertaining gentry who visited him; afterwards met with losses, yet continued to live high; simultaneously decreased his credit and increased his debts in connection with the Customs; altered his circumstances so seriously that his wife died of grief on account of the change; got into a lawsuit, about some tobacco, and lost it; next took the case to London—brought it before twelve judges, who confirmed the decision given against him; then, through inability to meet his pecuniary liabilities, was imprisoned in Lancaster Castle, where he died some years afterwards. Hodgson's estate, in Lancaster, was mortgaged for £500 to Sir Nicholas Sherburn; but, as there was owing to the Crown a larger amount, "upon bond, for Customs," Sir Nicholas lost the whole of the money he had advanced. Many other persons (creditors) had also to be content with—nothing. Hodgson had several sons, some dying early, in this country, and others dying abroad. His only daughter, Isabella, became the second wife of Mr. Edward Cole, of Beaumont Cote, near Lancaster; the issue of the marriage being a daughter, Isabella, who was married to Mr. Thomas Whitehead, of Fleet-street, Claughton, near

Garstang—one of the ancestors of the Forton Hall Whiteheads. Stout, whose story I have thus epitomised, as well as slightly corrected (in respect to the Christian name of the gentleman whom Hodgson's daughter married), and to which I have also made a small addition (regarding the Whiteheads), explains and moralises as follows concerning Customs evasion in Hodgson's time, &c. : " It was not accounted of as a crime to bribe the officers of the Customs or defraud the King of his Customs, which seldom or never improves men's estates, but rather is a canker to eat away that which is got by honest industry."

One-third of a mile north-east of the Preston and Lancaster main road, up the side way past the two " Abbey " houses in Ellel, Bay Horse railway station is situated ; but, strange as it may seem, though the station is thus designated, there is no village, nor hamlet, nor locality at all which bears such name. All the buildings, &c.—and there are but few—in the quasi or supposed Bay Horse region are, properly speaking, in Ellel. At the time when the Preston and Lancaster length of railway was made, a station was required between Scorton and Galgate, for south Ellel, Forton, Cockerham, and Dolphinholme people, and as the place selected for it had no name it took that of the nearest building, which was the one originally used as the Bay Horse Inn, directly adjoining the old coach road—about 40 yards distant, and on the lower side. In a

south-west, and quite close to a length of the new main road going past it. Coaches were drawn up and horses changed at this " New Bay Horse " from

NEW BAY HORSE INN BUILDING.

the time of its opening until the railway system put an end to their running. After being closed as an inn, the Old Bay Horse premises were used as a dwelling-house, &c., and eventually the district post office business was done here. In 1892, after being considerably enlarged and improved, the old place was re-opened as an inn—the license of the New Bay Horse going to it, whilst the postal business was transferred from the " old " to the " new " premises. And so matters remain. Up to about 1895, when he died, there lived at one of the cottages on

OLD BAY HORSE INN (ENLARGED).

hollow at the side of the old coach road, about 200 yards north-west of the station, there are three thatched cottages, all in one block. Here there used to be a public-house called the Rising Sun. It was done away with, as a licensed place, about 1815, being supplanted—so it has been conjectured by an inn which took the name of the Bay Horse (the present " Old Bay Horse") at the corner of the road opposite the station, and which was kept open until 1825, when its license and name were transferred to a house, built in that year, a quarter of a mile

the south-east side of the station a man, named Richard Brockbank, who supped the last glass of ale supplied at the Old Bay Horse prior to its closure in 1825, and partook of the first glass sold at the place when it was reopened 67 years afterwards !

In the forties, some time after the railway had been opened, a curious mishap occurred at Bay Horse station. At the time referred to, and for many years afterwards, there was a level crossing, with the customary kind of gate, on the north side

H

of and quite near to the station. A man called Jack Smith was, in his turn, the driver of the engine which brought up the Sunday morning train from Lancaster to Preston, and having been several times obliged to stop, just before reaching Bay Horse station, in consequence of the crossing gate being closed against him, he at length vowed that he would put an end to the annoyance; so he told the stationmaster (Wadeson) that if the gate were shut in this way any more, on a Sunday morning, he would run his engine right through it. When Jack next came up with the Sunday morning train, the gate was again closed, and without any hesitation at all he dashed into it and broke it to pieces. But in those days locomotives were small and light, and some of the fragments of the crossing gate threw the engine off the rails, and it mounted the platform on the east side, running along some yards towards the station before it came to a standstill. No personal injuries were sustained; but Jack, the driver, was considerably astonished, for he had much exceeded the performance which entered into his original programme; whilst the stationmaster, on perceiving what had occurred, got greatly excited, and even infused, though unconsciously, an element of commingled mystery and comicality into the affair. When the crash occurred the stationmaster was shaving himself in his house; he heard it, rushed outside, and, noticing that the engine was on the platform and close to the station building, ran off instantly, here and there, for help. The people whom he bounded past, and those at whose houses he hurriedly called for aid, were greatly mystified and amused by his appearance, for one side of his face was quite smooth and clean, whilst the other was thickly covered with shaving lather! He had got through only half of his "scraping" when the crash occurred, and, in his excitement and eagerness to obtain help, he had forgotten all about the lather on his unshaven cheek! —hence the amazement and amusement created. An accident of a very serious character happened at Bay Horse station, on the 21st of August, 1848. An ordinary train from Preston to Lancaster, which had stopped to set down and pick up passengers at this station, was on the point of starting, when there suddenly appeared in the rear, at the lower end of the curve near Foxholes bridge, the express for the North, coming at full speed. The danger signal was at once put up; but it was too late. The express dashed into the train at the station, and the consequences were very serious—a woman, named Ann Airey, wife of James Airey, labourer, Poulton-le-Sands (now called Morecambe), was so shockingly hurt that she died soon afterwards, whilst about 20 other passengers were injured. Mrs. Airey had with her a child—a boy about 18 months old—who was thrown out of one of the windows of the carriage, on to some ground near the fence on the lower side of the line, and who, when afterwards picked up and examined, was found to have sustained hardly any injury at all! The little one who thus escaped so marvellously is now a man of middle age, living at Morecambe. One of the adult passengers in the unfortunate train had

also a very remarkable escape. This was a grocery traveller from Lancaster—a little man, named Ralph Beckett. The carriage he was in was centrally smashed, and he fell right through the bottom of it, but sustained no personal injury whatever, and in a trice—so went the story—he was seen knocking about, making inquiries as to a parcel containing tea samples, which he had lost! On the 24th of October, 1861, the mail for the North ran into a goods train at Bay Horse Station—at the identical spot where the collision occurred in 1848; some waggons and a van being smashed, and one of the drivers along with a fireman somewhat hurt, but only one passenger was injured.

The tree-surrounded, rather elaborately fronted residence on a slight eminence, about a quarter of a mile south-east of Bay Horse railway station, is Foxholes. Dr. Christopherson, of Lancaster (presumably a son of Dr. P. Christopherson, of Lancaster, ob. circ. 1765), built the house here, about 1779, and when he died it was bought, along with certain adjoining property forming the Foxholes estate, by Dr. Carter, of Lancaster, who afterwards made additions by purchase; the entire property area, when thus increased, being 105 acres. Dr. Carter at first—after buying Foxholes—occasionally resided at the house; and eventually he regularly lived at it. He was very fond of shooting; and, when too advanced in years to go about on foot in pursuit of this particular kind of pleasure, he used to sally forth on a pony; a local youth—the now aged yet genial Mr. Richard Hall, builder, &c., Forton—usually accompanying him, and holding the pony every time he fired off his gun. About 1836 Dr. Carter died, and he was succeeded at Foxholes by Mr. W. Talbot Rothwell, who had some time before married his daughter, Miss Anne Carter. She died in 1842, at the age of 35, and was interred at Lancaster— in the Parish Churchyard, opposite the tower, at the west end, and a little below the footway which crosses the ground. A recumbent female figure in white marble—a very beautiful piece of statuary carved in Italy—was placed over the grave by Mr. Rothwell; and it is still in its original position; but in some parts it has been seriously broken. Not very long after being put up it was mischievously damaged; and since then it appears to have sustained some additional mutilation. After remaining for some time a widower, Mr. Rothwell took for his second wife Miss Elizabeth Conn, a native of Truro, in Cornwall. To the original Foxholes house very considerable additions, chiefly on the south-eastern side, were made by Mr. Rothwell. The residence on the north-eastern side, called Upper Foxholes, was also built by him: and he erected the long, plain-looking building just above—a portion of it, at the lower end, for a barn, and the remainder for a corn mill. He fitted up the mill portion with machinery. In 1860 one of Mr. Rothwell's children—a little boy between seven and eight years of age—happened to get too near an outside horizontal shaft, in connection with the corn mill, and, his clothes becoming entangled, he was drawn round by it and killed. The mill was afterwards accidentally gutted by fire, and this closed its career as a corn-grinding place: Mr. Rothwell simply put on the roof, and left the mill part empty, as it has virtually been ever since. His original idea, in respect to the mill, included not only extensive corn-grinding, but, as occasion required, the liquid-manuring of portions of the Foxholes estate! From

spects generous, but not unfrequently very eccentric in his ways, and rather fond of the " war path." For a while, after the railway which runs close to Foxholes had been opened, he was " down on " the locomotive engines, or rather the smoke which they emitted. Upon a bridge which crosses the line, right in front of Foxholes, he fixed some sort of an article for the purpose of gauging the quantity of soot or smudge emitted by the engines as they passed. The

FOXHOLES.

one or more tanks he laid a ramification of pipes into certain of his fields; the pipes, in the outer lengths were perforated, and he purposed forcing through them, by steam power, at the mill, as much liquid manure as would effectually drench the ground. But the scheme did not when in operation realise his expectations, and it was eventually abandoned. Mr. Rothwell was either connected with a commercial house in the East or had some property interests out there. Certain people in his home locality reckoned him to be a "Turkey merchant." Occasionally he was away for a while, and the supposition then was that he had gone to Smyrna or some other place in that region. For sport, Mr. Rothwell had a considerable fondness. He kept greyhounds for coursing; and at one time he had 17 thoroughbred stallions and mares—in fact, he had a regular stud, and went in for breeding and keeping "thoroughs" until they were about two years old, when they were sent off to be trained on Middleham Moor, in the North Riding of Yorkshire. A notable racehorse, bred by Mr. John Noble, maltster, of Preston, became his property: this was Lerywheut, which won numerous prizes at race meetings, but at length came to grief —shied or bolted one day, when on a course, broke a fetlock, and thus put an end to its racing career. For some time afterwards, when the injured part had got sufficiently better to allow of moderate walking, Lerywheut was utilised for stud purposes. Mr. Rothwell was one of the stewards of Lancaster Races in 1840 and 1850. He was a man of energy and integrity—exceedingly resolute, in some re-

railway men called this registering apparatus a "smoke jack." More than once Mr. Rothwell had the Railway Company fined for causing a nuisance by the excessive emission of smoke from the engines. He had on one occasion a rather peculiar tussle with the Company about a signal post. The Company began to fix a post of this kind on some of his land without asking permission to do so. He waited quietly till the work was finished; then he wrote to the secretary's office, at Lancaster, stating that a trespass had been committed; but a distinct unwillingness to change the position of the signal was evinced by the Company, so he tackled the post forthwith—had it cut off, close to the ground, and no attempt was made by the Company to fix another in the same place. Several men were once engaged to make drains, of a particular depth, in some of the fields on the Foxholes estate; in various places, however, the men did not go to the stipulated depth; Mr. Rothwell noticed the way in which the job was being dodged through or trifled with; but he said nothing until it was announced that everything had been finished, when he got all the drains professionally tested in respect to depth, and, after clearly proving the deficiencies which existed, made those concerned rectify them at their own cost. In his latter days Mr. Rothwell appeared to develop a curious spirit of isolation or indifferentism. He died in 1875, at the age of 62, and was interred in Shireshead old churchyard. His second wife died in 1896. Mr. Rothwell's son (Mr. Francis Talbot Rothwell) now resides at Foxholes.

A mile north-east of Bay Horse Railway Station

there is Newland Hall—medium-sized, and freed by an environment of trees and shrubs from what would otherwise amount to considerable bleakness. It is on the breast of an eminence, the base of which is at Bay Horse and the apex on Ellel Crag. About 400 yards below Newland Hall there is a very unusual convergence of lane ends. Commonly enough four lane ends, in proximity, are met with; but at this spot there are five. The Roman road from Ribchester to Lancaster ran through this region—the present way from the Fleece Inn, Ellel, to Galgate being on a portion of its line, and intersections of the latter by other roads form the five lane ends alluded to. The summit of Ellel Crag is, by the ordinary road, about three-quarters of a mile north of Newland Hall, and

heard (he has resided in this region all or the greater part of his life, as also did his father) the place now called Newland Hall went by the same name and has had no other. For a time Newland Hall belonged to the late Mr. Richard Hinde, wine and spirit merchant, Lancaster. He sold the place to Mr. Robert Daniel, formerly of Woodacre Hall, in Barnacre. Afterwards Mr. H. C. Owtram, cotton manufacturer, Preston, who for some years resided at Kirkland Hall, near Garstang, purchased the house and the land attached to it (84 acres). In 1878, after making great improvements at the place, including a large addition to the old building, at the south-east end, the ornamental laying out of a quantity of ground in front, the planting of trees, shrubs, &c., Mr.

NEWLAND HALL.

from it there is a finely-varied and very extensive view. It is conjectured that the original portion of Newland Hall was built in the last quarter of last century—probably between 1776 and 1786—during the time when attempts were made to reclaim waste or common land in the township: it was first a farmhouse, and the presumption is that it got its name through certain land being brought into agricultural use—virtually transformed into new land—shortly before or at the time of its erection, and in the neighbourhood of or directly adjoining its site. Some persons suppose that Undercroft, a residence a short distance off, on the south-east side, was the original Newland Hall, that after it had been in existence several years it was called Undercroft, and that the discarded name was applied to the farmhouse—the present Newland Hall. But there is no available evidence of a really reliable character to justify this supposition. The oldest man I have met with in the locality informs me that as far back as he can remember and according to everything he has

Owtram came to reside here. But he did not live long to enjoy the improvements thus made: he died in July of the following year. Mrs. Owtram, his widow, continued to live at Newland Hall till the spring of 1896, when she let the place to Mr. John Healey, cotton manufacturer, Preston, and went south. Mr. Healey left Newland Hall early in 1900, since which time it has been occupied by Mr. Herbert H. Owtram (son of the late Mr. H. C. Owtram), who is the owner of the place. In clear weather there is a splendid, wide-reaching view from the front of the Hall, and sometimes the Isle of Man can be seen from it.

Undercroft, as already mentioned, is situated on the south-east side of Newland Hall: it is about a third of a mile distant, in a straight line, but something like a mile off by the customary road. Upon a moderate eminence Undercroft stands—an eminence with a gentle slope of about 300 yards down to the road in front, which takes the line of the old Roman road. Some of the Hindes who belonged to the original firm of worsted manufacturers, at Dolphinholme, resided at Undercroft for numerous years, and one of the Derhams who were partners in the firm at a later date also lived here for a while. Various persons afterwards successively occupied the place. The Hindes used to own Undercroft. From them it passed, by purchase, to Mr. Thompson. It is now, as it has been for several years, the property of Major Allen, of Lancaster. In or about 1889 he rebuilt the whole or greater portion of the house. It is gable-fronted, has a neat, antique-looking facade, whilst trees on each side and at the rear, including not a few of the ornamental kind, make the general aspect cosy and picturesque. The Misses Peel, whose grandfather was a brother of the great Sir Robert Peel, are the present tenants of Undercroft. They have resided here about eleven years. Shireshead old Church and Scorton are in direct line, due south, with Undercroft, and from the front of it they come pleasantly into view.

UNDERCROFT.

CHAPTER XIX.

WYRESDALE—LANDOWNERS—PLACES OF WORSHIP—DOLPHINHOLME, PAST AND PRESENT—
ABBEYSTEAD—WYRESIDE.

To the east of Undercroft, a mile or so distant, there languishes, as if hopelessly ostracised or paralysed, and certainly, in some respects, undergoing disintegration, the once busy and prosperous village of Dolphinholme. In Wyresdale—the Nether portion of it—Dolphinholme is situated. When the Doomsday Survey was made the whole or the main portion of the land in Wyresdale was wild—had never been touched by the hand of the cultivator; and at or about this time a large quantity of the land here belonged to the great Norman baron Roger de Poictou. Early in the 12th century Wyresdale was owned by Henry I. William de Lancaster held the manor about the middle of the 13th century; and a few years later the "vaccary and forest of Wyresdale" became, by Royal grant, the property of Edmund son of Henry III. In the 14th century Robert de Guynes and John Rygmayden held the manor of Wyresdale—the interests here of the former descending to the Duke of Bedford, who died in 1435, and those of the latter to members of the Rygmayden family, who held them in succession until 1573, when they were settled upon Anne, daughter of Edward Tildesley, of Weardley, on her marriage with Walter, son and heir of John Rygmayden. In the next century the Gerards of Bromley, followed by the Hamiltons, were considerable landowners in Wyresdale—very much of the lower portion eventually becoming the property of the latter, by whom it was held until the great Hamilton sale in 1853. The Cawthornes were for a great number of years—600 or 700 it has been alleged—owners of land in Wyresdale; and the last of them having a connection with the locality (Mr. J. Fenton Cawthorne) possessed about 3,000 acres in the dale. In the 13th century this district was one entire vaccary, bearing the simple name of Wyresdale; but some time afterwards it was divided into twelve vaccaries, viz., Abbeystead, Marshaw, Dunkenshaw, Haythornthwaite, Green Bank, Ortner, Lentworth, Tarnbrook, Lee, Emmetts, Hayshaw, and Catshaw. These names still exist, and are applied now to farms, small clusters of cottages, &c. The word vaccary means a cow place or dairy house or cow pasture; and in Wyresdale, when the multiform succeeded the single vaccaral system, it must have applied to either large pastures and dairying places or to groups of them in the respective vaccaries named. As to the present divisional names, Nether and Over Wyresdale, they are of relatively recent application. The work of enclosing land in Wyresdale, on a systematic plan, was commenced in 1798. Much lime was afterwards applied to quantities of it—about 85 loads or 255 bushels per acre. The lime was made in kilns at Sykes, in Bowland, and brought into Wyresdale on the backs of ponies. Mr. J. Fenton Cawthorne enclosed, drained, and applied lime to a large quantity of land in the dale. He likewise planted many acres of land with trees. Wyreside, an excellent, beautifully-situated residence, about half a mile south of Dolphinholme, and concerning which some particulars will be given hereafter, was his ancestral home and his own country seat for many years. From November, 1806, to May, 1807, also from 1812 to 1818, and again from 1820 to the early part of 1831, he was one of the parliamentary representatives of Lancaster (borough). He died at his London residence, on March 1st, 1831, in the 79th year of his age. In 1570 there was an Episcopal "chapel" in Wyresdale, about a mile west of Abbeystead. In 1645 the "Committee for the Relief of Plundered Ministers" ordered the payment of £50 per annum out of the tithes arising in the parish of Bolton, sequestered from Sir Henry Compton, Knight, recusant, to increase the maintenance of the minister of the "chappell in Whirsdall" (Wyresdale), which at that time was only £4 a year. In 1731 this place of worship was rebuilt; in 1853 it was restored; and since then it has undergone various improvements. It is now a church, with a distinct ecclesitstical district assigned to it. Formerly it was, ecclesiastically, in the parish of Lancaster: in 1854 it was separated therefrom. Recently stained-glass windows have been put in the church—two by Lady Rose Mary Molyneux, in memory of her father, the late William Philip, Earl of Sefton, K.C., and one by the Hon. Richard Frederick Molyneux, in memory of the late Emily Cecil, Countess of Sefton. The present vicar is the Rev. D. Schofield. For many years there have been followers of George Fox (founder of Quakerism) in Wyresdale: they have a meeting house and a school in the "Over" division, a mile from the church, on the north side. At Emmetts, in the same division, about a mile and a quarter north-east of Abbeystead, there is an old Methodist chapel. But it is not used now for the purposes of worship: it was supplanted, about 1893, by a new chapel, nearer Abbeystead, &c. In June last there died, at Well Brook, in Over Wyresdale, a very old and much respected Methodist—Mr. John Winder, farmer. He had been a leader amongst the Methodists of the district for about half a century. When he died he was in the 84th year of his age. In the early part of this century there was a somewhat extensive cotton manufactory at Catshaw, in Over Wyresdale; and here for a time the late Mr. John Thompson, afterwards corn dealer, Preston (father of Alderman W. Thompson, Preston), was employed as a cardmaster.

Reverting now to Dolphinholme, it appears to have come into existence as a village through the establishment of a worsted factory, in the lower part, by Messrs Hindes and Patchett, towards the end of last century. It is said that before the factory was built there stood upon a portion of its site, or in contiguity thereto, a small, primitive corn mill. Not, however, until Messrs. Hindes and Patchett began operations was there a collection of dwellings or conflux of population here. Neither village nor hamlet bearing the name of Dolphinholme was there prior to the commencement of the works of this firm. But there was, many generations back, a farmstead called "Dolfynholme" in this locality— presumably in the vale, on part of the site as well as some distance east of what became the older portion of Dolphinholme village. In 1604-5, Lord Gerard had 55 tenants in "Wyresdale quarter," and the principal of them was "John P'kinson, of Dolfynholme," whose holding consisted of "xv. acr." Concerning the origin of the name Dolphinholme, there is a tradition that once a dolphin was found in the locality—at the side of the river Wyre, which runs through the lower or older part of the village —and that, owing to such circumstance, the place was designated Dolphinholme. But this is a very improbable story. The name dolphin comes from the word dolf, which means a curve or winding; and the application of such name to a place is no proof at all of there ever having been a cetacean of the dolphin kind at or about it. A mile and a half N.E.E. of Lancaster there is a farmstead called Dolphinlee; but a dolphin could not possibly get up to that place of itself, for the simple reason that it would have no water to swim in. According to the Ordnance map, the outline of a number of fields, at Dolphinlee, when they are taken in the aggregate, is curved, and somewhat resembles the form of a dolphin. Lee (lea, ley, or lay) signifies an expanse of meadow or pasture land—originally it meant an open space or cleared part in a wood; so that it is not improbable this configuration of a number of fields—originally, perhaps, they were a single clearing, without intersecting fences—suggested the name Dolphinlee. In the vale, about 300 yards east of the older part of Dolphinholme village, there is a flat field, along the north-west side of which the Wyre flows. On that side the course of the river curves considerably—as viewed from the south, it assumes a full line of convexity; and, probably, the water cut or race of the old corn mill—a mill most likely working anterior to John Parkinson's tenancy under Lord Gerard in 1604-5—took the same course from the river as that used, though on an enlarged scale, for the worsted works. If so, then the race of the corn mill would have a somewhat

outward curve on the south side of the flat field before named. The river and the race would thus give the central ground a distinctly curved appearance on each side, justifying the application of the root or primary portion of the word dolphin, and it would have the general outline of a dolphin's body as well, whilst a narrow piece, at the west or fore part, would assume the shape of a projection or snout, and a tapering strip at the east end, terminating at the inflow, would present the form of a tail; the whole intermediate land thus having in a striking degree the general configuration of a dolphin. A smaller piece of land just below would, as its present appearance shows, take a somewhat similar shape, through a continuation of the mill-race; but the former would, in outline, bear a closer resemblance than the latter to the general form of a dolphin; and its environment by the Wyre and the mill-race—its practical surrounding by fluviatile water—would make it a holme, i.e., a river isle: hence the appositeness of the name Dolphinholme. Messrs. Hindes and Patchett built a considerable number of cottages in the hollow, near their works, for the hands they required. Some years afterwards the firm here (changed in name to Messrs. Hindes and Derhams) built for additional workpeople and their families two rows of houses, called Corless Cottages—33 in number—at the top of the bank westward, near the Wyresdale-road, and on land evidently taken from an agricultural holding close by, named Corless Farm. But, notwithstanding this extra accommodation, there was a deal of overcrowding in the village generally: the houses were of the small, four-roomed kind, and as a rule each of them was occupied by two families. The water-wheel used at Dolphinholme works was the biggest in England, indeed the biggest in the United Kingdom with the exception of that at Laxey, in the Isle of Man; and if in one respect smaller, it was in another even larger than that—it was only four feet less in diameter than the Laxey wheel, but was twice as wide. Dolphinholme, it is said, was the first place in the kingdom lighted with gas. This luminant was originally made here about 1801, and was stored in a holder on the east side of the works. The gas was made for the factory; but in one or more of the shops in the older part of the village, as well as at the side of the road going through that part, gas was also used. One or two of the old lamp frames still remain in their original position at the road side. When the firm at Dolphinholme were at the zenith of their activity and prosperity, about 1800, they employed about 1,400 persons—something like 1,000 at the factory, who worked day and night in sections, the remainder, who could not be accommodated there, doing wool-combing, &c., at their own homes in Wyresdale, Quernmore, Scorton, Forton, Galgate, and in some cases, it is said, at Scotforth, near Lancaster. The total population of Dolphinholme, at this throng, flourishing time, was between 2,000 and 3,000. Some of the wool sorters at the factory could earn £4 per week each. For a considerable time there has been only one public-house in the locality; but in the old, prosperous days there were two or three drink places in the neighbourhood of the village, on the western side, and they were kept pretty busy. One of the landlords made his fortune with ale-selling. Mr. James Derham, a member of the Dolphinholme firm, had a great aversion to the drinking which went on, and if he happened to meet in the road a child carrying a jugful of ale, and going towards the village, he would up with his foot and punch the jug to pieces. In the early part of this century an engineering or trans-posing feat of a very peculiar character was per-formed at Dolphinholme, namely, the bodily re-moval, for the sake of securing a better draught, of a tall stone chimney from the works to the top of an eminence about 100 feet off, at the eastern end. This chimney, or a very considerable portion of it, is still standing. The wool-combers of Dolphin-holme thought a good deal of the patron saint of their order (Bishop Blaise), and more than once they celebrated his birthday by walking in proces-sion, headed by a band of music, to Lancaster, and there dining festally at one of the inns. Dolphin-holme factory works were noted for being very well kept: they were exceedingly clean. In the days of good trade, manufactured goods were regularly taken from Dolphinholme on waggons, each drawn by six horses, to Leeds and Bradford; and from one or both of those towns loads of raw material were brought, on the return journey, to Dolphinholme. When it was made known that a waggon thus laden was approaching the village, workpeople connected with the factory would go down the main road, and, on meeting with the home-comer, would push at the rear and pull with ropes, so as to ease the horses and expedite the transit. Once a quarter a heavy load of goods used to be sent from the Dolphinholme works to Norwich (then one of the greatest seats of the worsted trade in England), whence it was for-warded to the Continent. Between 60 and 70 years ago a merry receptional programme was gone through, by the operatives, at Dolphinholme, in respect to new-comers at the works. For instance, in the summer of 1833, when some fresh hands appeared on the scene, they had to "pay their footing," and in connection with this pecuniary process there was quite a festive stir: a large number of the work-people assembled in a neighbouring field, dancing and amusements of various kinds were indulged in, refreshments were provided by the firm, and alto-gether the proceedings were of a very pleasurable character. When the times were good, the masters at Dolphinholme were very considerate towards their workpeople, and did a great deal for their benefit. Originally, educational and religious facilities, in ac-cordance with Episcopal principles, were provided for the village, in a large room known afterwards as the old school or library building, and now used as a reading and recreation room. In 1839 Messrs.

Hindes and Derhams gave some land on the western side, above the older portion of the village—oppo-site Corless Cottages—for a new Episcopal place of worship, which was built during the same year, but by no means internally finished then. It contained sitting accommodation for 668 persons, and was, in reality, a sort of private chapel, maintained by Messrs. Hindes and Derhams, and in the first instance attended to by a resident schoolmaster whom they also provided. Afterwards the services, held on Sunday afternoons only, were conducted by the curate of Ellel (Galgate) Church, &c. Once a quarter, weather being favourable, the people met on a Sunday morning, at the school, and then walked in procession to Shireshead old Church for Holy Communion, headed by the wardens, and accompanied by the schoolmaster—the father of Mr. J. T. Preston, late principal of Ripley Hospital, Lancaster. It is said that on the way to Shireshead Church they sang hymns. The intro-duction of steam power into factories, &c., in many parts of the country, followed by greatly improved facilities, per railway, for the transit of goods, soon materially affected the works at Dolphinholme. Messrs. Hindes and Derhams, having to compete under old conditions, were greatly handicapped in the markets, and, in order to modify the diffi-culties which confronted them, they were obliged to resort to a reduction of wages. Several of the hands objected to this, and a number of them struck work. The operatives who thus "came out" were called "black sheep," whilst those who stuck to their employment were designated "white sheep." Much ill-feeling was engendered: a spirit of mutual hatred took possession of the two lots of work-people. In the course of this discord the "whites" decided to burn out the "blacks," and went to the houses they occupied for the purpose of pouring oil close to the front doors, and then applying a light to it; but this was too savage or illegal a scheme to be carried out, and it was stopped before any-thing really serious had been done. A large meet-ing was afterwards held at Lancaster, to consider the state of affairs at Dolphinholme, and it was decided that the strike should cease, and that the masters' terms should be complied with. Mrs. Derham, wife of one of the masters, residing at Undercroft, when apprised of the result of the meet-ing, drove over to Lancaster, found that the report she had heard was correct, then got her carriage gaily decorated, and, amid acclamation, returned home. The termination of the strike was the occa-sion of rejoicing throughout the Dolphinholme re-gion. There was a procession of a novel character; a man in kilts, playing bagpipes, and riding on a donkey, headed it; a live black sheep was carried, in a sort of cage, amid the throng of moving people; gladness—commingled satisfaction and hilarity—prevailed; and at the conclusion of the processional proceedings the black sheep was taken into a field, roasted, eaten with a due supply of bread, and copiously washed down with ale, &c.

But, though peace came with the termination of the strike, prosperity of the old kind never returned to the village. Owing to the retention of primitive manufacturing processes, increased competition, waggon and cartage expenses, distance from the markets, &c., the Dolphinholme firm (Messrs. Hindes and Derhams) ultimately failed, and the factory was stopped. This was a most serious blow to the village : several workpeople left ; gloom prevailed ; and the chapel was closed. But some time afterwards Messrs. John Swainson and Son commenced operations at the factory, in the wool or worsted line ; and in the summer of 1843, when the state of affairs in the village had improved, the chapel was re-opened. Messrs. Swainson and Son continued operations at Dolphinholme until about 1853, when the factory was again stopped. Some of the workpeople, who had been very careful and provident, then retired on their savings ; others went to Rochdale, Bradford, &c. ; several sought employment in fresh departments of industry at different places ; and a number emigrated. Later, Messrs. Cook and Margerison began work, at Dolphinholme factory,

to pieces ; the big water wheel has been broken up, and the main portion of the wheel house is in ruins ; all that remains of the gas system is the circular stone tank which once contained the holder, &c. ; several of the original cottages have been pulled down ; and, what with natural decay and the demolition personally effected, a most remarkable change has taken place here. On the north side of the river bridge—a very good one, of stone—there is a large building, apparently of the warehouse kind, which is in a very sound condition. It was built for the purposes of the factory, and a peculiarity in its construction is this—it has no roof-tree, rafters interlocked at the angle being sufficient without one. Of its kind, it is said to be a very strong and excellent structure. The older part of the village contains a few dwelling-houses, occupied ; but it has a singularly silent, forsaken look ; the number of " goers-in or comers-out " is exceedingly small, and a sort of Balcluthan desolateness prevails. One day, when I passed through this part, it could not have been quieter if it had been deserted : there was no sound save that made by the river, and I did not see a single human being

DOLPHINHOLME (1900).

in the cotton domain (weaving) ; and in a while they were succeeded by Mr. H. Rushton, of Preston, who, on coming to Dolphinholme, resided at a large house between the factory and the bridge, and who in 1864 took into partnership Mr. W. Slater, of Preston. This firm built a shed, near the factory, and carried on both cotton spinning and weaving. But success could not be secured at Dolphinholme ; its day here had gone by ; and in 1867 Messrs. Rushton and Slater closed the works. This meant "finis." Since then the older portion of the village has, practically, been in a dying-out condition ; and as to the works—the shed and the factory are in ruins, and quantities of stone which their walls once contained have been utilised in the construction or repair of buildings, &c., in the Dolphinholme district and elsewhere ; the offices and adjoining structures are falling

in the place. Eventually I encountered—out of the village, and at the back part of the old works—a man who was engaged in clearing away some of the ruins. The total population of Dolphinholme (upper and lower parts together) is now only about 400—a contrast, verily, to the time when 1,000 of the inhabitants were engaged at the worsted works, and when the aggregate number of the residents amounted to between 2,000 and 3,000 ! The chief property owners in this locality at present are Captain Garnett, of Wyreside, Captain Ormrod, of Wyresdale Park, Major Allen and Mr. H. Bradshaw, of Lancaster, and Mr. Matthew Procter, of Dolphinholme. The greater portion of the dwelling-houses in Dolphinholme are owned by Mr. Procter. These are Corless Cottages —originally 33 and now 30 in number—which he purchased in 1885. Singular to say, his father, James Procter, who was Messrs. Hindes' gamekeeper for 39 years, cut the first sod for the first of these cottages, and helped to prepare the foundations for the others. A school, of the "national" order, is located at the north-eastern end of the higher part of the village. The late Mr. Henry Garnett, of Wyreside, gave the site, and, with the assistance of grants from the National Society, erected the school. At the four lane ends, a few hundred yards beyond the school, there used to be four houses (since transformed into one), in which, during the palmy days of Dolphinholme, a man regularly employed seven shoemakers.

The chapel previously referred to, opposite Corless Cottages, Dolphinholme, was closed when the woollen or worsted trade collapsed here. In 1858 the late Mr. Henry Garnett, of Wyreside, purchased the chapel and a good deal of adjoining land from the executors of the late factory masters. He afterwards restored the chapel building, made it suitable for services of the Episcopal kind, partially endowed it, and also provided a graveyard. The work of restoration, &c., was completed in 1861; on the 25th of July, 1862, the consecration ceremony was performed; and a separate ecclesiastical district was assigned to the place—now a church. The Bishop of the diocese, taking into account the generosity which had been shown by Mr. Garnett, vested in that gentleman and his heirs the patronage of the living. The first incumbent was the Rev. W. J. Adams, B.A. Some time after the church had been consecrated, Mr. Garnett built a Vicarage; he also contributed towards the augmentation of the living. The Vicarage of Dolphinholme was built mostly of old materials brought from Wyresdale Tower, when that place was pulled down, by the late Mr. Henry Garnett, some 30 years ago: the doors of the entertaining rooms are of solid mahogany. Wyresdale Tower was in Marshaw vaccary, and is said to have been "a pretentious looking building," with a stone over the front door bearing the following inscription:—"John Fenton Cawthorne, 1802. This Tower shall live in song, and Wyresdale is its name." I have never met with any song relating to it. The present new church stands on the site of the old one, under the foundation stone of which there was found a brass plate, face downward, which bore the following inscription:—"This stone was laid to the glory of our Lord and Saviour Jesus Christ, on June 17th, 1839, by the Rev. John Dodson, M.A., Vicar of Cockerham; the Rev. John Gaman, B.A., incumbent; Thomas Foster Hinde, Walter Alen Hinde, Robert Derham, James Derham, donours of the land." A cavity in the stone which had been covered by the brass plate (now in the vestry) contained various coins of the realm, ranging in date from 1823 to 1838, and a Victoria coronation medal. The new church, which was opened on the 25th of January, 1899, cost £3,500, nearly one-third of which was subscribed by members of the Garnett family. It will accommodate about 250 persons. Externally, it has an ancient appearance, which is due to the character of its architecture—the late decorated style of the 14th century. The present vicar is the Rev. W. Poole, M.A., who took a very active and praiseworthy part in the movement for the new church. In Dolphinholme there are a few Wesleyans and some Independents. The Wesleyans utilise as a chapel part of a building formerly connected with the old works. The part in question was first used as a Wesleyan place of worship when Messrs. Rushton and Slater had the mill, &c., and since then, by permission of the Ormrod family, services in connection with the same body have been held in it. The place thus used will accommodate about 200 persons. The Independents first had religious services, at Dolphinholme, in a small room. In 1881 they opened a new iron chapel of their own (on the higher side), capable of accommodating about 200 persons. The Rev. P. Webster, Congregational minister at Forton, attends to this chapel.

On the eastern side of Dolphinholme, just behind the old mill chimney already named, there is a pasture called Scot field. A local tradition runs to the effect that in this field a "battle" took place, in 1745, between some of the King's troops and a number of the followers of the "Young Pretender." In Volunteer Ray's "Complete History of the Rebellion" there is no reference to a conflict having occurred here, or to even any of the Royal or rebel forces being in this particular locality at all; still, it is definitely stated in the district that small cannon balls have been found in Scot field, and it is a fact that, not long ago, a local gamekeeper picked up one in it.

Towards the head of Wyresdale, at Abbeystead, there is a large, handsome building which was erected in 1885-1887, as a shooting box, by the late Earl of Sefton, K.G. It more resembles a splendid, massive mansion than a building of the "box" kind. The land on which it stands, as well as a great quantity in the neighbourhood of it, was purchased by the late Lord Sefton from Mr. Henry Garnett, of Wyreside. In the reign of Edward III. some land in Wyresdale passed by marriage into the Molyneux family of Sefton—it was afterwards disposed of; so that certain old family associations as well as suitability for game shooting may have induced Lord Sefton to purchase land and erect such a building as the one referred to in this locality. His lordship, who died in 1897, left the mansion to his daughter, Lady Rose Mary Molyneux, who has an allowance of £5,000 per annum to maintain it. In case her ladyship marries, the place will revert to the titled estates. A short distance south-west of it there is a large compensation reservoir—it looks like a beautiful lake, which was made by the Lancaster Corporation, who tap the region above for their town's water supply.

Some time after the founding of Furness Abbey, in 1127, a number of monks (Cistercians) from that establishment settled in Wyresdale; and Abbeystead (meaning an abbey place) is understood to be the spot where they took up their quarters, and where they erected an abbey or a building of a cognate character.

It is supposed that their external operations pertained very considerably to farming. These monks left Wyresdale some time between 1188 and 1200, went to Ireland, and founded Wythney Abbey. The exact spot on which stood their abbey or the building they occupied, in Wyresdale, is not positively known. The Ordnance map (6in. scale) specifies the "supposed site of an abbey" at a point about 110 yards south of Abbeystead School. Some persons suppose that its site is covered by the reservoir. One Lancashire antiquary (Mr. W. O. Roper, F.S.A.) thinks that its position was between Abbeystead and the Lee. No ruins of stonework—no remains of any kind—capable of being identified with the establishment of the Cistercian detachment in Wyresdale have been found. The Rev. D. Schofield, vicar of Wyresdale, says, in a letter I have received from him: "The farmhouse at Higher Lee [about a mile and a half north of Abbeystead] has in it some excellent stonework—moulded cornices round the kitchen, with three arched doorways entering it, from the entrance hall, of exactly similar pattern to the old church windows and doors; while the farm at Lower Swainshead [about a mile and a half west of Abbeystead] has windows at the back that suggest a scholastic or ecclesiastical origin. These are the only architectural items I can find in the parish which even suggest connection with the old monks' place." In 1674 William Cawthorne, an ancestor of J. Fenton Cawthorne, built and endowed a free school at Abbeystead—the school which stands on the north side of the road there. This said William Cawthorne, by will dated September 22nd, 1683, proved in the Prerogative Court of Canterbury, and reciting amongst other things the erection by him of a free school, as well as a convenient house for the master, in Wyresdale, gave to Abraham Partington, Mayor of Lancaster, Seth Bushell, D.D., Vicar of Lancaster, Laurence Shawe, Vicar of Cockerham, and eleven other persons (whom he appointed visitors and governors of the school), and their heirs, the said school, master's house, and a quantity of property in the locality, upon trust, so that the school might remain a free one, for the benefit primarily of 50 scholars (whose parents had to reside in one or more of the vaccaries of Wyresdale), deemed fit objects of charity; his own kindred to be always preferred before any others, though they might live three or four miles from the said vaccaries; the schoolmaster to be a graduate of one of the Universities, and not under 23 years of age, and to hold the property referred to for his own advantage on entering into a bond to refrain from undertaking any "lecture or preaching in any church or chapel," whereby the scholars might be neglected in their education, to provide an usher at his own expense, in case the number of scholars, including those of the foundation, exceeded 60, to do certain repairs, and to deliver up all the property named, as well as all the books in his custody belonging or relating to the school, when required to do so. The revenues of the school now amount to about £280. Opposite the school there is a house which was built by William Cawthorne, and in front of it there is a stone which bears the date 1677. The schoolmaster with the longest record at Abbeystead appears to have been Thomas Richardson. He died in 1793, after having held the post of master for about 60 years. The school was put under a new scheme in 1844. Its operations are now in full unison with the requirements of an ordinary public school.—Lentworth Hall, or Lentforth, situated a mile and a quarter west of Abbeystead, is, in its foundation, very old—is, indeed, supposed to be one of the most ancient places in the parish of Wyresdale.

Selectly and beautifully placed is the Garnett residence—Wyreside. It is situated on the south side of Dolphinholme, about half a mile from the village in a direct line, but considerably more by the ordinary road. Wyreside is a spacious, handsome, stone-built mansion, and for 45 years it was the residence of the late Mr. Henry Garnett. The great grandfather of Mr. Henry Garnett was a farmer, at Casterton, near Kirkby Lonsdale; and his grandfather (Mr. John Garnett) was a merchant, trading with Jamaica, who for a time lived at Ulverston, subsequently removing to Manchester, and whose third son, Robert, in 1836, purchased a large quantity of property in Wyresdale (Wyreside included) from the executors of Mr. Fenton Cawthorne: he also purchased the office of Master Forester of Wyresdale from the Duchy of Lancaster. He resided at Wyreside, at which he made some alterations in 1843. In 1852 he died, and, by arrangement, his successor at Wyreside was his third son, Mr. Henry Garnett—a gentleman who was High Sheriff of Lancashire in 1860, and Chairman of the Lancaster Quarter Sessions for many years, and who died in 1897. The office of Master Forester of Wyresdale (purchased for two lives by Mr. Robert Garnett) passed over to Lord Sefton when he bought the Over Wyresdale property; but, as both his Lordship and Mr. Henry Garnett died in the same year, no complications arose respecting it. When Mr. Henry Garnett died, he was succeeded at Wyreside by his eldest son, Captain Charles Henry Garnett, who continues to reside at the mansion. Wyreside stands on a picturesque eminence sloping to the south-west: it has a select, commanding appearance, and from the front of it there is a charming view down Nether Wyresdale and away beyond into the Fylde country. On each side of the mansion and at the rear of it there are choice woodlands; the Wyre meanders prettily and flows with a gentle cadence at the base of the eminence which Wyreside crowns; hills, fine in their reposeful strength and beautiful in their empurpled vesture, fill up the horizon right and left and rearward. The old house here was built at different times and in different styles of architecture. The centre part was of the Tuscan order, with a large portion supporting a spacious gallery in front, surrounded by an elegant balustrade. The wings were more ancient. In the "Lonsdale Magazine" (1821) there is a full-page illustration of Wyreside, as it appeared when occupied by Mr. J. Fenton Cawthorne, and a description of the mansion, apparently by Mr. John Briggs, the editor of that periodical. The description not only relates to the architecture of the mansion, but to the size and character of the chief rooms, and the general contents thereof. In some of the rooms, it is stated, there was silvered glass placed against the wall opposite the front window, whereby the outside landscape was reflected; the centre of the bookcase in the library contained a concealed spring lock, which gave communication with the drawing-room; and in the dining-room there were two secret closets to which access was obtained by "invisible doors." Wyreside was refronted with massive masonry about 1804, and at the same time a servants' hall was built at the rear. Taken in its entirety, Wyreside is a very substantial, excellent structure, in a strikingly picturesque position, and with a varied and delightful outlook.

WYRESIDE.

CHAPTER XX.

To the point from which divergence into the higher parts of Ellel, &c., was made I now return, and thence go forward some distance on the old coach road. About 400 yards north-west of Bay Horse Railway Station there is the Hole of Ellel. To the uninitiated the mere name of this place—on paper—is somewhat suggestive of the mysterious or the gruesome; whilst the cursory reference made to the Hole, by some historical or topographical writers, would prompt the inference that it is either an important pass or a strait, deep valley. In reality, the name refers to a rustic-looking depression, through which the river Cocker flows, and to a farm immediately adjoining. As a curious coincidence, I may here just remark that there is a small farm called Hole of Ellel near the village of Holker, in the ancient district of Cartmel. The Hole of Ellel farmhouse, in Ellel, is a neat, substantial building, on the breast of a small hill which forms the north side of the Hole. The old coach road crosses this hill, and the farmhouse is close to it, on the east side. Mr. George Yeats built this farmhouse. Previously he had resided in Ashton, near Lancaster. In 1757 he leased Ashton Hall for five years. When the Duke of Hamilton came of age, Mr. Yeats left Ashton Hall, took up his abode at a dwelling in Ellel (probably an old place at the Hole), and in 1775 built the present farmhouse here. Over the front door of the house there is a stone which bears the date just named, and the initials "Y. G. E."—Yeats George and Elizabeth (his wife). In 1797 Henry Smith, who married Ellen, daughter of George Yeats, went to the Hole of Ellel, and resided here until his death, in 1831. He was succeeded by his eldest son William, who lived here till his death, in 1866, since which time the farmstead has been tenanted by different persons. Henry G. Smith, of Moor House, Ellel (son of William Smith), now owns the Hole of Ellel farm: he also owns property in the adjoining township of Forton, which was bought by one of his ancestors (James Smith) in 1674. A little way past the Hole of Ellel, and on the west side of the old road, there is a farm house called Stirzakers. This is evidently the place to which the Rev. Peter Walkden alludes in his diary when, under date January 15th, 1730, he says, "Came from Lancaster to Thomas Storzacre's, near the Hole of Ellhill." In the front part of the house there are some stones which appear to have belonged to an older building on the same site, or to some substantial structure in the district. Here—at Stirzakers—and for about a quarter of a mile to

the north there exists a very remarkable nearness, perhaps unique parallelism, of past and present transit or travelling ways: the railway, the old coach road, the main road lower down which superseded it, and the canal, all run parallel, and are all within a transverse space of 600 yards for the distance named! And opposite the same part, about 730 yards east of the railway, there is a portion of the course which the Roman road from Ribchester to Lancaster took. So that there are in this locality, within a distance of not more than three-quarters of a mile—in a diagonal line extending from a point south-east of Crag Hall, across the summit of the old coach road, to the Cocker culvert north-west of Nuthurst—lengths of all the ordinary public travelling ways used in England from the days of the Romans until now! From the summit of the old road beyond Stirzakers there is, on a clear day, a very spacious and delightfully varied view: eastward, the uplands of Ellel, with their farmsteads and cottages, the Crag with its rugged front, &c.; south-east, the fine pastoral sweep of Nether Wyresdale, and the hill range above Soorton; west, right in front, palatial-looking Ellel Grange, with Hay Carr select and sheltered in a vale on one side, and away outward the lands of Cockerham, Pilling, &c., Lancaster Sound below the Lune estuary, Fleetwood, with its prominent line of front buildings, and its high ship masts in the rear, and the broad, bright waters of the sea to the right; whilst northward there are visible the fells of Furness, the mountains of Lakeland, &c. The old road, north of the summit, descends for about a quarter of a mile, and then, at a point near the entrance lodge of Ellel Grange, merges into the present main road.

Ellel Grange is on an eminence west of the main road, and about half a mile from the entrance lodge. Its facade is excellent in range and altitude: the building generally has a finely-balanced, opulently-serene aspect, and, viewed from a distance, with its stately surmounting tower, it strikingly reminds one of Osborne. There are many trees about it; the grounds in front, &c., are beautifully laid out; and down in a tranquil dell, to the south-east, there is an ornamental expanse of water. Many generations ago there was a "grange" in Ellel; and if not originally built for, it in all probability belonged at a very early period to, Cockersand Abbey. In the Lay Subsidy Roll of Lancashire, for 1330, there is the entry, "Robto del graunge, Ellel." From 1501 to 1729 ancestors of the Prestons now living at Ellel

Grange owned part of the present estate here, besides other property in the parish of Cockerham. In the Bursar's rent roll of Cockersand Abbey, for 1501, there appears, "Vx Ric Egremuds t z di Grange do E'lell r iii capon iiili," directly followed by "Nicol Pston [Nicholas Preston] t z aliu di Grange r iii capon iiili." The will of a descendant of the Prestons of Ellel Grange (Nicholas Preston) was proved or lodged in the Probate Court, Chester, in 1608. In 1638 the will of Alice Preston, widow, of Ellel Grange, was proved within the arch-deaconry of Richmond. There is an administration bond in Somerset House, dated 1661, respecting the will of Isabel Preston, of the Graunge, Ellel. The will of John Preston, of Ellell Graing, was proved, in 1683, within the archdeaconry of Richmond: and therein likewise were proved, in 1694, the will of Robert Preston, of Ellell Grange, and in 1729 that of another Robert Preston, of Ellell Grainge. Dr. Charles Leigh, in his "Natural History of Lancashire, Cheshire," &c., published in 1700,

(a descendant of the aforenamed Richard Gillow) lived at Ellel Grange. He was a cabinet-maker, and also had a good knowledge of architecture: he was the architect of Lancaster Custom House, which was built in 1764. Mr. Gillow, who was the father of Mr. Robert Gillow, who built and lived for several years at Clifton Hill, Forton, died in 1811 at Ellel Grange. Later, Mr. Richard Worswick, a nephew of Mr. Richard Gillow, and connected with the Worswicks of Leighton Hall (Yealand Conyers) and Lancaster, occupied the place. In 1823 Mr. Richard Atkinson, one of the "lords of Cocker-ham," became the owner of the Grange, and occupied it for several years. There were Atkinsons in Ellel—one named Richard—in the 17th century; but whether the gentleman who purchased Ellel Grange in 1823 was a descendant of any of them I have not been able to find out. The Grange and the estate connected with it went by purchase, in 1856, to Mr. William Preston, merchant, &c., of Liverpool. Mr. Preston was a native of Pilling, and was born at a

ELLEL GRANGE.

refers to a stag, the head and neck vertebra of which were found deeply embedded in marl at Larbrick, near Poulton-le-Fylde, and the horns of which were "preserved at Ellel Grange." Dr. Leigh does not say who was residing at Ellel Grange when his History was published: perhaps it would be Richard Gillow. Some time after the death of Robert Preston, whose will was proved in 1694, Richard Gillow resided at the Grange, and he died here in 1717, being succeeded at the place by Robert Preston, whose will was proved in 1729. A lady named Parkinson afterwards lived at Ellel Grange, and she died at it about 1742. Later, Edward Carter resided at the Grange, where he died about 1748. I have not been able to glean any information as to the occupation of Ellel Grange from 1748 till 1804. The Grange is described as being, in the latter year, the seat of Edmund Rigby. Afterwards Richard Gillow

farm which was the last remnant of the property formerly owned by the Prestons; and his ancestors were the old Prestons of Ellel Grange. There were several Prestons in both Ellel and Forton in the 17th and 18th centuries. In the list of Lancashire Royalists whose estates were sequestered, in 1652, there is the name of one William Preston, of Ellel. When a youth Mr. Preston's ambition was to buy back the land which had belonged to his forefathers, and for this purpose he went to the office of his uncle, Robert Preston, a Liverpool merchant, and by his industry and perseverance attained the object he had worked for, and bought the estate of Ellel Grange. He married Margaret, daughter of Mr. Thomas Gardner, of Pilling Hall, made a fortune in business, became a county J.P. and D.L., and was High Sheriff of Lancashire in 1865. When he purchased Ellel Grange estate he took the growing timber on it separately, by valuation. There was amongst the timber a wonderfully fine oak tree: it stood in front of and not far from the old Grange, and was valued at £100. The old Grange, which was of a strong and in some respects peculiar character (one of its cellars was hewn out of solid rock), was pulled down by Mr. Preston, and supplanted by the present Grange, which was built in 1857-59, on a site something like 400 yards to the south-east. As already observed, the existing Grange is a very handsome, stately-looking structure. The altitude or its position is also excellent—it gives the building a noble conspicuousness, and makes the tower visible for miles on every side. In 1871 Mr. Preston died. He was succeeded by his son, Mr. G. T. R. Preston, who was High Sheriff of Lancashire in 1891, who died in that year before the period of his shrievalty had terminated, and whose widow (nee Helena Cornelia, eldest daughter of Mr. George Bagster Denton, of Liverpool), and Miss Margaret Helena Preston, his daughter (sole issue), reside at Ellel Grange. Near the Grange, south-west, there is a church, which was built in 1869, the cost of it (about £7,000) being defrayed entirely by Mr. Preston. It is in the 13th century French Gothic style of architecture. The exterior work is excellent; but the body of the building is, owing to the surrounding trees, almost entirely screened from view, at a distance. The spire rises finely, and can be seen miles away. The interior of the church is very beautiful. There is sitting accommodation in it for about 100. Contiguous to the church there is a mausoleum, which contains the remains of Mr. and Mrs. W. Preston, a daughter, and their son, Mr. G. T. R. Preston.

Amid trees, in a hollow, about 300 yards south of Ellel Grange, Crag Hall is situated. It is plain in appearance, stands on the Ellel Grange estate, and is used as a farm-house. The building does not appear to be very old. It has evidently always been utilised, more or less, for farm purposes. According to Baines's Directory, &c., Captain Bennett Smith was living at Crag Hall in 1825. Amongst the subsequent tenants were Mr. George Lancaster and his son Richard, who were here, successively, for 42 years— the former from 1842 to 1852, and the latter from 1852 to 1884. The present tenant (Mr. James Melling) has been at the place since 1884.

Hay Carr, a select and substantial residence, is situated in a small vale somewhat park-like in aspect, and is about three-quarters of a mile south of Ellel Grange. It is built of stone, is beautifully screened by trees, looks picturesque at a distance, and under closer view has a particularly pleasing appearance. The name Hay Carr is derived from two very old words—Hæg (Anglo-Saxon) and Kærr (Scandinavian), and refers, in its original application, to enclosed land of a damp or swampy character, or to a fenced-in meadow reclaimed from bog. The land immediately adjoining Hay Carr house, Ellel, lies low, and in all probability it was at one time of a wet or boggy nature. In the 17th and 18th centuries there

were several persons in Ellel of the name of Richmond, and one of the later lot lived at Hay Carr. The will of Ann Richmond, described as of "Hay carr in Ellell," was proved in 1733, in the archdeaconry of Richmond. Then there came to "Haycarr in Ellell" John Bond, who died here about 1746. Subsequently there commenced the long and noteworthy career of the Lambs at Hay Carr. William Lamb, probably a descendant of one of the Lambs of Cockerham, was evidently the first of this name who lived at Hay Carr. In his will, proved in 1763, he is designated a yeoman of "Hay Car within Ellel." The person next distinctly connected with the place was Thomas Lamb. What the relationship between him and William Lamb was is not clear: if he were the latter's son, then he must have been either a very young infant when his father died, or of posthumous birth, for he was apparently born in the same year as that in which the will of William Lamb was proved (1763). He resided at Hay Carr, succeeded Mr. Michaelson, of Sion Hill, Bonds, as agent for the Duke of Hamilton's property in North Lancashire (about 13,000 acres), and died in 1823. He had a rather large family. The eldest of his sons (Mr. William Lamb, who served his time with Mr. William Miller, surveyor, &c., Preston) succeeded him in the agency, and became a well-known, indeed noted, man amongst landed proprietors and tenant farmers: he not only acted as agent for the Hamilton property in North Lancashire, but was in addition steward for other land owners in the same portion of the county. In his office, at Hay Carr, he had a large staff of clerks, &c. Mr. Richard Veevers, of the firm of Messrs. Myres, Veevers, and Myres, surveyor, architects, &c., of Preston, served his apprenticeship with Mr. Lamb—was with him from 1836 till 1842. Mr. Lamb was both an experimental and practical agriculturist, as well as a noted land agent. He introduced amongst the farmers within the sphere of his agency the subsoil plough: it was first tried successfully on some ground adjoining Hay Carr, on the 6th of January, 1840. He inaugurated ploughing matches, established one of the first and best agricultural societies in North Lancashire, and took much interest in all that concerned the real progress and prosperity of the numerous tenants he was connected with. In addition, he was very fond of greyhounds and coursing meetings. He kept between 20 and 30 greyhounds: he also bred such hounds, a favourite sire at his canine establishment being named "Gunpowder." Once a year he had a "weeding-out" day at the Old Holly, in Cabus: at such time all his greyhound puppies were concentrated there and carefully examined, the inferior animals being drafted on one side and afterwards hanged. In or about 1838, at the Holker Coursing Meeting, one of his greyhounds took the first and second main prizes, and nearly won the third. Mr. Lamb enlarged Hay Carr, at the south end, very substantially and excellently, in 1835: the north-eastern portions of the present building are later additions. Prior to the extension at the south end, Hay Carr was a comparatively small dwelling-house. Mr. Lamb died, at Hay Carr, in 1850, when he was 55 years of age. His brother (Mr. Thomas Lamb, solicitor) succeeded to the ownership of Hay Carr estate, also resided at the house, and continued

In due time he set off to Newcastle, arrived there about six o'clock in the evening, and decided to make the promised inquiry without delay. But Newcastle was a sort of terra incognita to him: he was not acquainted with the town, and did not personally know anybody in it likely to give him

HAY CARR.

the agency of the Hamilton property until the sale of it, in 1853, when fresh supervisional arrangements came into operation. Mr. Thomas Lamb had for many years an office, for the transaction of his legal business, in Sun-street, Lancaster. He took into partnership Mr. W. B. Mortimer (his nephew); and for a time this professional union was continued; but eventually Mr. Mortimer left Lancaster entirely. For several years afterwards Mr. Lamb heard nothing definite respecting Mr. Mortimer, but fancied that he was somewhere away north, though he did not, apparently, trouble himself much on the point. As time went on, however, he evinced a wishfulness to learn something positive as to where Mr. Mortimer was residing. This was in 1870, and before long he got the desired information through a source or in a way he had never for a moment anticipated. One day, in the year named, Mr. Richard Hall, builder, &c., Forton, received a message to the effect that Mr. Lamb wanted to see him. On getting to Hay Carr he was asked by Mr. Lamb if he could do a little work, in his own line, on or about the premises. Mr. Hall replied that he was on the point of paying a visit to Newcastle-on-Tyne, that he would be away there about a week, and that on returning he should be glad to attend to any instructions as to work which might be given to him. This proposed visit to Newcastle struck Mr. Lamb as something which might be turned to account by way of making an inquiry respecting Mr. Mortimer, so he asked Mr. Hall if he would, whilst on his visit, endeavour to find out, if possible, whether anything were known of him in that locality. Mr. Hall replied that he would do his best in the matter.

any reliable information on the matter he had in view. During the evening he pondered over the subject, and at length resolved that he would get up early next morning, proceed to the General Post Office, and question the letter-carriers, as they came out on their first delivery, if they could inform him whether there was in Newcastle or its suburbs a gentleman named Mortimer. So next morning Mr. Hall rose early, went to the Post Office, and planted himself near the doorway by which, he had been told, the postmen would emerge. By and bye they turned out with their bags, &c., and, strange to say, the very first of them accosted by Mr. Hall said that he knew where a gentleman named Mortimer resided in Newcastle. The address was then given to Mr. Hall, who afterwards found it to be actually that of Mr. W. B. Mortimer, the nephew of Mr. Lamb, of Hay Carr; and he furthermore ascertained that Mr. Mortimer was occupying an excellent official position in Newcastle. On returning, Mr. Hall reported the result of his inquiry to Mr. Lamb, who was much pleased with it. Some time afterwards Mr. Mortimer came to Hay Carr to see Mr. Lamb. The Rev. Robert Lamb, who was for a time incumbent of St. Mary's Church, Preston—being deemed whilst there a most energetic, estimable minister—and afterwards for many years rector of St. Paul's, Manchester, and who died in 1872, aged 60 years, was Mr. Lamb's brother. In 1875, Mr. Lamb died, at Hay Carr, his age being 69 years. The burial vault of the Lamb family, of Hay Carr, is in Cockerham churchyard—west end. A short time before his death, Mr. T. Lamb presented a new funeral pall for use at interments in the churchyard named, and—how strange!—it was first required at his own funeral! After Mr. Lamb's death, Mr. W. B. Mortimer came to reside at Hay Carr, and he died here in 1880, in his 48th year; his remains being interred in the graveyard attached to Scorton Church. Mrs. Mortimer, his widow, resided at Hay Carr for some years afterwards; and the place is now occupied by Mr. R. G. E. and Miss Mortimer, son and daughter of the late Mr. Mortimer.

The hamlet of Hampson Green is about 500 yards from Ellel Grange entrance lodge, is on the east side of the railway, and is approached by a straight, tree-bordered lane which branches from the main road and crosses the line by a bridge. This is a very small place, and an air of tranquil aloofness or rural selectness seems to characterise it. When it originated, or by whom it was in the first instance occupied, I have not been able to find out. But it is evidently an old place. Amongst the wills now preserved at Somerset House, and proved in the years named, are those of James Winder, "Hamshead, Ellell," 1592; John Richmond, "Amsed in Ellel," 1635; James Richardson, "Amsdon in Ellell," 1675; and James Corles, senr., "Amsden parish of Cockerham," 1727. A bond of guardianship, dated 1763, and preserved at the same place, relates to the family of Thomas Ion, maltster, of "Amson Green in Ellel." In Baines's map of Lancashire, published in 1824, "Hampson Grn" (Green) appears; and amongst the names of the residents of Ellel given in the county directory (Baines's), published in 1825, there is that of "Gillgrass J., maltster, Hampsons." I take it that all or the bulk of these place names refer to one and the same spot, viz.,

north belongs to Mrs. Stackhouse, of Stackhouse; the other farm and houses are the property of Miss Preston, of Ellel Grange, the cottages having been erected by the late Mr. G. T. R. Preston, from a design by Mrs. Preston. Close by are two ponds, one being the scene of a sad and nearly forgotten event. Some 50 years ago, old Mrs. Wainman lived alone in the house at the top of the hill, or rather tenanted half of it, and one stormy night went to her son's neighbouring farm for some groceries. On returning, the wind swept her into the water. No one knew of this till the dawn of the following morning, when a man who had gone to one of the ponds with some horses to water noticed that they would not step to the edge of it because a red cloak was floating there. A shady lane leads southward to Malten House, a small farm, perhaps some time occupied by a maltster connected with the old malt kiln which stood below where a new farmhouse has lately been built. A certain Robert Gibson, not long deceased, would tell how he used to take malt from this kiln to Preston. Perhaps his load homeward in the autumn days would be the cannel coal whereby the spinners in neighbouring houses secured light for their work in the long evenings, before the flax merchant came round to buy it for export from Glasson. But malt and flax are not here now, nor newts in the sleepy pools, nor owls in the kiln; and not even the date can be recovered of that momentous day when the "Hampson Dobby" fought "Brunsa Hobby," and both were killed and interred in Dobb's field. The Dobby was not unamiable, and once in housing the cattle fastened up a hare also. 'Tis said that one good lady presented the creature with a suit of clothes; but, on the whole, its life history is obscure. Pasture

HAMPSON, NEAR HAMPSON GREEN.

Hampson Green. This place does not include more than a dozen houses, six of which—pretty cottages—nestle under the trees, being flanked by other dwellings and some farm buildings. The farm to the

fields cover nearly the whole little district of Hampson. The hedges which divided the small paddocks and barley fields have mainly been removed, though some of the trees remain to witness the fulfilment of that condition inserted in the leases granted by Viscount Molyneux, Lord of the Manor, which required that each year the tenant " shall and will during the said term, set and plant upon the said premises or some part thereof four plants or young trees of oak, ash, elm, or other wood such as are most proper and best adapted to the soil ; and, if any of them shall fortune to die or be casually destroyed, then the tenant shall at a proper season within one year next following set or plant a new tree or trees in the stead or place of those which shall so die or be destroyed." —Hampson proper, as distinct from Hampson Green, is the house on the adjoining eminence—a house which has lately been considerably enlarged, under the direction of Mr. Paley, of Lancaster ; the work being done by local workmen. The owner, Mr. W. G. Welch, resides here. He acquired the estate through his wife, who was one of the daughters of the late owner, Dr. James Johnson, who lived here for more than a quarter of a century, after inheriting the land from his mother (nee Mary Welch, of Ellel), a descendant of that Mary Welch who is said to have purchased the estate in the latter half of the seventeenth century, and whose descendants and their relatives have held it ever since. Other property in Hampson was held by the Welch family, for in 1745 Thomas Welch, of Hang Yeat, yeoman, made a will bequeathing to his son Timothy his property in Amson. This Timothy Welch was a flax merchant, in a considerable way of business : he became a freeman of the Russia Company, and acquired houses and farms in both Ellel and Forton. He was the great great-grandfather of the present owner of Hampson, and died in 1791.

CHAPTER XXI.

The village of Galgate—the centre of population in the township of Ellel—is about three-quarters of a mile north of the lane which branches from the main road and runs up to Hampson, &c. It consists of an old and a new part, which centrally run parallel, and at each end diverge considerably. In none of the old topographical works is Galgate mentioned : not even in Adams's "Index Villaris," which was published in 1680, and which is particularly comprehensive in its enumeration of places—villages as well as towns—does its name appear. But it must, notwithstanding, be very ancient. In old, far-away times, owing to the convergence of roads at the place, it must have been the scene of considerable activity, if even devoid of a definite residential population. The Roman roads from Walton-le-Dale and Ribchester met here—merged into one here, and then, as thus united, went on to Lancaster, &c. ; and at a later time, whilst the ordinary highway going north and south ran through it, roads from Cockerham, Thurnham, Wyresdale, Littledale, and other parts also met here, as they do now. Since it became cognizable at all, the name of this place (Galgate) has been spelled in a variety of ways, and there has been considerable guessing and theorising as to its meaning. There are now in Somerset House, London, two bonds of administration relating to the wills of John Clark and Hannah Banton, each bearing the date 1728, and both the persons named are described as of "Gangate in Ellell." This Gangate evidently refers to the place now called Galgate. The Rev. Peter Walkden states in his diary, under date May 4, 1730, that while on his way between Scotford (Scotforth) and Elhill (Ellel) Moor, &c., a man named Alexander Williamson accompanied him to "Gawgarth" (Galgate). In 1780 there was proved, within the archdeaconry of Richmond, the will of Edward Dickson, described as a victualler "of Galgate." This is the earliest instance I have come across of the name of the village being given in exact accordance with the way in which it is now spelled. In certain road-book and map definitions of a later date I have seen the village called Gaugut, Golgate, and Gallgate. The difficulty as to the meaning of the name relates entirely to the first syllable of it. Gate means, of course, a road, or passage, or way ; and gut—a form of the suffix in one preceding

instance—may here be taken as either a corruption of gate or as the equivalent of it (in some parts of Kent it is said that gut is used as a word in place of gate). In respect to the prefix variations mentioned, we have, first, Gan, which is an Anglo-Saxon word, meaning to begin. So that, in this case, it may have referred to the entrance or commencement of a road, or a road system, at the place (several roads converge at, and in the like ratio, of course, diverge from, it). Or Gan may have been a contraction of Gang, one meaning of which in the north, refers to going on foot, personally— thus conveying the idea that the place adjoined or included a walking way as distinguished from a pillion-riding, pack-horse, or vehicle-used road If the correct prefix were Gaw, then the full name would refer to a way or passage by the side of certain drained land—Gaw meaning a slit made by a spade or plough for field drainage purposes. Viewed from another point, Gaw might be a reduced form of Gawe—a word which implies demeanour of a staring, stupid kind—thereby making the full name to be indicative of a road on or near which there was considerable looking about of an insensate or doltishly inquisitive character. Curiously enough, there are now several cottages, on the south-west side of Galgate, which used to be called "Staring-row." But this name had nothing at all to do with that of the village : the cottages referred to are near the railway, and they were designated "Staring-row" on account of the manner in which persons living at them went to the front windows, or stood in the front doorways, and stared at passing railway trains. As to the prefix Gau, this is a Teutonic word, originally meaning a forest clearing ; and, if gut or gate were added, then, as thus formed, the full name would relate to a way or passage through or adjacent to an open place made in a wood. Gol is of far too Eastern an origin to admit of any consideration at all here. Gall would, if it were the real prefix, indicate in its application an awkward, unpleasant way—a road bad to go on, and productive of irritation or soreness. Taking the name of the village as it now stands (Galgate), the first part of it may have been applied in consequence of the passage of Gaels

115

(Highlanders) through the place—thus making it a Gael gate or way—in the old days of foraying and plundering. The foregoing nomenclative variations with the accompanying prefix and suffix definitions constitute the entire of the data I have been able to obtain, and form all the light I can throw on the subject; and with the reader I now leave the solution of the question as to what the name of Galgate may mean. The earliest mentioned building in the township is "Ellel Chapel," which, it is presumed, occupied a site near that of the present Episcopal Church, about half a mile from the centre of Galgate village, north-east. In a grant relating to Cockerham manor and church, made in the 12th century, the chapel of Ellel is named; and in a declaration connected with Cockerham Church, made in the 14th century, it is also referred to. In 1646, the Committee for the Relief of Plundered Ministers made an order that the sum of £50 should be paid yearly out of the tithes arising in the chapelry of Ellel, sequestered from John Bradshaw, "recusant and delinquent," "to and for increase of the maintenance of the minister" of Ellel Chapel. The order afterwards states that the chapel is above four miles distant from the parish church (Cockerham), that the communicants number "above 400," and that there is "noe maintenance for a minister belonging to the sd chappell." In 1662, when the Act of Uniformity came into force, the clergyman at Ellel Chapel was the Rev. Peter Atkinson, and it is said that he was such a favourite of, or on such good terms with, the better class people of the locality that he retained his ministerial position without complying with the Act. When he died the Uniformity or Conformist regime came into operation here, and the living has been held on the customary Episcopal lines ever since. In 1800 a new Episcopal chapel was built in Ellel (on a site about 20 yards south of the old structure, which was pulled down): it is now a church, with a separate district assigned to it, in accordance with the Blandford Act, and the Rev. G. Willes is the present vicar of it. Structurally, it is very plain and unpretentious—somewhat like the old church at Shireshead, but smaller. In 1804 the person who took the role of "parish clerk" in Ellel was one Thomas Harrison, and on the 22nd of May in that same year, when he had reached the age of threescore and ten, he got married, at Cockerham Church, to a woman named Jane Whittingham, who was 20 years younger than himself. It is said that he "bought her twelve years previously for 4s. 9d.," and that during the unmarried interval "they had lived together." There were, evidently, Nonconformists in the township of Ellel at a pretty early time; and no doubt here, as elsewhere, statutory "pains and penalties" would tend to secretly increase rather than diminish the number of them. Under date 1699, William Stout, the Lancaster Quaker previously mentioned, refers in his diary to "John Ashton, of Ellel, a rigid Presbyterian, who married a 'pretended' Lancaster Quakeress widow, named Elizabeth Wales."

In 1797 Congregationalism put in an appearance at Galgate; the first service—at any rate, the first recorded one—being conducted, in the year named, by the Rev. W. Alexander, at that time connected with Lancaster Congregational Chapel. For a while afterwards, services of a like kind were held at various houses in the village. About the middle of this century the Congregationalists were fairly strong at Galgate: they had a congregation of upwards of 150, and a Sunday school attended by a similar number of children; the accommodation they required being secured in the upper room of a day school towards the south end of the village. But, though at one time strong—indeed, the strongest Dissenting body in Galgate—the Congregationalists, through different causes, gradually decreased in numbers and prestige, and about 1870 they ceased to have any distinct denominational status in the village. The Wesleyan Methodists have for a considerable time had a substantial footing at Galgate. For a while they held services, &c., on Sundays, in the lower room of the school named, when the upper portion of it was occupied by the Congregationalists; about 1860 they built a chapel of their own at the north end of the village; and they are now in a flourishing condition. The Wesleyans are, at present, the only Dissenting body here. In old times there was a yearly fair at Galgate: it was held on Low Sunday. On the 9th of April, 1808, the Churchwardens of Ellel made a stand against the fair being held on such day. They issued a notice, stating that all articles offered for sale, at Galgate, on Low Sunday, would be seized, and that the owner or owners thereof would be prosecuted; and in the notice they also cautioned the publicans of the village against permitting tippling in their houses on Low Sunday. Afterwards the fair was held, yearly, on Low Monday. There were horse races, &c., near the village, on the fair day. "Touch Duckett" (James Duckworth), a notorious Preston character, used to figure prominently here with horses. The proceedings—the "carryings on"—in connection with the races were of a rough character, and as time went on they got worse: indeed, so bad had they become in 1849 that the orderly and peace-loving portion of the local community viewed them as a very great nuisance—virtually as equivalent to a yearly calamity. About 1856 the races were done away with, and an end was put to the fair at the same time. For a number of years, on the day following the fair, there was a roughly-hilarious burlesque, called "Mayor choosing," indulged in at Galgate. Publicans had then no restrictions placed upon them, during the ordinary week days, as to the hours for selling drink—they could keep their houses open as long as they liked. This being the case, it is hardly necessary to say that the drinking places at Galgate were particularly busy all through or during the greater portion of Low Monday—the fair day—night. And upon this moistening procedure depended the "Mayoral election." The first man found drunk and asleep anywhere in the village on the morning after the fair day—and there was not very much difficulty in finding one—was chosen "Mayor" for the ensuing year! And the ceremony was commenced by blacking the fellow's face with soot, and then dredging him with flour, after which he was seated on a chair fixed upon two or three light, short planks, fastened together, and carried about to different houses, where he made speeches replete with nonsense, and at which he and those carrying him supped all the drink, strong or weak, brought out for them; the whole farce being afterwards wound up by a dance and a spree at one of the village inns. This custom ceased about 1840. At one time considerable transactions took place in the cattle trade at Galgate. Dealers with droves of cattle, brought from the north on the highway, halted in the village, near where the roads cross, and butchers from Preston, Garstang, &c., met them and made purchases. There are now three inns and three beerhouses at Galgate. The inns (Green Dragon, Plough, and Whittle and Steel) are old ones. The present population of Galgate is about 900; and the life of the place chiefly depends

of it; later the partnership was dissolved, when Mr. Armstrong alone kept the mill going in connection with the cotton trade. The large five-storey mill, at the north-east end of the village, opposite the old factory, was built by Mr. Armstrong, for silk-spinning, and work was commenced in it in May, 1852. For some time prior to this Mr. Armstrong had been the proprietor of the old factory opposite, and he remained master of and continued working both places until his death, in 1858, in his 84th year. His brother (Mr. R. Baynes Armstrong) then took charge of the works, and they were kept going by him up to the time of his death, in 1867, when his trustees carried on the business for a while, after which the proprietary became of the joint stock kind. The concern is now worked by a company, viz., William Thompson and Company, Limited. For very many years the frontal name of this Company has been associated with silk spinning at Galgate. About 300 hands are now employed at the works. The cottages forming a long row at the north end of Galgate, facing the railway, were built in sections by Mr. John Armstrong:

GALGATE.

upon silk-spinning. For many years there has been silk spinning at Galgate. Amongst the diary entries made in 1713, by Tyldesley, there are several allusions to "Ellal Milles," and the presumption is that they were in or about the village of Galgate; but nothing is stated by him as to the kind of work done at them. At the north-east end of the village, on the left side of the road, going towards the Church, there is an old silk factory. I have not been able to ascertain when or by whom this factory was built; but it has been in the silk line since 1797. There was also at one time a silk mill on the south-west side of the village, near the bridge which crosses the Conder. In the early part of this century it was worked by Messrs. Thompson and Co.; afterwards it was turned into a cotton factory, and Mr. John Armstrong (brother of Mr. Robert Baynes Armstrong, who was successively recorder of Hull, Leeds, and Manchester and Bolton, and M.P. for Lancaster from 1848 to 1853) joined the proprietary

he first erected twelve, then twelve more, and afterwards the remainder making up the row; and in constructing them he had two objects in view—additional accommodation for mill hands, and extra voting power at election times. The village streets are lighted at night time with gas purchased from the silk spinning company by the Parish Council. A gaslight flower show, of the annual kind, was established at Galgate, several years ago, for the purpose of raising money to pay for the lighting of the village streets with gas, in winter time. The cost of this lighting is now covered by a rate laid by the Parish Council; but the gaslight flower show is still annually held, and the profits which accrue are appropriated by the Committee to deserving local objects. The bulk of the oldest portion of the village runs parallel with, and a short distance east of, the main road. A stone in front of one of the cottages in this part bears the inscription—

"E. Carter, 1676." The date thus recorded is the oldest I have noticed in the village. The stone containing the inscription came out of a building which was originally a farm-house on the same site, and which was pulled down in 1851. The first school for the children of Galgate—indeed, the children of the locality generally—was in a high, bleak part of the township, about three-quarters of a mile from the village: it was on the east side of the road which runs between Galgate and Dolphin-holme. Evidence is lacking as to when this school was founded; but it was certainly in existence in 1753, and the trustees or governors of it at that time possessed, presumably towards endowment, a school field, a small cottage and garden, and a portion of land on Ellel Moor. In their entirety,

OLD SCHOOL BUILDING, ELLEL.

however, these properties were of but little annual value. One of the masters of this school was John Briggs, who, in after years, became the editor of the "Lonsdale Magazine" (a scarce and much valued work now) and the "Westmorland Gazette." Briggs was born in a little cottage, near Cartmel village, in 1788; learnt his father's trade—basket-making; to a considerable extent educated himself; when 20 years of age got married, went to Ulverston, and "without a shilling in his pocket" opened a school there; in two years afterwards (1810) became a candidate for the mastership of Ellel old school, and obtained the post, the salary being about £35 a year; and then, according to a biographical sketch, attached to his "Remains," he "considered that Fortune had chosen him for her adopted child," that "the dark cloud which through life had hung over him was dissipated," and that "the unsetting sun of happiness had arisen upon him." But, before very long, his dream of bliss in the region of Ellel lost much of its charm, and in four years he was thoroughly disillusioned. This was the way in which facts took the place of fancies and reality supplanted imagination during his Ellel schoolmastership: "One part of his emoluments should have arisen from teaching a Sunday school, supported by voluntary subscriptions—which after the first year were

never collected. A small piece of land, belonging to the school, should have been another source of his receipts; but the rent was unjustly withheld, through the intrigues of an inveterate enemy, who wished to instal one of his own relatives in the situation. Besides, during the winter, itinerant teachers took up their quarters at Galgate, and occasionally succeeded in drawing scholars from the established school. . . situated at an inconvenient distance from the village. And in summer the farmers found sufficient employment for their children in the fields. Under these circumstances, finding himself unable to support his family, he relinquished his school in 1814," went to Cartmel, and there commenced basket-making. But, in addition to making baskets, Briggs found time to write letters to a Kendal newspaper, and these communications attracted favourable notice. In 1820 he became the editor and part proprietor of the "Lonsdale Magazine"—an excellent production, but so unsuccessful, financially, that, whilst working like a slave, he had to be content with the "county pittance of a common day labourer." Afterwards he became the editor of the "Westmorland Gazette," published at Kendal, and for a time he concurrently looked after that journal and the Magazine; but the latter, when the third volume of it had been completed, was discontinued, the editor being "buried more deeply than ever in debt and difficulties." Then the health of Briggs gave way: he did not, however, apprehend anything serious, and had, it is said, some intention, on the approach to convalescence, of "taking part in a controversy on Emancipation which was raging between the Protestants and Catholics of Preston;" but there was no "approach to convalescence," and on the 21st of November, 1824, when but 36 years of age, he died.

At the Lancaster Assizes in March, 1817, there was a trial—Wakefield and others v. Threlfall—for the purpose of determining whether the small cottage and garden previously named really belonged to or formed part of the old school field in Ellel. The trial was commenced on a Saturday morning; much contradictory evidence was given; the Judge did not conclude his summing up until one o'clock on Sunday morning; and then the Jury stated that they would have to see the property in dispute before they could give their verdict. The proceedings were consequently adjourned till the following Monday, when the Jury went to Ellel, looked at the property, returned to the Assize Court, and gave a verdict for the plaintiffs. It was afterwards reported that the defendant in the case (a Miss Threlfall) intended to "move for a new trial without delay." On the 14th of July in the same year a new trial was moved for in the Court of Chancery, but the application was refused, and the motion dismissed with costs. For some years the only steps taken or movement made by the parties concerned in this case had reference

to the costs, and at last—on the 16th of March, 1825—
the order made against Miss Threlfall for the payment
of them was discharged in the Court of Chancery.
The value of the property which formed the bone of
contention was only about £100; the total law costs
amounted to something like £5,000! George Blezard was the last master of the old school: he had
charge of it from 1828 till the time when it was closed,
in 1844. There is no date on either the outside or inside of the building. It belongs to the parish, and is
now occupied as a cottage. The old school was supplanted by a new one, at the bottom of the same

THE ARMSTRONG SCHOOL, GALGATE.

road, close to the south end of Galgate. A stone in
front of the latter bears the inscription—" Erected by
John Armstrong. A.D. 1844." Mr. Armstrong built
this school chiefly for the benefit of his workpeople's
children; but any of the children in the village and
the township were allowed to attend it as well.
The first master at the new school was Mr. Robert
Newton, and the first mistress was Miss Jane Watson
(sister of a gentleman subsequently referred to who
became M.P. for the Ilkeston Division of Derbyshire).

PRESENT SCHOOL.

On Sundays, as already stated, the Congregationalists
and Wesleyan Methodists of Galgate used to have
services, &c., in this school. But, like the old school
which it took the place of, this one in time got superseded in respect to educational work, and now it is
chiefly utilised for concerts, miscellaneous entertainments, &c. Its successor—the present school—was

erected in 1858, on a site a short distance south of
Ellel Church, near the road side: it is a substantial,
neat-looking building, but, owing to its distance,
somewhat inconvenient. In order to meet the requirements of very young children, an infants' school is
provided at the north end of the village.

Faber suæ fortunæ. Clarior e tenebris. Thomas
Watson—a very enterprising and successful
manufacturer in the domain of silk, a man
distinguished for his liberality, and for some time
a member of Parliament—was a native of
Galgate. He was born here in 1821, and was one of a
family of seventeen. His parents were in humble circumstances, and for several years he worked as a silk
spinner at Galgate. In 1846 he left the village and
went to Rochdale. After working for a while as a
journeyman, in a silk and hatting establishment there,
he was thrown out of employment, through the failure
of his master. But Watson was a man of skill and
energy; he had also saved a little money; and, being
thoroughly acquainted with silk spinning, he entered
into partnership with two thrifty, industrious men, one
of whom could make hats, whilst the other had a practical knowledge of the finishing process. Their united
capital was £500. For a time, their business operations, conducted at Rochdale, were financially successful; but, by and bye, depression set in, and this un-
favourable change caused Watson to put on his " study-
ing cap." He made numerous experiments, involving
a considerable expenditure of money, with the view
of producing a new sort of velvet, from spun silk, in
imitation of sealskin. Eventually he succeeded in
making the desired article, and the manufacture of it
brought back prosperity, on a very enlarged scale, to
the establishment. At length, through the death of
one of his partners, and the withdrawal into a private
life of independence of the other, he became the sole
proprietor of the works. The success of the business
was sustained; Mr. Watson built some excellent mills
in Shawclough valley, near Rochdale; and he likewise
erected, near them, a family mansion. At this time
he was very wealthy; and he was liberal as well. With
the accumulation of riches his generosity seemed to
extend. At his own expense solely he built two chapels
near Rochdale—one, which cost him £4,000, being for
his own denomination (the United Methodist Free
Church), and the other for the Baptist body, with
which certain members of his family were connected.
He was a generous supporter of the Home and Foreign
Mission Fund of the first-named denomination, and
he subscribed £3,000 towards the commemoration fund.
He defrayed the cost (£27,000) of Rochdale Infirmary,
which was opened, in 1883, by John Bright. For 17
years he was a member of the Rochdale School Board,
and during his connection with it he gave £1,000, or
£100 per year for ten years, for Board school scholar-
ships. He was likewise a member of the Rochdale
borough bench of magistrates. Furthermore, Mr. Watson was the first Free Methodist member of Parliament in the country, being elected for the Ilkeston
Division of Derbyshire, in 1885, and re-elected for it
in 1886. In 1887, after a short illness, he died. He

left a family of eight—four sons and four daughters. Mr. Watson was a practical, genuine man. Though wealthy, there was no pride about him. He never sought to disguise the fact that his origin was of the humble kind, and he always spoke well of his poor parents of Galgate. At a banquet which he gave, in Rochdale Town Hall, in 1874, to celebrate the coming of age of his eldest son, Mr. Watson made use of these words: "I never blush when I think of my parentage, for, though humble, it was honest and upright, and I received from my parents an example which has been worth the copying—an example of scrupulous integrity and honest and upright dealing in life."

Only once does the London and North-Western Railway go over the main road between Preston and Lancaster, and this particular traversion occurs at the south end of Galgate. There is here a high

many years ago, when Lancaster again became, as it has since remained, the post town of the village.

Quite near to Galgate, on the west side, Ellel Hall is situated. It is a plain, substantial, stone structure, and was apparently built—at any rate, the principal portion of it—about 1700. Possibly, there was before that date a building on the same site: if so, it would be considerably smaller than the present Hall. There is now, in Somerset House, a bond of administration, dated 1708, pertaining to the will of one William Charnock, of "Ellel Hall." About 1720 Thomas Jackson resided at this Hall. The Fords for a long time owned Ellel Hall. The first of the family whose name appears in connection with it was John Ford (eldest surviving son of John Ford, of Lancaster, and Morecambe Lodge, Yealand Conyers), who was the son of Isaac Ford, a Manchester merchant, by his marriage, in 1759, with Elizabeth, third daughter

ELLEL HALL.

bridge of the skew kind. Whilst being constructed it was the subject of a trial, at Lancaster Assizes, in March, 1839. The trustees of the Garstang and Heiring Syke section of the main road—turnpike road as it was then called—considered that this bridge would be an obstacle to public travelling, and brought an action against Mr. E. Sharp, architect for the Lancaster and Preston Railway Company, with the view of securing some change in the form or construction of it; but they failed to make out a case, and the verdict was given for Mr. Sharp. A very curious postal arrangement, affecting Galgate, was made in 1840. The inhabitants were officially informed, on the 7th of March in that year, that Preston, not Lancaster, would henceforth be their post town. Considering that Preston is 17 miles from Galgate, whilst Lancaster is only four miles from it, this alteration was a very singular one. But the regulation then made is not in force now—indeed, it was done away with

of Thomas Hutton Rawlinson, of Lancaster. He died in 1819, and his eldest son, Abraham Rawlinson Ford, who came of age in 1834, succeeded to the property. In 1849 Abraham Rawlinson Ford died, when the Ellel Hall estate passed to his only surviving brother, William Ford, by whom it was held till his death, in the early part of 1898. Lord Ashton, in the latter part of 1898, purchased Ellel Hall and certain associated property, including two farms. As to the occupation of Ellel Hall, the two earliest recorded persons who resided at it were, as before-stated, William Charnock and Thomas Jackson. In respect to the names of occupiers, after the latter, there is a hiatus extending over many years: indeed, nothing definite is available until 1812, when "A. Rawlinson" is residentially associated with the Hall. This was Mr. Abraham Rawlinson, one of the M.P.'s for Lancaster from 1780 to 1790, and presumably a relation of Elizabeth Hutton Rawlinson, whom Isaac Ford married. Mr. Abraham Rawlinson seems to have resided at Ellel Hall for about a dozen years. Then it was successively occupied by Mr. William Hinde, Mr. E. G. Hornby (the first M.P. for Warrington), Mrs. Ford (widow of Mr. John Ford, who died in 1819) and family, and Mr. William Ford (son of the same gentleman). The family referred to consisted of three sons and two daughters. Mr. William Ford, the only surviving son, occupied Ellel Hall nearly half a century, namely, from February, 1849, when his mother died, up to the time of his own death, in March, 1898. Since his decease the place has not been occupied. The view of Ellel Hall which appears on the preceding page is from a sketch which was taken in May, 1899. Since then the Hall has, internally, been put into better order; and the roof portion of it has also been slightly altered. Spacious grounds, containing numerous fine trees, extensive conservatories, large gardens, &c., adjoin the Hall.

CHAPTER XXII.

THURNHAM AND ITS HALL—OLD OWNERS—THE DALTONS—HIDING-PLACE—CATHOLIC
VIRGINS' TABLET—MISSION DEVELOPMENT—FINE OAK CHEST—TALENTED NATIVE—
COCKERSAND ABBEY.

Objects of considerable interest now necessitate a detour, west and north-west of the Ellel region, to the "capital" of which—Galgate—I shall at a later stage return, in order to deal with historic, anti-quarian, and other matters contiguous to and in the neighbourhood of the main road between that place and Lancaster. The points of interest will steadily accumulate as the divergence continues, and will at the end be found to amply warrant indulgence in it.

From the main road at the south end of Galgate there is visible the spire of Thurnham Roman Catholic Church. It rises, with peaceful picturesque-ness, above a mass of trees, to the west, and can be seen for miles on every side. Thurnham Hall, an old mansion, for generations the abode of the Daltons, is about 350 yards north-west of the church; but, owing to the many trees about the place, it is not visible from the Ellel side at all. In a straight line, the Hall is about a mile and a quarter from Galgate; but by the nearest available way—that along the Lancaster and Preston Canal, the Glasson Dock branch thereof, and the fields on the north side of the Hall—it is something like a mile and three-quarters from the village. The branch canal referred to extends from a point about 650 yards south of Gal-gate to Glasson, it is two and a half miles long, and was opened in 1826. When Halton, above Lancaster, was a Saxon manor (called Haltune), Thurnham (at that time designated Tiernun) was a portion of such manor, with a land area equal to 200 acres. The earliest property owner in Thurnham, whose name I have met with, was William de Forness, who, it is conjec-tured, took the name of William de Thurnham, and who in the 12th century made or confirmed a grant of land to the hospital of Cockersand. Alicia, sister and heiress of Michael le Fleming, and widow of Sir Richard de Cancefield, confirmed this grant. The manor of Thurnham descended from the Flemings to the Cancefields, and through the latter to the Har-ringtons, whose successors were the Bonviles and then the Greys. In 1483-4 the estates of Thomas Grey, Marquis of Dorset, which included the lordship of Thurham, were, on account of high treason, for-feited to the Crown; but in 1485-6 they were restored to him. In 1553 his son Henry, Duke of Suffolk, con-veyed, for £1,080, the manor of Thurnham to a Lon-don citizen and grocer, named Thomas Lonne, who in 1556 sold the same for £1,500 to Robert Dalton, of Bispham, in the parish of Croston. By his second marriage—his union with Elyza, daughter of William Hulton, of Hulton Park, near West Houghton—Robert Dalton had one son and seven daughters. When he died his son (Thomas) inherited his Thurn-

ham property, as well as some which he had in Bulk. This Thomas raised a troop of horse for the King, at the time of the Civil War: he was a colonel of cavalry, was wounded at the second battle of New-bury, on the 27th of October, 1644, and died within a week afterwards at Marlborough. His property in Thurnham and Bulk had previously been taken from him—it was sequestered in 1642-3—on account of his "delinquency." With respect to his seven sisters, some or all of them resided for a time at Aldcliffe Hall, near Lancaster. Their names were Margaret, Elizabeth, Jane, Ellen, Dorothy, Katherine, and Phillippa. They were very firm believers in the Roman Catholic faith; and it is said that Aldcliffe Hall was, when the Dalton sisters were at it, designated the "home of the Catholic Virgins." Two-thirds of their property at Aldcliffe was sequestered for "recusancy." In 1653[-4] they petitioned for per-mission to "contract jointly for the redemption of their interests"; and in the Record Office there is a certificate, dated May 11th, 1655, signed by Daubeny Williams, "showing that he had searched the books in his custody relating to Lancashire, Middlesex, and London, and found no conviction against Margaret Dalton or her sisters." The property referred to was afterwards leased from the Lancashire Commissioners to one of the sisters (Margaret) for seven years, at £40 a year. Through the marriage of Elizabeth Dal-ton (daughter and co-heiress of Robert Dalton, who was a descendant of the fore-named Robert, and died in 1704) with William Houghton, of Park Hall, in the parish of Standish, the Dalton property passed, in 1710, to their eldest son John, who took the surname and arms of Dalton. Thurnham Hall, a mansion built in the time of Queen Mary, was of course included in the property which he inherited, and he took up his residence at it. In 1715, when the Scotch Rebels reached Lancaster on their southward march, John Dalton, of Thurnham Hall, along with some friends, joined them. After the Rebels laid down their arms at Preston, he, with others, was sent to London, kept in confinement there for a time, and then tried for having participated in the Rebellion. He was found guilty, but, as the part he had taken in the revolt was not of a very serious character, the sentence did not involve capital punishment: his landed property was forfeited to the King, and he was imprisoned for a considerable time. It is said that, when liberated, he walked all the way back to Thurnham! Tradition also says that when he arrived he found his wife at the rear of the Hall, gathering kindling wood. He re-covered his confiscated property by the payment of £6,000 to the Government.

Originally, Thurnham Hall had a picturesque, antiquely-effective front, which included mullioned windows and massive bays, with a large tower-flanked courtyard, and an exterior connecting curtain wall; but in 1823 the then Squire of Thurnham (John, son of Robert Dalton) took down this front, and put in its place the present facade—a facade of the ashler kind, having a castellated parapet with small flanking turrets, and a large, projecting, castellated porch, containing in carved stone, above the door, the arms of the Daltons impaling those of the Gages, and surmounted by the crests of the two families (John Dalton married one of the daughters of Sir Thomas Gage). The Hall stands pleasantly on a moderate eminence, and commands a finely-varied view—a view which embraces the fertile marsh lands below Glasson, portions of the winding, silvery Lune, the broad, light-hued bay of Morecambe, and several of the mountains which fill in with a grand sweep the north-western horizon. John Dalton was a well-known figure in Preston—

couple who had brought up the greatest number of their own children, and it was awarded to William Warbrick and his wife, of Torrisholme, who had brought up a family of 15. In 1837 Mr. Dalton died. Miss Elizabeth Dalton, his daughter, resided at Thurnham Hall for many years: she was the "last lineal member of the family bearing the name of Dalton," and died at Thurnham Hall in 1861, aged 81 years. After her death the estate went to Sir James George Fitzgerald, Bart., of Castle Ishen, County Cork, a grandson of Sir James Fitzgerald, who married Bridget Ann, daughter of Mr. Robert Dalton, of Thurnham Hall, by his third wife Bridget More, of Barnborough Hall, Yorkshire, "the heiress and last lineal descendant of the once famous Chancellor Sir Thomas More." On the death of Sir James George Fitzgerald, without issue, in 1868, Sir Gerald Fitzgerald succeeded to the Dalton property. The estate now belongs to Mr. William J. Dalton, who succeeded to it in 1894, on the death of Sir

THURNHAM HALL.

amongst Roman Catholics particularly; and he had a residence in the town. He lived for a time at Avenham House, and subsequently—about 1804—he built a house on the east side of Winckley-square (the present No. 8), and occupied it periodically for a while. But his principal residence was Thurnham Hall. He was, of course, in the habit of putting in an appearance at Lancaster, where he had property. One of the public squares in Lancaster bears his surname; an adjoining thoroughfare takes his Christian name; several adjacent streets, made or improved in his time, have had applied to them the names of members of his family, &c., and one has the maiden surname of his wife. In the square referred to, the annual show of the Lancaster Agricultural Society was held for several years in the first half of the present century. Some of the prizes offered by the Society were of a rather curious character: for instance, at the show in 1803 a premium was offered to the married

Gerald Fitzgerald without issue; and it is a somewhat remarkable fact that when Mr. John Dalton died, in 1837, there were 11 lives (tenants for life) in existence between Mr. William J. Dalton and his chance of inheriting the estate. Mr. William J. Dalton is the son of Mr. John Dalton's half-brother, and is now, at length, the absolute owner of the property. No one has regularly resided at Thurnham Hall since the death of Miss Dalton, in 1861. The entrance hall of the mansion is very spacious, and over its fire-place there are the commingled armorial bearings of the Dalton, Fleming, and Middleton families. On one side of the entrance-hall is the dining-room, and on the other side the library. Above, approached by an oak staircase, there is the drawing-room, the proportions of which are 39ft. by 24ft. There is no furniture in the hall now. Up to the time of Miss Dalton's death, it contained a full complement of furniture, also a fine collection of family portraits, as well as a painting of Cockersand Abbey chapter-house, by Sir Thomas Gage, bart. In Thurnham Hall there is a priest's hiding place, which was apparently made some time after the erection of the general building. A blocked-up doorway, leading to a room on one side of which the secret place is directly located, was at a comparatively recent date discovered. Originally this room

small sitting-room; and it was whilst certain repairs or alterations were being made in the Hall that curiosity was excited as to what might be behind the western wall of this small room. The paper on the wall—paper of a highly ornamental pattern—was torn off; a bricked-up, stone-bordered doorway at one end of the wall was then noticed; the bricks were knocked out; and—complete darkness prevailed beyond. On

OPEN DOORWAY OF ROOM ADJOINING PRIEST'S HIDING PLACE.

APERTURE OF HIDING PLACE (LEFT SIDE.)

was an open one, or easy of access, consequently unsuitable for immediate contiguity to any hiding quarters, and obviously pointing to the making of this place of concealment at a time subsequent to the building of the Hall. The hiding place is in the second storey of the Hall, north side, and it was discovered accidentally. On the same floor, immediately adjoining, towards the south side, there is what may have been a parlour, in one corner of which there is a doorway leading to an apartment somewhat resembling a

a light being obtained, the space beyond was found to be a room, about 8ft. by 6ft. in size, on one side of which—within the wall—a priest's hiding place, about 6ft. high and a foot and a half square, was afterwards discovered; the entrance to it being by a square opening about 4ft. from the floor, and capable of being closed by means of a stone slab moving on a pivot. Owing to the peculiarity of the aperture, entrance had to be effected on the "feet foremost" plan. It was also found that the adjoining room giving access to the opening of the hiding-place could be only entered —when the doorway was blocked up—by a trap-door in the floor above, which floor was got to from the outside, through the roof leads. It has not transpired that there was ever any necessity felt at Thurnham Hall to actually secrete a priest in the hiding place. The foregoing illustrations of the doorway of the dark room and outer side of the hiding place, and likewise the square wall aperture of the latter, are from photographic views taken by limelight. Thurnham Hall is now in a semiruinous state. Some of the stonework of the facade is giving way—cracking in several parts, and becoming discoloured by rust in front of the iron dowel pins; the ceilings are falling; the floors above have in certain parts got unsafe; and I believe that no attempt will be made to restore the structure: rebuilding would, in fact, be less expensive than restoration. In the north gable of the Hall, near the front corner, and about three yards from the ground, there is a flag-like stone of an interesting character: it is about two feet broad and two and a half feet in depth, and it bears the following inscription:—"Catholicæ virgines nos sumus: mutare vel tempore spernimus. Ano Dni 1674." This, freely translated, is—"We are Catholic virgins, who scorn to change with the times." Originally, this stone was fixed in one of the walls of Aldcliffe Old Hall, in 1674, when only two of the seven daughters were living there; and, when that building was pulled down, in 1817, it was removed to Thurnham Hall, and fixed in the north gable,

CATHOLIC VIRGINS' TABLET.

where it has ever since remained. In front of the Hall there is still visible a parterre or grass plot, circular in form. A few ornamental trees adjoin it. Westward, the land slopes down gently, and then broadens considerably, assuming a park-like aspect. From the south-west corner of the front ground, near the Hall, to the main entrance gate, there is a winding avenue of large, old trees. At the south end of the Hall, close to it, there is a small, neat-looking domestic chapel, in the Gothic style of architecture. The rear of the Hall has an antiquely-imposing appearance. Contiguously located, at the north-east corner, are the buildings which originally formed the kitchens, &c., of the Hall, and which are now used for farm-house, barn, and kindred purposes.

The spired Roman Catholic Church, in the neighbourhood of the Hall, was built in 1847-8, as the successor of a smaller place of worship on the same site. In 1780 a bequest of £1,000 was made by Miss Jane Daniel, of Euxton, near Chorley, in order to establish a "clergy priest" at Thurnham; a condition attached to the gift being that Mr. John Dalton, of Thurnham Hall, should either give a sum of money annually or provide a house and a little land for the priest. In 1785 (prior to which local Roman Catholics met for worship at Thurnham Hall) a new mission, based upon these advantages, was established; and the first priest associated with it was the Rev. James Foster, who was born at Ashton Hall, and whose father rented the farm belonging thereto from the Duke of Hamilton. For nearly 40 years the Rev. James Foster was the priest at Thurnham, and whilst here he was instrumental in securing the erection of a brick chapel (in 1810) and also the present presbytery. He was succeeded by the Rev. Thomas Crowe, who in time contrived to raise £1,000 towards a new church; Mr. Dalton left £200 in aid of the building fund and a similar sum on behalf of the priest's maintenance; Miss Dalton, after the death of her father, generously provided the balance of the money required for building purposes, &c.; and the result was the present beautiful church, which was consecrated on the 25th of August, 1848. It stands on elevated ground, is environed by trees, and its spire, rising gracefully above them, can be seen for miles. The Rev. P. Byrne is the priest at present in charge of Thurnham mission. I have seen a statement in print to the effect that there is in Thurnham Roman Catholic Church the muniment or plate chest of Cockersand Abbey—that it is of 13th or 14th century make and very beautiful, that at the time of the break-up of Cockersand Abbey it was removed to Rawcliffe Hall, and remained there till 1861, when it was sold to Captain Whitle, of Whalley Abbey, and that it was some time afterwards bought by Sir J. G. Fitzgerald, removed by him to Thurnham Hall, and placed in the neighbouring church. In this statement there is a little truth and a good deal of inaccuracy. Amongst the furniture of Miss Dalton, sold after her death in 1861, was a very fine chest—the purchaser of it being Colonel (then Captain) Whitle. Subsequently it was purchased by Sir James Dalton-Fitzgerald, and taken back to Thurnham Hall, where it was used as a muniment chest. It contained some old charters relating to Cockersand Abbey, which the late Sir Gerald Fitzgerald sent to the Record Office, in London. This is the chest supposed to have been at the Abbey. It is a very handsome one, of oak; but the appearance of it—the style of its workmanship—does not warrant the assumption that it is a very ancient article. A judge of old oak, who some time ago examined this chest, informs me that it is "the creation of an age long subsequent to Henry VIII.," hence it could not have been in use in Cockersand Abbey, which was dissolved eight years before that monarch died, and that it is "comparatively a modern one." When Mr. Lawrence Holden, solicitor, &c., of Lancaster, acted for Sir Gerald Fitzgerald, he had the chest removed to the priest's house, at Thurnham, where it is now. But it does not appear to belong to the mission: it belongs to, or at any rate is claimed by, the present owner of the Dalton estate in Thurnham (Mr. W. J. Dalton). Dr. Leigh, in his "Natural History of Lancashire," &c., published in 1700, refers to the existence of "feathered alum" in Thurnham. Simon George Bordley, the originator or propounder of a peculiar kind of shorthand writing, was a native of Thurnham. He was born here in 1709 (was probably a relative of William Bordley, yeoman, of Thurnham, whose will was proved in or about 1750), became a Roman Catholic priest and a schoolmaster, and it is said that a book which he wrote, entitled "Cadmus Britannicus," was the first work ever published for the purpose of advocating and teaching a system of quick writing, called Cursive Shorthand, Graphic Shorthand, or Scripthand. He died at Ince Blundell, in 1799. Only four original copies of his shorthand work are now in existence. Some years ago 100 facsimiles of it were produced by Mr. Robert Mc.Caskie, of Westhampstead. In 1848 a project was initiated for a new railway between Lancaster and Preston—the main route to be on the west side, with a junction from Higher Thurnham, which is about half a mile north-west of Thurnham Hall; but the scheme fell through. Thurnham is a purely agricultural township, with the exception of the Glasson portion of it, and during the past 50 years there has been but little change in the numeric character of its population.

The burial place of the Daltons of Thurnham Hall is at Cockersand Abbey, the Chapterhouse there

the never-wearied sea rises and falls on its western side; the adjoining land, eastward, is very flat, having evidently, at some time, been tidally touched, if not covered at low water; and it has been conjectured that the Abbey originally stood upon an island. The position is a very exposed one, and the Abbey must have been, as old Leland observes, an "object to al Wynddes." The original building here was a hermitage, established some time between 1154 and 1189, by a poor recluse, "an heremyt of great perfecc'on," named Hugh Garth, who afterwards, by means of alms which he gathered in the county, turned it into a hospital. In 1190 the place was transformed, by charter, into a Monastery or Abbey of the Premonstratensian Order, and it found much favour or was sympathised with by many; land was given to it, immunities, &c., were variously extended to its possessions; and in 1292 property and prerogatives in many parts—in something like 200 townships, it has been estimated—were held for its benefit. But in less than 100 years after this the Canons of the Abbey designated themselves, in an application for charter-renewal, "the King's poor chaplains," and supplicated regard for their "poverty," &c. The cause of this indigence—if it were real, and not feigned—is a mystery. In 1535-6 Cockersand Abbey was included amongst the religious houses ordered to be suppressed; but, through a re-examination of its value, by a Commission appointed in 1537, letters patent from the King were issued for its preservation. The anti-monastic spirit, however, grew stronger in Regal and Reforming circles, and in 1539 this place was dissolved. It is said that, at the time of its dissolution, Cockersand Abbey contained 22 priests, all "of honest conversation," five aged, helpless men, "kept dayle of charitie," and 57 servants. In 1544 Cockersand Abbey site and lands were sold, for

COCKERSAND ABBEY RUINS (1900).

having been set apart for this purpose. Many members of the Dalton family and some of the relatives thereof have been interred here. Cockersand Abbey now a poor, thinly-scattered ruin, the Chapterhouse being the only substantial and comparatively complete portion of it now standing—is situated two and a half miles west of Thurnham Hall, on a piece of land which juts out between the Lune estuary and the sands of Cocker, quite close to the shore. Its site is somewhat elevated, very bleak and lonely;

£798 8s. 6d., to John Kechyn or Kitchen, of Hatfield, Herts, whose daughter Ann afterwards carried their possession into the Dalton family, by marriage with Robert Dalton, of Bispham (his first marriage), who, as previously stated, was the purchaser of the Thurnham Hall estate in 1556; and they have been held by the Daltons and their successors ever since. The Abbey buildings "covered nearly an acre of land," and tradition says that they stood in an enclosure of seven acres. The only portions now visible are the Chapterhouse at the east end; two lengths of masonry north of it—all that remain of four or five small chapels which were at the head of the north and south transepts; two parallel pieces of wall on the north side of what was the main structure, being parts of the nave of the Church; a few lateral remnants of the Cellarer's buildings, south-west of the nave; and an angle of the Fratry, south-west of the Chapterhouse. Numerous stones are scattered about on the ground, and protuberances on it in various places indicate the existence of subjacent masonry connected with foundation walls. Amongst the ruins there are between 30 and 40 old, high thorn trees, bent landward by steady breezes and stormy winds from the sea. On the tops of walls, near an adjoining farmhouse, there are all sorts of curiously-shaped stones—angular, triangular, oblong, &c.— obviously from the Abbey buildings; but neither a date nor a name of any kind has thus far been found on any of them, or indeed on any other of the Abbey stones. On the north side of the ruins there are two or three carved stones embedded in the ground. They are oblong, and evidently of the sepulchral kind: one has an angular surface, with a pair of shears, or something similar thereto, on one side; the others bear inscriptions or emblematic representations of some kind, but the carving is so very far worn that they cannot be definitely made out. The Abbey was built of red sandstone, quarried from the shore either directly west or laterally. And at the time of its erection the highwater line must have been farther off—more westward—than it is now. There appears to have been considerable disintegration—breaking down and washing away of earth and stones—west of the Abbey. At present one or two portions of the ruins stand in perpendicular line with the edge of the shore. Formerly there was a circular aperture at the base of the shore breast, immediately in front of the Abbey ruins, and by some persons this was supposed to have been connected with a subterranean passage for boats going to and from the interior of the establishment. The aperture was walled up a good many years ago, and it remains closed. In 1881 a Garstang man told me that a few years previously he made an inward expedition at this spot— that after he had got 40 or 50 yards along the passage he found it blocked with sand, that it contained nothing of particular interest, and that in all probability it had been a main drain in connection with the Abbey. Occasionally human bones have been found near the north end of the Abbey ruins, having apparently been washed out of the burial ground by the sea, during storms.

In respect to the Chapterhouse at Cockersand Abbey, it is now in fairly good condition. It is octagonal in shape; in diameter it is 30 feet; and its walls are two and a half feet thick. The oldest part of it, externally viewed, seems to be the doorway arch—a heavy, broad-bordered piece of masonry. The structure is plain all about the doorway, and at the sides; at the back it has been re-built, and surmounted with modern castellated work. The roof rests upon a central pillar, and is of slate—it was slated about 1859, having previously been covered with lead. The ceiling is of the groined kind; the supporting pillar being well carved, with a low-set, floriated capital. At the sides there are seven arched panels, laterally ornamented with quaintly carved stone heads; the majority being in a fair state of preservation. The floor is flagged, and upon it, in different parts, chiefly on the centre flags, the following names, &c., are inscribed—the bulk of those to whom they refer having, at time and time, been interred in the Chapterhouse: J. Bushell. L. Bushell. R. D., senr. E. Dalton. March 15th, 1865. B. D. M. D., junr. John Dalton, senr. M. D., senr. C. D. R. D., junr., E. N. senr. E. N., junr. Upon a panel-shaped slab fixed on the south-western side, there is this inscription:— "To the memory of Mary, wife of John Dalton, Esq., of Thurnham Hall, who died April 25th, 1819, aged 65 years; of Mary, their daughter, who died August 17th, 1820, aged 44; of Beatrice, their daughter, who died August 15th, 1821, aged 37; and of Charlotte, their daughter, who died February 26th, 1802, aged 16, who lie here interred. Also John Dalton, junr., Esqr., their son, who died May 18th, 1819, aged 41, and was interred in the Cathedral at Bath. R.I.P. And of John Dalton, senr., Esqr., husband and father to the above, who died March 10th, 1837, aged 90; also Lucy Bushell, their daughter, who died November 4th, 1843, aged 67; and Joseph Bushell, her husband, who died January 27th, 1860, aged 69 years. Also Elizabeth, daughter of John Dalton, senr., Esqr., who died March 15th, 1861, aged 81 years. R.I.P." On the opposite side, upon a similar slab, is this inscription:—"To the memory of Robert Dalton, Esq., of Thurnham Hall, who died 22nd July, MDCCLXXXV; also Cecily his wife, who died 3rd May, MDCCXLIX; also Elizabeth, his second wife; also Frances, his daughter to his first wife; also Robert, his son to his second wife; also Bridget Metcalf, daughter to his third wife; who lie here interred. This stone was placed by John Dalton, Esqr., of Thurnham Hall, in the year of Our Lord MDCCCX. R.I.P. Elizabeth Naylor, died Aug. 13, 1816." To the left of this a diamond-shaped slab, fixed against the wall, bears the inscription:—"Charlotte Dalton, obt. 26 Feb., 1802, aged 16. R.I.P." And on the other side, on a similar stone, is the following:—"Elizabeth Mary Angelina Naylor, obt. 24 July, 1810, aged 14. R.I.P." The inscriptions on the flags in the floor are evidently a sort of resume or condensation of the names contained on the mural slabs. Mr. Joseph Bushell, who married one of Squire Dalton's daughters, and whose name appears amongst those in the Chapterhouse, was a magistrate, and for some time chairman of the Lancaster and Preston Railway Company, and he resided at Dolphinlee, near Lancaster. The earliest date recorded amongst the foregoing inscriptions relates to Robert Dalton's first wife, who was interred in the Chapterhouse in 1749. But nearly 40 years before that time there was an interment at the Abbey, and probably in the Chapterhouse. During the interval as well as more remotely there may also have been burials in it. When the Chapterhouse was first used for the interment of members or relatives of the Dalton family it is now impossible to say. Tyldesley has the following entry in his diary, under date December 10th, 1712:—"Went to Thurnham to poor W: Houghton ffunerall, where most of the neigring [neighbouring] gentlemen was. Wee carryed him to the Abbey." This " poor W: Houghton " was an army officer, and younger brother of John Houghton, who assumed the name and arms of Dalton; and he was a great grandson of Thomas Houghton, the Royalist colonel, who was fatally wounded at the second battle of Newbury, in 1644. The last person interred in the Chapterhouse of Cockersand Abbey was Miss Elizabeth Dalton. Her funeral, which took place on the 21st of March, 1861, was of a very imposing character. After Mass, in Thurnham Church, the remains—preceded by upwards of 40 of the tenantry, on horseback—were conveyed to the Chapterhouse, the interment therein being accompanied with all the solemn funereal rites of the Catholic Church. At Thurnham Hall there was subsequently a large gathering, and during the proceedings 81 loaves—a number corresponding with the years forming the deceased lady's age—were distributed.

CHAPTER XXIII.

Glasson Dock is, by bee line, not quite two miles north-east of Cookersand Abbey ruins. By the road which goes through Thurnham it is upwards of four miles from them; but by another way, which runs near the shore of the Lune estuary for some distance and then strikes inland, it is only two and a quarter miles. The latter way is here and there somewhat rough through shore shingle, &c.; but this defect is compensated for by the comparative shortness of the road; and, in addition, it is for scenic purposes much preferable to the other. On a fine, clear day the views from it—especially from that portion which goes close by the shore—are very varied and charming. This is due not to any particular altitude—indeed, the road is generally low and flat—but to the far-reaching openness of the outlook on every side. The water of the Lune estuary, flanked with long sandbanks, flecked with sea birds, flows gently by; higher, Glasson, with its ship masts and tall warehouses, occupies one side, whilst Sunderland, with its scattered buildings fringing the shore, reposes on the other; straight ahead there rises in majestic strength "Gaunt's embattled pile," with the tall tower of Lancaster Parish Church by its side; whilst in the back ground there are distinctly visible round-headed Warton Crag, the sloping ridge of Farleton Knot, the high fells above Kirkby Lonsdale, and the lonely, stately form of Ingleborough; north-west the light-surfaced expanse of Morecambe Bay, Peel Castle, Walney Island, Barrow, the fells of Furness, and a multiform range of mountains—gently curved, serrated, piked, ponderously crested—stretching from Blackcombe to Helvellyn, come into view; due west there is the broad, shining "multitudinous sea"; southward, the baylets and tide-washed strands of Cockerham and Pilling, the heights of Preesall, and Fleetwood projecting conspicuously and picturesquely against the horizon; south-east, dark-purple hills and wood-sprinkled vales ranging for miles—Clougha, the flanking heights and gently concave base of Wyresdale, the sloping plantations above Scorton, and the sombre moors of Bleasdale; whilst southward the scene is made up of a large expanse of the Fylde district—level, many-hued, and fertile in aspect—as well as a very considerable portion of the country between Lancaster and Preston, looking like a long, finely-timbered plateau, and forming, with lateral accessories, a most delightful landscape. On the way from Cockersand Abbey to Glasson Dock there are two estuary structures for nightlight purposes—one being quite close to the channel, and the other, with a place to live in adjoining, slightly inland, on the east side. Both were put up about 1848. Within half a mile of Glasson

Dock, southward, the coast way from Cookersand Abbey, the road from Old Glasson, and that which goes by the school house converge into one, going over an eminence, and so passing down to the dock and the adjoining buildings, workshops, &c. From an old wooden seat, on the north-west side of the eminence, intended for both rest and sight-seeing, and made, apparently, of timber taken from some wrecked or used-up old vessel, a very extensive and delightful view can be obtained.

As to Old Glasson, it is situated half a mile from Glasson Dock, or 150 yards below the point where the roads before mentioned converge. It is a very small, primitive-looking place, consisting of a few thatched cottages, some farm buildings, &c. Apparently the farm buildings are of a considerably later date than the cottages. The probability is that Old Glasson was originally made or occupied by a little colony of fisherfolk. Passers by may now occasionally see in front or near some of the cottages one or more nets stretched out to dry, along with odds and ends of fishing tackle, suggestive of a continuation or remnant of the occupation pursued by the primary male dwellers here. The cottages, &c., surround an open space, partially green-swarded—a space analogous to an old village green. Altogether, the place has a quaint, secluded, ancient aspect. This is the original Glasson; it was in existence for generations before Glasson Dock; and, in order to distinguish it from the latter place, the adjective Old has been prefixed to its name. Amongst the Lancashire wills proved within the archdeaconry of Richmond, in 1561, was that of Humphrey Gardiner, " of Glasson." I have met with no earlier mention of Glasson, as thus spelt. Several persons of the name of Gardner (a variant of Gardiner) lived at Glasson in the 17th century—the principal portion of them between 1629 and 1660. In a map of Lancashire, dated 1598 (drawing No. 6,159, HL., MSS.), there is a spot designated " Glassa," and the location of it exactly coincides with the position of the present Old Glasson. Speed's map of Lancashire, dated 1610, and evidently prepared for his " Theatre of the Empire of Great Britain," &c., first published in 1611, contains " Glason on the Loyn " (Lune), and the mark relating to it seems to be just where Old Glasson is situated. In Adams's " Index Villaris," published in 1680, " Glason, Lancaster, Loynsdale " (evidently Old Glasson), is mentioned; and immediately under it there is " Glasen Castle, Lancaster, Loynsdale." On the face of it, this might prompt the idea that at the time the work referred to was compiled there was either an entire or ruinated castle at or in the neighbourhood of Glasson. But there was not. Whilst indicating by the names Lancaster and Loynsdale, after Glason and Glasen Castle, a certain nearness of location, the "Index" next dissipates this idea and to some extent complicates the matter by the "bearings" which it gives. All the places it mentions have their bearings—latitude and longitude—specified. Those for Glason are described as 54·06 lat., 2·36 W. lon., and those for Glasen Castle as 54·15 lat., 2·55 W. lon. With the exception of the castle at Lancaster, that at Peel, across Morecambe Bay, is the nearest structure of the kind (on the north-west coast) to Glasson, and it is in lat. 54·3 N. and 23' (minutes of lon.) West of Lancaster. But, of course, Peel is not the place referred to. The spot corresponding to the bearings of Glasen Castle, as given in the "Index," is proximately three minutes west of Whitbarrow Scar, Westmorland (S.W.). But the latitudes as well as the longitudes of various places named in the "Index"—certainly those on the eastern side of the Lune and its estuary,

reference to the connection of the Harringtons with both the manor in which "Glasen Castle" was situated and that containing "Glason," and, after mentioning the latter place in his "Index," he evidently went on, alphabetically, to "Glasen" (Gleaston) Castle, on the other property of the Harringtons, and, whilst altering the bearings, inadvertently duplicated the immediately preceding location; hence, "Glasen Castle, Lancaster. Loynsdale." And now as to the name Glasson. Glass (Saxon, Glæs; Welsh and Gaelic, Glas; German and Scandinavian, Glas) refers primarily to colour—to a blue, green, fresh, light, or bright hue; and as a name or prefix to a name, with either a single or a double s, it is invariably indicative of the immediate presence, adjacency, or palpable nearness of water. Glass is the name of a loch in Ross-shire and of a river as well as some water-surrounded land in Inverness-shire; in the United Kingdom there are numerous places—towns, villages, &c.—all quite close to or in the neighbourhood of rivers—bearing names with Glas or Glass as a prefix; and in certain parts there are

OLD GLASSON.

from Lancaster to Cockerham, Glasson included, of course—seem to be particularly wrong. Presuming that the latitudes are relatively correct, then the longitude named—lon. 23' west from Lancaster—would locate "Glasen Castle" at Furness Abbey. There is, however, no castle at that place. But if the calculation be reduced somewhat, say to the extent of about two and a half miles in a direct line eastward from Furness Abbey, then a spot will be come to where there are now some ruins visible—the ruins of Gleaston Castle. This is, no doubt, the "Glasen Castle" named in the "Index." It was built early in the 14th century by the Harringtons, lords of Aldingham. The same Harrintons were also the owners of Thurnham manor in the 13th and 14th centuries. Glasson—the "Glason" of the "Index"—is in the township of Thurnham. Adams had, probably, in the course of his reading or inquiries, met with some

place-names closely resembling Glasson on the Lune; their origin, evidently, being due to river proximity. For figurative or poetic purposes, water, bright and smooth, has long been specified as the analogue or equivalent of glass. For instance, in one of Shakspere's plays (Mid. N. Dr.) there are the words —"Her silver visage in the watery glass"; and in another (Henry VI.) are these—"The sun upon the glassy streams." Milton, in his great epic (P.L., 1st ed.) says—"The cleer Sun on his wide watrie Glass Gaz'd hot." And Addison observes (Salma. and Herm.)—"In the limpid streams she views her face, And drest her image in the floating glass." Old forms of the word glass include glase, glaso, and glasshe. By a phonetic process, the last letter of the different suffixes here given might, in time, respectively become a, as in glassa—one of the earliest forms of the name Glasson on the Lune which I have met with. Possibly, the terminating a may have originated, or been applied, during the temporary presence and conversation of certain far-northern sailors in this region. In some of the Scandinavian languages a is the equivalent of on, which, in a suffix, might here indicate freshness, clearness, brightness, &c., over the bulk, or ostensibly in contact with the upper part, or forming a surface characteristic, of the water; and the substitution of on for a would be merely a change of form, without any alteration in the meaning of the terminal. The letter a is also an abbreviation of the Anglo-Saxon word on; but, as such, it seems to be exclusively used for prefixing purposes. The name Glasson may, however, at a very early time have been Glassavon (avon is the Celtic word for river); the final a in Glassa being, on this hypothesis, a remnant of the suffix avon, and on in the present as in the earliest form of the name which I have seen (will, temp. 1561) a residual of the last syllable of it. But all that I have here stated as to the suffix must be taken as hypothesis only. There can be little, if indeed any, doubt as to the meaning of Glas or Glass: the remainder of the name I must place in the category of the uncertain, if not actually inexplicable. In

tons gross register, and discharging a cargo of upwards of 1,600 tons of manufactured wood goods) is the largest steamer which has thus far been in the dock. In addition to the dock, there are at Glasson a timber pond, or canal basin, with an area of about 13 acres, and a graving dock with an entrance of 35 feet, a length " over all " of 197 feet, and a length " on blocks " of 184 feet. A block of five-storey warehouses, some timber yards, &c., are at the south-eastern end. There are likewise at Glasson Dock a shipbuilding yard (the proprietors being Messrs. R. Nicholson and Sons, who in addition to being builders are repairers, sail makers, &c.), steam saw mills, and brick and tile works. The " Sprightly," from Duddon, with a cargo of slate, was the first boat which sailed on the canal from Glasson Dock to Preston. She started on her " voyage " on the 16th of May, 1826. The first " vessel " launched at Glasson was a superior sort of canal boat, called the " Acorn "—a boat 70 feet long and 14 feet broad. The launch of it took place on the 8th of March, 1837. Glasson Dock is the port of Lancaster. The state of trade in connection with the shipping at Glasson has entirely changed within the last few years: this has been due to a great falling off in the timber trade, and

GLASSON DOCK.

1738 an Act was obtained for the erection of a mole, on the east side of the present dock, at Glasson, in order to secure shelter and a place of convenience for vessels to discharge at. In 1749 an Act was got which had for its object " the improving of the river Loyne [Lune], and for building a quay or wharf "; and 23 years afterwards an Act was secured " to extend the same." In May, 1787, a wet dock was opened at Glasson—hence the name Glasson Dock. Previous to this, the place had been merely a tidal harbour, dry at low water. The area of the dock is a little over two acres. Up to the present time, the " Louise " (1,065 tons) is the largest sailing vessel which has been here; and the " Ardancorrach " (1,488

to an increased influx of iron ore. The imports are iron ore, manufactured wood goods, timber, deals, cork, cement, china clay, whiting, and other general articles. The exports are coals and pig iron. A line from Lancaster to Glasson—a branch of the London and North-Western Railway—was opened on the 9th of July, 1883. There are three public-houses at Glasson Dock. That which seems to be the most structurally substantial—the Pier Hotel—was erected about 1779, when the place was but a small harbour, with a mere sand or gravel bank for vessels to rest on at low water. The oldest of the public-houses is on the opposite or western side of the wet dock: this is the Dalton Arms—a small, whitewashed building,

closely adjoining and in line with some cottages of a
kindred external hue. There is an Episcopal church
at Glasson Dock. It was opened on April 12th, 1840;
its ecclesiastical district consisting of Glasson and parts
of Thurnham, Ashton-with-Stodday, and Cockerham.
The church is at the south-east end of Glasson Dock:
it stands amid trees, and, though but small, has a neat,
pleasing appearance. The east window was put up in
1866, to the memory of Le Gendre Nicholas Starkie,
of Huntroyde and Ashton Hall, by his widow, Anne
Starkie. In another part there is a window in memory
of John Piers Chamberlain Starkie, of Ashton Hall.
This window was given by the parishioners—Mr. R.
Nicholson, shipbuilder, taking a very active part in
the movement for it—and was put up in 1889. On the
north side there is another memorial window; this
is to the memory of Matthew Henry Simpson (only son
of Mr. M. Simpson, formerly of Glasson parish), who
died in 1892, at Moramhanna, British Guiana, in the
39th year of his age. The Rev. C. E. Golland is the
present incumbent. The population of Glasson Dock
is now about 300, and, strange to say, it has varied only
about three during the past 40 years. Mr. W. O.
Roper, F.S.A., in his collection of "Weather Say-
ings, Proverbs, and Prognostics," gives this—"When
the Welsh mountains are visible from Glasson Dock, it
is said that a gale is sure to follow from the south-west-
wards, and a bad one too." This saying is, no doubt,
correctly set forth by Mr. Roper. But Glasson Dock
is not the only place where rough atmospheric change
is predicted when Cambrian eminences are conspicuous.
There are different parts of Lancashire whereat such
visibility is deemed a certain sign of bad weather. For
instance, one day, some time ago, whilst standing on
the south platform of Lea Road station, near Preston,
I heard a local gentleman, close by, remark: "The
Welsh mountains are now quite distinct; whenever
they are visible from Lea a change in the weather
soon takes place; and we shall have a storm before
long." I turned round and saw the mountains in
question very distinctly. Next day there was a gale,
accompanied by heavy rain. Recently, whilst in
Ellel, I heard a gentleman, who resides in
the higher part of that district, observe that when
the Welsh mountains were visible from his house bad
weather was sure to speedily follow.

As the predecessor of Glasson Dock, for shipping
purposes—as, in fact, the port of Lancaster for some
time—reference must be made here to Sunderland.
West of Glasson, on the opposite side of the Lune
estuary, the hamlet of Sunderland is located. It is
conspicuously situated on the edge of a strip of land
which stretches south of it for something like
half a mile, getting gradually narrower right along
to its termination—Sunderland Point. The strip of
land is now, at ordinary full tide time, surrounded
by water, with the exception of about half a mile at
the north end. Formerly, before the inner edge of the
marsh was fenced off or bank-protected, water might,
when the tides were very high, pass up some sinuous
dyke or channel, and virtually make the strip an
island—separated or sundered from the main land;

and hence the name Sunderland. The oldest date I
have observed on any building at Sunderland is 1707.
About that time Mr. Robert Lawson, a merchant,
settled at Sunderland. He put up several buildings,
including two warehouses, and opened a shipbuilding
place. It is said that he was the original importer of
cotton wool into Lancashire: the first cargo of it,
which was brought to Sunderland, was deemed such
a curiosity that many persons went to look at it.
Nobody at that time, however, who saw this cotton
wool, seemed to know how to utilise it; and for
several months it remained on Mr. Lawson's hands as
an unsaleable article. The Scotch Rebels—the 1715
lot—when they got to Lancaster, on their southward
march, were informed—by "a gentleman of influence," it was afterwards said—that there were six
guns (brass cannons) on a ship at Sunderland; a detachment was sent down for them; the guns were
brought back; and a few days afterwards two of them
were used, on the Rebel side, at a barricade in
Church-street, Preston, against some of the Royal
forces commanded by General Wills; but, through
being either improperly charged or badly handled,
they were useless. As to the remainder of the guns,
it has not been recorded what was done with them
while they were in charge of the Rebels at Preston.
After the surrender of the Rebels, their weapons, am-
munition, &c., were transferred to the Royal forces;
and it is said that the six guns taken from the Sunderland ship are now in the Tower of London. When
the dock at Glasson was made, the local shipping
trade was drawn to it, and Sunderland, as a "port,"
went down. The population of Sunderland now
amounts to about 50. The principal occupation of the
male adult inhabitants is fishing. There are no inns at
Sunderland; formerly there were two. At the north
end there is a temperance hotel. And not far from it
there is a small place of worship, of red brick,
with a little bell in front. A good many
persons visit Sunderland in summer time. On
the seaward side of the land on which Sunderland is situated there is Sambo's grave.
About 1736 there arrived at Sunderland, on
one of the ships from the West Indies,
a negro, who had been acting as the captain's
servant. In the interval between the unloading and
re-freighting of the vessel this negro—they called him
Sambo—was kept, by arrangement, at one of the
inns; but he somehow got it into his head
that he had been abandoned, and he became so de-
jected that he refused to take food, and in a very
short time died. At a spot on the lonely western
side, close to the shore (it is now one corner of a field),
some sailors dug a grave for Sambo, and—coffinless,
simply covered with his own clothes—he was buried
in it. Sixty years afterwards the story of Sambo's
death and burial was told to the Rev. James Watson,
whilst he was temporarily staying at Sunderland, in
summer time. The solitary grave by the sea side,
about 600 yards west of the hamlet, was likewise
pointed out to him; and afterwards, by means of
subscriptions from visitors, he placed over it, hori-
zontally, a monumental stone, containing in the

centre, on a copper plate, the following inscription :—

Here Lies
Poor Samboo,
A Faithful Negro,
who
(Attending his Master from the West Indies)
Died on his arrival at Sunderland.
Full sixty years the angry winter's wave
  Has thundering dashed this bleak and barren shore
Since Sambo's head, laid in this lonely grave,
  Lies still, and ne'er will hear their turmoil more.
Full many a sand bird chirps upon the sod,
  And many a moonlight elfin round him trips;
Full many a summer's sunbeam warms the clod,
  And many a teeming cloud upon him drips.
But still he sleeps, till the awakening sounds
  Of the Archangel's trump new life impart;
Then the Great Judge His approbation founds
  Not on man's color, but his—Worth of Heart

James Watson, Scrt.   H. Bell, del., 1796.

Both the stone and the inscribed plate are now in good condition. The Rev. James Watson who composed the above epitaph and elegy was the son of James Watson, labourer, of Airton, a few miles from Settle. From 1737 to 1767 he was curate of Wyresdale Church. Two years prior to relinquishing the curacy there he was appointed Head Master of Lancaster Grammar School—a position he held till 1794. He was also—probably during the whole or greater portion of the time he was connected with the Grammar School—Chaplain of Lancaster Castle. And it is said that he was, some time anterior to 1786, appointed a prebendary of Lincoln Cathedral. During his Head Mastership at Lancaster he on one occasion (in 1770) got into "hot water" in consequence of his "behaviour" towards one of the scholars—a son of Mr. Thomas Hinde, Mayor of the borough. The matter was brought before a meeting of the Corporation (the Corporation owned or had control of the Grammar School at that time), and it was resolved that Mr. Watson's behaviour had been "improper and inhuman and unjustifiable" (he had probably given the youth referred to a specially heavy thrashing); that he had by means thereof, and owing to his conduct at the Corporate meeting (may be, he had vigorously vindicated his "behaviour," and told the members that they knew nothing at all about the duties of a schoolmaster) "highly incurred the displeasure of the Council;" and that if he persisted in such a course as that complained of steps would be taken to "amove [obsolete word, meaning remove] him from his office of schoolmaster." Fifteen years afterwards, when Mr. Watson resigned the Head Mastership, the Lancastrian Corporate mind had swung round very strongly in his favour, for at a meeting of the Town Council at that time (evidently at Midsummer, 1794) it was resolved—"That the thanks of this Corporation be given to the Reverend James Watson, Clerk, for the faithful discharge of the Duties of his office of Master at the Free Grammar School in this Town for a period of near Thirty years, for the great services he hath thereby rendered to the Publick, and also for the honourable manner in which he hath now resigned."

Near the western edge of the Lune, and a mile north of Glasson Dock, there stands conspicuously, on an eminence, a very old place of worship—Overton Church—though not so ancient, it has recently been contended, as one Lancashire antiquary in particular—the venerable and much-esteemed Mon-

Overton Church.

signor Cradwell, of Claughton-on-Brock—supposes it to be. Monsignor Cradwell apparently thinks that the foundation of Overton Church dates from "some time after the settlement of the Angles in

North Lancashire," that "the great thickness of the walls and the absence of courses in the stone work suggest a British rather than a Saxon origin of the building," that the structure "takes us back to the sixth or seventh century," and that it is " the oldest church in Lancashire." At the Congress of the Royal Archæological Institute, held at Lancaster, in July, 1893, Mr. W. O. Roper, F.S.A., said the antiquity of Overton Church had been considerably over-rated, and that the old ruined church at Heysham was of far greater antiquity; and the Rev. J. C. Cox, LL.D., F.S.A., afterwards stated that he visited Overton Church in 1897, that there was not a bit of Anglo-Saxon work about it, that with the exception of a Norman archway there was nothing of more than ordinary interest about the place, and that it was impossible to imagine how the delusion that it was the oldest church in the county had come about. In Yorkshire there are certain churches somewhat like that at Overton; and probably structures similar to them exist in other counties. Amongst those in Yorkshire the following may be specified:—The church at Adel, near Leeds (date, 1139); St. Mary's, Scawton, near Helmsley (1146); and Redmire Church, Wensleydale (earliest mention of it, 1484). At Heck, near Snaith, there is a new church very like that at Overton, in respect to the belfry and side windows, and the style of its architecture is mentioned as of the 14th century. In all the edifices named there are numerous variations from Overton Church; but, taken as a whole, there is a strong "family likeness." A movement is now on foot for the restoration and alteration of Overton Church, the estimated cost of the work being about £1,100. The Rev. T. W. Greenall is the present Vicar of Overton.

CHAPTER XXIV.

THE CONDER AND CONDER GREEN—ASHTON-WITH-STODDAY—ASHTON HALL, PARK, AND
ESTATE—LUNECLIFFE—ALDCLIFFE AND ITS HALL, &C.

There is a very small, rustic-looking place called Conder Green, a mile or so from Glasson Dock, on the east side. The road to it, from Glasson Dock, goes by the side of a marsh, and is a very sinuous, in-and-out one; but it is not so crooked as the lower course of the river Conder which adjoins, and which is crossed by a good stone bridge about 300 yards south of Conder Green. The Conder takes its rise near Littledale Fell. Drayton alludes, in his "Polyolbion," to the Conder. He says:—

To Neptune lowting [bending] low, when Chrystall Lun
  [Lune] doth cease,
And Conder comming in, conducts her by her hand,
Till lastly shee salute the poynt of Sunderland,
And leaues our dainty Lun to Amphitrites care.

Conder Green is in Ashton-with-Stodday—a compound township in the Union of Lancaster; and, though a particularly little place, it contains a very old public-house. Nowadays, this public-house is called the Stork; for many years, up to about 1854, its sign was the Hamilton Arms; and previously its name was the Cocks. It is conjectured that there used to be cock-fighting at this house or in its immediate vicinity. Tyldesley, the diarist, now and then dropped in here and had something to drink. His first reference to the place occurs under date May 3rd, 1712. After stating that he had on that day "spent 6d. at Preston," he says, "thence to ye Cockes at Condre Green." The present Stork seems to be a well-regarded bird by mortals of the thirsty order. Once a year there is a flower show, in a marquee, at Conder Green.

Ashton Hall is about a mile from Conder Green, in the direction of Lancaster. It stands about 250 yards west of the Lancaster and Cockerham road, and, with its combination of anciently-strong and modernly-elaborate architecture, its towers and turrets—multiform and embattled, its spacious bays—single and superposed, its lofty porch, and its intermediate masonry, all most substantial and castellated, it is at once impressive and admirable. In the Doomsday Survey Ashton is specified as Eshtun—a name meaning an enclosure in a clearing amid or near ash trees. Stodday, on the north side, is not mentioned in the Survey. A very early form of this name appears to have been Stodale, which may, primarily, have been Stowdale, meaning fenced-in or stockaded land of a low-lying or dell-like character, or land of the like kind containing a "fixed place or mansion." The earliest recorded owners of Ashton were the Lancastres, barons of Kendal, one of whom (William de Lancastre), it has been conjectured, gave, amongst

other property, the manor and church of Cockerham to the canons of Laycestre (Leicester), in the latter half of the 12th century. In the 13th century a William de Lancastre gave to the priory of Lancaster a rent of 12d., payable out of his mill at Stodale (Stodday), in order that he might have a chapel on his manor at Esseton (Ashton). The Lyndeseys or Lindsays afterwards held Ashton; then it passed to the De Coucys; and next it became, either through marriage or Royal gift, the property of John de Coupland, who, at the battle of Neville's Cross, in 1346, made a prisoner of David II., King of Scotland, and was knighted for his excellent services during that conflict by the King of England (Edward III.); and to the Harringtons (Lords of Aldingham, and originally of Harrington, in Cumberland) Ashton, in all probability, next passed. They owned the adjoining manor of Thurnham for many years—from the early part of the 13th to the middle of the 14th century; and as the Laurences, supposed to be descendants of the Harringtons, owned Ashton at a later period, it is not at all improbable that proprietary rights had previously been exercised here by the Harringtons themselves. In 1377 mention is made of "Edmund Laurence, son of John Laurence, of Asshdon" (Ashton). In 1442 a license, for three years, was granted for an oratory and a priest in the house of Sir Robert Laurence, Knight, of Ashton. Sir Robert, who died some time between 1450 and 1454, was succeeded by James Laurence, conjectured to have been his son, who was knighted in 1484, at Hutton Field, in Berwickshire, when Lord Stanley, at the head of 4,000 Lancashire and Cheshire men, was with the army which Edward IV. sent against the Scots. Sir James Laurence died in 1501, and was succeeded by Thomas Laurence, his son and heir, who, in the same year, when the marriage of Prince Arthur took place, was created a Knight of the Bath. He was also one of the commissioners employed in Lancashire to collect "aid" for Henry VII. when that monarch's career was drawing to a close. As to the immediate successor of Sir Thomas, in Ashton, the evidence is so conflicting that it is impossible to definitely say who the person was. But it is certain that in 1527 John, the second son of Sir James Laurence (the eldest son having pre-deceased his father), was at Ashton Hall, and, apparently, its owner. He had several daughters and co-heiresses. His daughter Elizabeth married John Butler, of Rawcliffe; and their daughter and heiress, Isabel, married Thomas Radcliffe, of Winmarleigh, whose daughter

135

Anne married Sir Gilbert Gerard, through which union the Ashton property passed to the Gerards, of Gerard's Bromley, in Staffordshire. For several years in the early portion of the 16th century the Ashton property was held by the Crown; the principal or sole grantee being Sir Thomas Parr (father of Catherine Parr, the sixth and last wife of Henry VIII.), who in 1513 secured it, at an annual rent, for 40 years. For some years subsequent to 1532 Sir James Leyburn rented and resided in Ashton, presumably at the Hall. One of the Gerards (Thomas), who was elected M.P. for the borough of Lancaster in 1584 and 1586, and for the county of Lancaster in 1588, and who in 1590 was raised to the peerage as Baron Gerard of Gerard's Bromley, was at Ashton Hall in 1603; but it is supposed he had been residing here prior to that time. On the 12th of August, 1617, he entertained James I., who was on his way from Edinburgh to London, at Ashton Hall. About two months afterwards Baron Gerard died, when he was succeeded by his eldest son Gilbert, who died in 1622, and was succeeded by his son Dutton. A branch of the Bindloss family, of Borwick Hall, occupied Ashton Hall for a time, between 1620 and 1650. "Drunken Barnaby" (Richard Brathwaite) was twice at Ashton Hall during this occupation. In

"Drunken Barnaby" was born in or near Kendal. in 1588; his father was a barrister and Recorder of Kendal, and married a daughter of Robert Bindloss, of Haulston, in Westmorland: he ("Barnaby") was well educated, and wrote several poems—24 books in all his principal production being "Barnabæ Itinerarium," or "Barnabee's Journal," frequently reprinted as "Drunken Barnaby's Four Journeys," and consisting of rhymed Latin, with an accompanying English translation, in doggerel verse. For some time he lived as an independent gentleman, in Westmorland, and became a deputy lieutenant of that county; afterwards he removed to East Appleton, near Catterick, in Yorkshire, became lord of the manor of East Appleton, died there in 1673, and was buried at Catterick Church. His mother (nee Dorothy Bindloss) was a sister of Sir Robert Bindloss, of Borwick Hall, so that "Barnaby" was the cousin of Sir Francis Bindloss (Sir Robert's son), who was one of the Parliamentary representatives of the borough of Lancaster in 1627-28, and who resided at or tenanted Ashton Hall for some time. This accounts for "Barnaby's" reference to the "friend and kinsman" who invited him to Ashton. The Hon. Elizabeth Gerard (daughter of Dutton, Lord Gerard, who succeeded to the title in 1622) had for her first

ASHTON HALL.

part 2 of his "Journal," after a reference to "John o' Gant's old towne-a" (Lancaster), he says:—

> Thence to Ashton, good as may be
> Was the wine, brave knight, bright ladie;
> All I saw was comely specious,
> Seemly gratious, neatly precious;
> My Muse with Bacchus so long traded,
> When I walkt, my legs denaid it.

And in part 4 he observes—

> Now to Ashton I'm invited
> By my friend and kinsman cited;
> Secret cellars entertain me,
> Beauteous-beaming stars inflame me;
> Meat, mirth, musick, wines are there full,
> With a count'nance blith and cherefull.

husband Colonel Philip Wenman, or Wainman, and they resided at Ashton Hall. When Charles II. was proceeding south, in the summer of 1651, he "lodged at Ashton Hall," which is described as being at that time "Colonel Wainman's house." The Colonel did not live very long, and the Hon. Elizabeth Gerard, his widow, afterwards became the wife of the Hon. William Spencer, third son of William, second Lord Spencer, of Wormleighton, in Warwickshire. They lived at Ashton Hall for some years. The Hon. William Spencer died in or about 1687, Lady Elizabeth surviving him, along with a daughter. Some time afterwards this daughter married Robert Hesketh, of Rufford, whose daughter and heiress Elizabeth became, in 1714, the wife of

Sir Edward Stanley, afterwards 11th Earl of Derby. Later, the Ashton property passed, by marriage, to the ducal family of Hamilton, and it remained a possession of that family till 1853, when it was sold. For some time prior to the disposal of the property the Duke of Hamilton had ceased to reside at Ashton Hall. The park grounds, which environ the Hall, are well laid out, choicely wooded, and enclosed by a high stone wall, &c. The plantations and northern belt of trees in Ashton Park have long formed a very striking and picturesque feature of the estate. A topographical work, published 76 years ago, says, "there is here some of the finest park scenery in the county." It is still of a very charming character. Formerly, a quantity of the land, north of the Hall, was used as a deer park. One of the Dukes attempted to establish a heronry in a portion of the grounds. He brought some herons from Hamilton Palace, placed them in what was deemed a suitable spot, and for a time they bred; but afterwards they became unsettled, and eventually died or flew away. In Lancaster Parish Church there was a Hamilton vault. The remains of Harriet, Lady Archibald Hamilton, who died in 1788, whilst proceeding to Bath, were brought to Ashton Hall, and afterwards placed in a vault in the centre of the church named. The funeral procession was a very large and imposing one. It consisted of six mutes on horseback; a hearse, bearing escutcheons of the family, and drawn by six horses; two favourite servants in deep mourning; a mourning coach containing the chief mourners and drawn by six horses; her ladyship's empty coach and four, draped; ten gentlemen in carriages; seventy-two tenants on horseback, in couples; twenty-four tenants on foot, wearing hat bands and gloves; and a numerous train of servants and other attendants. Lord Archibald Hamilton, who succeeded to the Dukedom in 1799, died at Ashton Hall, on the 16th of February, 1819, in the 79th year of his age. He was interred in Lancaster Parish Church, by the side of Lady Archibald, his wife, "the vault being situated under his pew." It is said that the front gates of Ashton Hall had never been opened from the time of the funeral of Lady Archibald, till the day when the remains of the Duke were removed for interment. (The remains of both the Duke and Lady Archibald were transferred from the vault in Lancaster Parish Church to a mausoleum at Hamilton Palace, Lanarkshire, about 1865). The Duke bequeathed the deer in Ashton Park to his daughter, the Duchess of Somerset. On the 1st of March, 1820, during the attempts made to secure the deer (120 in number), one of them impaled itself whilst trying to jump over a fence, and 26 died from exhaustion through being pursued so keenly. The others were removed, in covered carts, to the Hon. F. West's park, in Denbighshire. The Duke's racing stud, when offered for sale, a few weeks after his death, realised 2,130 guineas. At the Lancaster Assizes, in March, 1820, Dr. Baxendale, of Lancaster, brought an action against the executors of

the Duke to recover £1,007 for professional attendance, &c., during the last illness of his Grace. The sum of £500 was paid into Court; but the jury gave Dr. Baxendale a verdict for the full amount claimed.

The Duke of Hamilton, who died at Ashton Hall, in 1819, was succeeded in the dukedom by his son Alexander. Not unfrequently, in the early part of his ducal career, Alexander was at Ashton Hall, and at a later stage he periodically resided at it; but eventually he appeared to abandon the Hall as a place of residence. He died in 1852, and in the following year the Hamilton property, in North Lancashire, was sold by auction. Alexander was succeeded by his son William Alexander Anthony Archibald, who married Princess Mary of Baden, a cousin of the Emperor Napoleon III., and who died in Paris, in 1863; his successor in the dukedom being his eldest son William Alexander Louis Stephen, who died in 1895, leaving as his only issue a daughter, Mary Louise, who at that time was but eleven years of age. The dukedom then devolved upon a kinsman, the present Duke—Alfred Douglas Hamilton—who is a descendant, in the fifth generation, of James Earl of Arran, was born in 1862, and for some time served as a lieutenant in the Royal Navy. He is the 13th Duke of Hamilton. The Hamilton estates now consist of about 157,400 acres, and are held in trust, according to the will of the 12th Duke. When the Hamilton Lancashire property was sold, in 1853, that portion of it in Ashton, including the Hall and 1,558 acres of agricultural land, with nine grazing farms, was purchased by Mr. Le Gendre Nicholas Starkie, of Huntroyde, near Padiham, who was for some time M.P. for Clitheroe. He rebuilt a considerable portion of Ashton Hall, and resided alternately at it and at Huntroyde. In 1865 he died, when the Ashton estate became the property of his second son, Mr. J. P. Chamberlain Starkie (one of the M.P.'s for North-east Lancashire from 1868 to 1880), who resided at Ashton Hall, and died here in 1888. On the 7th of July, 1884, the Ashton property was offered for sale by auction, at Lancaster; but there was only one bid—a bid of £80,000, made by the late Alderman Charles Blades, of Lancaster—and, as this did not come up to the reserve price, the property was withdrawn. It was purchased, by private treaty, for £100,000, a few months afterwards, by Mr. James Williamson (the present Lord Ashton), who has since spent many thousands of pounds in improvements, the principal object in making them being to "enable the farmers on the estate the better and more profitably to carry on their business." After the death of Mr. J. P. Chamberlain Starkie, his widow continued to reside at Ashton Hall till 1895, when it became one of the residences of Lord Ashton. Half a century ago, a lingering tradition associated the occasional presence of "a lady in white" with one or two of the rooms in Ashton Hall; but subsequent regular occupation of the place eliminated that delusion—"laid" that ghost—and, Hibernianly speaking, there has since been no re-appearance of the spook, which never existed here at all. It also used to be said that there was a "dobby"—a sort of rough, inferior ghost—in the Ashton district, and that it appeared at night time chiefly in the ordinary road opposite Ashton Hall, and usually near the main entrance gate, indulging in a variety of contortional movements, and manifesting a predilection for mauling or getting hold of passers by. For many years, however, the "dobby" has been non est; and as an old Lancaster friend of mine observed, in a letter I lately had from him, even in the days when the "dobby" was believed in, it merely presented itself "to the befuddled vision of a belated sailor, as he wended his way from Lancaster to Glasson Dock, at the witching hour of midnight, after a debauch which made him see double." There used to be a story current in the locality regarding a sailor, who had a good deal of faith, for monetary purposes, in a tree opposite Ashton Hall. The story was to the effect that, having no person to trust or caring nothing for banks, the sailor deposited a quantity of his money in a high part of one of the big trees near the main entrance gate, that he afterwards joined a ship at Glasson Dock and sailed away on a long voyage, and that on returning he proceeded to the tree, climbed to the hiding-place, found his money quite safe, and went off with it in a very joyful, triumphant style.

Lunecliffe, formerly called Stodday Lodge, is about a mile and a half north of Ashton Hall. It occupies an eminence, about 300 yards west of the Lancaster and Cockerham road. There are now at Lunecliffe two Roman milestones (milliaria). The evidence as to where and when they were found is conflicting. One statement I have seen favours the presumption that both were discovered between Burrow and Stodday, in 1793 or 1794, when some excavations in connection with the Lancaster and Preston canal were being made; another affirms that one stone was dug up near Burrow, in 1793, and that the other was found during some ploughing operations in a field in Ashton, near the canal; and yet another statement is to the effect that the former stone was discovered in 1811, in the field referred to, and that the latter was found in the same field in 1834. Anyhow, they are evidently genuine milliaria. One, bearing the name of the Emperor Philip, who reigned between 244 and 249 A.D., is now in Lunecliffe garden; the other, which is in a better state of preservation, and was for some time in an old barn, in the village of Stodday, from which it was removed to Lunecliffe by Mr. E. B. Dawson, when he pulled down the barn, has on it the name of the Emperor (Decius) who succeeded Philip in 249 A.D. The latter stone is now in a sheltered position close to the side door of Lunecliffe. The Rev. R. Simpson, in his "History of Lancaster," makes reference to a "Roman well" adjacent to Lunecliffe; but his statement is quite a mistaken one. This "Roman well" is, in reality, a small dipping basin for garden-watering purposes, at Lunecliffe, and does not date further back than 1807.

Aldcliffe Hall is something like a mile north of Lunecliffe. The name Aldcliffe (meaning old cliff) appears in Doomsday Book as Aldeolif; and the land area associated therewith is specified in the same Book as being two carucates, or about two hundred acres. In early times the manor of Aldcliffe was held under lease by the Prior of Lancaster. In the reign of Henry VIII. there appears to have been some township or land tenure connection between Aldcliffe and Bulk. Aldcliffe Old Hall was built in the days of William Rufus, and was, it has been conjectured, enlarged about the time of Henry VII. It was in the possession of the Dalton family in the reign of Elizabeth, and some of the property, being left for the benefit of the secular clergy of the Church of Rome, was confiscated to the Crown. About 1680 the Rev. Peter Gooden (Roman Catholic priest), of Leighton, became a missioner at Aldcliffe Hall, where he kept a school or seminary "for the education of youths, who were afterwards sent to Popish colleges abroad to be trained as priests." Gooden, who died at Aldcliffe in 1694, was buried at Lancaster Parish Church. The confiscated portion of the property, including the Hall, was let by the Crown to Benjamin Leigh, some time prior to 1720, and on his death it passed to the husband of his eldest daughter Isabel—Robert Dawson, of Warton, near Lancaster. In 1769 this gentleman died; his widow's demise occurring in 1781. Their successor was an only son, John, who purchased the Aldcliffe estate from the Crown. Dying in 1804, at the age of 60, he was succeeded by his only son, Edward, then but 10 years old. In 1817 this son Edward, having a short time before purchased the remaining portion of the township of Aldcliffe from Mr. Ralph Riddell, of Felton Park, in the county of Durham—the representative of the Dalton family—pulled down the old Hall, and built the present one, on a better site, 50 yards from where the ancient structure stood, and 48 feet above the sea level. In 1820 Mr. Dawson enclosed by an embankment, at a cost of £2,000, 166 acres of Aldcliffe Marsh, which belonged to the estate, and for this work of reclamation the Society of Arts and Sciences presented him with a suitably inscribed gold medal, in 1821. The present Aldcliffe Hall stands picturesquely on the north-west side of the village of Aldcliffe. The trees in its grounds are amongst the finest in the North of England. On the 18th of September, 1899, one of them—an elm, 4ft. in diameter, and 80ft. high—was blown down. When the burial ground at High-street Chapel, Lancaster, was closed, Mr. Dawson prepared a small private cemetery under the shade of the great trees referred to. He died in 1876. So far, though 46 years have elapsed since the private cemetery within the grounds of Aldcliffe Hall was made, there have been only four interments in it. On the death of Mrs. Dawson, widow of Mr. Dawson, in 1884, their eldest son (Mr. E. B. Dawson) made some improvements at the Hall, including a private installation of electric light. Aldcliffe Hall, a good-looking, substantial stone building, now the residence of Mr. E. B. Dawson, is situated about a mile from the centre of Lancaster, and is within half a mile of the river Lune, of which and the upper portion of the estuary there is, from the front of the mansion, a full and very fine view. On the 19th of July, 1893, an ornamental, rusticated arch was erected over a well in the village of Aldcliffe, in commemoration of the birth of Mr. E. Dawson one hundred years previously. The keystone of the arch bears his coat of arms and crest, with various devices emblematic of continuance, the Greek AEI, the classic bat, and the Egyptian lotus, encircling the dates 1793 and 1893; while in allusion to Mr. Dawson's transformation of the property during his long tenure of it there is introduced part of the epitaph on Sir Christopher Wren, in St. Paul's Cathedral—"Si monumentum quæris, circumspice." By many—indeed, by the generality of people—the name Aldcliffe is pronounced Awcliffe; and for many generations it has, apparently, been articulated in the same way. There was proved, in 1618, within the archdeaconry of Richmond, the will of Katherine Sheirson, widow, "of Awcliffe," and five years afterwards that of Margaret Shierson, spinster, also "of Awcliffe," was proved within the same archdeaconry.

ALDCLIFFE HALL.

CHAPTER XXV.

ROAD IMPROVEMENT—FOOT RACES—LONGEVITY—LIVELY "ANCIENTS"—A TRAGIC AFFAIR—
BURROW—BAILRIGG—HORSE-RIDING AFFAIR—SELECTED AND DISCARDED BATTLE-FIELD
—SCOTFORTH—A THEOLOGIAN AND A JOURNALIST—CLOUGHA PIKE—INCREASE OF
BUILDINGS—THE GREAVES—CHARMING SCENERY, &C.

A reversion must now be made to Galgate: this go-back is necessary in order to deal with sundry historical matters and objects of interest adjacent to or not far from the main road between Galgate and Lancaster, as well as with a few farther off, but more or less visible on the eastern side. Nearly half of the way from Galgate to Lancaster—the length extending from Galgate to Burrow Bridge—is of the entirely "new" kind: it was made to supersede a corresponding length of the old coach road—still in usable condition, though grass-covered in some parts—on the western side, along a ridge with a steep brow at each end; and it was opened on the 1st of March, 1824. The remainder of the road, from Burrow Bridge to Lancaster, underwent improvement about the same time: it is entirely on the line of the old route. Immediately north of Galgate police station—a recently-built station, which an old Galgatian one day pointed out to me, with a sort of pride, as "a sign of progress" in the village—there is a straight, level length of main road, on which formerly foot races were run. Old inhabitants of Galgate remember them well enough. And there are not a few persons of that kind in the village now. Parenthetically, I may here just observe that persons of the old order, residing in the place, have an annual treat—a dinner, followed by a concert—at Christmas; and some of them are of a decidedly lively character. At Christmas, 1899, a free dinner was provided for 100; the oldest man present being 99 years of age. This was George Dixon, who is still alive, and who attained his 100th year on the 19th of June, 1900. As a proof of the liveliness of the "ancients," I cull the following lines from a paragraph I met with one day respecting the concert which took place after the last dinner:—The oldest lady, Mrs. Huntington, 75, sang in a pleasing manner "Men are not so kind as they used to be." Mrs. Swarbrick, 65, received an encore for her song, "A Parrot in a Pear Tree." Mrs. Lambert also received an encore for the "Mistletoe Bough." Mr. W. Taylor, 71, Mr. W. Price, 71, and Mr. Charnley, 66, sang with good effect the popular songs of their young days; and altogether the proceedings were very interesting.

About half a mile from Galgate, northward, the main road, the railway, the old coach road, and the canal run parallel for a short distance, all within a space of 600 yards.

A little over a mile north of Galgate there branches from the main road, on the east side, an initially zig-zag way, out of which—about 500 yards from the entrance—there slants to the left a grass-covered lane which leads to Hazlerigge, &c., and the lower or western portion of which is called Green-lane. At a secluded spot, on the north side of this lane, just past a bend, and about 100 yards from the entrance, a murder was committed on the evening of January 11th, 1866; the victim being a young woman named Elizabeth Nelson, of Skerton, near Lancaster. Next morning a man named Thomas Wilkinson, of Burrow Beck, discovered her dead body partially covered with snow (there had been a fall of snow during the night), at the spot named. The body was very badly bruised, and bore traces of a desperate struggle. A young man, connected with a farm in the neighbourhood, was soon afterwards apprehended, and taken before the magistrates at Lancaster, on the charge of having committed the murder; but the evidence adduced against him was not of a conclusive character, and he was set at liberty. Since then nothing has come to light as to the person or persons who committed the murder. At the place where the dead body was found there afterwards was fixed up an inscribed memorial slab, of a blue, slate-like kind, in a base of freestone. The money required for it was raised by public subscription. The stone bears the following inscription:—" In memory of Elizabeth Nelson, of Skerton, spinster, aged 31, who at this spot, on the evening of Thursday, January 11th, 1866, was barbarously murdered in defence of her chastity. 'O Lord, Thou hast seen my wrong; judge Thou my cause.'—Lam. c. 3, v. 59. Erected by public subscription." The top and sides of the slab have been considerably disfigured, in consequence of pieces having been chipped off as "souvenirs" by various morbid-minded, senseless persons.

The road from which Green-lane diverges has a connection, north-westward, across the main road, near Oubeck House, with the old coach way between Galgate and Burrow Bridge, and by such way with the rural district of Burrow. In this district, which forms part of the township of Scotforth, there is a small, hamlet-like place called Burrow. The major portion of the district is centrally traversed, north and south, by a ridge; the land in the highest part being nearly 200 feet above the level of the sea. The name Burrow means a prominence, a hill, a defensive or protective place. The north-west Roman road passed through Burrow.

The mansion whose ruddy roofs, picturesque gables, and well-set windows come prominently into view, on the right side (about half a mile from the main road) soon after Burrow Bridge has been passed, northward, is the new residence—not yet entirely finished—of Mr. H. L. Storey, son of the late Sir Thomas Storey, of Lancaster. It is called Bailrigg. South-west of it, about a quarter of a mile distant, on lower ground, there is Bailrigg farm-house, which, with its outbuildings, has been considerably improved in recent times, and which is either the original structure in part or the successor of a building which appears to have been here for generations. In the British Museum there are abstracts of the wills of Richard Hynde, " of Ballrigge," yeoman, proved in 1636, and James Lund, " of Baylerig," proved in 1638. There are also now in Somerset House the wills of the following persons, proved in the years named:—John Langton, " of Balerigg," 1661; Anne Thomasson, " of Balerigg," 1667; John Shaw, " of Balerigg," 1670; and Christopher Bracken, "of Balerigge," 1680—a descendant, no doubt, of Christopher Braken, " of Stotforth " (Scotforth), whose will was proved in 1626. As a name, Bailrigg signifies either a living place on or adjacent to a ridge or a boundary within a

accommodation. The house will be lighted by electricity, and water will be obtained from the Lancaster Corporation new supply. In front there is a well-proportioned terrace. Adequate carriage and stabling accommodation has been provided. At the western entrance way, near the main road, a lodge has been erected. Messrs. Woolfall and Eccles, of Liverpool, have been the architects; and Mr. Isaac Dilworth, of Wavertree, Liverpool, has been the sole contractor. The grounds adjoining the house are being artistically laid out, from plans made by Mr. H. E. Milner, of Victoria-street, London. Down the slope in front, as also on each side and at the rear of the house, there are trees, fields, &c.; and altogether the environment is very pastoral and pleasing. Structurally, Bailrigg is an excellent building. Its well-defined gables and antique-looking half-timber work, its carefully elaborated façade and pretty frontal terrace, its contiguous grounds and woodland surroundings give it a picturesquely effective, serenely select appearance. From the front extensive and charming views are commanded—views which range, transversely, from the Fylde country to the Lake mountains, and embrace, right ahead, choicely diverse landscapes, with Morecambe Bay and the Irish Sea beyond.

BAILRIGG.

large expanse of woodland. Bal and balla respectively mean an abode; bail refers to a certain limit in a forest. The suffix rig or rigge means a ridge: in its application to land, a steep, narrow-topped elevation or a piece of long, rising ground. Mr. Storey's new residence is built in the Elizabethan style; the walls being of brick up to the first floor, with half timber above; and the roofs are tiled. The entrance to the building is on the north side: it gives access to an oak-panelled hall, from which open the dining-room, also oak pannelled, the drawing and morning rooms, and a billiard room, all of large size and superior finish. On the first floor are a boudoir, a day and night nursery, a sewing room, bedrooms, dressing rooms, baths, &c.; and on the second floor are a playroom, bedrooms, and other

About 300 yards north of Burrow Bridge the main road goes over Burrow Beck. In 1821 Mr. Jeremiah Walmsley, flour dealer, Lancaster, rode on horseback from the White Cross in that town to the old obelisk in Preston Market-place and back again as far as Burrow Beck Bridge—a distance of about 40 miles—in two hours and fifty-five minutes. Mr. Walmsley, whose weight at the time was 13st. 4lb., made a wager that he would ride his horse from the White Cross, at the top of Penny-street, Lancaster, to Preston (round the obelisk), and back again to the Cross in four hours. He started at six o'clock one morning, got to Preston in good time, reached Burrow Beck Bridge, on his return, five minutes before nine o'clock, and here incautiously struck his horse between the ears with the butt end of his whip. Through this the horse fell, but it afterwards got up, was led forward, and reached the White Cross, Lancaster, at 9 51, or nine minutes within four hours from the time of starting. An objection was raised to the manner in which the distance had been covered; but eventually it was decided, on reference, that Mr. Walmsley had won the wager. It is very probable that some land directly north-east of Burrow Beck Bridge and about half a mile south of Scotforth—land which slopes from a hollow up to a somewhat commanding eminence—is that which, according to Maclaughan and Wilson's "History of the Scottish Highlands, Highland Clans, and Highland Regiments," was selected by some of the officers of Prince Charles as suitable for a battle, during the retreat north of his rebel army in 1745. The history named says that the Prince reached Lancaster on the evening of the 13th of December, 1745; that next morning, having intimated his determination to fight the Royal forces, some of his officers, &c., proceeded to make a reconnaissance, south of Lancaster, with the view of seeing if there were any ground in the neighbourhood of the highroad suitable for a battlefield (the Royal forces being at this time on the march north, after the rebels); and that when the reconnoitring party had got about two miles from Lancaster they found "a very fine field upon a rising ground sufficiently large for the whole army, and which was so situated that, from whatever quarter the enemy could come, the army would be completely covered till the enemy were close upon them." The suitability of this field was reported to Prince Charles; but, instead of accepting it as a fighting place, he said he had altered his mind, and intended to resume his northern march next day. So there was no battle. The ground in the neighbourhood of Burrow Beck Bridge, before mentioned, corresponds in its position, surface characteristics, and distance from the town of Lancaster with that selected by the officers; it is about two miles south of Lancaster, is covered at the base by the edge of a depression as well as by a bend in the road, rises rearward considerably, and seems to be the very ground which was picked out for a battle, and then rejected by Prince Charles, who afterwards with his followers went north and sustained a complete defeat at Culloden—a defeat which would, no doubt, have been experienced in the field between Burrow Beck Bridge and Scotforth if the rebels had assembled there and encountered the Royal forces.

Scotforth village is a little over half a mile north of Burrow Beck Bridge; it occupies elevated ground—something like 160 feet above the level of the sea—and the main road passes right through it. Near the village, as approached from Burrow Beck Bridge, there stands on the west side of the road a broad, gable-fronted building, formerly used as a toll gatekeeper's place. It is now a little shop and a private house in combination. One of the most singular incidents illustrative of equine memory and stolen property restoration that I have seen recorded occurred at Scotforth in the same year as did the horse-

riding performance previously mentioned. The record of it is to this effect—that a mare, with a man asleep on her back, walked up to the stable door of a man named Salthouse, of Scotforth, and was identified as one which had been stolen from him two years before; that Salthouse, of course, kept her; that when inquiries were made it was ascertained that after being stolen she had passed through various hands; that eventually she was purchased in Yorkshire, for 38 guineas, by Mr. H. Dewhurst, of Preston; and that the man on the mare's back had been to fetch her, and was taking her to Preston, but fell asleep near Scotforth, thus allowing her to go as she liked, and thereby causing her to bring memory freely into play, and restore herself to her real owner! Scotforth is of high antiquity. In the Doomsday Survey its name appears as Sco3forde In a map of Lancashire, apparently prepared near the end of the 11th century, it is designated Scoyford. Another map of the county, bearing the date 1598, has in it, a little to the south of Lancaster, a spot marked Scofield—evidently intended for Scotforth. Speed's map of Lancashire, dated 1610, gives the name as Skotford In Adams's "Index Villaris" (1680) it is called Scotford. A map of a considerably later date, issued in connection with one of the editions of Camden's "Britannia," styles the place Stotforth. Sixteenth and seventeenth century wills designate the place, or district, as Scotforthe and Scotforth. In 1564 one proved within the archdeaconry of Richmond was that of Thomas Crooke, who is described as "of Scotforthe"; and another, proved in 1568, was that of Stephen Mackerell "of Scotforth." The name invariably takes the latter form—Scotforth—in the local wills proved within the same archdeaconry during the 17th century. About 200 acres of land in Scotforth, subject to Knight's service, were, according to the "Testa de Nevill," given by William Fitz Gilbert to Hugh Norman. In the fifteenth century, a quarter of the manor of Scotforth was held by John Duke of Bedford. Later, the land of Scotforth was owned, successively, by the Lancastre, Coucy, Coupland, Laurence, Gerard, and Hamilton families. It is now variously possessed. Scotforth village is plain, small, and somewhat quaintly formed; but there are no very old buildings in it now, so far as dates give one a clue thereto. The oldest date here that I have seen is 1676, which appears on a stone in front of a cottage on the east side of the village. On the western side there is a road which branches from the centre of the village and goes down to Ashton-with-Stodday and neighbouring places. On the eastern side a road runs down some distance and then up towards the hills, branching variously—to Quernmore, Littledale, Wyresdale, &c. A short way from the village, and connected with the latter road, there is a small ford.

As to the name Scotforth, the meaning of the latter part of it is obvious enough; but there is an element of uncertainty, or ground for some speculation, in regard to the former portion of it. The prefix of the name, as given in the Doomsday Survey, may be the equivalent of the now obsolete word Scoss, meaning to change—a word which, if applied to forde or ford (forth being a mere orthographical variant of ford), would refer to a variable or fluctuating passage across a stream—a passage sometimes to be made a little higher or lower, or across water liable to much surface change, in dry or wet weather, owing to the character of the channel, &c. The Doomsday prefix may, however, be the equivalent of or derived from the Teutonic word Schosz, which means Scot, and signifies payment, tax, or toll (the terminal word of the English phrase " pay the shot " comes from Scot) ; and, if this were the case, then it would refer to a ford the passage of which involved a certain payment. The prefixes Sco and Stot seem to be pure blunders in spelling. As to the prefix Skot, which appears in Speed's map, it may be a reduced form of Skott—a far northern

their stay. It is very probable that the old Scots never crossed the stream adjoining Scotforth at all in either their southern or homeward marches. They would, in all likelihood, keep to the principal way on the western side—to a considerable extent on or near the route of the lower Roman road, which would be more direct. If they did not—if they marched by the other way, on the eastern side—fording would have to be done by them not only at Scotforth but elsewhere, and in some parts on a more extensive scale ; but as their name has not been associated with any of those places, why, it may be asked, should it be linked specifically with a passage across a stream at Scotforth? The definition before given of the name of this place, as it appears in the Doomsday Survey, viz., Sco3forde, may be correct ; but there is room for another—and possibly the right—explanation. The final letter (3) of the prefix is a semi-Saxon one in form ; it was used to represent the consonant y ;

SCOTFORTH VILLAGE.

word, meaning a free or uninterrupted course: if so, then either the immediately preceding supposition would not be applicable, or else a " free or uninterrupted course " would relate specifically here to an unimpeded, easy-flowing, fordable stream.

The general modern idea is that the name Scotforth is due to the passage of certain Scots across the little stream on the east side of the village. If this be correct, then the Scots in question cannot, of course, have been any of those connected with the Rebellion of 1715 or that of 1745, for the name—somewhat varied in the spelling, but easily recognisable—was clearly in existence very many years before. If the name originated through any passage of Scots, they must have belonged to the wild ones who in the 10th century were forced to march with King Æthelstan's soldiers or to those northern marauders who made incursions into England in the 14th century. In 1745 several Scotch rebels were quartered for a short time at Scotforth, and—this was rather wonderful—they behaved quietly during

and y, definitely shaped, afterwards took its place ; but frequently, at a somewhat later period, w was substituted for y ; so that the Sco3forde of the Doomsday Survey would thus become Scowforde. Scow is the name of a flat-bottomed boat (the northern words Skoutt and Skuba—a small boat—apparently come from the same root) ; in very remote times the stream at Scotforth was, perhaps, somewhat deeper or broader than it is now, and, if so, then in the absence of a gangway bridge or stepping stones, and particularly when the stream was in flood, a small boat would be required here by foot passengers, and it would have to be of shallow draught—would most likely be a flat-bottomed one of the scow sort ; and hence, according to this theory, the propriety of the Doomsday Survey name—Sco3forde, or Scowforde. In a very old map of Lancashire, or topographical work pertaining thereto, which I saw some time back, the name of Scotforth appeared as Scoyford, the prefix of which is the equivalent of that in the Doomsday Survey. About 1845 a brown earthenware pottery was established at Scotforth, on the east side, near the ford; but operations at it ceased about 1869. Recently the village has undergone some expansion on the south side, where several new, nice-looking dwelling-houses have been built. Part of Scotforth has for some time been within the borough boundary of Lancaster, and it is understood that shortly in the latter part of this year (1900)—the remainder will be incorporated. Dr. John Taylor, a famous Nonconformist scholar and theologian, was born in the township of Scotforth, in 1695. He was the son of a master joiner, &c., in Lancaster, was educated in a Dissenting Academy at Whitehaven, afterwards became pastor of a chapel at Kirkstead, in Lincolnshire, next took duty in a similar capacity at Norwich, and then, owing to his able and scholarly theological works, became the first President of a Nonconformist Academy at Warrington. It is said that he was "one of the first Arians who ministered to the English Presbyterians." Amongst his works was a Hebrew Concordance—a very scholarly production, and so highly appreciated that in 1754 twenty-two members of the English and fifteen members of the Irish Episcopal Bench became subscribers to it. Burns, the poet in his epistle to John Goudie, makes reference to Taylor's influence as an opponent of superstition and a promoter of the cause of religious progress. In 1761 Taylor died at Warrington; he was interred in the graveyard attached to the old chapel at Chowbent;

1824 and 1834 Mr. Quarme, who was a native of Exeter, held the post of editor of the "Preston Pilot." On vacating the editorial chair, he was presented with a piece of plate, by his Preston friends, "as a mark of respect for his private character during a period of ten years." From Preston Mr. Quarme went to Lancaster; and with the latter town he was journalistically associated for a long time. In the first instance he went thither to become the proprietor and editor of the "Lancaster Gazette." Four years after he had been on the scene—in 1838—a deputation of Lancaster gentlemen waited upon him, and presented him with a silver salver and a purse containing 150 sovereigns, "in approbation of his independent conduct," as editor of the "Gazette," "in advocating Conservative principles." In 1848 he sold the paper to the late Mr. G. C. Clark, but he continued his connection with it as editor for many years afterwards. In 1879 Mr. Quarme died, at the age of 84. Politically, he was a Church and State Tory of the old school: personally, he was precise and courteous; he evinced a considerable regard for correct sartorial form, when out generally displayed a button-hole flower, and he had very much the appearance of a retired military officer.

The hill which comes prominently to the fore, a few miles east of Scotforth village, is Clougha Pike. It forms the western end of a range of hills, the highest of which—Ward's Stone, near the head of Wyresdale—has an altitude of 1,836 feet. Clougha

OLD FORD AND POTTERY BUILDINGS.

and his wife, who died a few months afterwards, was buried in the same ground. In the chapel there is a mural tablet on which is the following inscription: —"Near to this place rests what was mortal of John Taylor, D.D. Reader, expect no eulogium from this stone; enquire amongst the friends of Learning, Liberty, and Truth. These will do him justice. While taking his natural rest, he fell asleep in Jesus Christ, the 5th of March, 1761, aged 66." On the south side of the lane near the brook, at Scotforth, there is an ivy-fronted house in which the late Mr. Charles Edward Quarme resided for many years. Between

Pike is 1,325 feet high. In a map of Lancashire which was forwarded, along with a report as to the state of the county, in 1590, to the Privy Council, by the Lord Lieutenant, and which is now in the Record Office, Clougha Pike is marked as a beacon hill, and designated "Claighoe." Some antiquaries doubt the correctness of Macaulay's remark, in his Armada verses, as to "the fire that burned on "Gaunt's embattled pile" (Lancaster Castle) being seen from Skiddaw; and, presuming he were in error on this point, it has been suggested that a beacon on Clougha Pike was what "Skiddaw saw." Owing to its excellent frontal position, Clougha Pike, though by no means a very high hill, has a decidedly conspicuous appearance from the west and north sides, and a beacon fire on its summit at night time would be visible at a great distance in those directions. But it is a "far cry" from Clougha Pike to Skiddaw, and one may fairly doubt the possibility of such a thing as direct beacon communication being established between them. Yates's map of Lancashire, published in 1786, gives as the "lines of sight" of Clougha Pike the Parish Church of Lancaster, Warton Crag, Kirkham windmill, Preesall mill, Parlick Pike, Pendle Hill, and Ingleborough. In 1803 the northern defences were inspected by Prince William of Gloucester, and on the afternoon of September 22nd in that year he rode from Lancaster to Clougha Pike, accompanied by his suite and two local gentlemen; afterwards returning to the town, and next day proceeding south-west, halting for a short time at Preston, where he reviewed a number of Volunteers.

The distance between Scotforth village and Lancaster Town Hall is about a mile and a half. A great portion of the connecting main road is flanked with buildings—chiefly dwelling-houses. Up to about the end of the first quarter of the 19th century the only buildings near the road, on the east side, between Scotforth and Lancaster, were three cottages, not far from Scotforth, known as Marshall's Houses (they were called this name after one Marshall), and a barn a little south of the canal bridge at the top of Pennystreet, Lancaster; whilst a few cottages (the Pointer Houses) formed the whole of the buildings on the west side. Even up to 1844-45 there were only about half-a-dozen buildings on the former side, and on the latter simply what is now known as the "old station" and three houses in addition to the Pointer lot. Scotforth Church, on the western side of the main road, and about 500 yards north of the village, was consecrated in 1876. It occupies a good, commanding site, but structurally has a rather oddly composite appearance—seems to be in some respects very substantial and in others rather more ornate than durable. In 1891 the chancel underwent considerable extension. This church, of which the Rev. W. F. Armitage is the Vicar, has a separate district, under the Blandford Act.

Immediately north of Scotforth Church there is the summit of the Greaves, over which the main road passes. The name Greaves indicates the existence here, at some time, of a grove or a series of groves. William Heysham left, by will dated April 22nd, 1725, an estate called the Greaves, for charitable purposes. The will of Samuel Towers, proved within the archdeaconry of Richmond, in 1727, describes him as "of Greaves, parish of Lancaster." Presumably the Greaves region between Lancaster and Scotforth is here meant. The foregoing are the earliest references to the place-name Greaves, near Lancaster, that I have met with. Very fine views, north-

west and south-west, are obtained from the Greaves. Pennant, the traveller and naturalist, who journeyed along here, northward, in 1772, says:—"From a common called the Grave [Greaves] have a fine view of Lancaster." Prebendary Gilpin, of Boldre, who passed this way during the same year, refers in his "Observations" to a view evidently obtained from the Greaves. He says:—"At a mile's distance Lancaster Castle rises to view. Its lofty situation, its massy towers and extensive buildings—for it is connected with the Church [it is not, though it seems to be, as noticed from the Greaves, owing to the close rearward position of the Church], give an air of grandeur to its appearance"; and then he remarks, inaccurately and with a curious lack of taste, "as the parts are neither well shaped nor well combined, it is but an indifferent object from any point."

His Imperial Highness the Grand Duke of Russia (afterwards the Emperor Nicholas), during his travels in this country, in 1816-17, rode over the Greaves, on the south side of Lancaster, and intimated that the view from it was one of the most charming he had ever seen. A strikingly fine sketch made by William Westall, A.R.A., is a view of Lancaster, Morecambe Bay, the Furness Fells, and the Lake Mountains, taken from the Greaves about 1825. William Black, the novelist, gives, in his "Strange Adventures of a Phæton," a finely-graphic description of the scenery commanded from the Greaves. On a clear day the distant scenery—that which the water, mountains, &c., constitute—is very conspicuous and delightful; but the town of Lancaster is not, owing to the growth of trees, and the erection of buildings on its southern side, by any means so fully visible as it used to be, and the sketch which Westall made could not now be taken, on this account. The Castle, the Parish Church, and certain buildings which front and partially flank them, are visible when the atmosphere is clear; but the bulk of the town, especially the south-eastern portion of it, is very considerably obscured through the causes named. The view on the next page is from a sketch made near the Golgotha entrance to Williamson Park (about three-quarters of a mile from the Greaves), at a point which commands the nearest and best full-front view of the town now obtainable. The first houses built on the higher part of the Greaves are those near the lane which branches up on the east side, from the main road. They now constitute Brunton House, of which some particulars will be given subsequently. Lower down, on the west side, there is a short cross-way leading to Ashton-with-Stodday, &c., called Dog Kennel-lane. There used to be a kennel on the south side of this lane. I remember seeing harriers in it about 1853: they were removed to this part when the old kennel, which stood on a portion of the site of the Grammar School (eastern side of Lancaster) was pulled down, but they did not remain here very long. The house on the top of the eminence on the eastern side of the main road, and opposite the entrance to

L

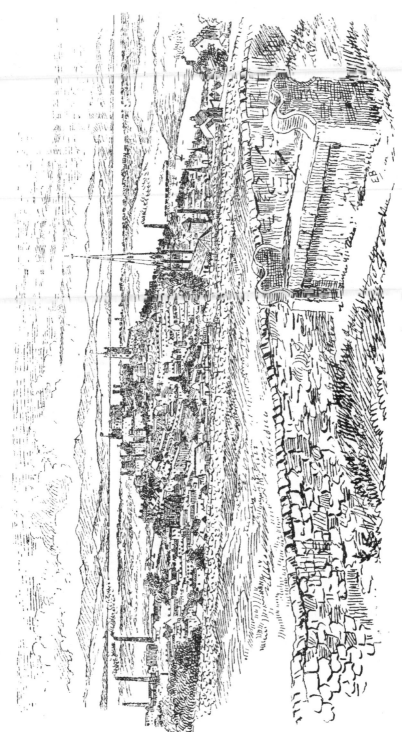

LANCASTER (1900) FROM THE SOUTH-EAST.

Dog Kennel-lane, is named Belle Vue. At the Lancaster Assizes, in March, 1830, four persons—Paul Rigby, John Grimes, Mary Grimes, and Michael Mc.Gibbons—were charged with robbing on the highway, opposite Belle Vue, a man named Robert Stanley. It was alleged by Stanley, who said he came from Oswestry, that the prisoners fastened him by wire to a gatepost, opposite Belle Vue, and then robbed him of £60 (he was found wired to a gatepost, at the place named, on the 23rd of the preceding February). All the prisoners were sentenced to be hanged. Soon after the trial, the sentence passed on the female prisoner was commuted to transportation for life. Mc.Gibbons was executed, after declaring with great earnestness that he was innocent; and the remaining condemned prisoners narrowly escaped a like fate. The time for their execution was rapidly drawing near when information was received to the effect that the man Stanley had previously, in several places, been found fastened with wire, in a style somewhat similar to that which he alleged the four prisoners had subjected him to opposite Belle Vue, his object having been to evoke sympathy and obtain money; that before he could be apprehended he had in each instance made off; and that his story as to having been wire-fastened and robbed, near Lancaster, was a pure fabrication; so the two men, Rigby and Grimes, were removed from their condemned quarters and set at liberty. Stanley got out of the way shortly before or at the time the information mentioned reached Lancaster, and no more was heard of him.

Parkfield House, which stands prettily in its own well-laid-out grounds, on the east side of the main road, below Belle Vue, and is now occupied by Mrs. Blades, widow of Alderman C. Blades, was the first of the modern residences erected on the Greaves. (The house of the Greaves person whose will was, as before mentioned, proved in 1727, does not appear to have been in existence for many years. Nobody now living seems to have ever seen it). Parkfield House was built by Mr. William Satterthwaite, grocer, New-street, Lancaster, and afterwards of the local Quaker firm of Satterthwaite and Barrow. Greaves House, a short distance below Parkfield, and on the same side, was the second residence built on the Greaves; and the house a little above Parkfield, on the same side, was the third erected in this quarter. The Pointer Houses—some small cottages lower down, at the bend of the road, west side—evidently got their name through being adjacent to a guide post, which stood on the opposite side, northward, at the junction of Bowerham-road. In the Ordnance map, based on the survey of 1844-5, there is a small mark for this guide post, which is called "The Pointer." Nearly all the buildings on the north side of Bowerham-road are of recent construction—some being quite new. The Barracks, on the summit of the eminence eastward, were erected in 1876-80. The substantial, well-finished stone structure in the angle between the roads below the Pointer Houses was erected as the Lancaster Station (north terminus) of the Lancaster and Preston Railway. Near the end of July, 1840, or about a month after the railway had been opened, I saw the Queen Dowager (Adelaide, widow of William IV.) at this station. Her Royal Highness—a rather tall, somewhat pale-featured lady, in very dark attire—had been staying at the King's Arms Hotel, Lancaster, during the previous night, and was going south. The first time I remember riding on the Lancaster and Preston Railway was, perhaps, a year after its opening. I started from the station at Lancaster; the carriage in which I rode was of the "parliamentary" order—something like a present-time cattle truck, with transversely ranged wooden forms, without backs, for seats, the top being covered with common board-like material, immediately below which was an opening, all round, about two feet deep, through which the wind blew strongly when the train was in motion. The only incident of the journey which I recollect was this: shortly after the train left Lancaster, one of the passengers, a man, who was standing in the middle of the carriage, lost his hat—it was blown right off his head into a field; and this odd incident induced some of the passengers to tie pocket-handkerchiefs closely round their hats, &c., and under their chins, so as to obviate further wind antics with headgear. When the railway was extended north of Lancaster (first to Kendal, in 1846, and then, a short time afterwards, to Carlisle), the building below the Pointer Houses was superseded by a fresh station on the western side of the town—a station which has to be supplanted by a very much larger one, on and about the same site, and for which purpose operations are now in progress. The rather heavy-looking, castellated building a short distance below the first railway station, and on the opposite side of the road, was originally erected for Militia barracks purposes. It now serves as the headquarters of the local Artillery Volunteers. The very high chimney at the rear of the Artillery quarters is connected with the spacious works of Messrs. Storey Brothers and Co., Limited, the well-known manufacturers of table cloths and baise, toilet covers, &c. Formerly, a cotton factory, called White Cross Mill, and some cottages a little west thereof, stood upon portions of the site of these very fine works. From the road near the canal bridge, below the Artillery quarters, some of the chimneys of the immense and excellent works of Lord Ashton, on the western side of the town, for the manufacture of linoleum, oilcloth, &c., can be seen.

CHAPTER XXVI.

Royal Albert Asylum—Brunton House—Ripley Hospital—Royal Lancaster Infirmary—Springfield Park—Canal Bridge—Agricultural Shows—Old Cross, Toll Bars, and Inns—Penny's Hospital—King's Arms Hotel—Storey Institute—Ancient Lanes and Buildings—Lune Bridge, &c.

Three most useful and excellent institutions (the Royal Albert Asylum, the Ripley Hospital, and the Royal Lancaster Infirmary), situated west of the main road, and forming, positionally, a sort of curve, extending from a point near the railway junction to the road angle below the old railway station, must now be referred to. But the reference will be comparatively brief, as these institutions have already been described, by various newspaper writers, &c., very comprehensively, if not quite exhaustively.

The Royal Albert Asylum occupies the crown of an eminence between Ashton road and the London and North-Western Railway, and is a mile and a quarter south of Lancaster Town Hall. From the front of the

wards he obtained information from different parts of the country as to the treatment of mentally weak persons; and then he conceived the idea of making Mr. Brunton's proposal the nucleus of a scheme for the treatment and amelioration of idiots and imbeciles in the counties of Lancashire, Yorkshire, Westmorland, Cumberland, Northumberland, and Durham (Cheshire being subsequently included). A meeting, presided over by the late Sir J. P. Kay-Shuttleworth, in favour of this scheme, was held in the Shire Hall, Lancaster, on the 21st of December, 1864; financial support warranting a commencement was promised; an estate of 42 acres, on the south side of Lancaster, was afterwards purchased; it was decided to erect upon this estate an asylum, primarily for 400 patients,

ROYAL ALBERT ASYLUM.

Asylum there is, on a clear day, a very fine view of Lancaster, the estuary of the Lune, Morecambe Bay, the Lake mountains, &c. In 1864 a plain, unassuming Lancaster Quaker, named James Brunton, suggested to Dr. De Vitré, a well-known local medical gentleman and consulting physician to the Lancaster County Asylum, the desirableness of renting a house as an asylum or home for idiots, and at the same time he offered to give £2,000 on behalf of such a place. Whilst duly appreciating the generous spirit evinced by Mr. Brunton, Dr. De Vitré thought that the suggested scheme was of too limited a character; after-

and of such a design as to admit of easy and comparatively inexpensive enlargement so as to accommodate 1,000; Messrs. Paley and Austin, of Lancaster, were selected as the architects, and they prepared a suitable building design, the style of the architecture being domestic Gothic of an early type; the foundation stone was laid, with Masonic honours, by the Earl of Zetland, on the 17th of June, 1868; a considerable portion of the building—about two-thirds of it, including the Brooke wing, erected at the cost of the Rev. R. and Mrs. Brooke, of Selby, who gave £30,000 to the Asylum fund—was

148

opened on the 14th of September, 1870, by the late Duke of Devonshire; and on the 8th of October, 1873, a banquet, presided over by the late Earl of Derby, was held, to celebrate the completion of the Asylum—subject to the expansion arrangement before named. (Mr. James Brunton, who did not live to see this opening, was the son of Mr. John Brunton, cooper, of Lancaster; was born in Sun-street, in that town, in 1801; was at one time a clerk in the service of Mr. Carlisle, a local wine and spirit merchant; was never married; died at his residence, Lune-terrace, in 1871; and was interred in the Friends' burial ground, adjoining Meetinghouse-lane, Lancaster.) The cost of the Asylum undertaking, including lodges, farmhouse and buildings, with separate accommodation for a dozen boys to be employed on the farm, architects' commission, salary of the clerk of the works, &c., was about £80,000. The furniture and fittings involved an additional outlay of about £10,000. The land forming the original estate of the Asylum also cost some thousands of pounds, and the extension of the estate has necessitated a large expenditure of money. There are many well-arranged rooms, &c., in the Asylum, all essential to the convenience and treatment of the patients; whilst the accommodation for officials, attendants, servants, and the like is necessarily considerable, and is equipped in a very practical, effective manner. The main dining-room is a large and excellent one. It is called "The De Vitré Hall," is well fitted up, and contains stained-glass windows to the memory of various deceased benefactors. In addition to the buildings already named, there are some cottages for trade attendants, &c., erected at the sole expense of Dr. De Vitre (they cost £2,375), and presented by him to the institution; an isolation infirmary, towards which the late Mr. Edward Rodgett and Mrs. Rodgett, his widow, of Darwen Bank, near Preston, gave £5,000, and which has since been enlarged at a cost of £4,136; a recreation hall, on behalf of which the late Lord Winmarleigh gave a handsome donation of £500; and a home for feeble-minded senior girls, erected, furnished, and equipped at the great cost of about £7,000 or £8,000 by the late Sir Thomas Storey, of Lancaster, in commemoration of the 60 years' reign of Queen Victoria. The housework at this home is done by the inmates, who are "much in request at the asylum," some being trained there to be useful in various ways, whilst others are very good assistant nurses. The foundation stone of a new south wing for epileptic, crippled, and feeble boys was laid on the 28th of September, 1898, by the Right Hon. Sir J. T. Hibbert; the estimated structural cost being about £15,000. In November, 1899, Lord Ashton handed to the Principal and Secretary (Mr. J. Diggens) a donation of £10,000 in aid of the funds of the Asylum. At a meeting of the Central Committee, on the 24th of the same month, it was resolved "that as this splendid act of munificence relieves the Committee from all anxiety with regard to the completion of the Extension Fund, they cordially request his Lordship's permission to call the new south wing 'The Ashton Wing.'" And his Lord-

ship, when this resolution was forwarded to him, gave the requisite permission. There is an industrial training department connected with the Asylum, and in it numerous boys are employed. A wood-carving class has also been formed: it is in charge of one of the trained joiner patients. Various boys are likewise engaged in the stores, bakehouse, and garden, whilst some work on the farm. At present there are in the Asylum about 600 boys and girls, and "the arrangements comprise every convenience for the specific treatment of idiots and imbeciles." The average number of patients resident at the Royal Albert Asylum during the year which ended on the 30th of June, 1900, was 594. Dr. A. R. Douglas is the present medical officer of the Asylum.

Brunton House, before mentioned, is at the side of the main road, on the upper portion of the Greaves, and about 350 yards east, by direct line, of the Royal Albert Asylum, of which institution it forms a special branch. The block of buildings here originally consisted of three dwelling-houses, which were erected about 1852 by Miss Dalton, of Thurnham Hall. They were designed by Mr. J. A. Hansom, the distinguished architect and inventor of the "hansom cab." Over two or three of the doors there are carved, on stone, the Dalton arms and the initials of Miss Dalton (E.D.). Miss Dalton, who died in 1861, bequeathed this block of houses to Miss English, who had been with her for some time as "lady's companion." The block is now made up of four gabled sections, which face the main road; three of them belonging to Brunton House proper, and the fourth, with annexe, to the house called Quarry Hill, occupied by Mr. James Diggens, the Principal, &c., of the Royal Albert Asylum. Mr. Diggens went to Lancaster, from Halifax, in October, 1865, and shortly afterwards he took up his abode in a portion of the previously named block, which at that time was still in its original condition. By and bye, this property came into the market, and Dr. De Vitré commissioned Mr. Diggens to negotiate for its purchase; but, when the latter went to see the agent (Mr. T. Fair, of Lytham), he found that he was just a day too late—the property had been purchased on the previous day by Mr. Roger Wright, builder, of Lancaster, for Mr. Edmund Sharpe. Dr. De Vitré's idea was to let Mr. Diggens remain in the house he then occupied (and at which he now resides) and to utilise the rest of the block as a temporary asylum for a few cases, whilst the Royal Albert Asylum was in course of erection, as the subscribers were pressing for the early admission of imbeciles. Mr. Sharpe made sundry extensive alterations in the property, laid out the adjoining grounds, &c., and went to live at the block, having thrown two of the houses into one: the other house Mr. Diggens continued to occupy for a short time, until it was required by Mr. Sharpe's married son (Mr. Edmund Sharpe). Some time after Mr. Sharpe's death the property, then in the occupation of his son, came into the market again. It was put up for sale by auction, but was not sold. The idea now struck Mr. Diggens that as the Royal Albert Asylum—at this time open—had been built by the wealthy and well-to-do for all sections of the community they ought to share in its benefits. He talked over the matter with the late Lord Winmarleigh, Sir Thomas Storey, and Mr. Higgin, Q.C. Sir Thomas urged the necessity of his making an offer for the block of buildings, with the view of their being used as a house for special private patients, who would attend the Asylum daily for instruction; the block was afterwards purchased, on behalf of the Central Committee of the Asylum; and, remembering Mr. Brunton's original idea, Mr. Diggens suggested that it should be called Brunton House—the name subsequently given to it. On the Queen's Jubilee Day, in 1887, it was opened; and at the same time Mr. Diggens returned to his original habitation here. There are beautifully laid-out grounds, gardens, &c., at the rear. The house is for private special pupils attending the schools and other departments of the Royal Albert Asylum: the object of it is to provide for such pupils (whose admission involves payment of a remunerative character) "all the seclusion and comfort of a private residence, with the hygienic, educational, and training resources of a public institution under responsible management." A short distance east of the rear grounds there is a quarry, from which was obtained all the stone required in the construction of the Brunton House block and the Royal Albert Asylum.

From the time the Royal Albert Asylum was opened, up to the present—a period of about 30 years—2,100 boys and girls have been received at it; and 1,112 discharged after seven years' training; the results being as follow:—Seven entirely cured, two sufficiently improved to be admitted into the Army, 266 much improved, 450 materially improved, 259 slightly improved, and only 128 unimproved. Viewed generally as to management and work achieved, this Asylum is a most excellent institution. Speaking at the annual meeting, in October, 1899, the Lord Mayor of Leeds said that the Royal Albert Asylum was not only by far and away the best of its kind in the North of England, or in England, but, from what he had been told, perhaps the very best institution anywhere for the treatment of imbecile children. Mr. James Diggens is the Principal and Secretary of the Asylum, and its adjuncts are likewise under his control; he has been officially at work in connection with the Asylum from the time its erection was commenced; and he has all along discharged his arduous and very responsible duties with thorough fidelity and efficiency.

The Ripley Hospital—a high, massive pile of masonry, stately and spacious in appearance—stands in an angle of Springfield Park, between Ashton-road and the London and North-Western Railway, and about a third of a mile north of the Royal Albert Asylum. This Hospital is a very admirable institution—it is somewhat similar in its objects and intention to Christ's Hospital, London. It was founded by the late Mrs. Julia Ripley, widow of Mr. Thomas Ripley, a Liverpool merchant and a native of Lancaster; and the original cost of it was about £25,000. The foundation stone was laid by Mrs. Ripley, on the 14th of July, 1856, and the building was formally opened by her on the 3rd of November, 1864. The architectural style of the Hospital is of the 12th and 13th centuries, usually designated Early English; the architect being Mr. J. Cunningham, of Liverpool, who, according to a florid, yet accurate, statement of one of the reporters present at the opening ceremony, "thoroughly succeeded in combining beauty with convenience, and in associating elegance of detail with imposing general effect." In founding this Hospital, Mrs. Ripley was fulfilling the wishes of her husband, who had intended, if he had lived, carrying out the work himself. Mrs. Ripley kept the management of the Hospital in her own hands up to the time of her death, in 1881. She bequeathed the whole of her estate to the foundation, and the endowment now realises a sum equal to nearly £10,000 a year. The benefits of the foundation are open to 300 fatherless or orphan children of Lancaster and Liverpool, and within a radius of 15 miles of the former and seven miles of the latter place—in each case in the county of Lancaster only. Up to Mrs. Ripley's death, the number of children maintained at the Hospital was about 150. The buildings were considerably extended in 1885-6 (in respect to the boys' and girls' schools, &c., and according to designs prepared by Messrs. Paley and Austin); and this enlargement was intended to make the Hospital capable of accommodating a total of 300 children, at which point the number has since stood. In connection with the Hospital there is a beautiful chapel, designed by Messrs. Paley and Austin, and opened on November 3rd, 1888. During 1899 various additional extensions were made, including a handsome gymnasium, a manual instruction school (wood and metal work) for boys, a domestic economy school for girls, and four fives-courts. There has also been an installation of electric light through the whole place. In Springfield Park, which forms part of the Hospital estate, there are cricket and football grounds; five full-sized pitches for the latter enabling 150 boys to play the game simultaneously. The ornamental grounds surrounding the general block of buildings constitute a striking feature. Large kitchen gardens are attached to the Hospital; and it likewise has a farm of about 40 acres. Through the very munificent character of the endowment the Hospital is almost unique; no finer institution of its kind can be found anywhere; and, if its benefits were not limited to an area so comparatively small, its fame would certainly be widespread. The charity is vested in seven trustees, the following being those now in authority: The Bishop of Manchester, the Bishop of Liverpool, the Vicar of Lancaster (these are ex officio trustees), Mr. C. J. Clark, Mr. William Garnett, Mr. Edward Storey, and Mr. G. D. Killey. The first Principal of the Hospital was Mr. J. T. Preston, who retired in 1882, and was succeeded by the Rev. W. Langley

Appleford, M.A., who still holds the position, and who in addition to acting as Principal takes the duties of resident Chaplain. The present matron of the Hospital is Miss McLeod; the schoolmaster is Mr. C. Grime; schoolmistress, Miss M. Snalam; domestic economy mistress, Miss F. Ashburner; the band-

situated. In 1781 a small Dispensary was established at the residence of Dr. D. Campbell, on the south side of Castle Grove, Lancaster. Dr. Campbell was mainly instrumental in promoting the movement for it. Four years afterwards the Dispensary work was transferred to a house on the north side of Castle

THE RIPLEY HOSPITAL.

master and gymnastic instructor being Mr. W. J. Whitehead. In Lancaster Parish Churchyard there is the Ripley tomb, and over it is a stone bearing the following inscription:—" In memory of Thomas Ripley, who was born in Lancaster on the 11th October, 1790, and who died in Liverpool, August 20th, 1852; also of Julia Ripley, widow of the above Thomas Ripley, who died February 2nd, 1881, aged 76 years." In Scotforth Church there is a stained glass window to the memory of Mr. and Mrs. Ripley; it was subscribed for by "old boys" of the Hospital,

Grove. In 1815 a House of Recovery was established in Plumb-street, adjacent to Dalton-square. Some years afterwards the propriety of amalgamating these two institutions was mooted; eventually they were united; and in 1832 a new Dispensary, embracing the functions of both, was opened in Thurnham-street. The Royal Lancaster Infirmary is the direct successor of the Thurnham-street Dispensary. The foundation stone of the Infirmary was laid on the 12th of July, 1893, by Mr. James Williamson, M.P. (now Lord Ashton); and on the 24th of March, 1896,

THE ROYAL LANCASTER INFIRMARY.

and at the dedication service, on November 3rd, 1898, an impressive address was delivered by the Rev. G. F. Eyes, M.A., vicar of St. Philip's, Bolton, and formerly a Ripley Hospital scholar.

On a gentle slope, at the north-east corner of Springfield Park, the Royal Lancaster Infirmary is

their Royal Highnesses the Duke and Duchess of York opened this excellent new institution, and, in doing so, announced that the Queen had given her assent to its being designated the Royal Lancaster Infirmary. Messrs. Paley and Austin, of Lancaster, were the architects of the building, which is of a very substantial, superior character. The site cost £2,471, and the sum incurred in erecting and completing the structure, including wards, offices, machinery, and general appurtenances, was about £23,800. By voluntary subscriptions and interest from an endowment fund the Infirmary is sustained. The Committee of Governors consists of gentlemen who thoroughly represent the supporters of the institution—upper, middle, and working-class people; the president being Mr. Albert Greg. Various internal matters are under the supervision of a Medical Committee. Mr. W. J. D. Bromley, M.B., &c., is the present House Surgeon and Mrs. Crewe the Matron. Mr. Alexander Satterthwaite acts as Hon. Treasurer and Mr. Allan Sewart as Hon. Secretary of the Infirmary. The Trustees of the real estate of the Infirmary are—Lord Ashton (who has been a very munificent donor to the funds of the institution), Drs. Hall and Harker, Messrs. William Oliver Roper, Alexander Satterthwaite, Herbert L. Storey, William Swainson, and William Gibbins Welch. The funds of the Infirmary are at present in the hands of four of these gentlemen, viz., Drs. Hall and Harker, and Messrs. Satterthwaite and Swainson. During the year 1899 the in-patients at the Infirmary numbered 528 (there are now 47 beds in use), and the out-patients 2,367. The wards for private patients are a satisfactory feature of the institution.

On the east side of Springfield Park, between the Infirmary and the Ripley Hospital, there is Springfield Hall. It is a very substantial, good-looking building, and was erected by Mr. James Hargreaves, about 1792. When Mr. Hargreaves died he was succeeded at Springfield Hall by his son Henry. Anyhow Henry, his son, was residing here in 1824. He was a sort of character in Lancaster, owned property in the West Indies, and lived for a number of years at Springfield Hall, until his death, about 1838, when it went to a relative (Mr. Godson, M.P. for Kidderminster), who lived at the Hall a few years, after which it was occupied by Mr. S. E. Bolden, then by Mrs. Ripley (owner), next by Mr. W. H. Higgin, Q.C., and now it is tenanted by Colonel Kidston, C.B., of the 4th Queen's Own.

Below the Infirmary, northward, the main road passes over the canal bridge, and goes straight into what used to be the extreme south end of the town of Lancaster. The bridge was originally built between 1792 and 1797, when the canal was made. In 1900 it was superseded by one of stone and iron, which not only affords increased accommodation in respect to the main road, but, by an extension or increase in its width at the north-east corner, gives access to a new street, whereby an additional and direct way to the centre of Lancaster is secured. This bridge was opened by Councillor Preston, Mayor of Lancaster, on the 81st anniversary of the Queen's birthday (May 24th, 1900). The old offices and wharves of the Canal Company are on the north side of the canal, near the bridge, and in the hey-day of passenger "packets" and freight boats they were the

scene of much activity. In 1842 the packet service between Preston and Lancaster was stopped in consequence of railway competition. Immediately north of the canal bridge, and between the main road and the new street, there is some land, now used for fairs, miscellaneous shows, cattle sales, &c.: formerly it was a meadow or pasture called Prince William Henry Field—a name still given to it by many people. The annual shows of the Lancaster Agricultural Society were held in Prince William Henry Field from 1824 to 1846; and in this same field the first exhibition of the Royal North Lancashire Agricultural Society—the original predecessor of the present county association—took place on the 5th of October, 1847. On the west side of the road, a little beyond the junction of Aldcliffe-lane, there was in old times a pinfold, and about a score of yards north of it there stood in the centre of the road a "white cross," which was, perhaps, originally put up through some local regard for, or connection with, the ancient Knights Hospitallers: if not, then this cross possibly derived its name from the colour of the stone it was made of, and, unless it were utilised for some guiding or boundary purpose, it may—seeing that Lancaster was in old times a "place of sanctuary"—have been a cross of the "sanctuary" kind. Speed's map of Lancaster (date, 1610) specifies both the pinfold and the cross. But neither is in existence now: they were done away with many years ago. Between the sites they occupied there used to be a toll bar. It was directly opposite or contiguous to the Corporation Arms Inn, and was one of three in the borough of Lancaster which were owned by the Corporation, and periodically let (along with adjoining inns, also belonging to the Corporation) to the highest private bidder. The location of the second toll place was near the White Lion Inn, St. Leonard-gate, and that of the third near Skerton Bridge—at the Bridge Inn until it was closed as a public-house, and then for a time the person who looked after the toll had accommodation provided for him in a wooden hut at the south end of the bridge. The tolls were of the "through" or "passage" order, varied in amount, and were levied on pigs, sheep, and cattle generally, as well as miscellaneous goods, wares, and merchandise, brought into the borough. "Freemen" of the borough were exempt from the tolls. This system of toll-levying was, per se, a constant source of irritation, and the inquisitiveness of the toll-keepers, who sometimes lifted up the basket lids of farmers, &c., in order to see what they were carrying, used not unfrequently to cause much annoyance and bickering. The rents from the toll places were paid to the municipal Properties Committee, on behalf of the Corporation. By deed dated the 5th of January, 1887, Mr. James Williamson, M.P. (now Lord Ashton), secured the abolition of the tolls on the payment, out of his own pocket, of £1,500 to the Properties Committee; and this Committee now receives 3½ per cent. for the money from the Finance Committee. The monetary benefit, in reality, goes to the Corporation for the advantage of the borough. Two very old public-houses (the Corporation Arms and the White Cross) stood until 1900 on the west side of the road, not far from the site of the old cross. Both were sold by auction, in 1899 (by order of the Lancaster Corporation, whose estate they formed part of), for a total sum of £12,050. They were disposed of subject to conditions involving their demolition and rebuilding in accordance with plans specially prepared for and approved of by the Corporation; and this work will, it has been conjectured, necessitate an expenditure of upwards of £6,000. One of the conditions of sale had a touch of creditable antiquarianism in it hardly to be expected in Corporation procedure: it stipulated that a large stone in front of the Corporation Arms Inn, bearing an elaborately carved representation of the borough arms, should be retained by the Corporation. To ancient Corporation ownership, evidently, the name of one of these inns is due, whilst nearness to the cross, at one time in the middle of the road, no doubt accounts for the other. White Cross old cotton mill got its name through being in the neighbourhood; and the present extensive works of Messrs. Storey Brothers and Co., Ltd., in the same quarter, include White Cross in their appellation.

A little north of the two inns before mentioned the road bifurcates—divides into two branches, one way going down Penny-street, and the other along King-street. The latter is part of the original north road, so I will take its course, and go to the end of it, within the old boundary of Lancaster, which is no great distance. In the early part of the 17th century the length of this road from the point of division at the top to the intersection by Market-street was called Chennell-lane; some time afterwards it was named Back-lane; then one portion of it was named King-street, and the other—from Queen-square to Henry-street—Back-lane; now the whole of it is designated King-street. On one side of this street, near the north end, there is a charitable institution for poor ancient men and women within the town of Lancaster. This is Penny's Hospital. It was founded by money which Alderman Penny, of Lancaster, left, per will dated March 2nd, 1715. There is accommodation in it for fourteen persons. The Hospital has an air of quaint aloofness, or snug, ancient selectness about it, and the outer world seems in no way to affect its simple tranquillity. At the north end of King-street (west corner) there is a large and notable hotel—the King's Arms—which was originally erected in 1625, and rebuilt, in its present form, in 1879. With the exception of the Cross Keys, near the bottom of Market-street, which was built in 1613, the King's Arms is the oldest hotel, as per visible date, in Lancaster. Royal personages, noblemen, notable lawyers, celebrated literary men, &c., have at time and time "put up" at the King's Arms. In the immediate neighbourhood—just at the top of the street in which this

hotel is situated—there is the Storey Institute, erected through the munificence of the late Sir Thomas Storey, in commemoration of the 50th year of Queen Victoria's reign, and opened on the 23rd of October, 1891, by Lord Hartington (now the Duke of Devonshire). The substantial-looking building opposite, at the north-east corner of Fenton-street, is Fenton-Cawthorne House, which was for several years the Lancaster residence of Mr. J. Fenton-Cawthorne, for some time M.P. for the borough, and previously mentioned in connection with Wyresdale.

Nearly opposite the King's Arms, the old road I have so often referred to had its northern continuation, in China-lane, formerly called Kelne-lane—a name indicating some connection with a channel or water. Between 1894 and 1898, many of the old houses in China-lane were pulled down, and the road right through was opened out to its present width. This improvement, which involved the demolition of a "rookery," long notorious for its dirtiness and disorder, materially facilitates the convenience of the public, vehicularly and otherwise. Prior to the change, China-lane (now designated China-street) was only about eight feet wide. Just out of it, at the north end, and on the higher edge of Church-street, there are some buildings which at one time were the Lancaster residences of the Shuttleworths, the Wilsons of Dallam Tower, and the Fauconbergs. Down Church-street, a short distance, on the north side, there is a building now used as the Conservative Club, in which, according to tradition, Prince Charles (the Young Pretender) stayed from the 24th to the 26th of November, 1745, when on his march southward with the Rebels, and where he found quarters from the evening of the 13th to the morning of the 15th of December following, when on his retreat to Scotland. The large, prominently-bayed building above (on the same side of the street), which is set apart for County Club purposes, stands on the site of a house in which the Judges used to lodge at Assize time. The broad-fronted, step-approached structure at the head of the street, where the Judges have for many years been accommodated, and which is known as the Judges' Lodgings, occupies the site of a building which is specified on Speed's map of Lancaster (1610) as "Olde Hall," with a cross in front of it. The Covells once resided here. They were a family of considerable local status. It is said that one of them—Thomas Covell—was Mayor of Lancaster six times. He died in 1639, aged 78. In Lancaster Parish Church there is a memorial brass pertaining to him, the epitaph (ten rhymed lines) being rendered ridiculous by excess of laudation. Pennant, the traveller, &c., evidently saw this epitaph when he was in Lancaster, en route to the North, for in the record of his journey it is mentioned. He says that this is "an epitaph so very extravagant that the living must laugh to read, and the deceased, was he capable, must blush to hear" it. The cross in front of the "Olde Hall" was called "Covell Cross." In or about 1662 the residence referred to was sold to and reconstructed by a member of the Cole family, and designated New Hall. There is a tradition that the old Town Hall or Moot Hall of Lancaster stood at the Church-street end of China-lane (north-east corner). In Speed's map there is in this quarter a building designated " Newe Hall." Bridge-lane, on the north side of Church-street, is in line with China-lane, and, like the latter, was formerly a portion of the main northern road. It ranges in width from about eight to ten feet, and has in it many small, odd-shaped, dingy-looking houses, &c.; but, though still an immense way from being in the category of the handsome or the immaculate, it is much better—cleaner, less dissolute, more orderly—than it used to be. On the hill side, west of Bridge-lane, there is a remnant of the old Roman wall. The open, level part, at the bottom of the lane, is Lune-square. From it a view of part of the lane, and of some of the oldest houses in it, can be obtained.

Lune, at Lancaster, in the time of the Danes; and, though no actual proof of this has been adduced, belief in the existence of a bridge here at such time—seeing that the usage of one had, it is "almost certain," been established some hundreds of years before—is not unreasonable. In the reign of King John there was a wooden bridge, or one in which a considerable quantity of wood figured, across the river. In the 14th century the pontage of the bridge (duty payable for its repair) was on various occasions secured by letters patent. In 16th century documents there are several references to a stone bridge across the Lune; but when this bridge (which presumably crossed the river at the same part as the wooden one) was built there is no evidence to show. In a record left by three military officers who visited Lancaster (entering from the north), in 1634, Lune bridge is described as

LUNE-SQUARE.

I am now near the " pulling-up " point, for close to Lune-square there is a hiatus in the old north road—the bridge which formerly carried the road over the Lune here does not now exist, and the line of continuity is consequently severed entirely. There has been no available passage, by bridge, in this part since 1802. The end of this bridge, on the south or town side, was about 70 yards from the centre of Lune-square, or say 50 yards north-west of where the present branch of the Midland Railway crosses the road. It was of stone, had four arches, and was about 120 yards long. In his " Roman Lancashire " Mr. Thompson Watkin says:— " It appears to be almost certain that a Roman bridge must have existed across the Lune, at Lancaster, though no vestiges of it are known to remain; and the point where the road northwards crossed the station has not been ascertained." It is not improbable that this Roman structure was at or near the part traversed by the bridge which was closed in 1802. A conjecture has been indulged in to the effect that there was a bridge over the

" a fayre, lofty, long, archt bridge." When the Scotch Rebels were approaching Lancaster (going southward), in 1715, a proposal was made, and approved of by the Corporation, with the view of stopping their progress, that the bridge over the Lune should be pulled down; and the process of demolition was actually commenced, but was soon stopped. After a portion of the bridge parapet, at the north end, had been pulled down, it was pointed out to those who had sanctioned the scheme of destruction that at low water the Rebels could ford the river, so the work of demolition was abandoned. In the autumn of 1769, Gray, the poet, was at Lancaster for a short time, and in his diary or journal he says, under date October 10:—" Here [at Lancaster] is a good bridge of four arches over the Lune, that runs, when the tide is out, in two streams divided by a bed of gravel, which is not covered but in spring tides." In 1782 this bridge had in certain parts got into a state of decay—had, in fact, become so dangerous that an indictment was made respecting it at the Quarter Sessions. A few years afterwards (in 1788, when the handsome, five-arched bridge a short distance above, generally called "Skerton bridge," was opened) it was to a great extent abandoned. On the 9th of August, 1802, passage over the old bridge was stopped, by order. Soon afterwards the end arch on the north or Skerton side was taken down in order to allow a full-rigged vessel—the largest hitherto built on the higher side of the bridge, and launched from the shipyard of Mr. Brockbank, on the north-west side of Green Ayre—to pass down the river. It is said that some coins of the time of Canute were found amongst the debris of this arch. Through having been damaged by floods, the second arch on the north side fell in on the 22nd of September, 1807. The first arch at the south end gave way on the 6th of February, 1814, through ice pressure, and it was taken down. On the 29th of December, 1845, the second arch on the same side—this was the only arch left—fell somewhat unexpectedly; and

not long afterwards my father (Anthony Hewitson, stonemason, of Lancaster) helped with others, acting under authority, to demolish the last remains standing above water of this old bridge. Recently my brother William (editor of the "Bury Times") had a picture frame made out of one of the old oak piles from the bed of the river—piles with which the foundations of the bridge had been stayed (possibly, also, the foundations of the bridge which was in existence in the reign of King John), and which appear to have been about six feet long. The oak is in excellent condition, very dark, almost as hard as flint, and the piece in question makes a very appropriate frame for a large photographic view of some buildings, &c., not far from the site of the old bridge. I have thus, you see, got to the very last remnants of this ancient structure, and I have now also reached the end of my "Gleanings between Preston and Lancaster."

ERRATA AND ADDENDA.

The stone shields mentioned on page 13 may refer to the Singletons, who in early times were connected with Broughton township (evidently before the Langtons), and who subsequently owned or occupied Broughton Tower. The shields of both the Singleton and Langton families included chevrons; but that of the former bore three, whilst that of the latter contained only two, though there is an instance of a Langton shield (whether its possessor were a Langton of Broughton Tower or some other place is not stated) which had on it three chevrons.

It is stated on page 54 that Dewhurst's view of Greenhalgh Castle did not secure a place in the edition of Baines's History of Lancashire edited by Croston. The absence of the view from that portion of volume 5 which deals directly with the Castle, and contains a description of it from Camden, Kuerden, Whitaker, &c., prompted the inference that it was not in this edition; but a recent casual opening of volume 1 revealed the fact that the view alluded to is in a section dealing with the civil warfare in the 17th century, though only about two lines of the letterpress are devoted to the Castle.

In the sixth line from the bottom of page 141, first column, for *pannelled* read panelled.

The following are extracts from notes kindly supplied to me by Monsignor Gradwell. Respecting what may be deemed the theories which they contain, I neither endorse nor impugn them: I place them before the reader just as I have met with them in the notes, viz.:—

The name Claughton goes back to the time before the Romans entered Britain. Claughton was then little else but forest and moor, but still there were some inhabitants. And they had a religion, and worshipped Tuite and Sul. Tuite was the guardian of roads; rude pillars were erected in his honour, and one such was placed on the old British track, which served for a road between the ancient Ribchester and Galgate, on a spot still known as Tootle Hall. Sul, the autotype of the Goddess Minerva, had a temple dedicated to her on the summit of Sullum, and the hill even now bears her name. From Salisbury to Mam Sul in Aberdeenshire this false deity was worshipped, and we have her name in Lancashire in Salford and Salwick. The Claughtoners of those days had their place of worship, too. Just opposite Cross House was a circle of rude stones, where, on the day of the full moon, the inhabitants flocked from their huts of wattle and daub, and their patches of open ground won from the forest. The stones were called in the British language the "Clack-en" or stones; and they gave the name to the whole township, for Claughton really means "Stones Town." But one stone now remains, and this owes its preservation to its having

been chosen by the early Christian missionaries as the pedestal for a cross.

There are some reasons for believing that Christianity was introduced into this neighbourhood even in Roman times. Between the Brock and the slope of Beacon Fell is a farm called Eccles Moss. It is not far from the Roman road, by the side of which was situated a Roman homestead, still known as Windy Harbour, and probably an ecclesia or church, for the use of the proprietor and his dependants, once stood on the site of Eccles Moss. Not far from the top of Sullum there is another Eccles, and no doubt this is another relic of Roman Christianity, and suggests that a church or ecclesia was built on the ruins of the ancient temple of Sul. With the withdrawal of the Roman Legions, most of the arts of civilisation disappeared from the country districts, but not so the Christian religion. When the Pagan tribes of the North drove out the British Christians from the more fertile lands of the plain, the latter took refuge in Bleasdale, and there erected a church, dedicating it to the memory of their great hero King Arthur, under the name of St. Eadmaur. This was one of the titles of the blameless King, and means in Welsh "the great head" or "chief." Perhaps this is the oldest Christian church in Lancashire which is still used as a place of worship. It is now called Admarsh, and is about five miles from Claughton.

In the 6th century, St. Kentegern, Bishop of Glasgow, passed through North Lancashire on his way to and from Glasgow to Menevia. He took this long journey to visit St. David, the great Bishop in South Wales, and the historian Jocelyn, of Furness Abbey, records that he preached in Lancashire. Another trace of Christian Missionaries in that remote time is found in the names of places in the neighbourhood, formed from the Irish word Kil. One such, Kilbreck, is situated on the north bank of the Calder, between Calder Vale and Oakenclough. The name tells us that an Irish priest or monk settled down here, and erected an humble church for the use of the scattered people. Another relic of olden times found in Claughton, not far from "the Street," tells us a very different story. One of the finds was an earthen urn containing the ashes of a Danish chief. This heathen mode of burial suggests that the dead warrior was a Pagan, and died in one of the raids made in North Lancashire in the 9th century. The name of the adjoining field, the Sixacre, was probably composed of that of the chief, Sœx or Sax, and acre, meaning land, and meant Sœx's land.

Up to the time of the Norman Conquest, in 1066, the name of Claughton does not occur in any written document which is preserved to us. In Domesday Book we find the first written mention of Claugh-

Claughton formed a part of the Vicarage of
htown, and was subject to the rule of the
of Cockersand. In the 15th year of the Ponti-
of Gregory IX., 1241, by a Bull dated from the
he confirmed the rights of the Abbot of
rsand to the advowson of Garstang. In this,
ct mention of Claughton, with its posts Hey-
nd Duncunberg, is made; and it is stated that
icar shall collect the Peter's Pence. In the
of King John, a house of the Knights Hospi-
was established at Howorth, and it was en-
with four acres of land at Heigham, and
n pasture in Klactone. There is no evidence
that there was any separate provision for
ritual wants of Claughton before the coming
Brockholes family, though the Chapel of St.
the Baptist, at Howorth, might serve them to
Mass, and save them from the long journey to
htown. But about the year 1358 a more
ious era began. A few years before, the heirs
of William de Tatham conveyed various lands in
Claughton and the neighbouring townships, Bilsborrow and Catterall, to Roger de Brockholes, of
Byreworth, to be held by the service of one rose
yearly and the finding of a Chaplain to celebrate a
Mass at Claughton, or in the church at Garstang,
at a salary of 66 shillings and 8 pence. From this
time onwards we find occasional notices of the Chaplains, the first on record being Lawrence de Myres-
cough, another being John de Lethum. A chapel
was built in what is still known as the Chapel Croft,
at the western side of the Park, and adjoining "the
Street," and it continued to be used until the very
end of the 16th century, towards the close of the
reign of Elizabeth. Claughton suffered less from the
wicked conduct of Henry VIII. than most other
places. Of course, the Knights of St. John were deprived of their house and possessions at Howorth
and Heigham; and the poor, whose wants in times
of distress and sorrow had been so kindly attended to
and relieved, were left to the tender mercies of the

wasteful but greedy favourites of the King. But the
Chapel, in Chapel Croft, was allowed to stand, and
the priest continued to say Mass at its altar. The
name of the Pope was, however, by order of the
King, carefully erased from the Missal, and the
Office of St. Thomas of Canterbury run through with
a pen. At the Rectory an ancient *Black Letter*
Missal, printed in 1517, is still preserved. It has
been mutilated in this manner. The family of the
Brockholes remained substantially faithful to the
old religion; many of the smaller proprietors were
equally staunch, and the mass of the people clung
to their faith. And dearly many of them had to pay
for their fidelity. The Chapel in Chapel Croft does
not appear to have been disturbed, for in the year
1591 the Bishop of Chester instituted an inquiry as
to the existence of a Chapel in Claughton, and as to
certain lands given for superstitious uses, that is to
find a priest to say Mass in the Chapel. A second
action in the same matter was tried at Preston, in
1595. We hear no more of it, and no doubt it fell
into decay. There is yet in the Rectory a broken
piece of alabaster, representing the Angel Gabriel,
and this may have belonged to this ancient Chapel.
In 1607, the benefit of the recusancy of Mr. Brockholes was granted to a certain David Stewart, of
Lancaster, and in the following year, 1608, a similar
grant was made to Charles Chambers.

Two sons of the then Squire of Claughton
[17th century] became priests, and did good
service to the Church at home and abroad.
In the next generation, three more of
the family of Brockholes were raised to the
priesthood, and, through the generosity of one of
them, the Mission of Claughton became firmly established. The second spring for England at large, of
which Cardinal Newman has spoken in imperishable
words, took place two centuries later, but for
Claughton it began shortly after that year of gloom,
1646.

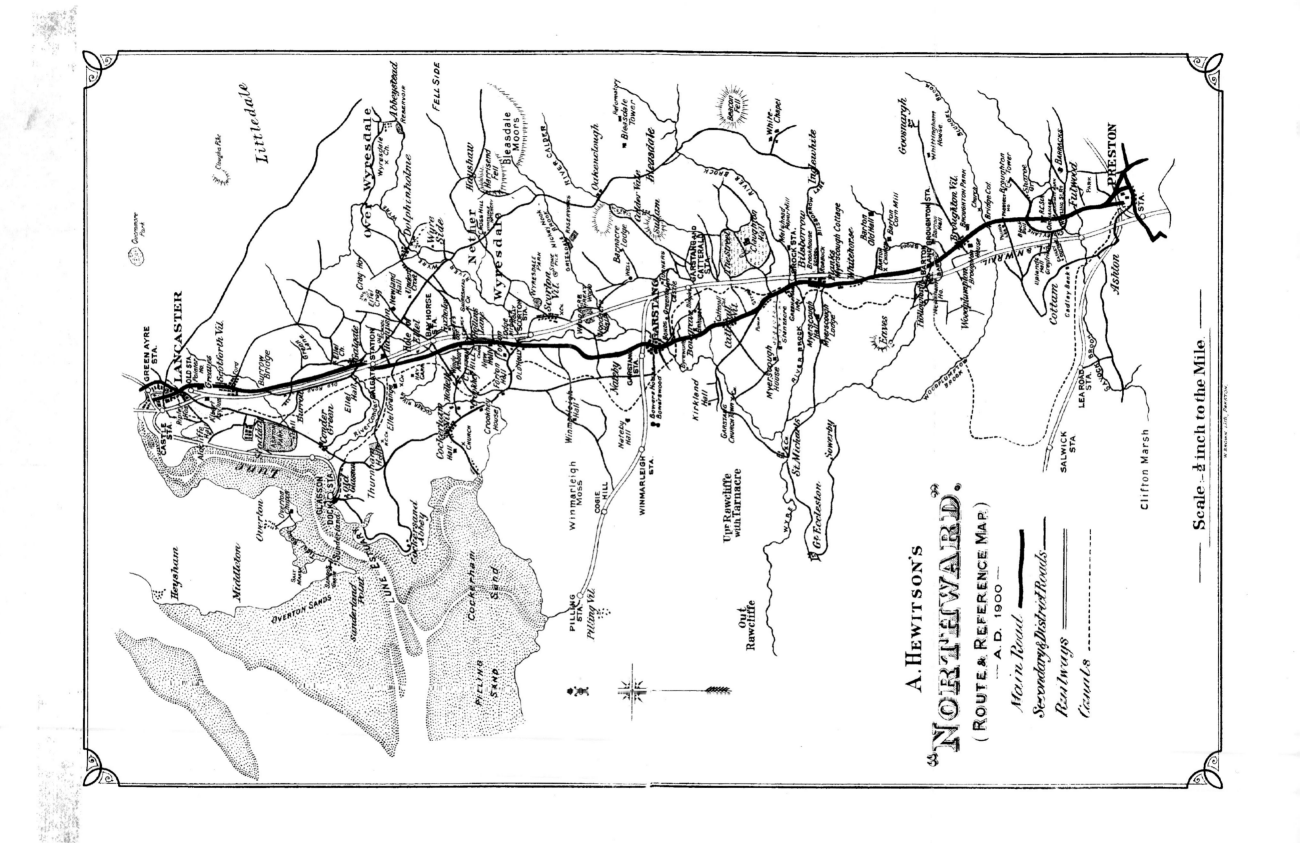

A. Hewitson's
"NORTHWARD."
(ROUTE & REFERENCE MAP)
— A.D. 1900 —

Main Road. ——————
Secondary & District Roads. ————
Railways ++++++++
Canals - - - - - - -

—— Scale :- ¾ inch to the Mile. ——

W. Brown, Lith, Preston.

INDEX.